PHOTO GUIDE
to the wildflowers
of South Africa

Supported by the South African
National Biodiversity Institute

Supported by the UK
Darwin Initiative (Department for
Environment, Food and Rural Affairs)

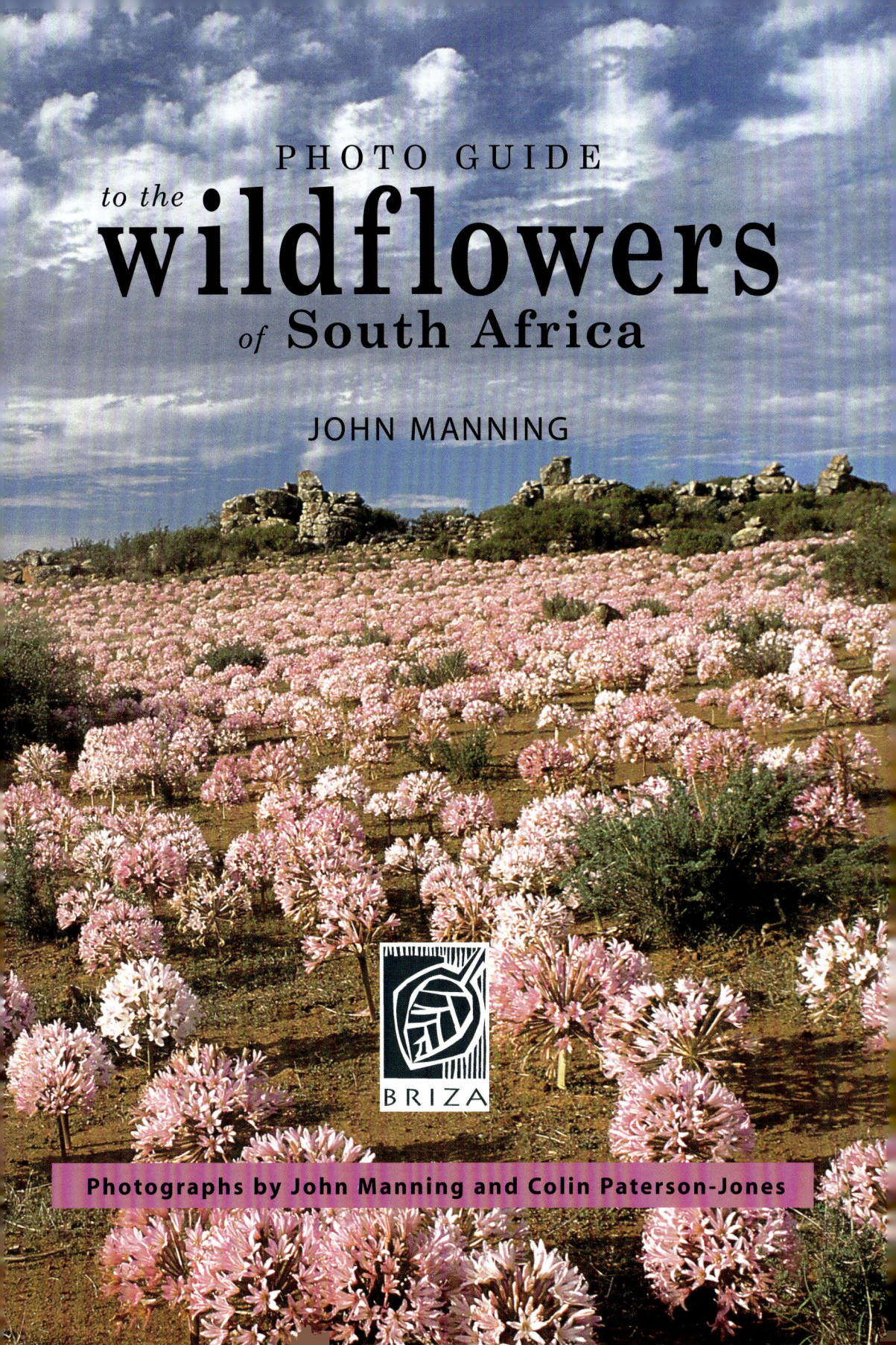

Published by

BRIZA PUBLICATIONS
CK 1990/011690/23

PO Box 11050
Queenswood 0121
South Africa

First edition, first impression, 2003
Second edition, first impression, 2012

Copyright © in text: John Manning
Copyright © in photographs: John Manning and Colin Paterson-Jones
Copyright © in published edition: Briza Publications

All rights reserved. No part of this publication may be reproduced or transmitted in any form or by any means without written permission of the copyright holders.

ISBN 978 1 920217 02 0

Project manager   Reneé Ferreira
Production coordinator   Douglas van der Horst
Copy-editor   David Pearson
Proofreader   Tessa Kennedy
Cover design   Sally Whines
Inside design   Lyndall du Toit
Typesetting   Gerhardt van Rooyen & Lebone Publishing Services
Distribution maps   Gavin Swingewood
Reproduction   Unifoto, Cape Town & Resolution Colour, Cape Town
Printed and bound by   PrintWORKS Global Services (Shenzhen) Company Limited, China

DISCLAIMER
Although care has been taken to be as accurate as possible, neither the author nor the publisher makes any expressed or implied representation as to the accuracy of the information contained in this book and cannot be held legally responsible or accept liability for any errors or omissions. This book contains numerous quoted examples of medicinal or other uses of plants. The publisher and author do not assume responsibility for any sickness, death or other harmful effects resulting from eating or using any plant in this book. Readers are strongly advised to consult professionals, and any experimentation or prolonged usage is done entirely at your own risk.

Acknowledgements

I would like to thank Hester Steyn of the National Herbarium for providing the distribution maps, Prof. Gideon Smith for his support of this project, Cornelia Klak and Pascale Chesselet for their help in identifying the Aizoaceae, and Julian Lloyd for very kindly checking the spelling of the vernacular names. These have been largely derived from two incomparable sources: Elsa Pooley's *A Field Guide to Wildflowers: KwaZulu-Natal and the Eastern Region*, published by the Natal Flora Publications Trust, and Auriol Batten & Hertha Bokelmann's *Wild Flowers of the Eastern Cape Province*, originally published by Books of Africa and subsequently rewritten by myself as *South African Wild Flower Guide 11: Eastern Cape*, published by the Botanical Society of South Africa in association with the National Botanical Institute. I am especially grateful to Colin Paterson-Jones, who did not hesitate in associating himself with this project, thereby making an impossible task feasible, and finally, it is with great pleasure that I thank all the friends and colleagues who shared their knowledge and field experience with me.

The map of the biomes is derived from Rutherford, M.C. (1997) 'Categorization of biomes', in Cowling, R.M., Richardson, D.M., Pierce, S.M. (eds) *Vegetation of Southern Africa*, Cambridge University Press, Cambridge, pp. 91–98. I am very grateful to Les Powrie of the National Botanical Institute for providing it in electronic format.

The Briza production team are to be complimented on their patience and professionalism. It has been a pleasure to work with them all.

Page 1:	Brilliant orange Arctotis fastuosa *brightens the granite hills around Springbok* (JCM)
Pages 2–3:	A pink froth of Brunsvigia bosmaniae *foams about the dolerite outcrops near Nieuwoudtville in autumn* (JCM)
Page 6:	Golden rivulets of Didelta carnosa *among the dunes fringing Table Bay* (JCM)
Page 8:	Bright yellow Rhynchopsidium pumilum *and magenta mesembs near Calvinia* (JCM)
Page 20:	Damp grassland in the KwaZulu-Natal Drakensberg (JCM)
Page 120:	Arid fynbos in the Olifants River Mountains (JCM)
Page 262:	Spring annuals among the granite outcrops in Namaqualand (JCM)

Contents

Introduction	9
Wildflower regions and climate	12
Recommended regional wildflower guides	17
Quick guide to wildflower groups	18
Grassland and savannah	21
Fynbos	121
Namaqualand	263
Index of scientific names	335
Index of vernacular names	342
Glossary	351

Introduction

SOUTH AFRICA IS A wildflower paradise, home to a rich flora of around 19 000 different species of flowering plants. These range from diminutive succulents little more than a centimetre high to towering forest giants. Many are extremely beautiful. The country has a long history of interest in its plants but the sheer number of species makes their identification difficult, even for professional botanists. The number of wildflower guides available in bookstores is eloquent testimony to this. Traditionally, and with good reason, these guides have concentrated on the plants from a more or less well-defined geographical area, possibly a region, province or even a single reserve.

To buy all the guides covering the country is expensive, and the alternative is to try to provide a single guide to all or most of the country. At first sight it would seem impossible to achieve even passable coverage of the whole country in a single volume but the task, although daunting, is not impossible, for two main reasons.

Firstly, not all of the flowering plants are likely to attract the attention of a passer-by. Among such is the group that comprises grasses, sedges and reeds. Although they are the dominant vegetation group over much of the country, and of the first importance in its ecology, grasses seldom draw attention except *en masse*. Another group that can be excluded comprises trees and larger shrubs. The small flowers that characterise many of these plants, combined with the difficulty in reaching them, means that their identification is a highly specialised discipline that relies on features of the leaves, stem and bark. In addition, there are several first-class identification manuals available about the trees of southern Africa. Of the remaining wildflowers, many are either very inconspicuous, in which case they are unlikely to attract attention, or they are rare or very localised in their distribution, which means that they are unlikely to be seen at all. By excluding trees, grasses and other grass-like families, as well as those plants that are not readily noticed or encountered, the number of wildflowers is substantially reduced. Of this smaller number, even less are common enough or interesting enough to attract attention. Quite which species fulfil these requirements can only be established by extensive field knowledge and I sincerely hope that mine proves equal to the task.

The second reason that such a guide is possible is that not all parts of the country are

Introduction

equally rich in wildflowers and therefore not equally likely to be visited by those interested in seeing them. The greater part of the western interior of the country, for instance, is arid and relatively poor in wildflowers. This is not to say that wildflowers cannot be found in the Karoo and Kalahari; some very striking species occur there but they are few and far between in comparison to the rest of the country. Excluding certain groups of plants, concentrating on those that are most likely to be seen, and focusing on those parts of the country in which one is most likely to see them, reduces the coverage necessary for a successful field guide. This reasoning has led to this book.

It illustrates nearly 900 of the most common and conspicuous wildflowers in South Africa and concentrates on those that are most likely to attract the attention of the average traveller in the more popularly visited parts of the country. These are particularly the Drakensberg of Mpumalanga, KwaZulu-Natal and the Eastern Cape, the eastern seaboard, the Western Cape and Namaqualand. Within these areas three main wildflower regions have been identified that coincide in broad terms with one or more of the main vegetation types that occur across the country. These three regions are Grassland and Savannah, Fynbos, and Namaqualand. The floras of these three regions are largely complementary, with little overlap, and the few common species that stretch across more than one region are featured in each.

Symbols used in this guide

The distribution maps for each species have been generated from specimens housed in the collections of the South African National Biodiversity Institute in Pretoria and the Compton Herbarium in Cape Town. As such they represent the recorded occurrence of each species and not necessarily the total actual distribution, although in most instances these will coincide. It is therefore very unlikely that the species will be found much outside of the ranges shown. Flowering time is illustrated by a bar with the main months of flowering highlighted in a darker colour and months in which sporadic flowering can be expected coloured in a lighter colour. For example:

Abbreviations used in vernacular names
(A) Afrikaans
(E) English
(N) Nama and related Khoisan languages
(SS) South Sotho
(Sw) Swazi
(X) Xhosa
(Z) Zulu

Introduction

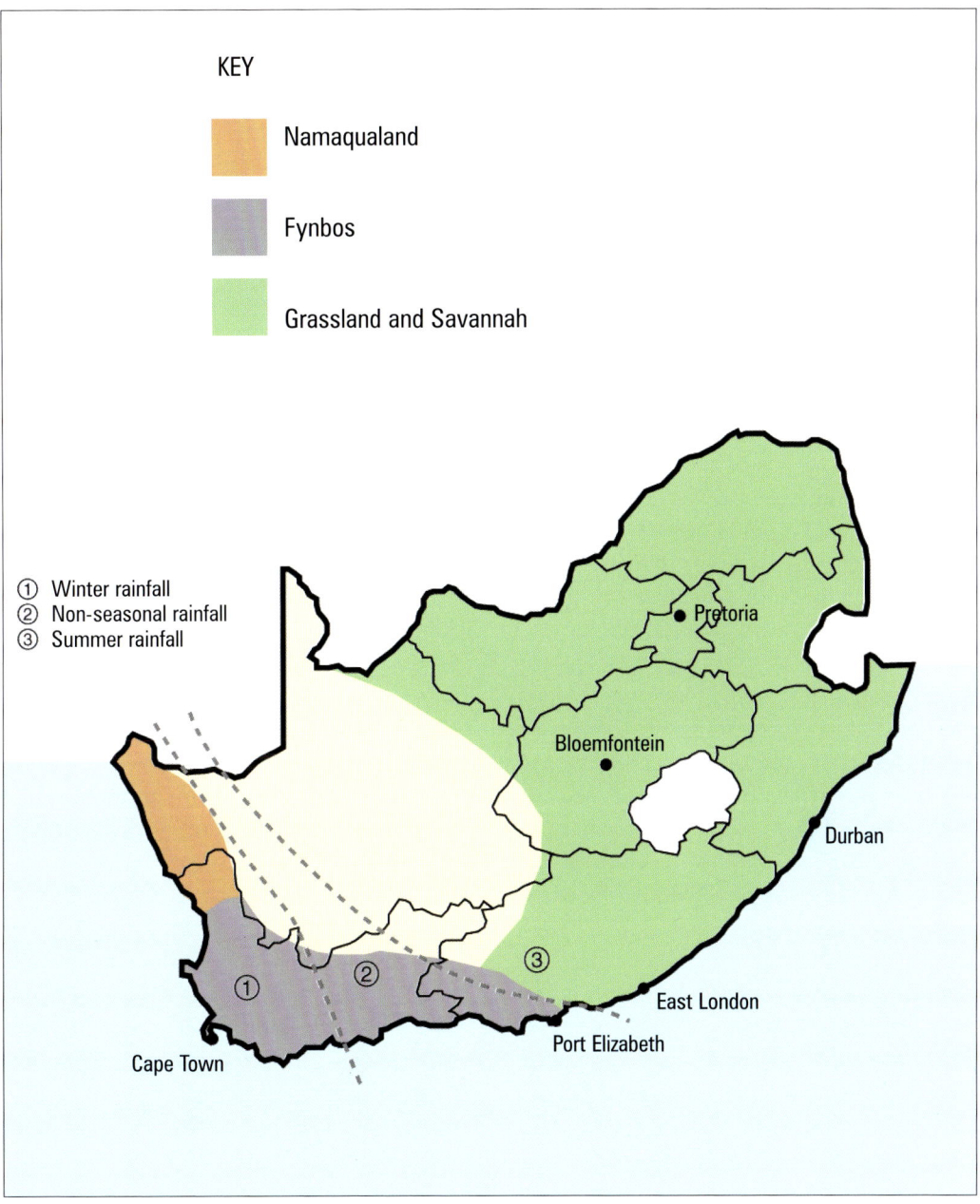

THE THREE WILDFLOWER REGIONS RECOGNISED IN THIS BOOK. THE SPECIES TREATED ARE GROUPED IN THESE THREE REGIONS.

Wildflower regions and climate

THE NATURAL VEGETATION of southern Africa can be divided into seven broad classes based on the dominant types of plants that occur in them, including such groups as trees, grasses and other herbaceous perennials, or annual herbs. The classes are termed biomes and each is defined by the dominant lifestyle found among its component plants. These lifestyles are a direct response to climatic factors, especially the average annual rainfall, the season in which most of it falls and the degree of summer aridity. The biomes are defined, therefore, on the structure of the vegetation rather than on the identity of the individual species. No less than eight different biomes occur in South Africa alone (although the Desert Biome is largely restricted to the Namibian coast and enters South Africa only along the lower reaches of the Orange, or Gariep, River). The large number of biomes that occur in South Africa is a reflection of the great variation in climate that occurs across the country. Climate is the prime determinant for the diversity of wildflowers that characterise a region and is, in turn, determined by its geography, latitude (and therefore the weather systems associated with it), and the ocean currents that pass along its coasts.

The eastern and western shores of southern Africa are washed by two very different currents, with dissimilar effects on their rainfall. In the east the Agulhas current flows southwards, bringing warm tropical water with it and raising the humidity of the air above it to levels that sustain the lush, subtropical vegetation that characterises the eastern seaboard. The west coast, in sharp contrast, is an arid desert, the result of the cold Benguela current that sweeps northwards from the southern polar region, lowering the humidity and reducing rainfall. Here the vegetation is dominated by a dwarf succulent shrubland. Between these two different coasts is the central plateau, which supports temperate grassland in the east and a semi-arid scrubland in the west. This plateau drops dramatically along the Drakensberg to the coastal plain in the east; to the west it slopes gently and then drops gradually to the coast.

To the south the coastal forelands have been folded into the parallel ranges of sandstone rock that form the towering ramparts of the Cape Fold mountains, which are the bastion of fynbos shrubland. Compounding the differences in the coastal currents is the

Wildflower regions and climate

influence of two distinct weather systems. The bulk of the country comes under the sway of a tropical high-pressure system that prevents warm, moisture-laden air from the Indian Ocean reaching the interior in winter. The result is that the central and eastern parts of the country receive the bulk of their rain during the summer months, in the form of thunderstorms and showers carried from the Indian Ocean by north-easterly winds. In contrast, the south-western part of the country receives the bulk of its rain in winter, when it comes under the influence of a low-pressure system that moves north at this time of the year. From April to September westerly winds drive a series of cold fronts across the southern part of the country, depositing rain in their wake. Sandwiched between these two regions is a narrow band that receives relatively little rain throughout the year.

South Africa's biomes are the result of the interplay between these geographical and climatological influences.

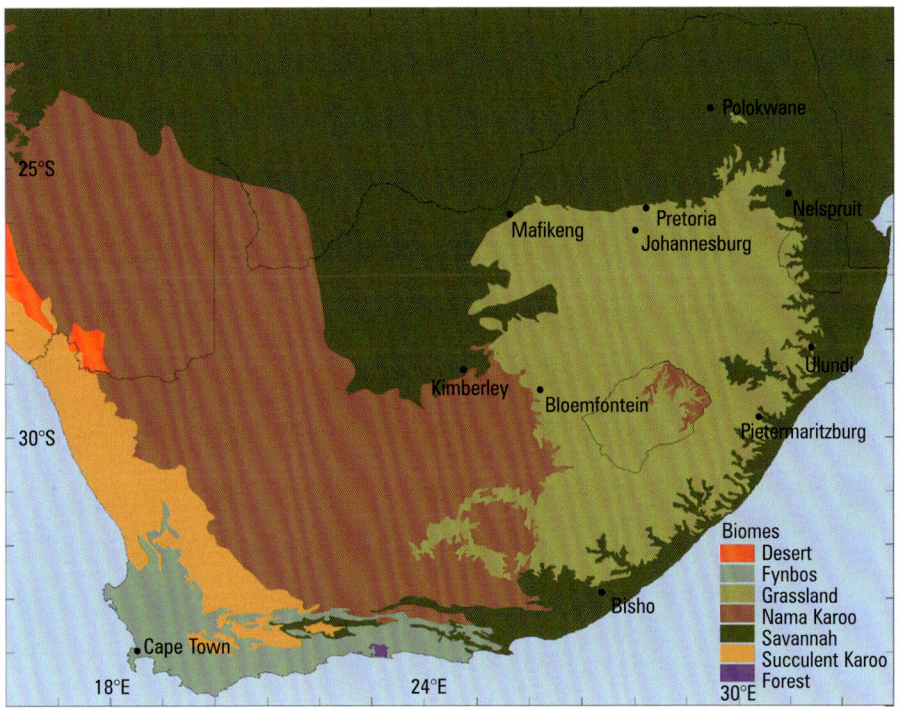

THE MAJOR VEGETATION CLASSES, OR BIOMES, RECOGNISED IN SOUTHERN AFRICA

Forest Biome

Forests are restricted to frost-free areas with a mean annual rainfall of more than 525 mm in the winter rainfall region and more than 725 mm in the summer rainfall region. They are sensitive to fire and persist only in places where fires are rare or absent, in humid coastal areas or protected valleys.

Forests cover only around 0,5% of South Africa's surface. They occur mainly as patches along the southern and eastern coast of the country, and inland along the eastern edge of the escarpment up to 2 100 m above sea level. They comprise a continuous canopy of mostly evergreen trees, beneath which is a multi-layered understorey of smaller trees and shrubs. The dense shade beneath the canopy prevents a distinct ground layer of plants from developing. Some 650 different woody plant species and almost as many herbaceous ones have been recorded from the forests of South Africa.

Scadoxus multiflorus *in coastal swamp forest*

Thicket Biome

Thicket replaces forest where the rainfall is too low to support true forest but where the absence of fires still allows the development of a vegetation type dominated by woody plants.

Thicket occurs as a series of narrow strips along the southern and especially eastern coasts, interdigitated among other vegetation types, mainly along river valleys. It covers just over 3% of the land area of the country. Thicket is a closed shrubland or low forest dominated by evergreen, small-leaved or succulent trees, shrubs and vines, many of which are armed with spines on their stems. It is often impenetrable and is not obviously layered, with little herbaceous cover on the ground.

Savannah Biome

The Savannah Biome is the largest in southern Africa, occupying around 46% of the land area. It is best developed in the northern and north-eastern parts of the country where it covers large areas of land, but small patches have also developed in the south-east. It is delimited largely by an average summer rainfall of 235–1 000 mm, which is insufficient to prevent the development of a woody canopy but enough to allow a grass layer to persist. Frost is a relatively uncommon occurrence.

Savannah is characterised by a grassy ground layer overtopped by a distinct upper layer of woody plants. The shrub or tree layer varies greatly in height, from 1 to 20 m, giving rise to a variety of different vegetation types, known variously as shrubveld, bushveld or woodland. Frequent fires are an important factor in maintaining them and almost all species in the biome are adapted to survive fires.

Grassland Biome

Grassland is found chiefly on the high central plateau and inland areas in the eastern part of the country, where it covers around 26% of the area, from near the coast to 2 850 m above sea level. The Grassland Biome is delimited by a combination of mean annual rainfall between 400–2 000 mm and low winter temperatures that prevent the development of a layer of woody plants.

Grassland is dominated by a single layer of grasses, and trees are absent except in a few localised habitats, such as rock outcrops. Fires are a frequent occurrence and the majority of associated plants are adapted to them, often flowering only after a fire has removed the grassy canopy. These plants form a class known as forbs, protecting their renewal buds and shoots from damage by fire and frost by keeping them underground, either in bulbs or other woody rootstocks. These underground organs also store nutrients and enable the forbs to sprout rapidly in the spring before the grass cover can re-grow after a fire. The combination of fire, frost and grazing ensures the dominance of grasses and other herbaceous perennials by preventing the establishment of trees.

Nama Karoo Biome

Nama Karoo covers around 23% of the country in the drier, western half of the central plateau between 500–2 000 m above sea level. The distribution of this biome is determined primarily by a low annual summer rainfall of 100–520 mm per year.

The vegetation is dominated by an open, grassy, dwarf shrubland and the relatively sparse cover means that fires are rare. In historical times large nomadic or migratory herds of springbok and other game traversed the area following patches of rainfall occurrences.

Succulent Karoo Biome

The Succulent Karoo occurs in a band below the western and southern edges of the central escarpment north of the Cape Fold Belt, mainly below 800 m but up to 1 500 m above sea level in the east, covering 6,5% of the land area. The biome is delimited essentially by a low winter rainfall of below 200 mm and extreme summer aridity. Fog is common near the coast but frost is rare.

The vegetation of the Succulent Karoo is dominated by a unique assemblage of dwarf, succulent shrubs of which the mesembs and stonecrops are especially prominent. Annuals are also common and provide mass displays in the spring but grasses are rare. The number of plant species, mainly succulents, is high and unparalleled elsewhere in the world for an arid area of this size. Around half of the biome falls within the area known as Namaqualand.

Gerbera viridifolia *in high grassland*

Fynbos Biome

Fynbos covers just over 6% of the land area in the extreme south and south-west of southern Africa but supports something less than half of all the species recorded in southern Africa. The distribution of the biome is determined by moderate to high winter rainfall, between 210–3 000 mm with moderate to high summer aridity.

Fynbos is an open or closed shrubland dominated by leathery and often fine-leaved woody shrubs and perennials together with a high representation (around 16%) of bulbous and cormous plants. Although seldom more than 3 m in height, it is more or less distinctly three-layered, with a canopy of medium or tall shrubs, especially members of the protea and erica families, a median layer of grasses, restios and small shrubs, and an understorey of herbaceous perennials. This basic structure is subject to the age of the vegetation as determined by the interval between successive fires, which affects the relative contribution that each of these classes makes. Fire is an essential element in the biome, serving to rejuvenate the vegetation. The frequency normally varies between 4 and 25 years. Many of the plant species in fynbos are highly localised in their distribution.

Desert Biome

The Desert Biome in southern Africa comprises the Namib Desert, which forms a broad belt along the west coast of Namibia and enters South Africa along the Gariep or Orange River. The climate is characterised by low summer rainfall of between 13–70 mm, resulting in extreme summer aridity. Coastal fogs are frequent and some strand plants are adapted to make use of this additional source of moisture, absorbing it through their leaves. The plant diversity is lowest of all the biomes.

The vegetation is dominated by annuals, which avoid water stress in the form of seeds. They include several grasses. North of the Swakop River is a narrow belt, no more than 200 m wide, of dwarf shrubs that depend on the coastal fogs for their survival.

Erica inflata *in montane fynbos*

Recommended regional wildflower guides

Grassland and Savannah

FABIAN, A. & G. GERMISHUIZEN. 1997. *Wildflowers of northern South Africa*. Fernwood Press, Cape Town.

MANNING, J.C. 2001. *Eastern Cape. South African Wildflower Guide 11*. Botanical Society of S.A. and the National Botanical Institute, Cape Town.

ONDERSTALL, J. 1984. *Transvaal lowveld and escarpment. South African Wildflower Guide 4*. Botanical Society of S.A. and the National Botanical Institute, Cape Town.

POOLEY, E. 1998. *A field guide to wildflowers: KwaZulu-Natal and the Eastern Region*. Natal Flora Publications Trust, Durban.

SHEARING, D. 1994. *Karoo. South African Wildflower Guide 6*. Botanical Society of S.A. and the National Botanical Institute, Cape Town.

VAN ROOYEN, N. 2001. *Flowering plants of the Kalahari dunes*. Ekotrust cc, Pretoria.

Fynbos

BURMAN, L. & A. BEAN. 1985. *Hottentots Holland to Hermanus. South African Wildflower Guide 5*. Botanical Society of S.A. and the National Botanical Institute, Cape Town.

MANNING, J. & P. GOLDBLATT. 2000. *West Coast. South African Wildflower Guide 7*. Botanical Society of S.A. and the National Botanical Institute, Cape Town.

MAYTHAM KIDD, M. 1996. *Cape Peninsula. South African Wildflower Guide 3*. Botanical Society of S.A. and the National Botanical Institute, Cape Town.

MORIARTY, A. 1996. *Outeniqua, Tsitsikamma and eastern Little Karoo. South African Wildflower Guide 2*. Botanical Society of S.A. and the National Botanical Institute, Cape Town.

MUSTART, P., R. COWLING & J. ALBERTYN. 1997. *Southern Overberg. South African Wildflower Guide 8*. Botanical Society of S.A. and the National Botanical Institute, Cape Town.

VANDERPLANK, H. J. 1998. *Wildflowers of the Port Elizabeth area: Swartkops to Sundays Rivers*. Bluecliff Publishing, Hunters Retreat.

VANDERPLANK, H. J. 1999. *Wildflowers of the Port Elizabeth area: Gamtoos to Swartkops Rivers*. Bluecliff Publishing, Hunters Retreat.

VAN ROOYEN, G. & H. STEYN. 1999. *Cedarberg, Clanwilliam and Biedouw valley. South African Wildflower Guide 10*. Botanical Society of S.A. and the National Botanical Institute, Cape Town.

Namaqualand

LE ROUX, A. & T. SCHELPE. 1988. *Namaqualand. South African Wildflower Guide 1*. Botanical Society of S.A. and the National Botanical Institute, Cape Town.

MANNING, J. & P. GOLDBLATT. 1997. *Nieuwoudtville, Bokkeveld Plateau and Hantam. South African Wildflower Guide 9*. Botanical Society of S.A. and the National Botanical Institute, Cape Town.

Wildflower groups

Quick guide to

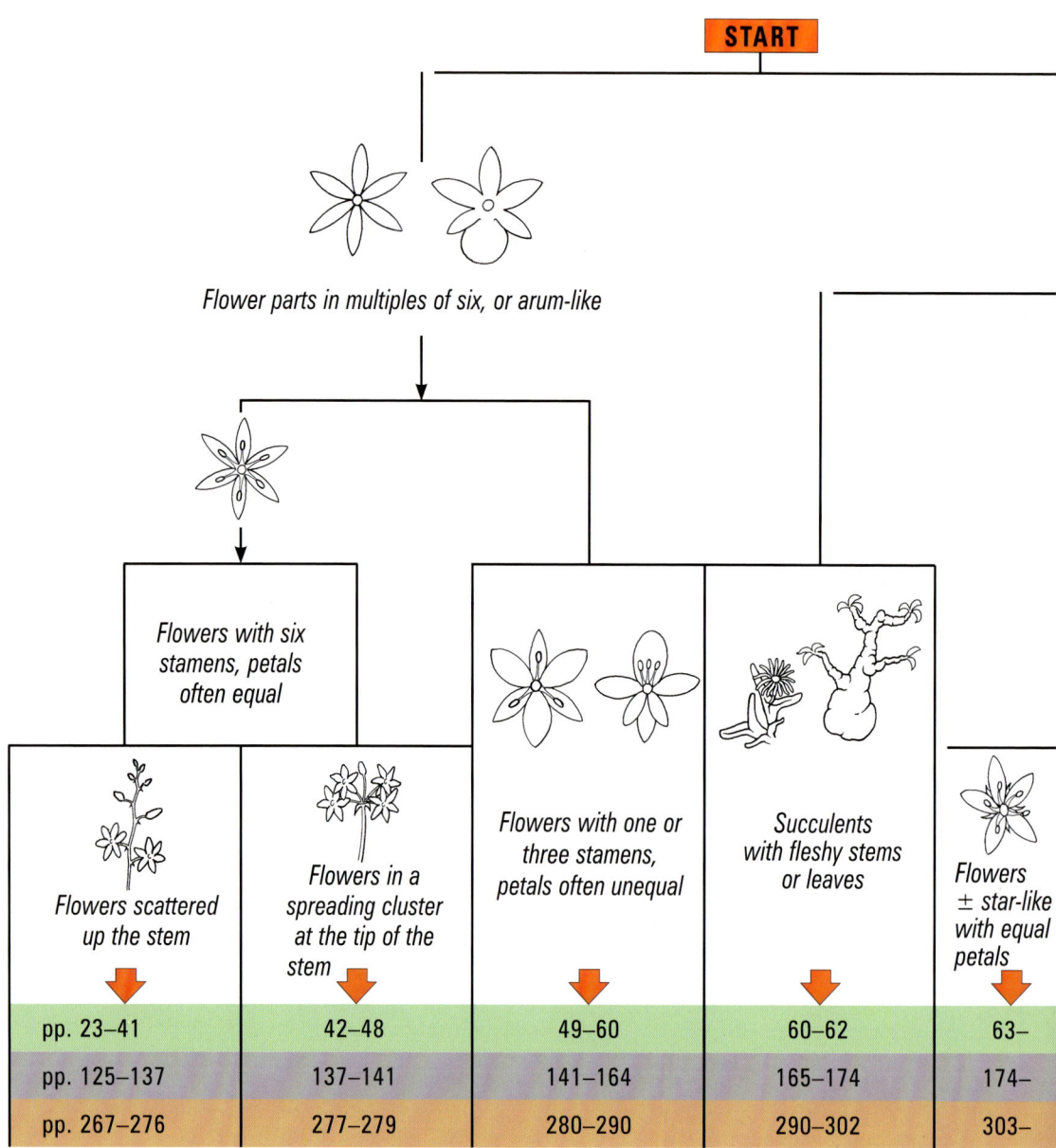

START

Flower parts in multiples of six, or arum-like

Flowers with six stamens, petals often equal		Flowers with one or three stamens, petals often unequal	Succulents with fleshy stems or leaves	Flowers ± star-like with equal petals
Flowers scattered up the stem	Flowers in a spreading cluster at the tip of the stem			
pp. 23–41	42–48	49–60	60–62	63–
pp. 125–137	137–141	141–164	165–174	174–
pp. 267–276	277–279	280–290	290–302	303–

Quick guide

wildflower groups

Use this pictorial guide to narrow down your options. Select the features shown by your plant from each successive pair of characteristics offered in the guide until you reach the group of species that displays this combination of features. Then turn to the relevant pages and match your plant to the illustrations. Read the descriptions carefully for details, especially colour variations.

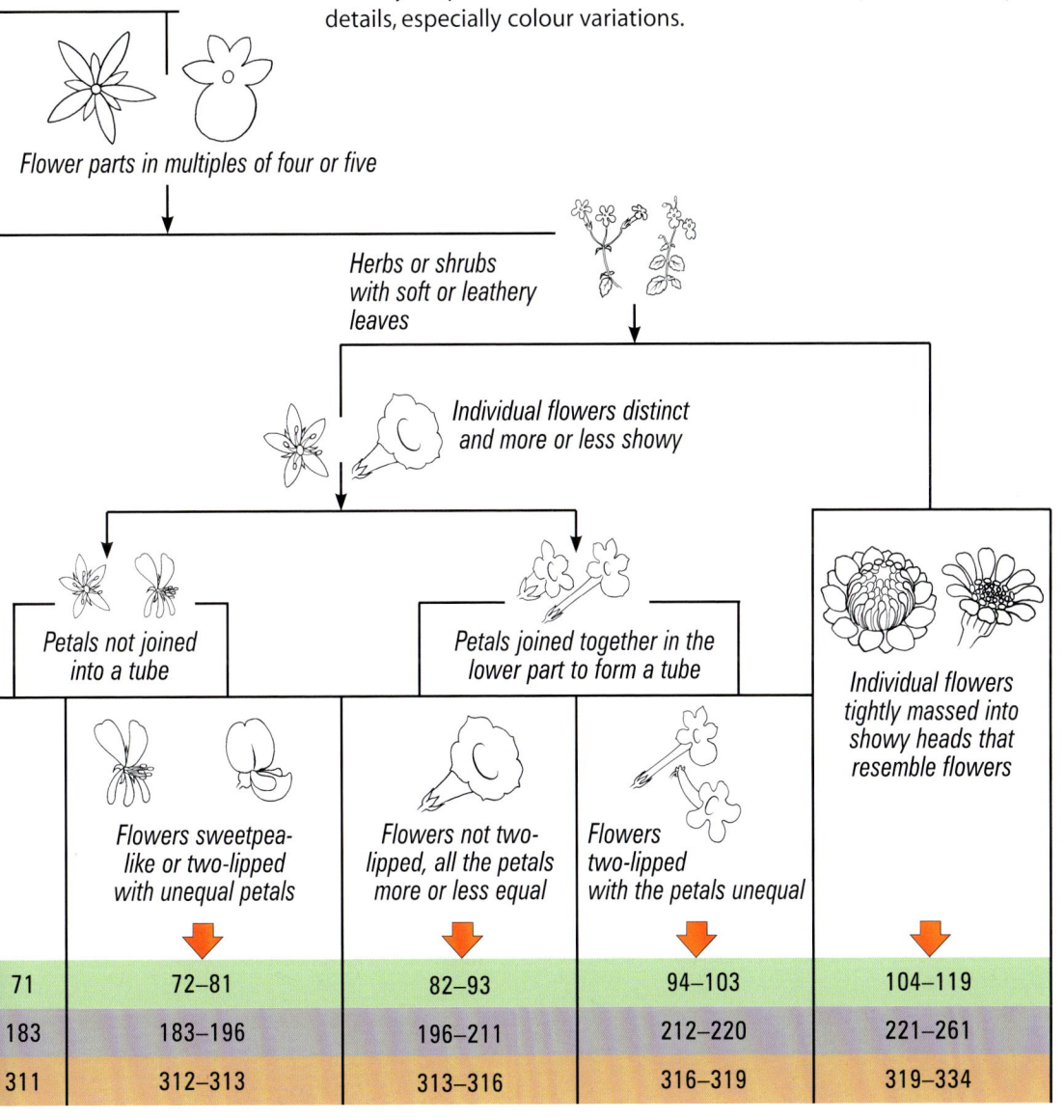

Flower parts in multiples of four or five

Herbs or shrubs with soft or leathery leaves

Individual flowers distinct and more or less showy

Petals not joined into a tube	Petals joined together in the lower part to form a tube		Individual flowers tightly massed into showy heads that resemble flowers
Flowers sweetpea-like or two-lipped with unequal petals	Flowers not two-lipped, all the petals more or less equal	Flowers two-lipped with the petals unequal	
71	72–81	82–93	94–103	104–119
183	183–196	196–211	212–220	221–261
311	312–313	313–316	316–319	319–334

Grassland and Savannah

GRASSLAND AND SAVANNAH are the most common vegetation types in South Africa and together they cover a little under two-thirds of the country. Along the eastern seaboard they are interpolated by fingers of thicket running up the river valleys, while patches of coastal and mistbelt forest are dotted along the east coast or form a discontinuous arc along the seaward side of the eastern escarpment. In the south-western interior the grassy vegetation gives way to a more arid scrubland called the Karoo. Together these various vegetation types cover almost 90% of the land area of South Africa and account for something in the region of 10 000 species of flowering plants, or around half of the total number found in the country.

These diverse vegetation types are all characteristic of the summer rainfall part of South Africa, unlike the Cape Region and Namaqualand, which occupy the winter and all-year rainfall portion of the country. The grasslands of South Africa are home to many of its most lovely wildflowers. The flowering season is lengthy, stretching throughout the rainy season from early spring through summer and into early autumn. There are two peaks in flowering over this period, one in spring and the other in late summer, with a slight dip in midsummer.

Blooming of wildflowers associated with grasslands, known to ecologists as forbs, is greatly stimulated by burning off the grass cover in winter. These forbs typically have tuberous large, woody rootstocks that burst into growth after the first rains, quickly sending up annual shoots that flower before the grass cover can re-establish itself and choke the smaller and more delicate species. In late October the burned grasslands of the KwaZulu-Natal Midlands and Mpumalanga present a colourful spectacle of daisies, milkweeds, wild peas, pelargoniums and other wildflowers. Among the daisies, the most conspicuous are several species of gerbera in various colours, purple vernonias, and yellow thistles in the genus *Berkheya*. The most spectacular of the gerberas are undoubtedly the orange-flowered *G. aurantiaca*, which is now rather rare, and the red-flowered *G. jamesonii*, which is fortunately quite common in bushveld around Lydenburg and Nelspruit. Other wonderful spring-flowering wildflowers are the several species of crinum and arum lily, especially the glorious golden *Zantedeschia pentlandii*. The jewels of the summer months are two lovely members of the Colchicum family, *Littonia* and *Sandersonia*, bearing elegant orange bells.

Grassland and Savannah

By late summer many of the more robust bulbous plants have grown up and are coming into flower. These include several species of gladiolus, watsonia, agapanthus and pineapple flowers. At this time of the year the most profitable areas to visit are the higher-lying grasslands along the edge of the Mpumalanga escarpment, especially around Wakkerstroom and Graskop, and the KwaZulu-Natal Drakensberg. Here the climate is cooler and moister and numerous montane and alpine wildflowers can be seen in bloom. All of the mountain resorts are worth visiting at this time of the year. In the northern KwaZulu-Natal Drakensberg the slopes of The Sentinel are an alpine garden while to the south the hillsides around the remote mountain village of Rhodes are studded with the almost impossibly large, scarlet flowers of *Gladiolus saundersii*.

Along the coast the flame-like flowers of *Gloriosa* can be seen shimmering in the coastal scrub while several species of orchid can be found in flower in the damper grasslands. One of the most breathtaking sights, however, must be the scarlet heads of the fireball lily, *Scadoxus multiflorus*, glowing like embers in the gloom of coastal forests. These glorious plants grow only in the dankest, darkest parts of the forest and the sight of a colony in full bloom is a magical experience. At this time of the year, too, the magnificent, balloon-sized flower heads of the brunsvigias can be seen in suitable grasslands. Their spherical heads bear the flowers on long spokes that stiffen in fruit to form a rigid ball that breaks free from the bulb and bowls along in the wind, scattering seeds along its path.

Any relatively pristine area of grassland will contain numerous wildflowers but overgrazing rapidly reduces the diversity, and plantations are the ultimate disaster for much of the richest grasslands along the eastern escarpment. Road verges and railway preserves, which are protected from grazing, can be rich refuges for wildflowers. The more arid western parts of the summer rainfall region are rather less rewarding although various annuals appear rapidly after rain and some lovely shrubs, such as the brilliant yellow *Rhigozum obovatum*, also burst into flower then.

Papaver aculeatum *growing in roadside scree in the KwaZulu-Natal Drakensberg*

Grassland and Savannah

Stylochaeton natalensis
ARUM FAMILY
Bushveld arum (E), umFana-nkomo (Z)
(Latin *natalensis*, from Natal)
Tuberous perennial, 10–40 cm high. Leaves arrow-shaped with netted venation. Flowers solitary at ground level, crowded in a narrow spike which is enclosed by a flask-shaped, leathery, creamy yellow bract.
Habitat: Stony grassland and open woodland.
Notes: Roots and leaves used medicinally for earache and chest complaints.

Zantedeschia rehmannii
ARUM FAMILY
Dwarf arum lily (E), pienkvarkoor (A), umFana-kamacejane (Sw)
(Named after Polish botanist Anton Rehmann who first collected the species)
Tuberous perennial, 20–60 cm high. Leaves narrowly elliptical. Flowers crowded in a narrow yellow spike 3–4 cm long which is enclosed by a narrowly funnel-shaped, leathery, white or deep pink bract.
Habitat: Rocky grassland and bush margins.

Zantedeschia albomaculata
ARUM FAMILY
Spotted-leaved arum lily (E), witvlekvarkoor (A), inTebe (Z)
(Latin *albomaculatus*, white-spotted, referring to the leaves)
Tuberous perennial, 40–60 cm high. Leaves arrow-shaped and usually flecked or spotted with white. Flowers crowded in a narrow yellow spike 4–8 cm long which is enclosed by a narrowly funnel-shaped, leathery, white to cream-coloured bract with a purple blotch in the base.
Habitat: Damp grassland, among rocks or in vleis.
Notes: *Zantedeschia aethiopica* has plain green leaves, a more flaring floral bract and fruiting stalks that remain erect instead of bending down.

Grassland and Savannah

Zantedeschia pentlandii
ARUM FAMILY

Yellow arum lily (E), geelvarkoor (A)
(Named after R. Whyte, Pentland House, who introduced it into cultivation in Britain in 1892)

Tuberous perennial, 40–60 cm high. Leaves arrow-shaped. Flowers crowded in a narrow yellow spike 8–9 cm long which is enclosed by a flaring, leathery, yellow or rarely a cream-coloured bract with a purple blotch in the base.
Habitat: Rocky grassland and open woodland among dolerite boulders.

Chlorophytum bowkeri
ANTHERICUM FAMILY

Bowker's chlorophytum (E)
(Named for Col. James Bowker, who first collected the species)

Robust rhizomatous perennial to 1 m. Leaves narrow and channelled, rather fibrous in texture. Flowers clustered in a long spike with more than one flower per bract, star-shaped, white, each lasting a single day, 20 mm diameter.
Habitat: Damp grassland.

Drimia altissima
HYACINTH FAMILY

Tall white squill (E), jeukbol (A), umGulube (Z)
(Latin *altissumus*, very tall)

Bulbous perennial to 1 m, with large, pinkish bulb. Leaves dry or just emerging at flowering, lance-shaped in a large tuft. Flowers in a cylindrical raceme on long, spreading pedicels, white or greenish, lasting a single day, 10 mm diameter.
Habitat: Hot bushveld and open thicket.
Notes: Leaves used as a soap and although poisonous traditionally used to treat colds and backaches.

Grassland and Savannah

Drimia macrocentra
HYACINTH FAMILY

Large snake-head (E), slangkop (A), inJoba (X, Z)

(Greek *macrocentron*, large spur)

Bulbous perennial to 1 m. Leaf solitary, cylindrical and hollow, not present in flowering plants. Flowers in a dense raceme, white or greenish, lasting a single day, 10 mm diameter, the lowermost bracts with a long, flat spur.
Habitat: Damp or marshy grassland near streams.
Notes: Poisonous and used traditionally as a vermifuge.

Schizocarphus nervosus
HYACINTH FAMILY

(= *Scilla nervosa*)

White squill (E), maGagana (X), iNgcolo (Z)

(Latin *nervosus*, veined, alluding to the fibrous leaves)

Bulbous perennial to 40 cm high, the bulb covered with fibrous sheaths. Leaves narrow or broader, stiff and often twisted with thickened margins. Flowers on long pedicels, white to cream with a green or blackish ovary, 5–8 mm diameter.
Habitat: Stony or open grassland.
Notes: Used to treat rheumatic fever and dysentery.

Albuca virens
HYACINTH FAMILY

(= *Ornithogalum tenuifolium*)

Common ornithogalum (E), bosui (A)

(Latin *virens*, green, referring to the flowers)

Bulbous perennial 30–80 cm high. Leaves narrow and channelled, rather drooping. Flowers in a long raceme, usually with long bracts, white or greenish with a green band on the petals, 10 mm diameter.
Habitat: Rough grassland or thicket, often along streams or roadsides.
Notes: Sap is an irritant on sensitive skin.

Grassland and Savannah

Albuca bracteata
HYACINTH FAMILY
(= *Ornithogalum longibracteatum*)
Pregnant onion, devil's onion (E),
maxabana (X), umBabaza (Z)
(Latin *bracteatus*, alluding to the large floral bracts)
Bulbous perennial 1–1,5 m high, with a smooth, green bulb exposed above the ground and producing numerous bulbils. Leaves strap-shaped and usually with a tail-like tip, rather drooping. Flowers in a long raceme with very long bracts, white with a green band on the petals, 10 mm diameter.
Habitat: Shaded slopes and forest margins.
Notes: Well known as a houseplant and widely used in traditional medicine.

Albuca abyssinica
HYACINTH FAMILY
Bushveld slime lily (E), bosveld slymlelie (A)
(Latin *abyssinicus*, from Ethiopia, formerly Abyssinia)
Bulbous perennial to 1 m high. Leaves strap-shaped and rather sappy, hairy on the underside towards the base. Flowers in slender spikes, spreading on short pedicels, green with darker keels, *c.*20 mm long.
Habitat: Rocky slopes on forest margins and shaded cliffs.

Albuca humilis
HYACINTH FAMILY
Drakensberg slime lily (E)
(Latin *humilis*, low-growing)
Deciduous bulbous perennial to 50 cm high, solitary. Leaves narrow, channelled and rather sappy. Flowers in slender spikes, held erect on long pedicels, white with green keels, scented of spicy vanilla, 15–20 mm long.
Habitat: Damp montane grassland and cliffs.
Notes: Common in the KwaZulu-Natal Drakensberg. *Albuca setosa* is similar but the bulb is topped with stout bristles and it occupies drier grassland and savannah.

Grassland and Savannah

Albuca nelsonii
HYACINTH FAMILY
Nelson's slime lily (E)
(Named for British nurseryman, William Nelson, who first collected the species)

Evergreen bulbous perennial to 1 m high, growing in clumps. Leaves strap-shaped and rather sappy. Flowers in stout spikes, held erect on long pedicels, white with green keels, 25–35 mm long.
Habitat: Grassland, especially near the coast.

Ornithogalum saundersiae
HYACINTH FAMILY
Giant white ornithogalum (E), Transvaalse tjienk (A)
(Named for Victorian flower artist, Katherine Saunders, who lived near Durban)

Bulbous perennial 1–1,5 m high. Leaves tongue-shaped. Flowers in rather flat-topped racemes, erect on conspicuous pedicels, petals rather thick-textured, white with a blackish ovary, 15 mm diameter.
Habitat: Localised on rocky banks and outcrops in thicket.
Notes: Bulbs very poisonous. An elegant and sophisticated cut flower.

Ornithogalum candicans
HYACINTH FAMILY
(= *Galtonia candicans*)
White berg lily (E), berglelie (A)
(Latin *candicans*, becoming pure white)

Bulbous perennial to 1,5 m high. Leaves strap- or tongue-shaped and channelled. Flowers in a conical raceme, nodding and bell-shaped, white or cream-coloured, 30–45 mm long, stamens 18–19 mm long.
Habitat: Rough grassland along streams and forest margins.
Notes: A statuesque plant popular in British gardens.

Grassland and Savannah

Ornithogalum regale
HYACINTH FAMILY
(= *Galtonia regalis*)
Royal berg lily (E), berglelie (A)
(Latin *regalis*, regal, from the type locality in Royal Natal National Park)
Bulbous perennial to 80 cm high. Leaves strap- or tongue-shaped and channelled. Flowers in a conical raceme, nodding and bell-shaped, greenish, 25–40 mm long, stamens 9–10 mm long.
Habitat: Wet basalt cliffs at high altitude.

Eucomis autumnalis
HYACINTH FAMILY
Common pineapple lily (E)
(Latin *autumnalis*, autumnal)
Bulbous perennial, 6–30 cm high. Leaves spreading in a basal cluster, tongue-shaped with undulate or crisped margins, uniformly green. Flowers tightly clustered on a plain green peduncle on pedicels 3–9 mm long, white to greenish, 13–25 mm diameter.
Habitat: Rocky, grassy slopes.
Notes: A decoction of the bulb is used for various ailments, including infections of the bowel and urinary tract.

Eucomis pallidiflora
HYACINTH FAMILY
Giant pineapple lily (E)
(Latin *pallidiflorus*, pale-flowered)
Bulbous perennial, 45–120 cm high. Leaves sub-erect in a basal cluster, tongue-shaped with undulate or crisped margins, uniformly green. Flowers more or less loosely clustered on a plain green peduncle on pedicels 15–50 mm long, white to greenish, 13–25 mm diameter.
Habitat: Marshy grassland, often along streams.
Notes: *Eucomis comosa* is another large species, with purple-spotted flower stalks that tend to lean sideways.

Grassland and Savannah

Eucomis bicolor
HYACINTH FAMILY
Bicoloured pineapple lily (E), bontpynappel-lelie (A), umBola (Z)
(Latin *bicolor*, bicoloured)

Bulbous perennial, 20–60 cm high. Leaves sub-erect in a basal cluster, tongue-shaped with undulate or crisped margins, spotted with purple beneath. Flowers more or less drooping, clustered on a spotted peduncle on pedicels 15–50 mm long, white with purple margins and speckling, 13–25 mm diameter.
Habitat: Montane grassland along streams and wet cliffs.

Pseudogaltonia clavata
HYACINTH FAMILY
Desert hyacinth (E)
(Latin *clavatus*, club-like, alluding to the flower shape)

Bulbous perennial, 50–100 cm high. Leaves usually emerging or present at flowering, sub-erect in a basal cluster. Flowers nodding in a dense, globose raceme, tubular and curved, white with pale green banding, 30–45 mm long.
Habitat: Stony and sandy flats.
Notes: Most often seen in the Kalahari.

Veltheimia bracteata
HYACINTH FAMILY
Forest sandlily (E), sandui (A)
(Latin *bracteatus*, with bracts, alluding to the conspicuous floral bracts)

Bulbous perennial, 20–40 cm high. Leaves glossy green, lanceolate or tongue-shaped. Flowers crowded in an ovoid or conical raceme, spreading to nodding, tubular, pink or pale yellow and finely speckled with red, 25–35 mm long.
Habitat: Coastal scrub and thicket.
Notes: A lovely garden plant for partly shaded situations.

Grassland and Savannah

Ledebouria cooperi
HYACINTH FAMILY
Cooper's ledebouria (E)
(Named after the English plant collector, Thomas Cooper)

Deciduous bulbous perennial to 15 cm high. Leaves sub-erect, narrow, more or less streaked and lined with purple beneath. Flowers spreading on pedicels 6–12 mm long, pink, the petals weakly recurved, 5 mm long.
Habitat: Damp grassland and seeps.
Notes: Variable but often distinguished by the bright pink flowers.

Ledebouria revoluta
HYACINTH FAMILY
Common ledebouria (E), inQwebebane (X), iCubudwana (Z)
(Latin *revolutus*, rolled back, referring to the petals)

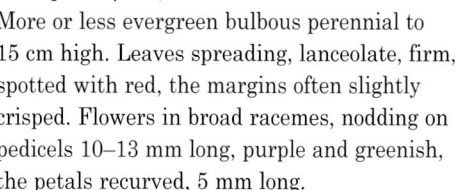

More or less evergreen bulbous perennial to 15 cm high. Leaves spreading, lanceolate, firm, spotted with red, the margins often slightly crisped. Flowers in broad racemes, nodding on pedicels 10–13 mm long, purple and greenish, the petals recurved, 5 mm long.
Habitat: Stony grassland. Used for various ailments.

Ledebouria floribunda
HYACINTH FAMILY
Green ledebouria (E)
(Latin *floribundus*, profusely flowering)
More or less evergreen bulbous perennial to 20 cm high. Leaves spreading, lanceolate, firm, spotted with red. Flowers in broad racemes, nodding on pedicels 12–16 mm long, usually uniformly greenish, the petals recurved, 7–9 mm long.
Habitat: Stony slopes, often in bushveld.
Notes: Common around Nelspruit. The heated leaves are used as a source of eardrops.

Grassland and Savannah

Merwilla natalensis
HYACINTH FAMILY
(= *Scilla natalensis*)
Large blue squill (E), blouslangkop (A), iCitha (Z), kherere (SS)
(Latin *natalensis*, from Natal)
Bulbous perennial to 1 m high, solitary or communal, the bulb covered with papery, brownish scales. Leaves usually just emerging at flowering, lance-shaped, smooth or velvety. Flowers in tall racemes, star-shaped, blue to lilac with white stamens, *c.*10 mm diameter.
Habitat: Damp grassland and cliffs.
Notes: Decoctions are taken as an enema for internal tumours and to enhance fertility and performance.

Cyanotis speciosa
COMMELINA FAMILY
Doll's powderpuff (E), uMagoswana (X), uMakotigoyile (Z)
(Latin *speciosus*, showy)
Perennial herb to 50 cm high. Leaves narrowly lanceolate with a sheathing petiole, hairy. Flowers in tight clusters subtended by a leaf-like bract, fragile, blue to mauve, 10 mm diameter, lasting a few hours, with prominent fluffy stamen filaments.
Habitat: Grassland.
Notes: Used to treat infertility and as a love charm.

Aneilema aequinoctiale
COMMELINA FAMILY
Clinging aneilema (E), iDangabane elikhulu (Z)
(Latin *aequinoctialis*, of the equinox or midday, when the flowers fade)
Erect or trailing perennial herb to 60 cm high. Leaves lance-shaped with a sheathing base covered in hooked hairs. Flowers in branched clusters, fragile, yellow with two prominent petals, 10 mm diameter, lasting a single morning.
Habitat: Coastal forest margins.
Notes: Used as a spinach.

Grassland and Savannah

Xerophyta retinervis
VELLOZIA FAMILY
Large black-stick lily (E),
bobbejaanstert (A)
(Latin *retinervis*, net-veined)

Tufted perennial with erect stems to 1 m high covered with the thickly fibrous remains of the leaf bases, usually blackened by fire. Leaves narrow and channelled with stiff hairs along the keel and margins, fibrous. Flowers solitary on slender stalks covered with stiff hairs, pale to deep mauve, 60 mm diameter.
Habitat: Rocky outcrops and hills.
Notes: Flowers after fire.

Xerophyta viscosa
VELLOZIA FAMILY
Small black-stick lily (E), lefiroane (SS)
(Latin *viscosus*, sticky, alluding to the flower stalks)

Tufted rhizomatous perennial to 50 cm high. Leaves narrow and channelled with stiff hairs along the keel and margins, fibrous. Flowers solitary on slender stalks covered with black, glandular hairs, white to pink or mauve, 60 mm diameter.
Habitat: Damp sandstone cliffs.
Notes: Leaves plaited into rope.

Rhodohypoxis baurii
STARGRASS FAMILY
Red star (E), rooisterretjie (A)
(Named for the missionary and plant collector, Rev. Leopold Bauer)

Cormous perennial, 5–10 cm high. Leaves narrow and channelled, covered with conspicuous hairs. Flowers on slender, roughly hairy stalks, white, pink or red, 20–30 mm diameter.
Habitat: Rock sheets and damp ledges in short grassland.
Notes: A popular plant among alpine enthusiasts in the northern hemisphere.

Grassland and Savannah

Hypoxis hemerocallidea
STARGRASS FAMILY
Medicinal star-flower (E), sterblom (A), inKomfe (Z)
(Latin *hemerocallideus*, resembling the day-lily, *Hemerocallis*)
Cormous perennial to 30 cm high. Leaves in three ranks, sickle-shaped and channelled with a prominent keel, covered with white hairs on the underside and margins. Flowers several per stem, yellow, 30–40 mm diameter.
Habitat: Grassland and open woodland.
Notes: The leaves are used to make rope and the bulb to blacken floors. Used to treat headaches, dizziness, mental disorders and cancer.

Hypoxis rigidula
STARGRASS FAMILY
Stiff-leaved star-flower (E), inKomfe (Z)
(Latin *rigidulus*, somewhat stiff or rigid)
Erect, cormous perennial, 30–60 cm high. Leaves erect, narrow and strongly ribbed, covered with white hairs and forming a false stem at the base. Flowers several per stem, 30–40 mm diameter.
Habitat: Stony grassland.
Notes: The leaves are used to make ropes.

Hypoxis costata
STARGRASS FAMILY
Ribbed star-flower (E), kharatsa (SS)
(Latin *costatus*, ribbed)
Cormous perennial, 10–15 cm high. Leaves rather broad and ribbed with strongly thickened margins, smooth or hairy, especially on the margins. Flowers several per stem, 30–40 mm diameter.
Habitat: Grassland.

Grassland and Savannah

Bulbine capitata
ALOE FAMILY
Narrow-leaved bulbine (E)
(Latin *capitatus*, with a knob-like head, referring to the flower head)

Rhizomatous perennial to 30 cm high. Leaves narrow and sappy, bright green, with broad membranous bases, decaying into membranous strips at the base. Flowers in a head-like raceme, bright yellow, lasting a single day each, with fluffy stamens, 10 mm diameter.
Habitat: Open grassland, conspicuous after a burn.
Notes: *Bulbine abyssinica* is similar but the leaves are pink at the base and decay into long membranous strips and the raceme is conical or cylindrical.

Bulbine narcissifolia
ALOE FAMILY
Strap-leaved bulbine (E),
komo-ea-balisa (SS)
(Latin *narcissifolius*, with leaves like a daffodil, *Narcissus*)

Rhizomatous perennial to 30 cm high. Leaves in a fan, twisted and strap-like, grey and firm, decaying into fine fibres at the base. Flowers in a conical raceme, pale canary yellow, lasting a single day each, with fluffy stamens, 10 mm diameter.
Habitat: Open grassland, common on overgrazed range land.
Notes: Used traditionally to induce pregnancy.

Kniphofia laxiflora
ALOE FAMILY
Slender poker (E), iCacane (Z)
(Latin *laxiflorus*, loosely flowered)

Perennial herb to 1 m, solitary or in small groups. Leaves slender and keeled, grass-like with smooth or minutely toothed margins. Flowers in a lax or loose spike, tubular with the anthers not protruding, orange to reddish or yellowish, 25–35 mm long.
Habitat: Rocky outcrops in grassland.

Grassland and Savannah

Kniphofia ichopensis
ALOE FAMILY
Ixopo poker (E)
(Latin *ichopensis*, from Ixopo)

Perennial herb to 80 cm, in colonies. Leaves slender and keeled, grass-like with smooth or minutely toothed margins. Flowers in a lax or loose spike, tubular with the anthers scarcely protruding, yellowish green to orange with yellowish buds, 25–35 mm long.
Habitat: Grassland vleis and marshy places.

Kniphofia triangularis
ALOE FAMILY
Mandarin poker (E),
leloele-le-lenye (SS)
(Latin *triangularis*, triangular, referring to the shape of the flower spike)
Perennial herb to 60 cm high, solitary or in small groups. Leaves narrow and keeled with the margins smooth or toothed, firm or softer in texture. Flowers in a conical head, tubular with the anthers scarcely protruding, coral-red to orange-yellow, 25–35 mm long.
Habitat: Montane grassland in damp places.
Notes: Pieces of the rhizome are threaded onto necklaces worn by pregnant women as protection against lightning.

Kniphofia thodei
ALOE FAMILY
Thode's poker (E)
(Named for the plant collector, Justus Thode)
Perennial herb to 50 cm high, usually solitary. Leaves narrow and keeled with the margins smooth or minutely toothed, soft in texture and greyish. Flowers in a conical head, tubular with the anthers scarcely protruding, reddish in bud opening white, 28–35 mm long.
Habitat: Montane grassland in damp places.
Notes: Easily seen near The Sentinel.

Kniphofia ritualis
ALOE FAMILY
Ritual poker (E)
(Latin *ritualis*, pertaining to the ritual usage of the plant)

Perennial herb to 80 cm high, solitary or in small groups. Leaves narrow and keeled with the margins regularly toothed, soft in texture. Flowers in an ovoid or cylindrical head, tubular with the anthers scarcely protruding, orange-red in bud opening greenish yellow, 25–30 mm long.
Habitat: Montane grassland in damp places, especially at the base of cliffs.
Notes: Easily seen near The Sentinel. Leaves used to make rope. Used traditionally during initiation of young women.

Kniphofia ensifolia
ALOE FAMILY
Pale poker (E)
(Latin *ensifolius*, sword-leaved)

Perennial herb to 1 m, in groups or colonies. Leaves strap-shaped and keeled with toothed margins, firm. Flowers in a dense cylindrical head, tubular with the anthers conspicuously protruding, yellowish to cream with pinkish buds, 15–20 mm long.
Habitat: Grassy vleis and marshes.

Kniphofia tysonii
ALOE FAMILY
Tyson's poker (E)
(Named for William Tyson, teacher and plant collector)

Perennial herb to 2 m high, in groups. Leaves narrow and keeled with smooth or minutely toothed margins. Flowers in an oblong or sub-cylindrical head, tubular with the anthers conspicuously protruding, orange to red opening yellow or greenish, 20–28 mm long.
Habitat: Vleis or seepage areas on hillsides.
Notes: *Kniphofia linearifolia* is similar but has slightly longer flowers with the anthers less conspicuously protruding.

Grassland and Savannah

Kniphofia caulescens
ALOE FAMILY
Lesotho poker (E), Basoetoe vuurpyl (A), leloele-la-loti (SS)
(Latin *caulescens*, developing a stem)
Evergreen perennial herb to 1 m high, with a well-defined stem, in groups or colonies. Leaves narrow and keeled with toothed margins, bluish grey and firm textured. Flowers in a cylindrical head, tubular with the anthers protruding, yellow with orange buds, 25 mm long.
Habitat: Damp mountainsides along streams.
Notes: The persistent, grey leaves are distinctive.

Kniphofia northiae
ALOE FAMILY
Marianne North's poker (E), leloele (SS)
(Named for the Victorian wildflower artist, Marianne North, who discovered the species on her travels)
Evergreen perennial herb to 1,7 m high, solitary or loose colonies. Leaves broad and without a keel, with toothed margins, leathery. Flowers in a cylindrical head, tubular with the anthers protruding, whitish or yellow to orange with reddish buds, 25 mm long.
Habitat: Damp mountainsides along streams and seeps.

Aloe kniphofioides
ALOE FAMILY
Poker aloe (E)
(Resembling a red-hot poker, *Kniphofia*)
Tufted perennial herb to 50 cm high with tuberous roots and swollen, bulb-like leaf bases. Leaves narrow and channelled, sometimes with small white teeth along the margins. Flowers in loose racemes, tubular, red with green tips, 50 mm long.
Habitat: Scattered in moist, stony grassland after fire.

Grassland and Savannah

Aloe cooperi
ALOE FAMILY

Cooper's grass aloe (E), isiPhukutwane (Z)
(Named for the English plant collector, Thomas Cooper)

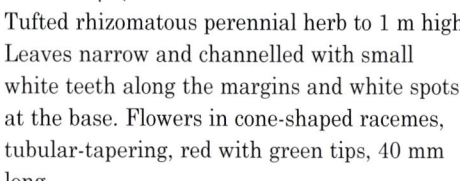

Tufted rhizomatous perennial herb to 1 m high. Leaves narrow and channelled with small white teeth along the margins and white spots at the base. Flowers in cone-shaped racemes, tubular-tapering, red with green tips, 40 mm long.
Habitat: Rocky grassland.
Notes: Flowers and leaves eaten as a vegetable. Used medicinally to promote easy birth.

Aloe ecklonis
ALOE FAMILY

Ecklon's grass aloe (E)
(Named for nineteenth-century German plant collector, C.F. Ecklon, who originally sent seeds of the species to Europe)

Tufted rhizomatous perennial herb to 50 cm. Leaves strap-shaped with white teeth on the margins and white spots at the base. Flowers in head-like racemes, ovoid, orange, red or yellow, 25 mm long.
Habitat: Grassy slopes.
Notes: Flowers and leaves eaten as a vegetable. Used traditionally to treat tuberculosis.

Aloe maculata
ALOE FAMILY

Common soap aloe (E), bontaalwyn (A), amaHlala (Z)
(Latin *maculatus*, blotched)

Stemless succulent perennial to 1 m. Leaves spreading and triangular with the tips usually curved down, densely spotted with white and with sharp, brown teeth on the margins. Flowers in head-like or flat-topped racemes, tubular with a swollen base, red to yellow, 45 mm long.
Habitat: Rocky outcrops, thicket and dry grassland.
Notes: Leaves eaten as a vegetable. Used traditionally for various ailments.

Grassland and Savannah

Aloe cryptopoda
ALOE FAMILY
Bushveld aloe (E), geelaalwyn (A)
(Greek *cryptopodus*, hidden foot, alluding to the large bracts that conceal the flower pedicels)

Stemless succulent perennial to 1 m. Leaves in a dense rosette, rather erect and lance-shaped, greyish green with small reddish teeth along the margins. Flowers in conical racemes, tubular and slightly upturned at the mouth, red to yellow or bicoloured, 30–40 mm long.
Habitat: In bushveld on open flats or rocky hills.

Aloe greatheadii
ALOE FAMILY
Greathead's aloe (E), Transvaalaalwyn (A)
(Named for Dr J.B. Greathead who collected the original material with the botanist, Dr S. Schönland)

Stemless succulent perennial to 1,5 m. Leaves spreading and triangular to lance-shaped with the tips often dead, shiny green and densely marked with pale spots arranged in bands and with sharp, brown teeth on the margins. Flowers in ovoid racemes, tubular with a swollen base, pink to red, 30–35 mm long.
Habitat: Rocky grassland.

Aloe chabaudii
ALOE FAMILY
Chabaud's aloe (E), inKalane (Z)
(Named for John Chabaud, who first flowered the species in his garden)

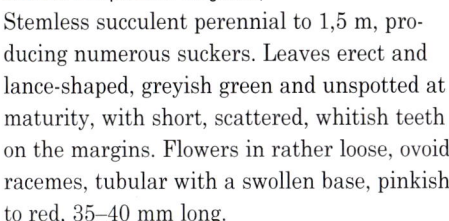

Stemless succulent perennial to 1,5 m, producing numerous suckers. Leaves erect and lance-shaped, greyish green and unspotted at maturity, with short, scattered, whitish teeth on the margins. Flowers in rather loose, ovoid racemes, tubular with a swollen base, pinkish to red, 35–40 mm long.
Habitat: Rock outcrops in bushveld.

Grassland and Savannah

Aloe marlothii
ALOE FAMILY
Marloth's mountain aloe (E), bergaalwyn (A), umHlaba (Z)
(Named after the chemist and botanist H.W. Rudolf Marloth)

Single-stemmed succulent to 5 m high. Leaves broad and dull green with dark brown spines on the margins and especially the lower surface. Flowers in well-branched panicles, each branch often more or less horizontal, the flowers facing upwards, tubular, red to yellow, 25 mm long.
Habitat: Rocky slopes and open bushveld.

Aloe castanea
ALOE FAMILY
Cat's-tail aloe (E), katstertaalwyn (A)
(*Castanea* is the chestnut, an allusion to the brownish nectar)

Single-stemmed succulent to 5 m high. Leaves narrow and dull green with small brown teeth on the margins. Flowers in dense, rather twisted, brush-like spikes, the flowers facing upwards, shortly tubular with very prominent, protruding stamens, orange-brown, 25 mm long.
Habitat: Rocky slopes and open bushveld.

Aloe ciliaris
ALOE FAMILY
Common rambling aloe (E)
(Latin *ciliaris*, fringed, referring to the leaf sheaths)

Shrublet with erect or sprawling stems to 6 m long. Leaves scattered along the branches, lanceolate with small white teeth on the margins and clasping bases that are conspicuously fringed at the mouth. Flowers in ovoid racemes, red with yellow and green tips, *c.*25 mm long.
Habitat: Coastal thicket and scrub.

Grassland and Savannah

Sandersonia aurantiaca
COLCHICUM FAMILY
Christmas bells (E), geelklokkie (A), uMagobongwana, uShayabhici (Z)
(Latin *aurantiacus*, orange)
Tuberous perennial to 75 cm high. Leaves lanceolate with three main veins, sometimes forming tendrils at the tip. Flowers nodding, lantern-like, orange, c.25 mm long.
Habitat: Damp grassland, often on the margins of bush.
Notes: Used as an aphrodisiac and a charm against evil.

Gloriosa modesta
COLCHICUM FAMILY
(= *Littonia modesta*)
Littonia (E), geelklokkie (A), iHlamvu lehlathi (Z)
(Latin *modestus*, modest, alluding to the coyly bowed flowers)
Erect or scrambling tuberous perennial to 75 cm high. Leaves lanceolate with three main veins, sometimes forming tendrils at the tip. Flowers nodding, cup-shaped, orange, 20-30 mm diameter.
Habitat: Damp grassland, often on the margins of bush.
Notes: Used traditionally as a fertility drug.

Gloriosa superba
COLCHICUM FAMILY
Flame lily (E), vlamlelie (A), iHlamvu, isiMiselo (Z)
(Latin *superbus*, superb)
Tuberous perennial with sprawling or climbing annual stems to 2 m high. Leaves lanceolate and tapering to a tendril at the tip. Flowers nodding, shaped like a turk's-cap lily, yellowish to orange and yellow with recurved petals crinkled along the margins, c.70 mm long.
Habitat: Coastal dunes and in thicket.
Notes: The whole plant is extremely poisonous but is used as an antiparasitic and remedy for ascites. The brightly coloured seeds are used in necklaces.

Grassland and Savannah

Colchicum melanthioides
COLCHICUM FAMILY

(= *Androcymbium melanthioides*)
Pyjama flower (E), patrysblom (A), khara (SS)
(Resembling the North American bunch-flower, *Melanthium*, in the form of the individual flowers)
Cormous perennial, 10–20 cm high. Leaves narrow and channelled. Flowers clustered between large creamy-white or lilac bracts with conspicuous green veins, the stamen filaments 8–10 mm long.
Habitat: Stony grassland.
Notes: *Colchicum orienticapense* has the stamen filaments only 4–5 mm long.

Haemanthus humilis
AMARYLLIS FAMILY
Rabbit's ears, common paintbrush lily (E), bobbejaanoor (A), sekitla (SS)
(Latin *humilis*, low growing)
Bulbous perennial, 12–20 cm high. Leaves appearing at flowering, two, tongue-shaped and usually hairy, curving backward onto the ground. Flowers in a loose terminal cluster on a reddish stem, pale pink or white, 25 mm long.
Habitat: Rocky grassland, among boulders.
Notes: Used traditionally for stomachaches, wounds and asthma.

Scadoxus puniceus
AMARYLLIS FAMILY

Blood lily (E), rooikwas (A), isiPhompo (Z)
(Latin *puniceus*, phoenician purple, crimson)
Bulbous perennial, 40–50 cm high. Leaves appearing at flowering, five to eight, soft-textured and bright green with the bases forming a false stem. Flowers in a dense terminal cluster subtended by large greenish to chocolate-brown bracts, red, 25 mm long.
Habitat: Coastal forest and inland bush clumps, often among rocks.
Notes: Used as a poultice, to treat coughs, stomach ailments, and headaches. The bulb is poisonous.

Grassland and Savannah

Scadoxus multiflorus
AMARYLLIS FAMILY
Fireball lily, Catherine wheel (E),
isiPhompo (Z)

(Latin *multiflorus*, many-flowered)

Bulbous perennial, 30–100 cm high. Leaves present at flowering, four or five, soft-textured, the bases forming a false stem. Flowers, many in a dense terminal cluster on a stout stem speckled with purple, borne on fairly long pedicels to form a rounded ball about 20 cm in diameter, pinkish to red, 40 mm long. Fruits fleshy, berry-like, red when ripe.
Habitat: Coastal and inland forests in damp places.

Clivia miniata
AMARYLLIS FAMILY
Clivia, bush lily (E), boslelie (A),
uMayime (Z)

(Latin *miniatus*, saturn-red, flame-red)

Rhizomatous perennial to 60 cm. Leaves strap-like, dark green. Flowers in a terminal cluster, spreading, funnel-shaped, pale orange with a yellow centre, 50–60 mm diameter. Fruits fleshy, berry-like, red when ripe.
Habitat: Coastal and inland forest, sheltered ledges and ravines.
Notes: Used for snakebite and relieving fevers. The leaves are used in delayed pregnancy and to ease childbirth.

Clivia caulescens
AMARYLLIS FAMILY
Transvaal clivia (E)

(Latin *caulescens*, developing a stem)

Rhizomatous perennial to 1 m, with a distinct, often sprawling stem. Leaves strap-like, dark green. Flowers in a terminal cluster, nodding, tubular, deep red with short greenish to yellow-tipped petals, 40 mm long. Fruits fleshy, berry-like, red when ripe.
Habitat: Forest floors along the Mpumalanga escarpment.

Grassland and Savannah

Cyrtanthus tuckii
AMARYLLIS FAMILY
Green-tipped fire lily (E), brandlelie (A), isiWesa (Z)
(Named for horticulturist and collector, William Tuck)

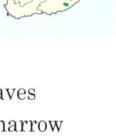

Bulbous perennial to 20 cm high. Leaves usually appearing after the flowers, narrow and strap-like. Flowers, several in a terminal cluster, tubular, strongly curved and nodding, red with yellowish or green tips, 50–60 mm long.
Habitat: Damp grassland, flowering best after veld fires.

Cyrtanthus sanguineus
AMARYLLIS FAMILY
Inanda lily, Kei lily (E), isiLawu esimhlope (X)
(Latin *sanguineus*, blood-red)

Bulbous perennial to 25 cm high. Leaves narrow and strap-like, channelled. Flowers one or two, funnel-shaped with a long tube, bright red with paler throat striped with red, 100 mm long.
Habitat: Riverine bush, shady rocks and cliffs.
Notes: Traditionally used as an emetic.

Cyrtanthus breviflorus
AMARYLLIS FAMILY
Yellow fire lily (E), geelvuurlelie (A), uVelabahleke (Z)
(Latin *breviflorus*, with short flowers)

Bulbous perennial to 15 cm high. Leaves often absent or just emerging at flowering time, narrow and strap-like. Flowers, several in a loose terminal cluster, funnel-shaped, yellow, 20–30 mm long.
Habitat: Marshes and damp grassland, flowering best after veld fires.

Grassland and Savannah

Cyrtanthus mackenii
AMARYLLIS FAMILY

Ifafa lily (E), ifafalelie (A)
(Named for Mark McKen, first curator of the Durban Botanic Gardens)

Bulbous perennial to 20 cm high, usually growing in clumps. Leaves shiny, narrow and strap-like, appearing with or after the flowers. Flowers narrowly tubular with short spreading petals, whitish or yellow to creamy-pink or red, *c.*50 mm long.
Habitat: Grassland, forest margins, stony slopes and along the coast.

Crinum bulbispermum
AMARYLLIS FAMILY

Orange River lily, Vaal River lily (E), vleilelie (A), lelutla (SS), umNduze (Z)
(Greek *bulbispermus*, bulb-seeded, referring to the fact that the seeds develop directly into bulbils)

Bulbous perennial to 1 m high. Leaves spreading, strap-like with wavy margins. Flowers nodding in bud and flower, narrowly funnel-shaped with a long slender tube, pale pink with darker stripes and white to pink anthers, strongly fragrant at night, 150 mm long.
Habitat: Damp grassland near streams and seasonal pans.
Notes: Used traditionally to treat colds and rheumatism and as a poultice for sores.

Crinum macowanii
AMARYLLIS FAMILY

MacOwan's river lily (E), rivierlelie (A), inTelezi (X), umNduze (Z)
(Named for Victorian botanist, Peter MacOwan, who first collected the species)

Bulbous perennial to 80 cm high. Leaves spreading, strap-like with wavy margins. Flowers erect in bud but nodding and funnel-shaped with a long slender tube at flowering, pale pink with black anthers, strongly fragrant at night, 150 mm long.
Habitat: Grassland near rivers.
Notes: Used as a treatment for urinary tract infections, rashes and as a charm.

Grassland and Savannah

Crinum moorei
AMARYLLIS FAMILY
Moore's river lily (E), boslelie (A),
umNduze (Z)
(Named for D. Moore, director of Dublin Botanic Gardens)

Bulbous perennial to 1,2 m high, often growing in clumps and forming large colonies. Leaves spreading and strap-like with wavy margins, forming a false stem at the base. Flowers nodding and bell-like with a long slender tube, white to pale pink, sweetly scented, opening more widely at night and more strongly scented, 150 mm long.
Habitat: Vleis and marshy sites, in shade or sun.
Notes: Used traditionally for urinary tract infections.

Nerine angustifolia
AMARYLLIS FAMILY
Ribbon-leaved nerina (E), lematlana (SS)
(Latin *angustifolius*, narrow-leaved)
Bulbous perennial, 20–50 cm high. Leaves narrow and strap-like or channelled. Flowers on shortly hairy pedicels, flaring with narrow, crisped petals, pink, 30–40 mm diameter.
Habitat: Grassy marshes.

Nerine bowdenii
AMARYLLIS FAMILY
Great nerina (E)
(Named for Mr Cornish-Bowden, a government surveyor, who first collected the species)
Bulbous perennial, 30–70 cm high. Leaves strap-like and channelled. Flowers on hairless pedicels, flaring with narrow, crisped petals, pink, 40–50 mm diameter.
Habitat: Wet cliffs at high altitude.
Notes: Abundant along the path up The Sentinel.

Grassland and Savannah

Boophone disticha
AMARYLLIS FAMILY
Oxbane (E), seerooglelie (A), inCwadi (X, Z)
(Latin *distichus*, arranged in two opposite rows, alluding to the fan of leaves)

Bulbous perennial to 45 cm high. Leaves dry or just emerging at flowering, strap-like and often twisted, many in a two-ranked fan. Flowers in a dense terminal cluster, borne on stalks that lengthen with age, funnel-shaped, deep pink, 30 mm diameter. Fruiting head a large tumbleweed, breaking loose from the plant when dry and blowing in the wind.
Habitat: Grassland, open bush, and rocky flats.
Notes: A poultice is used for boils and abscesses while the fresh leaf is applied to cuts to stop bleeding. The sap is toxic and was used by the San in the preparation of arrow poison.

Ammocharis coranica
AMARYLLIS FAMILY
Ammocharis (E), seerooglelie (A), isiDiya (Z)
(Name alludes to the tribe Korana San)

Bulbous perennial to 20 cm high. Leaves several, strap-shaped and spreading, greyish green. Flowers in a rounded terminal cluster, star-like with a slender tube, pink to crimson, sweetly scented, 40 mm diameter.
Habitat: Dry grassland and flats.
Notes: Paste from the bulbs used to waterproof clay pots and traditionally used for men's head rings.

Brunsvigia natalensis
AMARYLLIS FAMILY
Common candelabra (E), misryblom (A), lematla (SS)
(Latin *natalensis*, from Natal)

Bulbous perennial to 20 cm high. Leaves four to six, tongue-like and rough, flat on the ground. Flowers in a rounded terminal cluster on long pedicels, deep pink to maroon, 40 mm diameter. Fruiting head a ball-like tumbleweed, breaking free of the plant when dry and bowling across the veld in the wind.
Habitat: Grassland.

Grassland and Savannah

Brunsvigia grandiflora
AMARYLLIS FAMILY
Giant candelabra (E), kandelaar (A),
isiChwe (X), umQhele-wenkuzi (Z)
(Latin *grandiflorus*, large-flowered)

Bulbous perennial to 60 cm high. Leaves present at flowering, 10 to 15, oblong and wavy, more or less erect in a fan. Flowers in a rounded terminal cluster on long pedicels, pale to deep pink, 40 mm diameter. Fruiting head a ball-like tumble-weed, breaking free of the plant when dry and bowling across the veld in the wind.
Habitat: Grassland.
Notes: Bulb used traditionally to soothe and heal wounds, particularly after circumcision.

Agapanthus campanulatus
AGAPANTHUS FAMILY
Bell agapanthus (E), bloulelie (A),
uGebeleweni (X), uBani (Z)
(Latin *campanulatus*, bell-shaped)

Rhizomatous perennial herb, 40–70 cm. Leaves strap-shaped, deciduous. Flowers spreading in umbels, widely funnel-shaped with the petals much longer than the flower tube, blue to purple, 20–35 mm long.
Habitat: Rocky grassland.

Agapanthus inapertus
AGAPANTHUS FAMILY
Drooping agapanthus (E), bloulelie (A)
(Latin *inapertus*, without an obvious mouth, alluding to the tubular flowers)

Rhizomatous perennial herb, 40–150 cm. Leaves strap-shaped, deciduous. Flowers nodding in umbels, tubular with the petals shorter than the flower tube, blue to purple, 30–50 mm long.
Habitat: Damp grassland or stream sides.
Notes: Rhizomes used as a purgative antenatally and postnatally.

Grassland and Savannah

Aristea angolensis
IRIS FAMILY
Common branched aristea (E)
(Latin *angolensis*, from Angola, where the original material was collected)
Rhizomatous perennial, 60–100 cm. Leaves narrow and fibrous, in a loose fan. Flowers in small clusters on a branching stem, pale to deep blue, lasting a single morning, 10–15 mm diameter.
Habitat: Damp grassland and margins of bush clumps.
Notes: *Aristea woodii* is similar but the flower clusters are scattered along an unbranched stem.

Dietes iridioides
IRIS FAMILY
Wood iris, dietes (E), inDawo yehlati (Z)
(Resembling the genus *Iris* in its flowers and rhizomatous habit)
Evergreen perennial herb to 60 cm high, with a creeping rhizome. Leaves sword-shaped, in a loose fan, dark green. Flowers subtended by sheathing bracts, each lasting a single morning, white with the inner petals often marked with brown streaks near the base and the style branches lightly flushed with violet, 30–40 mm diameter.
Habitat: Evergreen forest or clearings in bush.
Notes: *Dietes grandiflora* has larger flowers that last for several days each.

Moraea brevistyla
IRIS FAMILY
Partridge moraea (E)
(Latin *brevistylus*, short-styled)
Cormous perennial, 20–50 cm high, usually branched. Leaf solitary, slender and channelled. Flowers white, the outer three petals speckled with brown at the base, the inner petals three-lobed and coiled at the tips, 20–25 mm diameter.
Habitat: Montane grassland, often in damper places.

Grassland and Savannah

Moraea inclinata
IRIS FAMILY
Common blue moraea (E)
(Latin *inclinatus*, inclined, alluding to the stem)

Cormous perennial, 30–90 cm high, the stem sharply inclined above the leaf. Leaves solitary and inserted well up on the stem, narrow and channelled. Flowers mauve, the outer petals marked with yellow and purple at the base, the inner petals tongue-shaped and spreading, 30–40 mm diameter.
Habitat: Montane grassland.

Moraea polystachya
IRIS FAMILY
Karoo iris (E)
(Latin *polystachyus*, many-spiked, alluding to the branched inflorescence)

Cormous perennial, 40–90 cm high, branched. Leaves several, narrow and channelled, trailing. Flowers blue, the outer petals marked with yellow at the base, the inner petals tongue-shaped and erect, 40–50 mm diameter.
Habitat: Stony slopes in karroid bush.
Notes: Common around Beaufort West. Parts of the plant are poisonous when green, causing death in stock and occasionally humans.

Moraea muddii
IRIS FAMILY
Early yellow moraea (E)
(Named for the English horticulturist, C. Mudd, who first collected the species)

Cormous perennial, 20–50 cm high, solitary. Basal leaf solitary, narrow and channelled, often overtopping the stem. Flowers pale yellow, the outer three petals with a darker yellow eye and the inner tepals tongue-shaped and erect, 40–50 mm diameter.
Habitat: Damp or marshy grassland.
Notes: Distinguished by its small stature. Common around Graskop.

Grassland and Savannah

Moraea spathulata
IRIS FAMILY
Large yellow moraea, teele-e-kholo (SS),
iHlamvu lentaba (X), iNdlolothi (Z)
(Latin *spathulatus*, spatula-shaped, referring to the petals)

Cormous perennial to about 1 m high, solitary or growing in small clumps. Basal leaf single, leathery, flat or channelled, often bent and trailing above. Flowers bright yellow, the outer three petals with a darker yellow eye and the inner tepals tongue-shaped and erect, 50–60 mm diameter.
Habitat: Grassland, often among rocks.
Notes: *Moraea huttonii* has a brown mark on each style crest and grows in clumps, while *M. moggii* is similar but the leaf is distinctly grey. Poisonous to stock.
Flowering: May to September in the south, November to February in the interior and north.

Dierama floriferum
IRIS FAMILY
Tufted hairbell (E)

(Latin *floriferus*, bearing many flowers)
Cormous perennial, 40–70 cm high, growing in dense clumps. Leaves narrow and fibrous. Flowers rather crowded in a slender, nodding spike, funnel-shaped, mauve, 15–20 mm long, the floral bracts densely speckled with brown in the centre.
Habitat: Well-watered grassland.
Notes: Common around Nottingham Road.

Dierama luteoalbidum
IRIS FAMILY
Large white hairbell (E)
(Latin *luteoalbidus*, yellowish white)
Cormous perennial, 70–100 cm high, solitary. Leaves narrow and fibrous. Flowers, rather few in a slender, nodding spike, funnel-shaped, ivory-white, 30–50 mm long, the floral bracts white.
Habitat: Well-watered grassland.
Notes: Common around Nottingham Road and Karkloof.

Grassland and Savannah

Hesperantha baurii
IRIS FAMILY

Common hesperantha (E), khahla-enyenyane (SS), isiDwa (Z)
(Named for the missionary and plant collector, Rev. Leopold Bauer)

Cormous perennial, 15–40 cm. Basal leaves two, slender and sword-like. Flowers with a tube 6–12 mm long, deep pink, 15–20 mm diameter.
Habitat: Well-watered grassland.
Notes: Common in the Drakensberg.

Hesperantha coccinea
IRIS FAMILY

(= *Schizostylis coccinea*)
Scarlet river lily (E), khahlana (SS)
(Latin *coccineus*, deep red)

Perennial with a short rhizome, 40–90 cm high. Leaves narrow and sword-shaped, in a loose fan. Flowers with a slender tube 30 mm long, bright red or pink, 30 mm diameter.
Habitat: Stream banks.
Notes: A popular garden plant, better known under the old name *Schizostylis*.

Freesia laxa
IRIS FAMILY

(= *Anomatheca laxa*)
Small forest freesia (E), bospaletblaar (A)
(Latin *laxus*, loose, not crowded)

Cormous perennial, 15–30 cm high. Leaves narrowly sword-like and soft-textured, in a loose fan. Flowers with a long, slender tube 20–40 mm long, red or lilac with darker marks on the lower petals, 20–25 mm diameter.
Habitat: Forest margins and edges of bush clumps or thicket.
Notes: The lilac form is found only along the northern KwaZulu-Natal coast.

Grassland and Savannah

Watsonia pillansii
IRIS FAMILY
Pillans' watsonia (E)
(Named for Cape Town botanist, Neville Pillans)
Cormous perennial, 50–120 cm high, growing in colonies. Leaves sword-shaped, leathery, mostly 10–18 mm wide. Flowers in a two-ranked spike, scarlet to orange, trumpet-shaped, the floral tube 35–50 mm long, the petals 20–26 mm long.
Habitat: Rocky outcrops in grassland.

Watsonia densiflora
IRIS FAMILY
Natal watsonia (E), khahla (SS), inCembuzane (Z)
(Latin *densiflorus*, densely flowered)
Cormous perennial, 60–120 cm high, growing in clumps. Leaves sword-shaped, leathery, mostly 10–18 mm wide. Flowers in inclined, two-ranked spike, pink, funnel-shaped, the floral tube 20–40 mm long, the petals 18–24 mm long.
Habitat: Well-watered grassland.
Notes: Distinguished from related species by its clumped growth habit and pale greenish-straw bracts with dark margins and pale veins.

Watsonia lepida
IRIS FAMILY
Drakensberg watsonia (E), khahla (SS)
(Latin *lepidus*, attractive)
Cormous perennial, 25–60 cm high, solitary. Leaves sword-shaped, leathery, mostly 5–15 mm wide, the lower leaves dry and brown or burned off. Flowers in erect, two-ranked spike, pink, funnel-shaped, the floral tube 20–35 mm long, the petals 20 mm long.
Habitat: Well-watered, montane grassland.
Notes: Distinguished by its solitary growth habit and dry lower leaves.

Grassland and Savannah

Crocosmia paniculata
IRIS FAMILY

Zigzag crocosmia, Aunt-Eliza (E), uDwendweni, umLunge (Z)
(Latin *paniculatus*, a branched inflorescence)

Cormous perennial, 1–2 m high, growing in large clumps. Leaves sword-like and longitudinally pleated, in a loose fan. Flowers in a one-sided, branched inflorescence, on zigzag branches, trumpet-shaped, orange and yellow with darker petals, 70 mm long.
Habitat: Rock outcrops in grassland and along road verges.
Notes: Used traditionally to treat dysentery and infertility.

Crocosmia aurea
IRIS FAMILY

Falling stars, Forest montbretia (E), umLunge (Z)
(Latin *aureus*, golden-yellow)

Cormous geophyte to about 1 m high. Leaves narrowly sword-like, in a loose fan. Flowers nodding, star-like with a slender, curved tube, bright orange, 40 mm diameter. Fruits yellow-orange on the inside with dark brown or black seeds.
Habitat: Forest margins and clearings and light bush.
Notes: Used traditionally to treat dysentery.

Gladiolus woodii
IRIS FAMILY

Wood's gladiolus (E)
(Named for John Medley Wood, first curator of the Durban Botanic Gardens, who collected the species)

Cormous perennial, 30–50 cm high. Leaves few and scattered up the stem with at most a short blade, with scattered soft hairs. Flowers in an angled, one-sided spike, funnel-shaped, yellow, dark brown or lilac, 25 mm long.
Habitat: Stony grassland.

Grassland and Savannah

Gladiolus longicollis
IRIS FAMILY

Moth gladiolus (E), aandblom (A), khala-enyenyane (SS), umBejo (Z)

(Latin *longicollis*, long-necked, referring to the slender floral tube)

Cormous perennial to 60 cm high. Leaves three, narrow, almost grass-like, X-shaped in section. Flowers often solitary, cream, often mottled with light to dark brown, somewhat closed during the day but opening and sweetly scented at night, trumpet-shaped with a long slender floral tube 50–100 mm long.
Habitat: Moist grassland.
Notes: Pollinated by hawkmoths.

Gladiolus crassifolius
IRIS FAMILY

Thick-leaved gladiolus (E), khala-enyenyane (SS), iGulusha (Z)

(Latin *crassifolius*, thick leaved)

Cormous perennial, mostly 50–100 cm high. Leaves narrow and fibrous with pale, thickened margins and midrib, in a loose fan, the bases often forming a stem. Flowers in a one-sided spike, funnel-shaped, cream flushed pink or orange and with darker marks on the lower lip, 25–40 mm long.
Habitat: Well-watered grassland.

Gladiolus papilio
IRIS FAMILY

Butterfly gladiolus (E), sidvwana (SS), iButha (Z)

(Latin *papilio*, butterfly)

Cormous perennial, mostly 50–100 cm high. Leaves narrow and relatively short, in a loose fan. Flowers few in an angled, one-sided spike, nodding, bell-shaped, yellowish green or cream, often flushed purple, with large dark marks on the lower lip, 50 mm long.
Habitat: Marshy or damp grassland.

Grassland and Savannah

Gladiolus ecklonii
IRIS FAMILY

Speckled gladiolus (E), khahla (SS)
(Named for nineteenth-century German plant collector, C.F. Ecklon)

Cormous perennial, mostly 25–40 cm high. Leaves sword-shaped with pale, thickened margins, in a tight fan. Flowers in a short, one-sided spike, in the axils of large, green bracts, funnel-shaped, mottled purple, red or brown on a cream to pink background, the floral tube 15–20 mm long, the petals 25–35 mm long.
Habitat: Marshy or well-watered grassland.
Notes: The corm may be eaten raw or cooked and is used for treatment of rheumatic pain.

Gladiolus sericeovillosus
IRIS FAMILY

Large speckled gladiolus (E), isiDwa (Z)
(Latin *sericeo-*, *villosus*, silky, shaggy)

Cormous perennial, 50–150 cm. Leaves narrow and fibrous with prominent margins, in a loose fan with the bases forming a stem, smooth or finely hairy. Flowers in a two-ranked spike on a woolly stem, funnel-shaped with a rather closed mouth, whitish or pink to greenish, 30 mm long.
Habitat: Rough grassland and edges of bush.
Notes: Used traditionally to treat dysentery and for sprains and swollen joints.

Gladiolus oppositiflorus
IRIS FAMILY

Large pink gladiolus (E)
(Latin *oppositiflorus*, with flowers in opposite ranks)

Cormous geophyte to 100 cm or more. Leaves narrow and fibrous, in a loose fan, often minutely velvety. Flowers several to many in a more or less two-ranked spike, narrowly tubular below, pink to salmon, the lower petals with darker streaks in the midline, floral tube 30–55 mm long, petals 40–40 mm long.
Habitat: Stony open grassland and mountain slopes.

Grassland and Savannah

Gladiolus dalenii
IRIS FAMILY

Parrot lily (E), khala-e-kholo (SS), isiDwi esibomvu (Z)

(Named in 1828 for Cornelius Dalen, director of the Rotterdam Botanical Gardens)

Cormous perennial, 70–100 cm high. Leaves sword-shaped, in a loose fan. Flowers in a one-sided spike, funnel-shaped, orange or greenish, sometimes flushed purple, the lower petals often yellow, the floral tube 30–50 mm long and the upper petals 20–50 mm long.
Habitat: Open grassland, rocky slopes and ledges.

Gladiolus saundersii
IRIS FAMILY

Saunders' gladiolus, Lesotho lily (E), khala ea maloti (SS)

(Named for the English grower, W. Wilson Saunders, who employed the collector Thomas Cooper)

Cormous perennial, 50–90 cm high. Leaves sword-shaped, in a tight fan. Flowers in a one-sided spike, drooping, funnel-shaped with the petals curled back, red with white speckles on the lower lip, the floral tube 35–40 mm long and the upper petals 50–70 mm long.
Habitat: Open grassland, rocky slopes and ledges.
Notes: Common near Rhodes.

Strelitzia reginae
CRANE FLOWER FAMILY

Crane flower (E), geel piesang (A)

(Latin *reginae*, queen, alluding to its regal appearance)

Evergreen stemless perennial to 1,5 m high. Leaves on long petioles with large, elliptical blades. Flowers enclosed in a leathery, boat-shaped bract, orange with blue styles, *c.*200 mm long. Fruit a woody capsule containing black, pea-like seeds bearing a tuft of bright orange hairs.
Habitat: River banks, in coastal bush and thicket.

Grassland and Savannah

Eulophia clavicornis
ORCHID FAMILY
Early fire eulophia (E), imFeyamasele eluhlaza (Z)
(Latin *clavicornis*, club-horned, alluding to the spur)
Rhizomatous perennial to 30 cm high. Leaves produced on a separate shoot, partly to fully developed at flowering, narrow and pleated. Flowers in a loose spike, white or lilac and purplish or yellow and brown, *c.*20 mm long, the lip covered with slender papillae and bearing a narrow spur 2–9 mm long.
Habitat: Grassland, especially after fire.

Eulophia ensata
ORCHID FAMILY
Yellow cluster eulophia (E), iPhamba lentaba (Z)
(Latin *ensatus*, sword-shaped, alluding to the leaves)
Rhizomatous perennial to 1 m high. Leaves produced on a separate shoot, partly to fully developed at flowering, narrow and pleated. Flowers crowded in a head-like spike, pale to bright yellow, *c.*20 mm long, the lip covered with slender papillae and bearing a narrow spur 4–7 mm long.
Habitat: Grassland and open bushveld, often coastal.

Eulophia foliosa
ORCHID FAMILY
Green cluster eulophia (E), lekholela (SS)
(Latin *foliosus*, leafy)
Rhizomatous perennial to 60 cm high. Leaves produced on a separate shoot, partly to fully developed at flowering, narrow and pleated. Flowers crowded in a dense spike, green with a purple lip, 20 mm long, the lip covered with stout papillae and without a spur.
Habitat: Grassland.

Grassland and Savannah

Eulophia angolensis
ORCHID FAMILY
Yellow marsh eulophia (E)
(Latin *angolensis*, from Angola, where it was first collected)

Stout rhizomatous perennial, 60–120 cm. Leaves produced on a separate shoot, stiff and pleated. Flowers in a loose spike, yellow with the upper tepals folded over the flower, fragrant, 25 mm diameter, the lip covered with rough crests and with a very short conical spur.
Habitat: Marshy grassland, often coastal.
Notes: Used traditionally as a love charm.

Eulophia streptopetala
ORCHID FAMILY
Bushveld harlequin orchid (E), amaBelejongosi (Z)
(Latin *streptopetalus*, with striped petals)

Stout perennial with partly exposed pseudobulbs. Leaves produced on a separate shoot, thin-textured. Flowers in a loose spike, thick-textured, yellow and brown with the upper tepals held like a roof over the flower, 30 mm diameter, the lip folded and with a short conical spur.
Habitat: Bushveld and open scrub.
Notes: Used traditionally as a love charm.

Eulophia speciosa
ORCHID FAMILY
Yellow harlequin orchid (E), umLunge omhlope (Z)
(Latin *speciosus*, showy)

Stout perennial with subterranean or partly exposed pseudobulbs. Leaves produced on a separate shoot, leathery and channelled. Flowers in a loose spike, thick-textured, bright yellow and green with purple streaks on the lip, 30 mm diameter, the lip bearing shallow ridges and with a short conical spur.
Habitat: Bushveld and open scrub.
Notes: Used traditionally as an emetic and charm against storms.

Grassland and Savannah

Brownleea macroceras
ORCHID FAMILY
Large false disa (E)
(Greek *macroceras*, large horned i.e. spurred)

Tuberous perennial, 6–20 cm high. Leaves one to three, narrow. Flowers few, pale to deep lilac, upper petals with a long, slender spur 25–40 mm long, lip vestigial.
Habitat: Damp montane grassland and wet ledges.

Disperis stenoplectron
ORCHID FAMILY
Purple granny's bonnet (E), moederkappie (A)
(Greek *stenoplectron*, narrow spur)

Tuberous perennial, 15–30 cm high. Leaves two to four, lanceolate. Flowers in a two-sided spike, dull pink to purple and greenish, with a sac-like hood, 20 mm diameter.
Habitat: Moist montane grassland.
Notes: One of several similar species. *Disperis fanniniae*, with larger, white flowers, is not uncommon on inland forest floors. Most species are pollinated by specialised oil-collecting bees.

Delosperma obtusum
MESEMB FAMILY
Mountain vygie (E), kransvygie (A)
(Latin *obtusus*, blunt, referring to the leaves)

Creeping, succulent dwarf shrub, to 5 cm high, with papillate branches. Leaves three-angled, succulent. Flowers in small clusters, brilliant magenta, 20 mm diameter.
Habitat: Rock sheets and outcrops at high altitude.
Notes: Easily seen at Witzieshoek.

Grassland and Savannah

Carpobrotus dimidiatus
MESEMB FAMILY
Sourfig (E), perdevy (A), gaukum (N)
(Latin *dimidiatus*, halved, alluding to the leaf pairs)

Robust succulent perennial with trailing stems that root along their length and form dense mats. Leaves succulent and three-sided, almost straight. Flowers solitary, purple, pink or white, 60–80 mm diameter, rounded at the base and narrowed abruptly into the flower stalk.
Habitat: Sand dunes and rocks along the seashore, and rocky coastal grassland.
Notes: The fruits are used for jam and syrup. The juice of the leaves is highly astringent and mildly antiseptic and is useful for burns, wounds and eczema. It is used as a gargle and is also taken internally for a variety of stomach ailments.

Portulacaria afra
PORTULACA FAMILY
Elephant bush (E), spekboom (A)
(Latin *afra*, from Africa)

Succulent shrub or small tree to 3 m high. Leaves opposite, fleshy, obovate. Flowers in clusters at the branch tips, pink, c.5 mm diameter.
Habitat: Dry rocky slopes.
Notes: Dry, powdered leaves used traditionally as a snuff. A valuable fodder plant in dry areas, particularly for the Addo elephants.

Crassula sarcocaulis
STONECROP FAMILY
Bonsai bush (E), uMadinsane (Z)
(Greek *sarcocaulis*, fleshy stemmed)

Succulent shrublet to 60 cm high, resembling a bonsai in form. Leaves narrow and fleshy. Flowers in dense, rounded clusters, cup-shaped, creamy white and pinkish, unpleasantly scented, 6 mm diameter.
Habitat: Damp or partially shaded rock outcrops, often at high altitudes.
Notes: Used traditionally as an emetic.

Grassland and Savannah

Crassula vaginata
STONECROP FAMILY

White stonecrop, yellow crassula (E), umDumbukane (Z)

(Latin *vaginatus*, sheathing, referring to the leaves)

Perennial herb with a leafy annual stem to 50 cm high from a tuberous rootstock. Leaves grading down in size up the stem, lance-shaped and smooth or hairy with a white-fringed margin. Flowers in a flat-topped, branched cluster, yellow or white, fragrant, 6 mm diameter.
Habitat: Moist grassland.
Notes: Used traditionally to treat earache and bruises. The ground roots are added to milk as a carbohydrate in times of famine.

Kalanchoe thyrsiflora
STONECROP FAMILY

White lady (E), meelplakkie (A), utywAla bentaka (X), utywAla benyoni (Z)

(Latin *thyrsiflorus*, with the flowers produced in the arrangement known as a thyrse)

Succulent biennial to 1,5 m in flower, producing a rosette of leaves in the first year and flowering in the second. Leaves mainly in a basal rosette, obovate, greyish with the margins tinged red. Flowers crowded in an elongate inflorescence, bright yellow, fragrant, 12–20 mm long.
Habitat: Dry rocky grassland.
Notes: Used to treat earache and colds, as a vermifuge and charm.

Cotyledon orbiculata
STONECROP FAMILY

Pig's ears (E), varkoor (A), iPhewula (X, Z)

(Latin *orbiculatus*, circular, referring to the rounded leaves)

Succulent shrublet to 1 m high. Leaves obovate to narrowly ovoid, smooth and with a grey bloom or sometimes velvety. Flowers nodding in terminal clusters, reddish, 8–30 mm long.
Habitat: Rocky outcrops in scrub.
Notes: Used traditionally to treat warts, corms, earache, toothache and as a poultice for boils.

Grassland and Savannah

Nymphaea nouchali
WATERLILY FAMILY
(= *Nymphaea caerulea*)
Blue waterlily (E)
(From the Hindi *nilkamal* or *niloo phal*)
Aquatic perennial with floating leaves. Leaves orbicular and deeply notched at the base with undulate or scalloped margins. Flowers blue to mauve, scented, 100–120 mm diameter, closing at night.
Habitat: Pools and sluggish rivers.
Notes: Used traditionally to treat colds and as a love charm.

Clematis brachiata
RANUNCULUS FAMILY
Traveller's joy (E), lemoenbloeisels (A), morarana-oa-mafehlo (SS), iTyolo (X), iHlonzo lezinduli (Z)
(Latin *brachiatus*, with spreading branchlets)
Climber with wiry stems. Leaves opposite, divided into ovate segments with coarsely toothed margins, sparsely hairy on the underside. Flowers in clusters, hairy, white, fragrant, 20 mm diameter. Fruits topped with the feathery style.
Habitat: Scrub and forest margins.
Notes: The dried plant is pounded as a snuff for clearing the head. An infusion of the leaves is taken as a vermifuge.

Anemone transvaalensis
RANUNCULUS FAMILY
(= *Knowltonia transvaalensis*)
Transvaal blistering leaves (E), brandblaar (A), umVuthuza (X, Z)
(Latin *transvaalensis*, from the Transvaal)
Slender perennial herb, 40–100 cm. Leaves mostly basal on slender petioles, deeply lobed and coarsely toothed on the margins. Flowers in clusters on slender pedicels, white, often tinged reddish, 15–20 mm diameter.
Habitat: Damp grassy slopes and river banks.

Grassland and Savannah

Ranunculus multifidus
RANUNCULUS FAMILY

Common buttercup (E), hlapi (SS), iShasha-kazane, uXhapozi (Z)

(Latin *multifidus*, divided into many parts, alluding to the leaves)

Silky, perennial herb, 20–50 cm high. Leaves divided and celery-like with toothed segments, hairy. Flowers on branched stems, bright glossy yellow, 10–15 mm diameter.
Habitat: Damp ground near streams or marshes.
Notes: The acrid juice from the pounded plant is used to treat skin irritations.

Ranunculus baurii
RANUNCULUS FAMILY

Nasturtium-leaved buttercup (E), qojoana (SS)

(Named for the missionary and plant collector, Rev. Leopold Bauer)

Perennial herb, 60–120 cm. Leaves in a basal tuft on slender petioles, circular and attached in the centre like an umbrella, finely toothed on the margin. Flowers on tall, branched stems, bright glossy yellow, 20–25 mm diameter.
Habitat: Along waterfalls and stream sides at high altitude.

Anemone fanninii
RANUNCULUS FAMILY

Giant anemone (E), groot anemoon (A), uManzamnyama (X)

(Named for George F. Fannin, who first collected the species)

Tufted perennial herb with annual stems to 1,2 m high from a woody rootstock. Leaves mostly basal, five- to seven-lobed on long petioles, leathery and velvety above with long hairs beneath, the margins with red-tipped teeth. Flowers on branched stems, creamy white, 80–100 mm diameter.
Habitat: Moist depressions along drainage lines and stream sides.

Grassland and Savannah

Dianthus basuticus
CARNATION FAMILY
Lesotho carnation (E), hlokoa-la-tsela (SS)
(Latin *basuticus*, growing in Basutoland, now Lesotho)

Tufted perennial, to 25 cm, often mat-forming. Leaves narrow and grass-like, greyish. Flowers on slender stems, white or pink with toothed or fringed petals, 20–30 mm diameter.
Habitat: Montane and alpine grassland in rocky places.
Notes: Used traditionally as a love charm.

Oxalis obliquifolia
SORREL FAMILY
Oblique-leaved sorrel (E),
skuinsblaarsuring (A)

(Latin *obliquifolius*, oblique-leaved)
Cormous perennial herb to 10 cm high. Leaves divided into three spade-shaped, thinly hairy leaflets. Flowers solitary on slender stalks, bright pink or white with a yellow or white centre, 10–20 mm diameter.
Habitat: Stony grassland.
Notes: *Oxalis smithiana* is similar but has narrow leaflets.

Hypericum aethiopicum
FLAX FAMILY
Small St John's wort (E), vlieëpisbossie (A),
iThalelimpofu (Z)

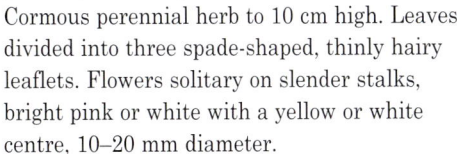

(Latin *aethiopicus*, from Africa usually South Africa)
Perennial herb with slender annual stems to 50 cm high from a woody base. Leaves narrow or elliptical with the lower ones opposite. Flowers in loosely branched clusters, yellow but reddish in bud, 10 mm diameter.
Habitat: Stony grassland.
Notes: Used traditionally to purify the blood.

Grassland and Savannah

Hypericum revolutum
FLAX FAMILY
Curry bush (E), kerriebos (A)
(Latin *revolutus*, rolled back, referring to the leaf margins)
Shrub to 2 m high. Leaves elliptical with translucent glands and the margins rolled under. Flowers solitary, deep yellow, 30–40 mm diameter.
Habitat: Stream banks and forest margins.

Acridocarpus natalitius
MALPIGHIA FAMILY
Moth-fruit (E), uMabopha (X, Z)
(Latin *natalitius*, coming from Natal)
Sprawling shrub or small tree with rust-coloured hairs on the young branches and leaves. Leaves elliptical and leathery. Flowers in loose racemes, bright golden yellow, 20–30 mm diameter.
Habitat: Forest margins and bushveld, often near the coast.
Notes: Roots traditionally used medicinally.

Papaver aculeatum
POPPY FAMILY
Orange poppy (E), doringpapawer (A), sehlolo (SS)
(Latin *aculeatus*, prickly)
Prickly, tufted annual to 1 m high. Leaves deeply lobed and toothed, covered with stiff yellow prickles. Flowers on slender stalks, orange, 50 mm diameter.
Habitat: Disturbed ground.
Notes: Young plants eaten as a spinach. The only poppy native in the southern hemisphere. Apparently allied to certain Mediterranean species.

Grassland and Savannah

Tricliceras longipedunculatum
WORMSKIOLDIA FAMILY
Lion's eye (E)
(Latin *longipedunculatus*, with a long peduncle i.e. flowering stalk)
Herb to 20 cm high with stems covered with coarse, purple bristles. Leaves narrow with smooth or somewhat toothed margins, sometimes bristle on the midrib beneath. Flowers on long, slender peduncles, velvety reddish orange, 20 mm diameter.
Habitat: Open grassland and savannah.

Triumfetta welwitschii
LINDEN FAMILY
Maagbossie (A)
(Named after the nineteenth-century Austrian botanist, Friedrich Welwitsch)
Perennial with annual stems from a woody rootstock. Leaves narrowly elliptical with toothed margins and covered with rough, star-shaped hairs. Flowers in loosely branched clusters with spreading sepals and the petals clustered in the centre, pale yellow, 10 mm diameter. Fruits burr-like and covered with reddish bristles.
Habitat: Grassland and rocky ridges, especially after fire.
Notes: *Triumfetta sonderi* is a shrublet from Gauteng and the Highveld.

Melhania prostrata
HIBISCUS FAMILY
Common melhania (E)
(Latin *prostratus*, prostrate, lying on the ground)
Low-growing shrublet with creeping branches covered with yellowish, star-shaped hairs. Leaves narrow and almost hairless above but greyish velvety beneath. Flowers solitary or in pairs, yellow, 15 mm diameter.
Habitat: Open woodland in rocky grassland.

Grassland and Savannah

Hermannia cristata
HIBISCUS FAMILY
Scarlet doll's rose (E)
(Latin *cristatus*, crested)

Low-growing herb with erect stems to 30 cm high from a woody rootstock. Leaves elliptical and covered with rough, star-shaped hairs. Flowers nodding in elongate racemes, bell-shaped, reddish orange, 20 mm long. Fruit erect, five-angled with fringed crests along the angles.
Habitat: Stony grassland.

Radyera urens
HIBISCUS FAMILY
Karoo pumpkin (E), pampoenbossie (A)
(Latin *urens*, stinging, referring to the rough hairs)

Coarse herb with trailing stems from a woody rootstock. Leaves resembling those of a pumpkin, rounded and paler beneath with crinkled margins, on long petioles and covered with rough, star-shaped hairs. Flowers on the ground concealed beneath the leaves, deeply cup-shaped, reddish orange with a dark throat, 15 mm diameter.
Habitat: Dry karroid flats along roadsides and waste places.
Notes: Used traditionally as a remedy for piles.

Hibiscus cannabinus
HIBISCUS FAMILY
Hemp-leaved hibiscus (E), umHlakanye (X), uDekane (Z)
(Latin *cannabinus*, resembling cannabis, *Cannabis sativa*)

Woody annual herb with stiffly erect stems to 2 m high, covered with short prickles. Leaves divided into three to seven, toothed lobes. Flowers solitary in the upper axils, pale yellow with a purple centre, 100 mm diameter, the calyx surrounded at the base by seven or eight narrow bracts.
Habitat: Disturbed ground and roadsides.
Notes: Grown as a source of fibre in India.

Grassland and Savannah

Hibiscus diversifolius
HIBISCUS FAMILY
Prickly-leaved hibiscus (E)
(Latin *diversifolius*, with variable leaves)

Erect perennial herb with stiffly erect stems to 2,5 m high, covered with short prickles. Leaves on long, prickly petioles, usually divided into three to five, coarsely toothed lobes. Flowers in terminal racemes, yellow with a dark centre, 100 mm diameter, the calyx surrounded by 10 to 12 narrow bracts.
Habitat: Forest margins and bush.

Hibiscus trionum
HIBISCUS FAMILY
Bladder hibiscus (E), terblansbossie (A), iYeza lentshulube (X), uVemvane olukhulu (Z)
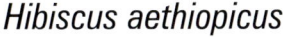
(From an old name for the species, *Trionum*, flower of an hour)
Stiffly hairy annual herb to 1 m high. Leaves mostly deeply three- to five-lobed and toothed. Flowers solitary in the upper axils, yellow with a dark eye, 25–40 mm diameter, the calyx bell-shaped with conspicuous purple veins and surrounded at the base by 10 to 12 narrow bracts, swollen like a gooseberry in fruit.
Habitat: Stony slopes and forest margins.
Notes: Introduced from the Old World tropics and now widespread in southern Africa. A decoction is traditionally used as a vermifuge.

Hibiscus aethiopicus
HIBISCUS FAMILY
Cape hibiscus, dwarf hibiscus (E), uVemvane (Z)
(Latin *aethiopicus*, from Africa, usually South Africa)
Roughly hairy subshrub to 30 cm high with stems produced from a woody underground base. Leaves oblong and toothed above with three to five veins from the base, nearly hairless above. Flowers cream to yellow or rarely pink, often with a dark centre, 50 mm diameter, the calyx surrounded by 10 to 12 bracts.
Habitat: Stony grassland and open scrub.
Notes: Used traditionally to treat sprains.

Grassland and Savannah

Hibiscus calyphyllus
HIBISCUS FAMILY
Large yellow hibiscus (E), wildestokroos (A)
(Greek *calyphyllus*, leafy calyx)
Shrub to 2 m high. Leaves rounded or three- to five-lobed and toothed, velvety. Flowers solitary in the upper axils, yellow with a dark eye, each lasting less than a day, 120 mm diameter, the calyx surrounded at the base by five broad bracts.
Habitat: Thicket and forest margins.

Dissotis canescens
PRIDE-OF-INDIA FAMILY
Marsh dissotis (E), imFeyenkala (Z)
(Latin *canescens*, becoming greyish)
Shrub with erect, reddish stems to 1,5 m high. Leaves opposite, dark green and rough above but velvety whitish beneath. Flowers in branched clusters, brilliant magenta, 35–45 mm diameter.
Habitat: Marshy grassland.
Notes: Used traditionally as a treatment for dysentery and hangovers.

Begonia sutherlandii
BEGONIA FAMILY
Orange begonia (E), uQamamawene (Z)
(Named for P.C. Sutherland, Surveyor-General of Natal and a keen plant collector)
Tuberous perennial with brittle stems to 50 cm high. Leaves asymmetrical, elliptical and often lobed with irregularly toothed margins. Flowers with the sexes separate, orange to red, to 35 mm diameter.
Habitat: Forest floor in humus or on mossy rocks.
Notes: Used traditionally to treat heartburn. Very variable in leaf shape. Other species have pink flowers: *B. sonderana* from Mpumalanga, *B. homonyma* and *B. dregei* from KwaZulu-Natal and Eastern Cape; *B. geranioides* has rounded leaves.

Grassland and Savannah

Monsonia attenuata
GERANIUM FAMILY
Narrow-leaved monsonia (E)
(Latin *attenuatus*, tapering to a slender point)
Perennial herb with an erect, annual stem from a tuberous rootstock. Leaves crowded, narrow and folded along the midline with toothed margins and often flexed downwards above the petiole. Flowers crowded at the top of the stem, chalky white and finely creased with fine charcoal veining beneath, the petals blunt and toothed at the tips, 30–40 mm diameter.
Habitat: Stony grassland.

Geranium wakkerstroomianum
GERANIUM FAMILY
White geranium (E)
(Latin *wakkerstroomianus*, from the Wakkerstroom district where it was first collected)
Straggling perennial herb to 1 m high from a taproot. Leaves coarsely lobed and toothed, thinly hairy above and variously hairy beneath. Flowers white with pink or red veins and notched petals, 15 mm diameter.
Habitat: Damp sheltered hollows and forest margins.

Geranium pulchrum
GERANIUM FAMILY
Silver geranium (E)
(Latin *pulchrus*, beautiful)
Robust shrublet to 1,2 m high with woody stems. Leaves deeply five- to seven-lobed and toothed, thick-textured and greyish above but silvery-velvety beneath. Flowers pale to deep mauve with rounded or shallowly notched petals, 30 mm diameter.
Habitat: Rocky stream banks and mountain slopes at high altitude.
Notes: Conspicuous on Sani Pass.

Grassland and Savannah

Pelargonium luridum
GERANIUM FAMILY

Starburst pelargonium (E), iNyonkulu (Z)
(Latin *luridus*, smoky or drab)

Perennial herb with annual stems from a tuberous rootstock. Leaves basal, variably lobed with broad to ribbon- or thread-like segments. Flowers in a round head on a slender, hairy stem, pink or pale yellow to white, 20 mm diameter.
Habitat: Grassland.
Notes: Used traditionally to treat nausea and vomiting and as a love charm.

Pelargonium schlechteri
GERANIUM FAMILY

Two-tiered pelargonium (E)
(Named for the German botanist and plant collector, Rudolph Schlechter)

Perennial herb with annual stems from a tuberous rootstock. Leaves basal, coarsely lobed and toothed. Flowers usually in two-tiered heads on a slender, hairy stem, greenish yellow with a more or less well-developed maroon blotch, 20 mm diameter.
Habitat: Grassland.

Pelargonium schizopetalum
GERANIUM FAMILY

Fringed pelargonium (E), muishondbossie (A)
(Greek *schizopetalus*, with deeply fringed petals)

Perennial herb with annual stems from a large, woody tuber. Leaves basal, deeply lobed and softly hairy. Flowers in a round head on a slender, hairy stem, pale yellow and variously tinged with purple with finely fringed petals, 30–40 mm diameter.
Habitat: Grassland.

Grassland and Savannah

Cleome gynandra
CLEOME FAMILY
Spider-wisp cleome, white mouse-whiskers (E), oorpynpeultjie (A), umZonde (Z)
(Greek *gynandrus*, female-male, alluding to the common stalk beneath both stamens and ovary)
Erect annual herb with glandular-hairy stems to 60 cm high. Leaves divided like a hand into several elliptical or paddle-shaped leaflets covered with glandular hairs. Flowers in slender racemes, white fading pink, 10–25 mm diameter.
Habitat: Savannah and open grassland, often in disturbed places.
Notes: A popular spinach in rural areas.

Cleome angustifolia
CLEOME FAMILY
Yellow cleome, yellow mouse-whiskers (E), peultjiesbos (A)
(Latin *angustifolius*, narrow-leaved)
Erect annual herb with wand-like stems to 1,5 m high covered with conical, whitish protuberances. Leaves divided like a hand into several thread-like leaflets. Flowers in slender racemes, yellow with reddish marks at the base of the two largest petals, closing at midday, 20 mm diameter.
Habitat: Savannah and open scrub.

Cadaba aphylla
CLEOME FAMILY
Black storm (E), swartstorm (A)
(Latin *aphyllus*, leafless)
Leafless, often tangled shrub with grey or purplish branches to 2 m, often spinescent at the tips. Flowers in clusters on side shoots, greenish to red, 40–50 mm long.
Habitat: Dry bushveld and semi-desert.
Notes: Palatable to game. The red flowers are pollinated by sunbirds.

Grassland and Savannah

Chamaecrista comosa
PEA FAMILY
Trailing dwarf cassia (E)
(Latin *comosus*, bearing a tuft of leaves)
Perennial herb with stems to 50 cm high from a woody rhizome. Leaves divided into numerous pairs of narrow leaflets, with the leaf axis grooved above. Flowers clustered at the branch tips, yellow with a reddish calyx, *c*.20 mm diameter.
Habitat: Grassland, often along roadsides.
Notes: The annual *Chamaecrista mimosoides* is somewhat similar in appearance but the leaf axis is crested.

Senna italica
PEA FAMILY
Wild senna (E), elandsertjie (A), imPengu (Z)
(Latin *italicus*, from Italy)
Perennial with glandular-hairy stems to 60 cm high. Leaves divided into several pairs of asymmetrically elliptical leaflets with the margins fringed with orange hairs. Flowers in short racemes, yellow with a dark brown calyx, *c*.20 mm diameter.
Habitat: Bushveld.
Notes: Seeds used as a coffee substitute and to treat pain and roundworm.

Bauhinia galpinii
PEA FAMILY
Pride-of-de Kaap (E),
vlam-van-die-vlakte (A)
(Named for the naturalist and plant collector, E.E. Galpin)
Sprawling shrub to 5 m. Leaves broad, folded along the midline and deeply notched. Flowers in clusters on side shoots, carried on brown, velvety pedicels, dull reddish, 40 mm diameter.
Habitat: Scrambling among bushveld and scrub.
Notes: Widely cultivated as an ornamental.

Grassland and Savannah

Erythrina zeyheri
PEA FAMILY

Ploughbreaker (E), ploegbreker (A), umNsinsana (Z)

(Named for the nineteenth-century German botanist and plant collector, Carl Zeyher)

Dwarf shrublet with short stems to 60 cm high from a large, underground stem. Leaves divided into three spade-shaped leaflets covered with hooked prickles on the veins. Flowers in slender, pointed racemes, drooping, bright red, 45 mm long.
Habitat: Grassland, especially after fires.
Notes: Red and black seeds used as beads.

Lessertia frutescens
PEA FAMILY

(= *Sutherlandia frutescens*)
Scarlet balloon pea (E), kankerbos (A)

(Latin *frutescens*, becoming shrubby)

Erect or sprawling shrublet to 1 m. Leaves divided into many small oblong leaflets that are rounded at the tips, greyish green and mostly thinly hairy above. Flowers in short racemes, bright red, 20–40 mm long. Pods large and balloon-like with smooth papery walls.
Habitat: Widespread on a variety of soils but usually along roads.
Notes: Enjoys a high repute for the treatment of cancer but there is no evidence in support of this belief.

Eriosema distinctum
PEA FAMILY

Scarlet eriosema (E), uBangalala olukhulu (Z)

(Latin *distinctus*, distinct, i.e. not confused with related species)

Erect herb with annual stems from a woody rootstock, 10–20 cm high. Leaves divided into three elliptical leaflets, shortly hairy. Flowers in short racemes, dull reddish with darker veins, 15 mm diameter, calyx with silvery hairs.
Habitat: Rocky grassland, especially after fire.
Notes: Unpalatable to cattle and flourishing in overgrazed grassland.

Grassland and Savannah

Eriosema kraussianum
PEA FAMILY

Pale eriosema (E)

(Named for the German naturalist and plant collector, Christian Krauss)

Erect perennial herb, 30–50 cm high, growing in clumps from a woody rootstock. Leaves divided into three narrow leaflets, thinly covered with silky hairs. Flowers in narrow racemes, pale creamy yellow, 10 mm diameter, calyx with golden hairs.
Habitat: Grassland, especially after fire.

Eriosema salignum
PEA FAMILY

Narrow-leaved eriosema (E), lesapho (SS), uQonsi (Z)

(Latin *salignus*, willowy, alluding to the slender stems)

Slender, erect herb, 30–60 cm, from a woody rootstock. Leaves divided into three narrow leaflets, folded and dark green above but velvety-white beneath. Flowers on silvery stalks, yellow to pale orange, 10 mm diameter, calyx shaggy.
Habitat: Grassland.
Notes: Used traditionally as an expectorant and diuretic.

Eriosema cordatum
PEA FAMILY

Heart-leaved eriosema (E), lesapho (SS), uQonsi (Z)

(Latin *cordatus*, heart-shaped)

Straggling perennial herb with creeping stems. Leaves divided into three, broadly elliptical leaflets, shortly hairy on the veins beneath. Flowers in erect racemes, yellow with brownish veins, 10 mm diameter, calyx very shortly hairy.
Habitat: Rocky grassland.

Grassland and Savannah

Rhynchosia cooperi
PEA FAMILY
Common creeping rhynchosia (E)
(Named after the English plant collector, Thomas Cooper)

Trailing perennial herb. Leaves erect, divided into three, broadly diamond-shaped, shortly hairy leaflets. Flowers in erect racemes on slender stalks, bright yellow, 8 mm diameter, calyx shortly hairy.
Habitat: Grassland.

Lotononis corymbosa
PEA FAMILY
Pincushion lotononis (E), iNcini (Z)
(Latin *corymbosus*, like a corymb, alluding to the rounded inflorescence)

Perennial herb with annual branches to 30 cm high from a woody rootstock. Leaves divided into three elliptical leaflets that are hairless above and silky on the margins and beneath. Flowers crowded in dome-like heads nestled in the upper leaves, yellow, 10 mm long.
Habitat: Grassland, especially after fire.
Notes: Used traditionally as a tonic.

Crotalaria globifera
PEA FAMILY
Round-pod rattle bush (E), jaagsiektebossie (A)
(Latin *globiferus*, globe-carrying, referring to the ball-like pods)

Shrublet with annual stems to 60 cm high from a woody rootstock. Leaves divided into three, narrow leaflets that are folded along the midline. Flowers in racemes, yellow with a sharply pointed keel, 10 mm long. Pods globular.
Habitat: Drier grassland, especially after fire.

Grassland and Savannah

Argyrolobium sandersonii
PEA FAMILY
Common liquorice bean (E)
(Named for John Sanderson, amateur nineteenth-century Natal botanist)
Bushy annual herb, 30–60 cm high. Leaves divided into three, narrowly elliptical leaflets, greyish and hairless. Flowers in elongated racemes, bright yellow, the flag petal narrowly wedge-shaped, scented of wistaria, 10 mm diameter, calyx hairless.
Habitat: Grassland, especially after fire.
Notes: Flowers turn black on drying.

Argyrolobium robustum
PEA FAMILY
Large liquorice bean (E)
(Latin *robustus*, robust)
Bushy annual herb, 30–60 cm high. Leaves divided into three, broadly ellipt-ical leaflets, hairless. Flowers in cylindrical racemes, pale yellowish and orange with darker veins, the flag petal rounded, scented of lemon and wistaria, 10 mm diameter, calyx hairless.
Habitat: Grassland, especially after fire.
Notes: Flowers turn black on drying.

Pseudarthria hookeri
PEA FAMILY
Velvet bean, bug-catcher (E), fluweelboon (A), uPhandosi (Z)
(Named after Sir Joseph Hooker, first director of Kew Gardens)
Shrub with erect, velvety stems to 3 m high. Leaves divided into three, elliptical leaflets that are rough and green above and pale and velvety beneath. Flowers in branched racemes, bright pink, 8 mm diameter, calyx velvety-brown or mauve.
Habitat: Rough grassland in damp places and forest margins.
Notes: The curved, velvety hairs act like Velcro, sticking to other surfaces.

Grassland and Savannah

Indigofera hilaris
PEA FAMILY
Red bush indigo (E), iGqokisi (Z)
(Latin *hilaris*, relating to the hilum, where the funicle attaches to the seed, an obscure reference)

Perennial with annual stems to 60 cm high from a woody rootstock. Leaves divided into five to seven, narrowly elliptical, greyish leaflets. Flowers in numerous, short racemes, reddish pink, 10 mm diameter.
Habitat: Grassland, especially after fires.
Notes: Becomes straggly if not burned.

Indigofera oxytropis
PEA FAMILY
Keeled indigo (E)
(Greek *oxytropis*, sharply keeled, referring to the flag petal)

Shrublet with creeping stems from a woody rootstock. Leaves divided into 11 to 15 elliptical leaflets that are folded along the midline and hairless above but covered with appressed hairs beneath. Flowers in racemes, the flag petal sharply keeled and folded over the other petals, silky on the upper surface, reddish pink, 10 mm long.
Habitat: Grassland.

Tephrosia grandiflora
PEA FAMILY
Pink bush pea (E), iHlozane (Z)
(Latin *grandiflorus*, large flowered)

Shrub to 1,5 m high. Leaves divided into numerous elliptical leaflets that are almost hairless and closely parallel-veined to the margins, subtended by large, many-veined stipules. Flowers in crowded racemes on naked stalks, pink or magenta, 15–20 mm long.
Habitat: Scrub and forest margins.
Notes: Used traditionally to treat chest ailments and as a fish poison.

Grassland and Savannah

Tephrosia macropoda
PEA FAMILY

Creeping tephrosia (E), visboontjie (A), iHlozane (Z)

(Greek *macropodus*, with large foot or support, i.e. flower stalk)

Straggling perennial herb with creeping branches. Leaves divided into numerous elliptical leaflets that are almost hairless above but silky beneath and closely parallel-veined to the margins. Flowers in crowded racemes on naked stalks, pink or magenta, 15–20 mm long.
Habitat: Open and rocky grassland.
Notes: Used traditionally to treat chest complaints, fevers and lice and as a fish poison.

Vigna vexillata
PEA FAMILY

Narrow-leaved sweetpea (E), wilde-ertjie (A), isiKhwali (Z)

(Latin *vexillatus*, with a (conspicuous) standard or flag petal)

Slender trailing creeper. Leaves divided into three leaflets ranging in shape from very narrow to elliptical, rough. Flowers, one or two on slender stalks, pale pink to lilac, sweetly scented, 25 mm diameter.
Habitat: Grassland or open woodland.
Notes: *Vigna unguiculata* is similar but the central leaflet always bulges at the sides near the base. Seeds and tubers edible.

Canavalia rosea
PEA FAMILY

Beach-bean canavalia (E), strandboontjie (A)

(Latin *roseus*, rose-pink)

Robust trailing creeper. Leaves divided into three broad, rounded leaflets. Flowers, few on upright stalks, pink to purple, sweetly scented, 25 mm diameter.
Habitat: Coastal dunes and along estuaries.

Grassland and Savannah

Polygala virgata
POLYGALA FAMILY
Purple broom (E), bloukappies (A),
iThethe (Z)

(Latin *virgatus*, with slender rod-like stems)
Slender shrub with wand-like stems to 1,5 m high, branching in the upper parts only. Leaves soon falling, narrow. Flowers in arching racemes, pink to magenta, 15 mm diameter.
Habitat: Rough grassland and forest margins.
Notes: Used traditionally as a blood purifier.

Impatiens hochstetteri
BALSAM FAMILY
Wild impatiens (E), iHlula (Z)
(Commemorates the German botanist, Christian Hochstetter)
Soft annual or perennial herb with brittle stems. Leaves ovate and scalloped along the margins. Flowers in small groups at the branch tips, pale pink or mauve, 'butterfly-like' with the lower part of the petals drawn into a slender 'tail', 20 mm diameter.
Habitat: Shaded and damp forest margins.
Notes: Used traditionally to treat eczema.

Impatiens sylvicola
BALSAM FAMILY
Transvaal impatiens (E)
(Latin *sylvicolus*, forest-dwelling)
Soft annual or perennial herb with brittle stems. Leaves ovate and scalloped along the margins. Flowers in small groups at the branch tips, pale pink or mauve with a distinct dark spot on the deeply two-lobed petals, 20 mm diameter.
Habitat: Shaded and damp forest margins.

Grassland and Savannah

Cucumis africanus
PUMPKIN FAMILY
Wild cucumber (E), agurkie (A)
(Latin *africanus*, from Africa)
Perennial herb with trailing annual stems from a tuberous root, covered in white, hooked hairs. Leaves with tendrils at the base, deeply lobed. Flowers unisexual, greenish yellow, 10 mm diameter. Fruits egg-shaped and covered with prickles, dark green with pale bands but turning yellow when ripe, up to 6 cm long.
Habitat: Sandy soils, often along seasonal streams, floodplains or disturbed areas.
Notes: The fruits are poisonous when raw but have been used as pickles after cooking.

Citrullus lanatus
PUMPKIN FAMILY
Tsamma melon (E), t'samma, karkoer (N)
(Latin *lanatus*, woolly)
Robust annual herb with trailing stems to 3 m long, covered in coarse, silky hairs. Leaves with tendrils at the base, deeply lobed. Flowers unisexual, greenish yellow, 15 mm diameter. Fruits globose, hairy at first, mottled yellow and green, up to 15 cm diameter.
Habitat: Seasonal streams, floodplains or disturbed areas.
Notes: The fruits are either bitter and then possibly poisonous, or sweet and then edible and consumed by animals and man for both food and water. The seeds are highly nutritious.

Trichodesma physaloides
BORAGE FAMILY
Chocolate bells (E), sjokaladeklokkies (A)
(Resembling the Cape gooseberry, *Physalis*)
Slender shrublet with annual stems to 50 cm high. Leaves produced after the flowers, lance-shaped and white-spotted on the margins and beneath. Flowers nodding in branched clusters, bell-shaped, bluish white fading brown, 25 mm long.
Habitat: Rough grassland on the edges of marshes and seeps, especially after fires.

Grassland and Savannah

Pachypodium saundersii
MILKWEED FAMILY
Kudu lily (E), koedoelelie (A), isiHlele (Z)
(Named after Sir Charles Saunders, brother of the botanical artist Katherine Saunders)
Succulent shrublet with a swollen stem to 1 m high bearing pairs of long, slender spines on small cushions. Leaves in tufts on the cushions above the spines, elliptical and leathery with the margins sometimes finely toothed. Flowers trumpet-shaped with a velvety tube 30 mm long, white, 50 mm diameter.
Habitat: Rock outcrops in savannah.

Adenium multiflorum
MILKWEED FAMILY
Impala lily, Sabi star (E), impalalelie (A), isiGubengubu (Z)
(Latin *multiflorus*, many-flowered)
Succulent shrublet with a swollen stem to 1,5 m high. Leaves in clusters at the branch tips, elliptical and leathery, appearing after the flowers. Flowers trumpet-shaped with a velvety tube 30 mm long, white with brilliant pink margins, 50 mm diameter.
Habitat: Dry woodland.
Notes: *Adenium swazicum*, which flowers in the summer, has uniformly pink to reddish purple flowers with a tube 50 mm long.

Adenium oleifolium
MILKWEED FAMILY
Tufted impala lily (E), pylgif (A), ouhiep (N)
(Latin *oleifolius*, with leaves like an olive)
Dwarf shrublet with a subterranean swollen stem to 40 cm high. Leaves in clusters at the branch tips, narrow and leathery, shortly hairy, especially beneath. Flowers trumpet-shaped with a velvety tube 22–35 mm long, pink to red with darker margins, 50 mm diameter.
Habitat: Stony ridges, limestone outcrops and sandy flats.
Notes: One of the ingredients of arrow poison. The dried tuber is used to treat insect bites.

Grassland and Savannah

Raphionacme hirsuta
MILKWEED FAMILY
False gentian (E), khadiwortel (A), inTsema (X)
(Latin *hirsutus*, hairy, referring to the leaves)
Perennial herb with softly woody annual stems from a large, flattened, tuberous rootstock, exuding milky sap when damaged. Leaves opposite, elliptical and smooth or hairy, often not fully developed at flowering. Flowers in clusters, bright purple with a white or purple central crown, 10–15 mm diameter.
Habitat: Grassland, especially after fire.
Notes: The tuber is used in brewing beer and also to treat ulcers but is possibly poisonous.

Asclepias cucullata
MILKWEED FAMILY
Hooded meadow-star (E), mohlatsisa (SS)
(Latin *cucullatus*, hooded, referring to the corona lobes)

Tuberous perennial herb with annual stems to 30 cm high, exuding milky sap when damaged. Leaves opposite, very narrow with the margins rolled under, roughly hairy. Flowers in flat-topped clusters, whitish flushed with dull purple, 10 mm diameter, the corona lobes pitcher-shaped and yellowish green at the base.
Habitat: Stony grassland, mainly after fire.

Xysmalobium undulatum
MILKWEED FAMILY
Uzura (E), bitterwortel (A), iShongwe (X, Z)
(Latin *undulatus*, undulating, referring to the leaf margins)

Tuberous perennial herb with annual stems to 1 m high, exuding milky sap when damaged. Leaves opposite, elliptical and roughly hairy with crisped or undulating margins. Flowers in round clusters at the nodes, greenish and covered with long white hairs, 10–15 mm diameter, the corona lobes knob-shaped. Fruits swollen and pear-shaped, covered with soft bristles.
Habitat: Stony open grassland.
Notes: Used traditionally to treat headaches, colic and dysentery but certainly poisonous.

Grassland and Savannah

Pachycarpus concolor
MILKWEED FAMILY

Astral-bell (E)

(Latin *concolorus*, uniformly coloured, i.e. not spotted or marked)

Perennial herb with annual stems to 60 cm high from a tuberous rootstock, exuding milky sap when damaged. Leaves opposite, elliptical and roughly hairy. Flowers in small clusters at the nodes, yellowish to brown, 15–25 mm diameter, the corona lobes slipper-shaped.
Habitat: Stony open grassland, especially after fire.

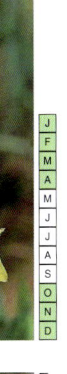

Pachycarpus schinzianus
MILKWEED FAMILY

Dark-eyed bell (E), bitterwortel (A)

(Named for the German explorer and plant collector, Hans Schinz)

Perennial herb with annual stems to 60 cm high from a tuberous rootstock, exuding milky sap when damaged. Leaves opposite, elliptical and roughly hairy. Flowers in small clusters at the nodes, white or flushed dull purplish, 15–25 mm diameter, the corona lobes scoop-shaped and marked with a black blotch.
Habitat: Stony open grassland, especially after fire.

Pachycarpus campanulatus
MILKWEED FAMILY

Fairy bell (E)

(Latin *campanulatus*, bell-shaped)

Perennial herb with slender annual stem to 60 cm high from a tuberous rootstock, exuding milky sap when damaged. Leaves opposite, narrow with the margins rolled under, roughly hairy. Flowers in a cluster at the stem tip, nodding and deeply cup-shaped, pale greenish or pinkish, 20–30 mm diameter.
Habitat: Grassland, especially after fire.
Notes: *Pachycarpus grandiflorus* has similar balloon-shaped flowers, usually speckled with purple, but the corona lobes are long and reach to the rim of the flowers.

Grassland and Savannah

Ceropegia ampliata
MILKWEED FAMILY
Bushman's pipe (E), boesmanspyp (A)
(Latin *ampliatus*, enlarged, referring to the swollen base of the flowers)

Leafless vine with smooth, greyish-green stems to 1 m long from a tuber, exuding clear sap when damaged. Leaves short-lived. Flowers vase-shaped with the petals remaining attached at the tips, cream coloured to greenish with fine green veins outside, 50–70 mm long.
Habitat: Scrub and thornveld.

Ipomoea obscura
MORNING-GLORY FAMILY
Yellow ipomoea (E), wildepatat (A), uSiboniseleni (Z)
(Latin *obscurus*, indistinct, possibly alluding to the colour, or rather lack thereof)

Slender twiner with shortly hairy stems to 2 m long. Leaves narrowly heart-shaped and softly hairy. Flowers pale creamy-yellow, sometimes with a deep red centre, 12–30 mm diameter, the sepals narrow.
Habitat: Grassland.
Notes: Leaves cooked as a relish. Used traditionally as a hallucinogenic.

Ipomoea crassipes
MORNING-GLORY FAMILY
Leafy-flowered ipomoea (E), wildewinde (A), uBoqo (Z)
(Latin *crassipes*, thick foot, i.e. stem)

Trailing perennial with softly hairy stems to 1-m long. Leaves ovate to lanceolate and thinly hairy. Flowers mauve to cream with a magenta centre, 35–60 mm diameter, the outer sepals arrow-shaped and leaf-like.
Habitat: Grassland and roadsides.
Notes: The roots are eaten raw. Traditionally used to treat dysentery, sores and hiccups.

Grassland and Savannah

Ipomoea cairica
MORNING-GLORY FAMILY
Common ipomoea (E), iHlambe (Z)
(Latin *cairica*, from Cairo)
Vigorous climber with slender stems. Leaves deeply divided into five to seven lobes, grey beneath. Flowers deep mauve, 40–60 mm diameter, the sepals small.
Habitat: Riverine bush and disturbed places along the coast.
Notes: Can become weedy. Used traditionally to treat rashes.

Ipomoea oblongata
MORNING-GLORY FAMILY
(= *Turbina oblongata*)
Turbina (E)
(Latin *oblongatus*, oblong-shaped, alluding to the leaves)
Perennial creeper with prostrate, hairy stems to 2 m long. Leaves oblong to elliptical, covered with yellowish hairs and held erect. Flowers deep magenta, 40–70 mm diameter, the sepals lance-shaped and tapering.
Habitat: Open grassland and savannah.
Notes: *Ipomoea pellita* is similar but the flower clusters are on long stalks and the sepals are narrow throughout and not tapering. The tuber is edible.

Wahlenbergia grandiflora
BELLFLOWER FAMILY
Drakensberg bellflower (E)
(Latin *grandiflorus*, large-flowered)
Perennial herb to 50 cm high. Leaves elliptical and hairy with wavy or crisped margins. Flowers on loosely branched stems, cup-shaped, pale blue, 20–30 mm diameter, the calyx lobes slender and tapering.
Habitat: Damp cliffs or in the shelter of rocks.
Notes: *Wahlenbergia undulata* is similar but has short calyx lobes.

Grassland and Savannah

Erica algida
ERICA FAMILY
Alpine heath (E), sehalahala (SS)
(Latin *algidus*, cold, alluding to the climate)
Dwarf shrub to 30 cm high.
Leaves in whorls of three, needle-like and curved upwards with the margins rolled under, coarsely hairy. Flowers in small clusters of four, urn-shaped, pale pink to white, downy, 3 mm long.
Habitat: Damp grassland.
Notes: Used as fuel.

Erica oatesii
ERICA FAMILY
Oates' heath (E)
(Named for the Victorian naturalist and traveller, Frank Oates)
Shrub to 1,2 m high. Leaves in whorls of three or four, needle-like and spreading or erect with the margins rolled under, coarsely hairy. Flowers in terminal clusters, urn-shaped, pink to red, hairless, 10–13 mm long.
Habitat: Stream banks and damp grassy slopes.

Gnidia compacta
DAPHNE FAMILY
Alpine yellow-head (E)
(Latin *compactus*, compact, alluding to the cushion-like form)
Cushion-forming shrublet to 20 cm high from a woody rootstock. Leaves narrow and bluish green above but softly silky on the margins and beneath, somewhat concave. Flowers in small clusters, bright yellow with a short tube bearing four teeth at the mouth, 5 mm diameter.
Habitat: Rocky montane grassland.

Grassland and Savannah

Lasiosiphon capitatus
DAPHNE FAMILY
(= *Gnidia capitata*)
Common yellow-head (E), gifbossie (A),
isiDikili (Z)
(Latin *capitatus*, with a knob-like head,
referring to the flowering stalks)
Many-stemmed shrublet with branches to 70 cm high from a tuberous rootstock. Leaves narrow and bluish green, the uppermost forming a whorl below the flowers. Flowers in heads on smooth peduncles, glistening mustard yellow with a slender tube bearing from none to five scales at the mouth, 7 mm diameter.
Habitat: Grassland, especially after fires.
Notes: Used traditionally to cure headaches.

Lasiosiphon kraussiana
DAPHNE FAMILY
(= *Gnidia kraussiana*)
Lesser yellow-head (E), gifbossie (A),
isiDikili (Z)
(Named for the German naturalist and plant collector, Christian Krauss)
Many-stemmed shrublet with annual stems to 50 cm high from a tuberous rootstock. Leaves narrow and bluish green, the uppermost forming a whorl below the flowers. Flowers in heads on hairy peduncles, yellow with a slender tube bearing five scales at the mouth, 8 mm diameter.
Habitat: Grassland, especially after fire.
Notes: Poisonous to stock. Used traditionally to treat stomach and chest ailments.

Glumicalyx goseloides
FIGWORT FAMILY
(= *Zaluzianskya goseloides*)
Gooseneck drumstick-flower (E)
(Resembling the genus *Gosela*)
Perennial herb with annual leafy stems from a woody rootstock. Leaves finely hairy. Flowers in a dense, nodding raceme that elongates and becomes erect in fruit, with a slender tube 20–30 mm long, bright orange with a creamy reverse, 8 mm diameter.
Habitat: Rocky scree, boulder beds, damp cliffs.

Grassland and Savannah

Zaluzianskya microsiphon
FIGWORT FAMILY
Diurnal drumstick-flower (E)
(Greek *microsiphon*, narrow-tubed)
Perennial herb with annual leafy stems from a woody rootstock. Leaves in a basal rosette, more or less hairy. Flowers in a cylindrical raceme, open during the day, with a slender tube 20–50 mm long and deeply notched petals, the upper two petals closely paired, white with deep red reverse, 15 mm diameter.
Habitat: Montane grassland.
Notes: Most other *Zaluzianskya* species open only at night and have evenly spreading petals.

Chascanum latifolium
VERBENA FAMILY
Broad-leaved chascanum (E)
(Latin *latifolius*, broad-leaved)
Erect or rounded shrublet to 50 cm high. Leaves opposite and elliptical, smooth or hairy. Flowers in cylindrical racemes, two-lipped with a slender tube 15 mm long, white to pale mauve, 12 mm diameter.
Habitat: Grassland, especially after fire.
Notes: Common in overgrazed grassland.

Plumbago auriculata
PLUMBAGO FAMILY
Plumbago (E), blousyselbos (A), uMabophe (X), umuThi wamadoda (Z)
(Latin *auriculatus*, eared, alluding to the little lobes at the base of the leaves)
Shrub or scrambler to 2 m high. Leaves oblong or paddle-shaped. Flowers in spikes at the branch tips, pale blue with a slender tube 20–30 mm long, the calyx covered with glandular hairs.
Habitat: Thicket and scrub.
Notes: Powdered roots or leaves are traditionally used as a snuff for headaches. Charred and powdered roots also used as an antiseptic.

Grassland and Savannah

Pentanisia prunelloides
COFFEE FAMILY
Pentanisia (E), sooibrandbossie (A),
setima-mollo (SS), iCishamlilo (X, Z)
(Resembling self-heal, *Prunella*)

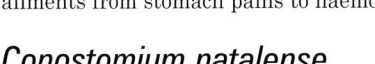

Perennial herb to 40 cm high. Leaves opposite, variable in shape and hairiness. Flowers in a round head on a leafless stem, with a slender tube 15 mm long, pale blue to lilac, 8 mm diameter.
Habitat: Grassland, especially after fire.
Notes: Used traditionally to treat a variety of ailments from stomach pains to haemorrhoids.

Conostomium natalense
COFFEE FAMILY
Wild pentas (E), umBophe, uNgcolosi (Z)
(Latin *natalensis*, from Natal)

Erect perennial or shrublet to 1 m high. Leaves opposite and narrow. Flowers in round heads surrounded by leafy bracts, with a slender tube 15 mm long, pale blue to lilac, 8 mm diameter.
Habitat: Forest margins, often in disturbed sites.

Chironia palustris
GENTIAN FAMILY
Marsh chironia, cerise stars (E),
bitterwortel (A)
(Latin *palustris*, swampy or marshy)

Perennial herb with slender, annual stems to 70 cm high from a woody rootstock. Leaves opposite, narrow and sometimes leathery. Flowers in loose clusters, deep pink with a slender tube 25 mm long, the calyx with short, sticky, triangular lobes.
Habitat: Damp and marshy grassland.
Notes: *Chironia purpurascens* is similar but the calyx lobes are long and slender. Used traditionally to treat colic and diarrhoea.

Grassland and Savannah

Sebaea natalensis
GENTIAN FAMILY
Alpine yellowwort (E)
(Latin *natalensis*, from Natal)
Perennial herb with annual stems to 25 cm high, often branching from the base. Leaves opposite and rather broad. Flowers in flat-topped clusters, bright yellow with a tube 5–7 mm long, the calyx lobes with a well-developed wing along the keel.
Habitat: Damp montane grassland.
Notes: *Sebaea sedoides*, from lower altitudes, is very similar but the calyx lobes lack a conspicuous wing on the keel.

Rhigozum obovatum
BIGNONIA FAMILY
Karoo rhigozum (E), wildegranaat (A)
(Latin *obovatus*, obovate, referring to the leaves)
Stiffly branched, spiny shrub to 4,5 m high. Leaves in tufts, sometimes divided into leaflets, elliptical with the margins rolled under. Flowers one to three on short shoots, funnel-shaped, yellow, 20–30 mm diameter. Fruit a flattened pod containing winged, papery seeds.
Habitat: Dry shale slopes in karroid scrub.
Notes: Common in the Great Karoo.

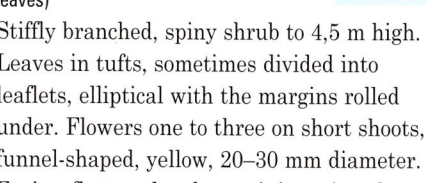

Rhigozum trichotomum
BIGNONIA FAMILY
Pale rhigozum (E), driedoring (A)
(Latin *trichotomus*, with branches in threes)
Stiffly branched, spiny shrub to 1 m high, with the branches in threes. Leaves often in tufts, spoon elliptical with wavy margins. Flowers one to three on short shoots, funnel-shaped, white to pink, 20–30 mm diameter. Fruit a flattened pod containing winged, papery seeds.
Habitat: Dry grassland and karroid scrub, often along riverbeds and edges of pans.
Notes: Not grazed and very common in the Great Karoo and the Kalahari.

Grassland and Savannah

Thunbergia atriplicifolia
ACANTHUS FAMILY

Natal primrose (E), isiPhondo esincane (Z)
(Latin *atriplicifolia*, with leaves resembling orache, *Atriplex*)

Perennial to 40 cm high from a woody base. Leaves opposite, ovate and softly hairy, almost stalkless. Flowers solitary in the leaf axils, trumpet-shaped, creamy yellow, 50 mm diameter, the calyx with about 10 slender teeth and concealed by greenish bracts.
Habitat: Grassland, especially after fire.
Notes: *Thunbergia dregeana* and *T. neglecta* are creepers in grassland with distinctly petiolate leaves, the former with heart-shaped blades and the latter ovate. The green fruits are used as a hair wash.

Thunbergia alata
ACANTHUS FAMILY

Black-eyed Susan (E), swartoognooi (A)
(Latin *alatus*, winged, alluding to the winged petioles)

Creeper with twining stems to 4 m long. Leaves opposite, heart-shaped with toothed margins. Flowers solitary in the axils, trumpet-shaped, deep orange or yellow with a blackish purple throat, 30 mm diameter, the calyx with about 12 narrow teeth and concealed by green bracts.
Habitat: Forest margins, often in disturbed places.

Thunbergia natalensis
ACANTHUS FAMILY

Natal bluebell (E), isiPhondo esikhulu (Z)
(Latin *natalensis*, from Natal)

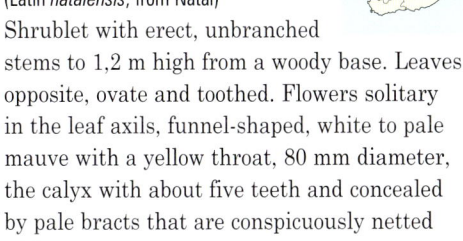

Shrublet with erect, unbranched stems to 1,2 m high from a woody base. Leaves opposite, ovate and toothed. Flowers solitary in the leaf axils, funnel-shaped, white to pale mauve with a yellow throat, 80 mm diameter, the calyx with about five teeth and concealed by pale bracts that are conspicuously netted with green.
Habitat: Thick grassland and forest margins.

Grassland and Savannah

Crossandra greenstockii
ACANTHUS FAMILY

Bushveld crossandra (E), rooiblom (A)
(Named for William Greenstock, clergyman and plant collector)

Perennial with annual stems to 20 cm high from a woody rootstock. Leaves mostly basal, elliptical and shortly hairy. Flowers in a tight spike, subtended by ovate bracts with short teeth on the margins, tubular with a single flaring lip, orange, 20–25 mm diameter.
Habitat: Rocky grassland and open woodland.

Adhatoda densiflora
ACANTHUS FAMILY

Adhatoda (E), valsmoeraskruid (A), umuSa omncane (Z)
(Latin *densiflorus*, densely-flowered)

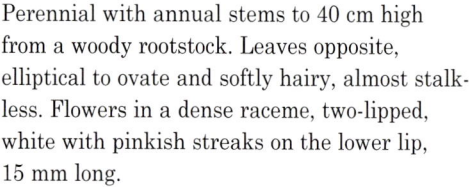

Perennial with annual stems to 40 cm high from a woody rootstock. Leaves opposite, elliptical to ovate and softly hairy, almost stalkless. Flowers in a dense raceme, two-lipped, white with pinkish streaks on the lower lip, 15 mm long.
Habitat: Stony grassland, after fire.
Notes: *Adhatoda andromeda*, from higher altitudes, is distinguished by its narrower, almost hairless leaves. Used traditionally to treat biliousness.

Tecoma capensis
BIGNONIA FAMILY

(= *Tecomaria capensis*)
Cape honeysuckle (E), trompetters (A), iCakatha (X), uDodo (Z)
(Latin *capensis*, from the Cape)

Scrambling shrub or small tree to 6 m high. Leaves opposite and divided into several toothed leaflets. Flowers in dense racemes at the branch tips, trumpet-shaped, orange, 50–60 mm long. Fruits a slender pod containing winged papery seeds.
Habitat: Thicket and forest margins.
Notes: Widely grown as an ornamental under the name *Tecomaria*.

Grassland and Savannah

Leonotis ocymifolia
MINT FAMILY
Broad-leaved minaret flower (E), klipdagga (A), isiHlungu sedobo (X), iMunyane (Z)
(Latin *ocymifolia*, with leaves like sweet basil, *Ocimum*)

Roughly hairy shrub to 2 m high. Leaves ovate and toothed. Flowers in well-spaced spherical clusters, velvety, orange, 40–55 mm long, the calyx unevenly toothed with the upper tooth larger.
Habitat: Rocky slopes and forest margins.
Notes: The tubular flowers are visited by sunbirds. Used traditionally to treat colds.

Rotheca hirsuta
MINT FAMILY
(= *Clerodendrum hirsutum, C. triphyllum*)
False violet, bush violet (E), khopa (SS), uMathanjana, uSikisiki (Z)
(Latin *hirsutus*, hairy, referring to the leaves)

Perennial herb with annual stems to 40 cm high from a woody rootstock. Leaves opposite or in whorls of three, elliptical and smooth to roughly hairy. Flowers solitary or in small clusters in the axils on slender stalks, pale to bright purplish blue with two white streaks, 20 mm diameter.
Habitat: Stony grassland and open woodland, after fire.
Notes: Used traditionally as a vermifuge and to treat kidney complaints.

Hybanthus enneaspermus
VIOLET FAMILY
Pink lady's slipper (E)
(Greek *enneaspermus*, nine-seeded)

Perennial herb with erect or trailing annual stems to 20 cm high from a woody rootstock. Leaves narrow or elliptical, smooth or thinly hairy with smooth or toothed margins. Flowers solitary in the axils on slender stalks, with a very large lower lip that is pouched at the base, pink or lilac, 10–20 mm diameter.
Habitat: Damp grassland.

Grassland and Savannah

Monopsis decipiens
BELLFLOWER FAMILY
Butterfly monopsis (E), isiDala somkhuhlane (Z)
(Latin *decipiens*, deceptive, alluding to the resemblance to the genus *Lobelia*)
Perennial rhizomatous herb with slender stems to 20 cm high. Leaves narrow and roughly hairy on the margins and midrib beneath. Flowers solitary, two-lipped, blue and purple with two yellow blotches on the lower lip, 12–15 mm diameter.
Habitat: Moist grassland in wet places.
Notes: Used traditionally to treat colds, skin afflictions and rheumatism.

Ocimum obovatum
MINT FAMILY
(= *Becium obovatum*)
Cat's whiskers (E), katsnor (A), iDada (Z)
(Latin *obovatus*, obovate, referring to the leaves)

Perennial herb with annual stems from a woody rootstock. Leaves opposite, elliptical and usually sparsely toothed. Flowers in well-spaced whorls at the branch tips, white to pale mauve with darker streaks, two-lipped with the upper lip four-lobed and fringed, 10–17 mm long.
Habitat: Grassland, especially after winter burns.
Notes: Used traditionally as an enema.

Ajuga ophrydis
MINT FAMILY
Blue bugle (E), moonyane (SS)
(Latin *ophrydis*, resembling the bee orchid, *Ophrys*)

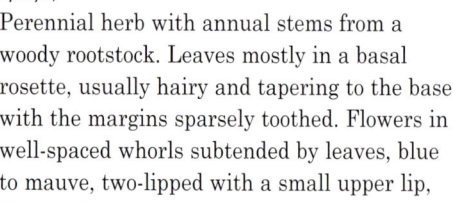

Perennial herb with annual stems from a woody rootstock. Leaves mostly in a basal rosette, usually hairy and tapering to the base with the margins sparsely toothed. Flowers in well-spaced whorls subtended by leaves, blue to mauve, two-lipped with a small upper lip, 12 mm diameter.
Habitat: Moist grassland.
Notes: Traditional cure for female sterility.

Grassland and Savannah

Syncolostemon densiflorus
MINT FAMILY

Pink plume (E), isiDleke senqomfi, iSolelemamba (Z)

(Latin *densiflorus*, densely flowered)

Aromatic shrub to 2 m high, with velvety white stems. Leaves opposite, elliptical and sometimes sparsely toothed. Flowers scattered in whorls along the branch tips, pink to crimson, tubular, 18–23 mm long.
Habitat: Rough grassland and forest margins.

Plectranthus saccatus
MINT FAMILY

Porch jacaranda (E), stoepjakaranda (A)

(Latin *saccatus*, with a sac, alluding to the flower tube)

Soft shrublet with purple-tinged stems to 1,2 m high. Leaves opposite and often leathery, broadly ovate and coarsely toothed. Flowers scattered in slender, one-sided racemes, with a swollen tube that is sac-like at the base, mauve to pale blue or white, 13–30 mm long.
Habitat: Forest margins and sheltered rocky places.

Salvia disermas
MINT FAMILY

Large blue sage (E), grootblousalie (A)

(The derivation of the name is obscure)

Soft, glandular-hairy shrub to 1,2 m. Leaves opposite and often crowded below, elliptical and roughly hairy with toothed margins. Flowers in whorls along the branch tips, whitish to mauve, 15–30 mm long.
Habitat: Stream sides, road verges and other disturbed sites in stony, often lime-rich soil.
Notes: Common around Calvinia and Kimberley.

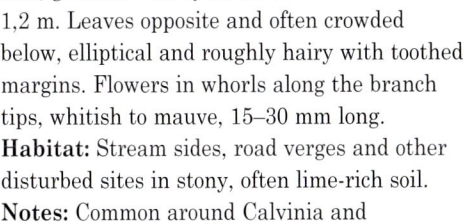

Grassland and Savannah

Sesamum triphyllum
SESAME FAMILY
Wild sesame (E), brandogie (A)
(Greek *triphyllus*, three-leaved, actually referring to the lobes of the divided leaves)
Annual herb with erect stems to 1,5 m high, foetid when bruised. Leaves opposite, the lowermost divided into three to five narrow segments. Flowers funnel-shaped, pink with red markings in the throat, 30–50 mm long. Fruits narrow with a sharply pointed tip.
Habitat: Grassland and roadsides.
Notes: *Sesamum alatum* has flowers 20–30 mm long, and winged seeds.

Ceratotheca triloba
SESAME FAMILY
Wild foxglove (E), wildevingerhoedjie (A), uDonqa (Z)
(Latin *trilobus*, three-lobed, alluding to the leaves)
Annual or short-lived perennial herb with velvety, purple stems to 1,5 m high, foetid when bruised. Leaves opposite, elliptical or three-lobed. Flowers funnel-shaped, pink with red streaks in the throat, 50–60 mm long. Fruits with two horns at the tip.
Habitat: Grassland, roadsides and old lands.
Notes: Used traditionally to treat painful menstruation, stomach cramps, nausea and fever.

Harpagophytum procumbens
SESAME FAMILY
Devil's claw, grapplethorn (E), bobbejaankloue (A), ghamaghoe (N)
(Latin *procumbens*, procumbent)
Prostrate perennial with a tuberous root. Leaves deeply lobed or toothed with white glands on the surface. Flowers funnel-shaped, deep pink or purple with a yellow throat or rarely yellowish, 50–60 mm long. Fruits armed with spiny horns dispersed by antelope.
Habitat: Sandy soils along roadsides and in waste places.
Notes: Used traditionally to treat rheumatism and arthritis and as a tonic.

Grassland and Savannah

Sopubia cana
BROOMRAPE FAMILY
Silvery sopubia (E), leilane (SS)
(Latin *canus*, greyish white)
Erect shrublet to 45 cm high, entirely covered with silvery grey hairs. Leaves narrow, with leafy short shoots in the axils. Flowers in dense racemes, pink to mauve and short-lived, 20 mm diameter.
Habitat: Grassland. Parasitic on the roots of various grasses.
Notes: Common in overgrazed grassland. Used traditionally to treat fevers, rashes and other sores.

Cycnium tubulosum
BROOMRAPE FAMILY
Small pink mushroom-flower (E)
(Latin *tubulosus*, tubular)
Erect, hairless half-parasitic herb with slender stems to 50 cm high. Leaves narrow and not toothed. Flowers in open racemes, white to pale pink turning black when faded, 30–40 mm diameter, the calyx cup-shaped with slender teeth, exposing the short, transversely oriented fruit at maturity.
Habitat: Moist grassland. Parasitic on the roots of certain grasses and sedges.

Cycnium racemosum
BROOMRAPE FAMILY
Large pink mushroom-flower (E), pienkinkblom (A), inJanga (X), uHlabahlangane (Z)
(Latin *racemosus*, with the flowers in a raceme)
Erect, rough or shortly hairy half-parasitic herb to 75 cm high. Leaves narrow and toothed. Flowers in open racemes, white to deep pink turning black when faded, 50–60 mm diameter, the calyx tubular and ribbed with very short, hooked teeth, enclosing the longitudinally elongated fruit at maturity.
Habitat: Moist grassland. Parasitic on the roots of certain grasses and sedges.
Notes: The root is used traditionally as an emetic and for general pains.

Grassland and Savannah

Cycnium adonense
BROOMRAPE FAMILY

White mushroom-flower, handkerchief flower (E), wit-inkblom (A)
(Latin *adonensis*, coming from Addo, where the type specimen was collected)

Low-growing, roughly hairy half-parasitic herb to 20 cm high. Leaves elliptical and roughly hairy with sharply toothed margins. Flowers in the leaf axils, white turning black when faded, 60–70 mm diameter, the calyx tubular with blunt teeth.
Habitat: Grassland, often in rocky places, especially evident after a fire. Parasitic on the roots of certain grasses and sedges.
Notes: Used traditionally as a remedy for snakebite.

Harveya speciosa
BROOMRAPE FAMILY

Great white inkflower (E), groot-inkblom (A), isiNama (X), umShelezana omhlophe (Z)
(Latin *speciosus*, showy)

Softly hairy parasitic perennial to 1 m high with scale-like leaves, turning black when bruised. Flowers in racemes, narrowly funnel-shaped with a long tube, creamy-white with a yellow throat, fragrant especially at night, 40–60 mm diameter, the calyx shortly toothed.
Habitat: Damp grassland and thicket. Parasitic on the roots of certain grasses and shrubby daisies.
Notes: The roots are pounded with water and used to clean and drain nasal passages.

Streptocarpus grandis
AFRICAN VIOLET FAMILY

Purple fountain (E)
(Latin *grandis*, large or great)

Short-lived herb to 45 cm high. Leaf solitary and velvety. Flowers in elongate or branched racemes, several open at once, trumpet-shaped with a cylindrical tube and relatively short petals, white or mauve to violet, 22–45 mm long.
Habitat: Forest floor in humus or on rocks.

Grassland and Savannah

Streptocarpus formosus
AFRICAN VIOLET FAMILY
Natal primrose (E)
(Latin *formosus*, beautiful)

Perennial herb to 20 cm high.
Leaves several in a rosette and velvety.
Flowers, one or two at the tip of a slender stalk, narrowly funnel-shaped with a straight, cylindrical tube, pale blue with darker streaks on the lower lip and yellow in the throat, 70–105 mm long.
Habitat: Forest floor among rocks.

Streptocarpus rexii
AFRICAN VIOLET FAMILY
Cape primrose (E), umFazi onengxolo (X)
(Latin *rexii*, named for George Rex, notary and pioneer of Knysna)

Perennial herb to 20 cm high. Leaves several in a rosette and velvety. Flowers, usually one or two, rarely up to six at the tip of a slender stalk, narrowly funnel-shaped with a straight, cylindrical tube, pale blue with darker streaks on the lower lip, 40–75 mm long.
Habitat: Forest floor or shaded banks at the forest margin.
Notes: Leaves and roots used traditionally as a love charm.

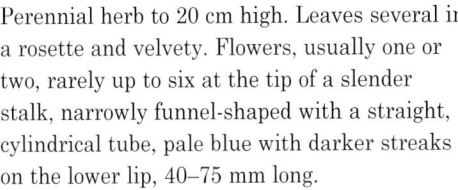

Streptocarpus dunnii
AFRICAN VIOLET FAMILY
Crimson streptocarpus (E)
(Named for E.G. Dunn who first collected the species)

Perennial or short-lived herb to 15 cm high. Leaves one to several and velvety. Flowers in an elongate raceme with several open at once, trumpet-shaped with a curved, cylindrical tube and relatively narrow petals, pink to reddish, striped on the floor, 40 mm long.
Habitat: In the shelter of rocks in damp grassland.

Grassland and Savannah

Scaevola plumieri
SCAEVOLA FAMILY
Scaevola (E), seeplakkie (A),
umQhapphu (X)
(Commemorates the eighteenth-century French missionary and explorer, Charles Plumier)
Evergreen perennial with spreading, underground stems that emerge at intervals to form colonies. Leaves rather fleshy or leathery and paddle-shaped. Flowers in small stalked clusters in the leaf axils, whitish with crumpled petals and narrow tube that is slit above and woolly within, 25 mm diameter.
Habitat: Coastal foredunes.
Notes: The leaf sap is used to treat bluebottle stings.

Phygelius aequalis
SUTERA FAMILY
Northern river bell (E), rivierklokkie (A),
mafifi-matso (SS)
(Latin *aequalis*, equal, contrasting with the oblique tube in *Phygelius capensis*)
Shrub to 2 m high. Leaves opposite, elliptical and toothed. Flowers nodding in dense panicles, the floral tube with a horizontal mouth, reddish with a yellow throat, 40 mm long.
Habitat: Montane stream sides at high altitudes.
Notes: Popular garden plant, both yellow and orange forms.

Phygelius capensis
SUTERA FAMILY
Southern river bell (E)
(Latin *capensis*, from the Cape)
Shrub to 1 m high. Leaves opposite, elliptical and toothed. Flowers flexed backwards in open panicles, the floral tube with an oblique mouth, orange with a yellow throat, 30–40 mm long.
Habitat: Montane stream sides at high altitudes.

Grassland and Savannah

Jamesbrittenia breviflora
SUTERA FAMILY
(= *Sutera breviflora*)
Scarlet sutera (E)
(Latin *breviflorus*, short-flowered, alluding to the short tube)
Straggling, aromatic perennial to 30 cm high. Leaves opposite or alternate, ovate and more or less toothed, covered with glandular hairs. Flowers solitary in the leaf axils, two-lipped with a short tube, reddish with a yellow throat, 15 mm diameter.
Habitat: Rocky slopes, roadsides and stream banks at high altitude.

Nemesia denticulata
SUTERA FAMILY
Natal nemesia (E), leeubekkie (A)
(Latin *denticulatus*, finely toothed)
Tufted perennial herb with annual stems to 40 cm high from a woody rootstock. Leaves opposite, ovate and toothed. Flowers in rounded racemes elongating in fruit, two-lipped, pink or mauve with paired yellow or orange crests on the lower lip and a pair of raised yellow bumps inside the throat at the mouth of the spur, 10 mm diameter.
Habitat: Stony grassland and open woodland.
Notes: *Nemesia caerulea* from higher altitudes lacks the raised bumps inside the flower.

Diascia anastrepta
SUTERA FAMILY
Drakensberg twinspur (E)
(Greek *anastreptus*, curved upwards, alluding to the spurs)
Loosely tangled perennial herb to 40 cm high. Leaves ovate and toothed. Flowers in elongate racemes, two-lipped with a pair of spreading spurs, the stamens in two diverging pairs, pink with a yellow and black window in the upper lip and scattered black glands on the lower lip, 20 mm diameter.
Habitat: Damp basalt cliffs and stream sides.
Notes: Most other *Diascia* species have the four stamens clustered together.

Grassland and Savannah

Protea dracomontana
PROTEA FAMILY

Drakensberg sugarbush (E)

(Latin *dracomontanus*, growing in the Drakensberg)

Low shrub, 50–150 cm high. Leaves elliptical, leathery with thickened margins. Flower heads cup-shaped, 40–60 mm diameter, the surrounding bracts cream-coloured to carmine, smooth.
Habitat: Sub-alpine grassland on basalt.
Notes: *Protea simplex* is very similar but has softer-textured leaves and shorter styles (20–40 mm vs 45–60 mm).

Protea caffra
PROTEA FAMILY

Common sugarbush (E)

(Latin *caffra*, from South Africa)

Shrub or tree, 3–8 m high.
Leaves linear to narrowly elliptical. Flower heads cup-shaped, 45–80 mm diameter, the surrounding bracts usually pink to carmine above but sometimes entirely creamy-green, smooth or silvery-silky.
Habitat: Grassland on sandstone and quartzite.

Protea gaguedi
PROTEA FAMILY

African sugarbush (E)

(*gaguedi*, the vernacular name for this species in Ethiopia)

Shrub or tree, 2–4 m high. Leaves elliptical to oblong, hairy when young but hairless at maturity. Flower heads bowl-shaped, 50–110 mm diameter, the surrounding bracts creamy-green and covered with silvery, silky hairs.
Habitat: Drier rocky grassland, often on quartzite.
Notes: *Protea welwitschii* is very similar but generally smaller with the leaves remaining hairy and the bracts with brownish hairs.

Grassland and Savannah

Protea welwitschii
PROTEA FAMILY
Welwitsch's sugarbush (E)
(Named for Friedrich Welwitsch, who collected the species in Angola)
Shrub to 1,5 m high, rarely more. Leaves elliptical to oblong, remaining hairy, at least at the base and on the midrib. Flower heads bowl-shaped, 50–110 mm diameter, the surrounding bracts creamy-green and covered with brownish silky hairs.
Habitat: Drier rocky grassland, often on quartzite.
Notes: *Protea gaguedi* is very similar but is generally a taller tree with the leaves becoming hairless at maturity and the bracts with silvery hairs.

Protea roupelliae
PROTEA FAMILY
Silver sugarbush (E)
(Named after the Victorian flower painter, Arabella Roupell)
Tree, 3–8 m high. Leaves narrowly elliptical, curved upwards. Flower heads conical, 80–100 mm diameter, the surrounding bracts pink to brownish and silky, the inner bracts spoon-shaped.
Habitat: Grassland and protea savannah, mostly on sandstone or quartzite.

Protea subvestita
PROTEA FAMILY
Waterlily sugarbush (E)
(Latin *subvestitus*, somewhat clothed, i.e. with hairs)
Large shrub or tree to 5 m high. Leaves elliptical, densely hairy when young. Flower heads cylindrical, 30–40 mm diameter, the surrounding bracts cream-coloured to pink, hairless or silky and fringed with silky hairs, the inner bracts recurved at the tips.
Habitat: Grassy slopes on sandstone.

Grassland and Savannah

Helichrysum glomeratum
DAISY FAMILY
Silver carpet (E)
(Latin *glomeratus*, collected together into a head, alluding to the flower heads)

Rhizomatous perennial herb with leafy stems to 45 cm high. Leaves closely overlapping and not decreasing in size upwards, lance-shaped and silvery-silky. Flower heads massed in rounded clusters matted with wool, yellow, 5 mm diameter, surrounded by several series of brownish bracts.
Habitat: Forming colonies in open grassland.

Helichrysum splendidum
DAISY FAMILY
Cape gold (E)
(Latin *splendidus*, shining)

Sprawling perennial herb with leafy stems to 1,5 m long. Leaves narrow with the margins rolled under and whitish woolly beneath. Flower heads in small, rounded or flat-topped clusters, yellow, 5 mm diameter, surrounded by several series of bright yellow bracts.
Habitat: Sheltered rocky places and forest margins.

Helichrysum cymosum
DAISY FAMILY
Straggling everlasting (E), imPepho (Z)
(Latin *cymosus*, with the flowers arranged in the flat-topped inflorescence called a cyme)

Straggling or sprawling shrublet to 1 m high. Leaves narrow with the margins slightly rolled under, thinly silky or with skin-like hairs above but white-felted beneath. Flower heads crowded in flat-topped clusters, cylindrical, yellow, 3 mm diameter, surrounded by several series of yellow bracts.
Habitat: Stony or sandy slopes or steep turf in damp places.

Grassland and Savannah

Helichrysum pallidum
DAISY FAMILY
Silver Hottentot's tea (E)
(Latin *pallidus*, pale, referring to the leaf undersides)

Tufted perennial herb to 65 cm high, the roots producing narrow tubers. Leaves mostly clustered near the base, elliptical and roughly hairy above but white-felted beneath, five to seven net-veined from the base. Flower heads crowded, bell-shaped, pale yellow or brownish, 5–7 mm diameter, surrounded by several series of blunt bracts that are papery at the tips.
Habitat: Grassland.

Helichrysum nudifolium
DAISY FAMILY
Hottentot's tea (E), Hottentotstee (A), letapiso (SS), iCholocholo (X, Z)
(Latin *nudifolius*, naked-leaved, i.e. without hairs on the leaves)

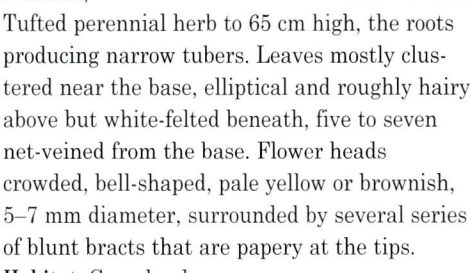

Tufted perennial herb to 1,5 m high, spreading by stout runners. Leaves mostly clustered near the base, oblong and more or less smooth but roughly hairy on the margins and veins, three to seven net-veined from the base. Flower heads crowded, bell-shaped, pale yellow or brownish, 4–5 mm diameter, surrounded by several series of blunt bracts that are papery at the tips.
Habitat: Grassland.
Notes: Used traditionally as a tea or as a poultice to treat various ailments.

Helichrysum ruderale
DAISY FAMILY
Weedy everlasting (E)
(Latin *ruderalis*, growing among rubbish)
Biennial herb to 1 m high, aromatic when fresh. Leaves decreasing in size upwards, elliptical and clasping the stem, glandular-hairy with the margins often white-woolly as well. Flower heads flattened, yellow, 20–25 mm diameter, surrounded by several series of golden yellow, papery bracts.
Habitat: Weed of roadsides and waste places.

Grassland and Savannah

Helichrysum aureum
DAISY FAMILY

Yellow everlasting (E), leabane (SS)
(Latin *aureus*, golden, referring to the bracts)

Tufted perennial herb to 80 cm from a woody rootstock, producing numerous leaf rosettes. Leaves mostly basal, elliptical and roughly hairy above but more or less grey-woolly beneath. Flower heads one to few at the branch tips, flattened, yellow or white, 15–25 mm diameter, surrounded by several series of golden yellow, papery bracts.
Habitat: Grassland.

Helichrysum adenocarpum
DAISY FAMILY

Pink everlasting (E), pienksewejaartjie (A), senko-toana (SS)
(Greek *adenocarpus*, with glandular fruits)

Tufted perennial herb with several leaf rosettes and flowering stems to 45 cm high from a woody rootstock. Leaves elliptical and greyish, usually woolly or cobwebby. Flower heads one to few, bowl-shaped, yellow, 25–30 mm diameter, surrounded by several series of white to red, papery bracts.
Habitat: Moist grassland, often in damp depressions.

Helichrysum ecklonis
DAISY FAMILY

Ecklon's pink everlasting (E), umuThi wechanti (Z)
(Named for the nineteenth-century German apothecary and plant collector, Christian Ecklon)

Tufted perennial herb with several leaf rosettes and flowering stems to 45 cm high from a woody rootstock. Leaves elliptical and greyish, usually woolly or cobwebby, the stem leaves much smaller with papery tips. Flower heads solitary, bowl-shaped, yellow, 30–40 mm diameter, surrounded by several series of white to red, papery bracts.
Habitat: Montane grassland, often on steep slopes.

Grassland and Savannah

Hilliardiella aristata
DAISY FAMILY
(= *Vernonia natalensis*)
Silver vernonia (E), iLeleva (Z)
(Latin *aristatus*, awned, referring to the pointed floral bracts)

Perennial herb with annual, leafy stems to 1 m high from a woody rootstock. Leaves narrow and silvery-silky on both surfaces. Flower heads in flat-topped clusters, purple, 8–10 mm diameter, surrounded by several series of silvery, bristle-tipped bracts.
Habitat: Open grassland, especially after fire.

Hilliardiella hirsuta
DAISY FAMILY
(= *Vernonia hirsuta*)
Quilt-leaved vernonia (E), wildeson-soekertjie (A), iKhambi lenyongo (Z)
(Latin *hirsutus*, covered with coarse hairs)

Perennial herb with annual, leafy stems to 1 m high from a woody rootstock. Leaves oblong or elliptical with toothed margins, clasping the stem at the base, roughly hairy above but greyish woolly beneath. Flower heads in flat-topped clusters, purple, 5–8 mm diameter, surrounded by several series of greyish, hairy, bristle-tipped bracts.
Habitat: Rough grassland, often on the edges of forest, especially after fire.
Notes: Used traditionally to treat colic, sore throats, coughs, headaches and rashes.

Gymnanthemum myrianthum
DAISY FAMILY
(= *Vernonia myriantha*)
Wild lilac (E)
(Greek *myrianthus*, with numerous flowers)

Much-branched shrub to 4 m high. Leaves elliptical with a lobed base and toothed margins, thinly woolly beneath, the petioles with a pair of deciduous, ear-like lobes at the base. Flower heads numerous in flat-topped clusters, purple, 3 mm diameter, surrounded by several series of oblong bracts.
Habitat: Forest margins.

Grassland and Savannah

Senecio barbatus
DAISY FAMILY

Sticky-plume groundsel (E)

(Latin *barbatus*, bearded, alluding to the conspicuous hairs on the flower heads)

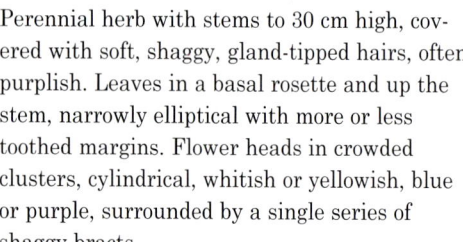

Perennial herb with stems to 30 cm high, covered with soft, shaggy, gland-tipped hairs, often purplish. Leaves in a basal rosette and up the stem, narrowly elliptical with more or less toothed margins. Flower heads in crowded clusters, cylindrical, whitish or yellowish, blue or purple, surrounded by a single series of shaggy bracts.

Habitat: Moist grassland.

Felicia filifolia
DAISY FAMILY

Needle-leaved felicia, fine-leaved felicia (E), draaibos (A)

(Latin *filifolius*, thread-leaved)

Well-branched shrub to 1 m high. Leaves in tufts on short shoots, needle-like and lightly dotted with glands. Flower heads solitary in the leaf tufts, yellow with blue to mauve ray florets, 20 mm diameter, surrounded by three series of narrow bracts.

Habitat: Rocky places in grassland, a weed in overgrazed veld.

Notes: Poisonous to sheep. Used for firewood.

Berkheya umbellata
DAISY FAMILY

Mop-headed berkheya (E), klossiedissel (A), iKhakhasana elincane (Z)

(Latin *umbellatus*, like an umbrella, referring to the clustered flower heads)

Perennial herb to 80 cm high from a creeping woody rootstock, usually in colonies. Leaves mainly in a basal tuft, elliptical with toothed and spiny margins, roughly hairy above and glandular hairy beneath. Flower heads in flat-topped clusters on spiny-winged stems, yellow, 25–30 mm diameter.

Habitat: Rough grassland, especially after fire.

Notes: Used traditionally as a fragrant body lotion by girls.

Grassland and Savannah

Berkheya speciosa
DAISY FAMILY
Showy berkheya (E), skraaldisseldoring (A), uMaphola (Z)
(Latin *speciosus*, showy)

Perennial herb with slender stems to 1 m high from a woody rootstock. Leaves in a basal tuft, elliptical and distinctly petiolate with toothed margins, roughly hairy above but white-cobwebby beneath. Flower heads yellow with yellow ray florets, 30–60 mm diameter.
Habitat: Stony, moist grassland, especially after fire.
Notes: *Berkheya setifera* has bristly leaves. Used traditionally to treat stomach problems, bilharzia and to bathe sore eyes.

Berkheya subulata
DAISY FAMILY
Transvaal grass berkheya (E)
(Latin *subulatus*, awl-shaped, referring to the leaves)

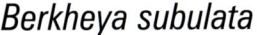

Perennial herb with clumps of annual stems to 50 cm high from a woody rootstock. Leaves narrow with the margins rolled under and bearing scattered short bristles, smooth or roughly hairy above and white-felted beneath. Flower heads solitary at the stem tips, yellow with yellow ray florets, 50–70 mm diameter.
Habitat: Rocky grassland, especially after fire.
Notes: *Berkheya insignis*, the Natal grass berkheya, has long, flexible bristles on the leaf margins.

Berkheya rosulata
DAISY FAMILY
Drakensberg berkheya (E)
(Latin *rosulatus*, rosetted, referring to the tufts of leaves)

Bushy shrub to 1 m high. Leaves in clusters at the branch tips, elliptical with toothed and spiny margins, glossy dark green above and white-felted beneath. Flower heads solitary on white-felted branches, yellow with yellow ray florets, 25–35 mm diameter.
Habitat: Basalt cliffs at high altitude.

Grassland and Savannah

Berkheya cirsiifolia
DAISY FAMILY
Lesser thistle-leaved berkheya (E),
mohata-o-mosoeu (SS)
(Latin *cirsiifolius*, with leaves like the thistle, *Cirsium*)

Perennial to 1 m high, branching above, often in colonies. Leaves decreasing in size upwards, oblong but deeply lobed with the margins toothed and spiny, shortly hairy above but white-woolly beneath. Flower heads few on spiny-winged stems, yellow with white or yellow ray florets, 50–80 mm diameter, the outer bracts tipped with a spine 5–8 mm long.
Habitat: Rocky montane grassland.
Notes: *Berkheya onopordifolia* has shorter spines on the outer bracts, 3–4 mm long.

Berkheya purpurea
DAISY FAMILY
Purple berkheya (E), bloudisseldoring (A),
sehlolo (SS)
(Latin *purpureus*, purple)

Perennial to 1 m high, often in colonies. Leaves in a basal tuft, lanceolate with the margins toothed and spiny, roughly hairy above but white-woolly beneath. Flower heads few on spiny-winged stems, mauve, 50–80 mm diameter.
Habitat: Montane grassland.
Notes: *Berkheya leucaugeta* (below) has white ray florets.

Grassland and Savannah

Berkheya multijuga
DAISY FAMILY
Spiny Berg thistle (E), mohatollo (SS)
(Latin *multijugus*, in many pairs, referring to the leaf lobes)

Perennial to 1.8 m high, in small colonies. Leaves mostly in a basal rosette, narrowly oblong and lobed to the midrib with the margins toothed and spiny, shortly hairy above but usually white-woolly beneath. Flower heads yellow with yellow ray florets, 50–80 mm diameter.
Habitat: Montane grassland.

Euryops tysonii
DAISY FAMILY
Tyson's rosinbush (E), sehlakoana (SS)
(Named for William Tyson, teacher and plant collector)

Shrublet to 1,5 m high with the branches leafless below. Leaves overlapping, elliptical and leathery, smooth except for white wool in the axils. Flower heads crowded at the branch tips, yellow with yellow ray florets, fragrant, 10–15 mm diameter, surrounded by a single series of smooth bracts.
Habitat: Rocky slopes, screes and boulder beds.

Senecio microglossus
DAISY FAMILY
Greater two-day cure (E)
(Greek *microglossus*, small-tongued, referring to the short ray florets)

Clump-forming perennial with erect stems, becoming leafless below, to 1,2 m from a creeping, woody rootstock. Leaves scattered along the stems, elliptical with two small lobes at the base, leathery with toothed margins, three-veined from the base. Flower heads orange with bright yellow ray florets, 10 mm diameter, surrounded by a single series of bracts.
Habitat: Rocky grassland, especially after fire.
Notes: *Senecio serratuloides* is similar but the leaves have a single main vein. Re-sprouts rapidly after fire, becoming rather untidy after a few years. Spreads by means of suckers.

Grassland and Savannah

Senecio polyanthemoides
DAISY FAMILY
Weedy ragwort (E)
(Greek *polyanthemoides*, resembling the polyanthus primulas)
Bushy annual with somewhat woody stems to 1,8 m high. Leaves elliptical with the margins rolled under and toothed, smooth or rough above and thinly woolly beneath. Flower heads yellow with yellow ray florets, 10 mm diameter, surrounded by a single series of bracts.
Habitat: Rough grass on forest margins, common along roadsides and old fields.
Notes: Reputed to cause death in horses.

Senecio bupleuroides
DAISY FAMILY
Yellow starwort (E), iDwarane (X), inDabula-luvalo (Z)
(Latin *bupleuroides*, resembling the genus *Bupleurum*)
Slender perennial herb with stems to 80 cm high from a woody rootstock. Leaves few, lance-shaped and leathery with thickened margins that are often rolled under, greyish and smooth. Flower heads yellow with yellow ray florets, 10 mm diameter, surrounded by a single series of short, smooth bracts.
Habitat: Grassland after fires.
Notes: Used traditionally to treat heart complaints.

Senecio macrospermus
DAISY FAMILY
Great alpine groundsel (E)
(Greek *macrospermus*, large-seeded)
Robust, clumped perennial herb to 1 m high from a woody rootstock. Leaves mainly basal, elliptical with finely toothed margins, covered with a grey woolly felt. Flower heads yellow with yellow ray florets, 25–30 mm diameter, surrounded by a single series of grey-felted bracts.
Habitat: Steep, damp mountain slopes in grass or scree.

Grassland and Savannah

Senecio speciosus
DAISY FAMILY
Magenta groundsel (E), iDambiso (X, Z)
(Latin *speciosus*, showy)

Perennial herb with stems to 70 cm high from a woody rootstock, often arched at the base then erect. Leaves mostly in a basal rosette, elliptical and lobed or toothed, somewhat fleshy and usually glandular-hairy. Flower heads deep pink to purple with similar coloured ray florets, 30–40 mm diameter, surrounded by a single series of hairless or glandular-hairy bracts.
Habitat: Damp grassland, often in marshy depressions.

Dimorphotheca jucunda
DAISY FAMILY
(= *Osteospermum jucundum*)
Mauve daisy (E), bergbietou (A),
uMasigcolo-nkonekazi (Z)
(Latin *jucundus*, delightful)

Spreading perennial herb to 30 cm high. Leaves narrow and tapering below, sometimes toothed, shortly hairy. Flower heads yellow and black with pale to deep pink ray florets that are coppery beneath, 20–30 mm diameter.
Habitat: Rocky grassland and cliffs.
Notes: Used traditionally to treat stomach complaints.

Dimorphotheca fruticosa
DAISY FAMILY
(= *Osteospermum fruticosum*)
Sea boneseed (E), rankmargriet (A)
(Latin *fruticosus*, bushy)

Evergreen perennial with sprawling to prostrate stems that root along their length and form mats. Leaves leathery, broad but narrowed below and minutely toothed along the margins. Flower heads purple with white or mauve ray florets, 30–40 mm diameter.
Habitat: Coastal dunes and rocks.

Grassland and Savannah

Aster bakerianus
DAISY FAMILY

Baker's wild aster (E), umThekisana (X), uDlatshana (Z)

(Named after the Victorian botanist, J.G. Baker, who published extensively on African flora)

Perennial herb with roughly hairy, annual stems to 70 cm high from a woody rootstock. Leaves roughly hairy and three- to five-veined from the base. Flower heads yellow with blue or white rays, 20–30 mm diameter.
Habitat: Rocky grassland, especially after fire.
Notes: *Aster harveyanus* is hairless. Used traditionally to treat stomach complaints, internal parasites, various infections and sores and for head ailments.

Callilepis laureola
DAISY FAMILY

Ox-eye daisy (E), wildemagriet (A), iHlamvu (Z)

(Latin *laureolus*, laurel-like)

Perennial herb with erect, annual stems to 60 cm high from a woody rootstock. Leaves three-veined from the base, smooth or softly hairy. Flower heads black with creamy-white ray florets, 20–30 mm diameter.
Habitat: Stony grassland, especially after fire.
Notes: *Callilepis leptophylla* from the Highveld has narrow, one-veined leaves. Used to treat tapeworm and maggots in cattle.

Haplocarpha scaposa
DAISY FAMILY

False gerbera (E), moarubetso (SS), isiKhali (Z)

(Latin *scaposus*, with a well-developed, leafless flowering stalk)

Tufted perennial herb with the flowering stalk to 30 cm high. Leaves in a basal tuft, ovate, hairy above but white-felted beneath with a fringed margin. Flower heads yellow with yellow ray florets, 25–40 mm diameter.
Habitat: Stony grassland or open woodland.
Notes: The white felt from the leaves was used in tinderboxes.

Grassland and Savannah

Gerbera piloselloides
DAISY FAMILY
Small gerbera (E), swarttee (A),
moarubetso (SS), ubuLawu (Z)
(Resembling the hawkweed, *Pilosella*)
Tufted perennial herb with the flowering stalk to 30 cm high. Leaves in a basal tuft, ovate and tapering below, softly hairy or cobwebby with a fringed margin. Flower heads yellow or white with white, pink, red or yellow ray florets, 10–25 mm diameter.
Habitat: Stony grassland or open woodland, often after fires.
Notes: Recognised by the swollen top of the flowering stalk. Used traditionally to treat tapeworm, earache, headache and coughs.

Gerbera ambigua
DAISY FAMILY
Common gerbera (E), griekwatee (A),
moarubetso (SS), uCabazane (Z)
(Latin *ambiguus*, doubtful or uncertain, suggesting the species was somewhat perplexing)
Tufted perennial with the flowering stalk to 35 cm high. Leaves in a basal tuft, elliptical and petiolate, silky or almost hairless above but white- or yellowish-felted beneath. Flower heads yellow or white to black with white or, rarely, yellow ray florets that are pink to coppery beneath, 25–40 mm diameter.
Habitat: Grassland or open woodland, often near moisture.

Gerbera viridifolia
DAISY FAMILY
Pink gerbera (E)
(Latin *viridifolius*, green-leaved, alluding to the almost hairless mature leaves)
Tufted perennial with the flowering stalk to 35 cm high. Leaves in a basal tuft, elliptical and petiolate, silky or almost hairless above and beneath. Flower heads yellow or white to violet with white or pink to purple ray florets that are pink to purple beneath, 25–40 mm diameter.
Habitat: Grassland or open woodland.

Grassland and Savannah

Gerbera aurantiaca
DAISY FAMILY
Hilton daisy (E)
(Latin *aurantiacus*, orange)
Tufted perennial with the flowering stalk to 30 cm high. Leaves in a basal tuft, elliptical and petiolate, velvety above but thinly woolly or smooth beneath. Flower heads reddish with orange to red ray florets that are coppery beneath, 25–35 mm diameter.
Habitat: Rocky grassland.
Notes: Hybridises with *Gerbera ambigua*.

Gerbera jamesonii
DAISY FAMILY
Barberton daisy (E)
(Named for Robert Jameson, businessman and plant enthusiast, who first collected seeds of the species)
Tufted perennial with the flowering stalk to 70 cm high. Leaves in a basal tuft, deeply undulating or lobed and distinctly petiolate, almost hairless except on the margins. Flower heads reddish with slender, red or rarely white or pink ray florets, 40–60 mm diameter.
Habitat: Rocky slopes in woodland, often under trees.

Grassland and Savannah

Hirpicium armerioides
DAISY FAMILY
Mountain gerbera (E), skynloodkruid (A)
(Resembling the sea-pink, *Armeria*)

Mat-forming perennial with flowering stalks to 25 cm high. Leaves in a basal tuft, narrow with the margins rolled under, hairy above but white-felted beneath. Flower heads yellow with white ray florets that are yellow or black beneath, 25–40 mm diameter.
Habitat: Poor stony soils and rock sheets.

Gazania krebsiana
DAISY FAMILY
Common gazania (E), bruingousblom (A), uBendle (X, Z)
(Named for Georg Krebs, who farmed near Bedford in the Eastern Cape in the nineteenth century)
Tufted perennial herb with flowering stalks to 20 cm high. Leaves in a basal tuft, narrow and sometimes lobed with the margins rolled under, roughly hairy above but white-felted beneath. Flower heads yellow with yellow to orange rays that are sometimes dark at the base, 30–70 mm diameter.
Habitat: Roadsides and stony grassland.
Notes: The flowers may be eaten raw, while the plant is used traditionally to treat sickly babies, earache and sterility in women.

Arctotis leiocarpa
DAISY FAMILY
Karoo arctotis (E), karoogousblom (A)
(Greek *leiocarpus*, smooth-fruited, referring to the occasional lack of hairs on the fruits)
Slightly fleshy annual to 45 cm high. Leaves elliptical or paddle-shaped and toothed or lobed and often eared at the base, cobwebby or woolly. Flower heads yellow with white ray florets tinged purple on the reverse, 50–60 mm diameter, surrounded by several series of bracts, the outer with long tails and the inner with rounded, papery tips.
Habitat: Arid sandy or gravelly flats, often along washes.

Fynbos

THE TERM FYNBOS has become synonymous with the floral wonderland that characterises the south-western tip of Africa. Derived from the Dutch term for fine-leaved shrubs, it describes the characteristic vegetation of the Cape Floral Region. Covering an area of around 90 000 km², the Cape Floral Region is an L-shaped area centred on Cape Town that stretches northwards about 150 km to the Bokkeveld Escarpment near Nieuwoudtville in the north, and eastwards for 350 km to Port Elizabeth. Nowhere is it more than about 100 km wide. Enclosed within this narrow belt is one of the most remarkable temperate floras in the world. Here over 9 000 different species of flowering plants are found, accounting for 44% of the total number of species in the country in a region that covers little more than 5% of its land area. Of this extraordinary diversity, a massive 70% of the species do not occur outside the boundaries of the Cape Floral Region.

Rainfall in the Cape region is largely restricted to the winter months, between April and August, especially in the west. Towards the east, however, the rainfall becomes progressively less seasonal. In addition, the seaward slopes of the southern coastal mountain ranges benefit from summer moisture that condenses on their upper slopes, while the West Coast is essentially hot and dry throughout the summer. The seasonality of flowering is closely related to the seasonality of precipitation, and while little can be found in flower along the West Coast in summer there is a relative wealth of plants in flower on the higher slopes in the south-east.

The distinctive fynbos vegetation of the Cape Floral Region is defined by the occurrence of members of the protea, erica and restio families, along with an abundance of bulbous species unmatched elsewhere in the world. True fynbos is an evergreen shrubland confined to acidic, nutrient-poor sandstone soils that predominate in the Western Cape. These soils are derived from the sandstone rocks of the Cape series, which have been dramatically folded into the parallel ranges of the Cape Fold Mountains that dominate the skyline wherever you might find yourself in the region. Some 7 000 species in the region occur in true fynbos, with perhaps an additional 1 500 in the second main vegetation type in the region, renosterveld. Occupying the richer shale soils that lie in the valleys between these fynbos-clad ranges, and forming much of the coastal forelands, renosterveld is an allied but quite distinct vegetation type. It derives its name from the renosterbos or rhinoceros bush, *Elytropappus rhinocerotis*, which gives it a characteristic dull grey cast. Although it receives far less attention than fynbos, renosterveld is much more endangered than its more charismatic cousin and today less than 10% of renosterveld has escaped the plough!

One of the characteristics of the vegetation of the Cape Region is the highly local nature of many of its species. This means that it is easy to see a great number of different wildflower species in a relatively short distance. It also means, of course, that great care must be taken not to overlook superficially similar species. The chances of doing this are greatly increased by another unusual feature of the Cape flora: the diversity is not evenly spread across the different plant families and genera. Out of a total of almost 950 genera of flowering plants that occur in the Cape Region, only 20 of these account for one third of all the species! Among the largest are *Erica* (660 species), *Aspalathus* (272 species), *Pelargonium* (148 species) and *Agathosma* (143 species). Distinguishing between many of these is extremely difficult. Many of these species, however, are rare or highly local in occurrence and therefore not often seen. In the Cape, a spring season after a summer fire is almost invariably spectacular, with large numbers of bulbs in particular responding to the removal of choking shrubbery.

The West Coast is a familiar destination for wildflower enthusiasts as its spring displays of annuals are quite spectacular. Despite the encroachment of housing estates, a significant stretch of this coast is preserved in the West Coast National Park. The sands along the West Coast are dominated by large tufts of restios and scattered shrubs of rhus and the rusty-flowered sages, *Salvia lanceolata* and *S. africana-lutea*. The most conspicuous shrub in flower in spring is the broom-like *Muraltia scoparia*, which forms large purple or lilac mounds thickly covered in small pea-like flowers that perfume the air. Among the numerous annuals it is the daisies that are

The slopes of Kogelberg ablaze with spring bulbs after a summer burn

Fynbos

Gladiolus cardinalis *cascades down a waterfall near Bain's Kloof*

most conspicuous, especially the glistening white *Dimorphotheca pluvialis*, orange *Ursinia anthemoides*, purple *Senecio arenarius* and yellow or white buttons of *Cotula turbinata*. The daisies close their flower heads at night or in inclement weather, making an early start to the day somewhat unrewarding. Another characteristic to take into account is that they face north towards the sun. This means that it is best to be driving south in the afternoon, when you will be able to return the bright gaze of the flowers.

Mixed in with the daisies are pale blue *Heliophila* and several species of nemesia, each with a different charming face. The granite outcrops that fringe the Langebaan lagoon and dot the landscape around the village of Darling are especially rich in lovely plants and repay a prolonged visit. Several small reserves around Darling are closely studded in brilliantly coloured bulbs in mid- to late September, including the charming winecups, *Geissorhiza*. The comparison between these verdant meadows and the millefiore on medieval paintings is not a difficult one to draw.

The granite domes on the West Coast are home to numerous bulbs that seek shelter from the depredations of baboons and porcupines in the rock crevices. Among these are various species of lachenalia, gladiolus, romulea, spiloxene and ornithogalum. Many striking succulents also cling to the smoothly rounded flanks of these domes. The most spectacular is undoubtedly *Carpobrotus quadrifidus*, which trails its greyish stems over the rocks and shrubs, dazzling in the sun with brilliant purple cups nestling among the fleshy leaves. One of the most characteristic annuals of the West Coast is the Bokbaai vygie. This popular garden plant appears in a bewildering variety of colours, mainly bright pink but more commonly white or lemon yellow around the Langebaan Lagoon. The Cape of Good Hope Nature Reserve is also well worth a visit, particularly for its lovely stands of several Proteaceae, notably *Mimetes hirtus*, *Leucadendron xanthoconus* and the endemic *Serruria villosa*. In early summer it is especially brilliant with glossy white stretches of *Syncarpha vestita* covering the ground in drifts like snow. The Breede River valley between Tulbagh and Bonnievale is another stretch of country that provides flowers over a long period. September is especially good for the many bulbous plants, including the charming orange *Gladiolus alatus*. This little species is easily among the most entrancing of the many gladiolus species that occur in the Western Cape. The glory of the Worcester valley must be its succulents, especially the endemic *Drosanthemum speciosum*. This small shrub bears flowers of almost impossibly brilliant reds and orange in late spring, in October. The best-known river valley in the region, however, is the Olifants River valley, between Citrusdal and Clanwilliam. Nestling on either side of the Cedarberg mountains, the Clanwilliam and Biedouw valleys can justly be described as the Valleys of the Flowers. Unfortunately, like Namaqualand, their glory is short-lived, and they are at their best between August and September.

Unlike Namaqualand, however, it is possible to extend the flower viewing season in the Western Cape by scaling the heights. The grandeur of the Cape mountains is enhanced by their relative accessibility via numerous mountain passes that cut through their jagged slopes. Their flanks are clothed in a rich shrubbery dominated by various proteas, among which the grey-leaved waboom, *Protea nitida*, is probably the most instantly recognisable. Forming a thick understorey here are numerous needle-leaved shrubs. Although these shrubs may appear to be a uniform and rather uninteresting mass, careful examination will disclose many different species, each with its own distinct flower. It is also one of the characteristics of fynbos that different sites support different suites of species despite appearances to the contrary, and so the secret is to stop frequently and look carefully. It is not unusual to find several different species of proteas, conebushes, ericas or buchus growing together. The record is eight different ericas in a square metre of mountain fynbos! All of the mountain passes are recommended, and they will yield something of interest in any month of the year. It is difficult to pick out particular plants or places but the Hottentots Holland, Outeniqua/Tsitsikamma and Swartberg mountains are all accessible by road. The coastal route along the southern foot of the Outeniqua/Tsitsikamma range, with its breathtaking vistas, is popularly known as the Garden Route, and provides an opportunity to see the largest stretches of forest in the country, between George and Knysna.

The easiest of the Cape mountains to scale is Table Mountain itself and late summer is the time when one of its most glorious wildflowers, *Disa uniflora*, the red disa, comes into flower. This blood red orchid is the flower emblem of the Western Cape and can be seen in bloom along streams and runnels on Table Mountain between mid-February and March. It is little wonder that this lovely flower is an object of annual pilgrimage by many local residents. Another wildflower worthy of a hike in summer is *Gladiolus cardinalis*, the New Year Lily, which cascades from the edges of waterfalls in the Hottentots Holland range. It is easily seen in certain side valleys off the Bain's and Du Toit's Kloof passes.

Erica schumannii clinging to the summit of the Stettynsberg

Fynbos

Zantedeschia aethiopica
ARUM FAMILY
Common calla lily, arum lily, pig lily (E),
varkblom (A)
(Latin *aethiopicus*, from Africa, usually
South Africa)

Tuberous perennial, 60–100 cm high. Leaves arrow-shaped, on long spongy petioles. Flowers crowded in a narrow yellow spike 8–9 cm long which is partly enclosed by a flaring, leathery, white bract.
Habitat: Seasonal wetlands or stream sides, often in quantity.
Notes: The warmed leaves are used as a dressing and the boiled rhizomes mixed with syrup as a gargle. Uncooked parts must not be eaten as the needle-like oxalate crystals cause painful inflammation.

Aponogeton distachyos
APONOGETON FAMILY
Edible pond blossom (E),
waterblommetjie (A)
(Greek *distachyos*, two-spiked)

Rhizomatous aquatic perennial. Leaves on long petioles with floating, oblong blades. Flowers in two rows in forked, floating spikes 20–30 mm long, white with one large petal, gardenia-scented.
Habitat: Pools and ditches.
Notes: Young fruits sold and eaten as a vegetable, particularly in *waterblommetjiebredie*, a traditional mutton stew.

Asparagus capensis
ASPARAGUS FAMILY
Thorny asparagus (E), katdoring (A)
(Latin *capensis*, from the Cape)

Thorny shrublet to 1 m high with widely spreading, brush-like branches bearing whorls or clusters of short branchlets closely covered with small 'leaves'. Flowers, one or rarely two at the tips of the branchlets, white with brown mid-veins, very fragrant of tuberose, 6 mm diameter.
Habitat: Stony clay flats in scrub.

Fynbos

Chlorophytum triflorum
ANTHERICUM FAMILY
Wire-root grasslily (E)
(Latin *triflorus*, three-flowered, referring to the several flowers per bract)
Tufted perennial to 1 m high, with hard, dark and tapering roots. Leaves strap-shaped with finely hairy margins. Flowers in loose racemes with several flowers in each bract, white with brown keels, each lasting a single day, 15 mm diameter.
Habitat: Sandy soils, often coastal.
Notes: Distinguished from similar species by its characteristic roots.

Ornithoglossum undulatum
COLCHICUM FAMILY
Cockatoo snakelily (E)
(Latin *undulatus*, wavy, a reference to the leaf margins)
Cormous perennial, 5–20 cm high. Leaves lance-shaped and greyish with wavy margins. Flowers nodding on slender stalks with the six petals arranged in a fan, white to pink with purple or maroon tips, fragrant, 20–25 mm diameter.
Habitat: Rocky sandstone or granite slopes.

Wurmbea stricta
COLCHICUM FAMILY
(= *Onixotis stricta*)
Greater waterphlox (E), rysblommetjie (A)
(Latin *strictus*, very straight, referring to the stems)
Cormous perennial with stiffly erect stems, 20–50 cm high. Leaves three, rod-like and triangular in section with the upper two set just below the spike. Flowers in a narrow spike, pink, lightly scented, 15 mm diameter.
Habitat: Marshes and pools.

Fynbos

Wurmbea variabilis
COLCHICUM FAMILY
Stinking spike lily (E)
(Latin *variabilis*, variable, traditionally in colour but here referring to general variability)

Cormous perennial, 5–20 cm high. Leaves three, broadly lance-shaped. Flowers in a cylindrical spike, star-shaped, the petals cream with a brown blotch near the base, 15 mm diameter. **Habitat:** Stony clay or sandstone soils in open scrub.

Bulbinella caudafelis
ALOE FAMILY
Cat's tail bulbinella (E), katstert (A)
(Latin *caudafelis*, cat's tail, alluding to the flower spike)

Rhizomatous perennial to 80 cm high. Leaves narrow and channelled, grass-like and often with finely toothed margins. Flowers in a slender, tapering raceme, white with a pink tinge, 7–8 mm diameter.
Habitat: Often on clay slopes, but also sandstone or granite in scrub.
Notes: Bulbinellas can be distinguished from bulbines by their long-lasting flowers with smooth, thread-like stamen filaments.

Bulbine annua
ALOE FAMILY
Annual bulbine (E)
(Latin *annuus*, annual, referring to the annual habit which is unique in the genus)

Annual herb with wiry roots, 15–40 cm high. Leaves many in a basal cluster, knitting needle-like and slightly fleshy. Flowers in a dense raceme on slender stalks, yellow, 10 mm diameter. Fruits spherical on spreading stalks.
Habitat: Sandy soils, often coastal.
Notes: The flowers, like those of all bulbines, last only a single day. This and the fluffy stamen filaments distinguish them from bulbinellas.

Fynbos

Trachyandra divaricata
ALOE FAMILY
Seaside tumbling starlily (E)
(Latin *divaricatus*, spreading widely, referring to the branching flower stems)

Tufted, rhizomatous perennial to 90 cm high, with many cylindrical, fleshy roots. Leaves many, narrow and oval in section, fleshy and smooth, each individually wrapped at the base in a brown, papery sheath. Flowers nodding in rounded panicles with sharply spreading branches, white, fragrant, 10 mm diameter.
Habitat: Coastal dunes and sandy flats.
Notes: The young flower buds can be eaten as a vegetable. The flowering stem dries into a tumbleweed that is blown about by the wind in summer to disperse the seeds.

Trachyandra muricata
ALOE FAMILY
Common tumbling starlily (E)
(Latin *muricatus*, rough, referring to the leaves)

Rhizomatous perennial to 90 cm high, with many cylindrical, fleshy roots. Leaves few to several, lance-shaped, rough or sandpapery, at least along the margins. Flowers nodding in rounded panicles with the stem rough at the base, white, fragrant, 10 mm diameter.
Habitat: Stony clay slopes in karroid scrub and renosterveld.

Aloe perfoliata
ALOE FAMILY
Cliff aloe, mitre aloe (E), kransaalwyn (A)
(= *Aloe comptonii, A. mitriformis*)
(Latin *perfoliatus*, of leaves that clasp the stem)

Sprawling, often branched succulent shrub with stems 1–2 m high. Leaves succulent and broadly lance-shaped, dark green with few or no white speckles and with coarsely toothed margins. Flowers crowded in branched, head-like racemes, nodding, scarlet, 40 mm long.
Habitat: Rocky sandstone or granite slopes and cliffs.

Aloe plicatilis
ALOE FAMILY
Fan aloe (E), waaieraalwyn (A)
(Latin *plicatus*, pleated, alluding to the appearance of the leaf rosettes)

Stout succulent shrub or small tree to 5 m high with more or less equally forked branches. Leaves in tight fans, oblong and greyish with dark margins that are rough but not toothed. Flowers nodding in short, loose racemes, scarlet, 40–50 mm long.
Habitat: Cool sandstone slopes.

Aloe microstigma
ALOE FAMILY
Cape speckled aloe (E)
(Greek *microstigma*, little spot, referring to the white speckling on the leaves)

Rosette-forming succulent to 50 cm high when not in flower. Leaves tapering and succulent, often reddish and usually with small white spots, the margins with sharp, reddish-brown teeth. Flowers nodding in conical racemes, usually red in bud but opening yellow, 20–25 mm long.
Habitat: Stony slopes among scrub.
Notes: Exceptionally common in the Little Karoo, dominating rocky hillsides in places.

Aloe arborescens
ALOE FAMILY
Krans aloe (E), kransaalwyn (A), inHlazi (Z)
(Latin *arborescens*, becoming tree-like)

Many-branched shrubs or small trees to 2 m high with the stems often tilted. Leaves sickle-shaped with sharp greenish teeth along the margins. Flowers nodding in conical racemes, usually pink but also orange to yellow, 30 mm long.
Habitat: Rocky slopes; exposed ridges in scrub.
Notes: Common and widespread, often cultivated, especially in the Eastern Cape where it is used as live fences. The sappy leaves are a convenient first-aid treatment for burns.

Fynbos

Aloe ferox
ALOE FAMILY
Bitter aloe (E), bitteraalwyn (A), iKhala (X)
(Latin *ferox*, fierce, alluding to the prickly leaves)

Robust single-stemmed succulent to 2 m high, rarely to 5 m, with the old leaves remaining on the trunk. Leaves tapering with sharp brown teeth on the margins and sometimes the leaf surfaces. Flowers nodding in dense, branched candelabras, usually orange to red, about 30 mm long.
Habitat: Widely distributed on stony flats and slopes.
Notes: Probably the most important medicinal plant in the region. For over 200-years the golden-brown leaf sap has been used to make the purgative known as Cape Aloe.

Kniphofia uvaria
ALOE FAMILY
Cape poker (E), vuurpyl (A)
(Latin *uvarius*, clustered like grapes, alluding to the flower spikes)

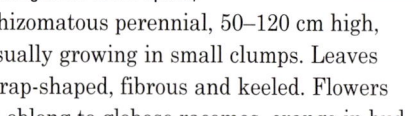

Rhizomatous perennial, 50–120 cm high, usually growing in small clumps. Leaves strap-shaped, fibrous and keeled. Flowers in oblong to globose racemes, orange in bud turning greenish yellow, 30–40 mm long.
Habitat: Seeps, marshes and streams, usually in peaty soils, flowering well after a burn.

Lachenalia bulbifera
HYACINTH FAMILY
Red lachenalia (E), rooinaeltjie (A)
(Latin *bulbiferus*, bearing bulbils, a reference to the propensity for producing bulblets)

Bulbous perennial, 8–30 cm high. Leaves one or two, lance- to strap-shaped, plain or blotched with dark colour. Flowers nodding, tubular with the anthers enclosed within the flower, orange to red with darker red or brown markings and green tips, 20–35 mm long.
Habitat: Sandy flats and lower slopes, mainly coastal.

Fynbos

Lachenalia aloides
HYACINTH FAMILY
Cape cowslip (E), vierkleurtjie (A)
(Resembling an aloe in its flowers)
Bulbous perennial, 5–31 cm high. Leaves one or two, lance- to strap-shaped, sometimes densely spotted with green or purple. Flowers nodding, tubular with the anthers enclosed within the tube, combinations of orange, red, yellow or greenish blue with greenish markings, 20–35 mm long.
Habitat: Granite and sandstone outcrops, often coastal.

Lachenalia mutabilis
HYACINTH FAMILY
Tasselled lachenalia (E)
(Latin *mutabilis*, changeable, a reference to the multi-coloured flowers)
Bulbous perennial, 10–45 cm high. Leaf solitary, lance-shaped with wavy margins. Flowers tubular or urn-shaped with the anthers enclosed within the tube, pale blue and white with yellow tips or yellowish green, the upper flowers often vestigial and sometimes electric blue, 8–10 mm long.
Habitat: Sandy and stony slopes.

Lachenalia pustulata
HYACINTH FAMILY
Warty lachenalia (E)
(Latin *pustulatus*, warty or blistered)
Bulbous perennial, 15–35 cm high. Leaves one or two, lance- or strap-shaped and smooth or densely warty. Flowers on long pedicels, urn-shaped with the anthers shortly or well protruding, shades of cream, blue or pink with green or brownish markings, 7–9 mm long.
Habitat: Clay or granite flats, often in large colonies.
Notes: Common on granite outcrops near Langebaan.

Massonia depressa
HYACINTH FAMILY
Common hedgehog lily (E),
bobbejaanboek (A)
(Latin *depressus*, flattened from above, alluding to the low growth form)
Bulbous perennial to 5 cm high. Leaves broad and rounded, flat on the ground, plain green or marked with purple. Flowers clustered between the leaves, with large bracts, deeply cupped below, green or yellowish to white or pink, 10–15 mm diameter.
Habitat: Mainly clay flats.
Notes: Pollinated by rodents that lap the thick nectar from the flowers at night.

Albuca grandis
HYACINTH FAMILY
Sandveld slime lily (E)
(Latin *grandis*, large or great)
Stout to slender bulbous perennial to 1 m high, the bulb sometimes with bulbils around the base. Leaves several, channelled, fleshy and oozing a slimy sap when torn. Flowers in racemes that droop in bud, nodding, yellow with green keels, fragrant, all six stamens with anthers although three are smaller, 25–30 mm diameter.
Habitat: Sandy slopes and flats, often coastal.

Albuca flaccida
HYACINTH FAMILY
Common slime lily (E), tamarak (A)
(Latin *flaccidus*, flaccid, referring to the rather limp leaves)
Bulbous perennial, 40–100 cm high, the bulb tunics membranous. Leaves several, channelled and clasping the stem below, fleshy and oozing a slimy sap when torn. Flowers in loose racemes, nodding, mostly yellow or with green keels, lightly fragrant, the inner petals with a hinged flesh flap at the tips and only three stamens with anthers, 25–30 mm diameter.
Habitat: Mostly coastal in stony sandstone and granitic soils.

Fynbos

Albuca canadensis
HYACINTH FAMILY
(= *Albuca altissima, A. maxima*)
Greater slimelily (E), wittamarak (A)
(Latin *maximus*, greatest, for its large size)

Stout bulbous perennial, usually 1–2 m high, the bulb tunics slightly fibrous at the top. Leaves several, channelled and clasping the stem below. Flowers in racemes that elongate markedly in fruit, nodding, white with green keels, the inner tepals with a hinged flap at the tip and only three stamens with anthers, 25–30 mm diameter.
Habitat: Rocky outcrops.
Notes: Can form dense colonies along roadsides.

Albuca suaveolens
HYACINTH FAMILY
(= *Ornithogalum suaveolens*)
Striped chincherinchee (E), bonttjienk (A)
(Latin *suaveolens*, sweetly fragrant)

Bulbous perennial, 10–50 cm high. Leaves few, sometimes dry at flowering, narrow and channelled. Flowers in loose racemes on slender stalks, greenish yellow with dark green keels, sweetly fragrant, 20–30 mm diameter.
Habitat: Dry stony slopes and flats.

Ornithogalum thyrsoides
HYACINTH FAMILY
Chincherinchee (E), tjienk (A)
(Resembling the inflorescence type known as a thyrse)

Bulbous perennial, 20–80 cm high, the outer layers of the bulb soft and whitish. Leaves sometimes dry at flowering, lance-shaped and usually with minutely hairy margins. Flowers shiny white and often darker in the centre, three of the stamen filaments with broad wings at the base, 20–25 mm diameter.
Habitat: Sandy flats and often in vleis.
Notes: Toxic to stock. *Ornithogalum conicum* lacks the conspicuous wings at the base of the inner filaments. Both species and their hybrids are popular cut flowers.

Ornithogalum dubium
HYACINTH FAMILY

Varicoloured chincherinchee (E), geeltjienk (A)
(Latin *dubius*, doubtful, reflecting the doubts regarding the true identity of the species)

Bulbous perennial, 10–50 cm high, the outer layers of the bulb often blackish. Leaves sometimes dry at flowering, lance-shaped with minutely hairy margins. Flowers in almost flat-topped racemes, yellow to orange or rarely white and often with a green or brown centre and a very short style, 20–25 mm diameter.
Habitat: Mainly clay or gravelly flats and lower slopes.

Empodium plicatum
STARGRASS FAMILY

Common autumn star (E), klipsterretjie (A)
(Latin *plicatus*, pleated, referring to the leaves)

Cormous perennial, 10–30 cm high, with pale basal sheaths. Leaves several but often only beginning to emerge at flowering, narrow and pleated. Flowers solitary on a three-angled stalk, bright yellow, 20–30 mm diameter.
Habitat: Clay and granite flats and lower slopes.

Spiloxene capensis
STARGRASS FAMILY

Painted peacockflower (E), poublom (A)
(Latin *capensis*, from the Cape)

Cormous perennial, 10–30 cm high. Leaves several, grass-like and channelled with the margins usually minutely toothed. Flowers one per stalk, the flowering stalk with a single leaf-like bract, yellow, white or pink and usually with black or iridescent markings in the centre, the reverse of the petals boldly striped, 30–70 mm diameter.
Habitat: Seasonally wet flats.

Spiloxene aquatica
STARGRASS FAMILY
Water star (E), watersterretjie (A)
(Latin *aquaticus*, living in water)

Cormous perennial, 20–45 cm high. Leaves two to five, knitting needle-like and somewhat triangular in cross-section. Flowers two to seven per stalk, the flowering stalk with two or more bracts, white with green backs, often scented, 20–30 mm diameter.
Habitat: Seasonal pools and streams.

Gethyllis afra
AMARYLLIS FAMILY
Kukumakranka (E), koekemakranka (N)
(Latin *afra*, from Africa)
Bulbous perennial to 15 cm high. Leaves withered at flowering, many, narrow and spiralled, usually hairless. Flowers appearing at ground level, cup-shaped, cream with pink stripes on the reverse, 30–40 mm diameter.
Habitat: Sandy flats.
Notes: Flowers are followed in the autumn by a narrow, cylindrical fruit that protrudes from the ground. This is the famed kukumakranka. It is highly fragrant, with a fruity scent. Although edible, the fruit was more often steeped in brandy or witblits, which was then taken for colic and indigestion.

Lanaria lanata
KAPOK LILY FAMILY
Kapok lily (E)
(Latin *lanatus*, woolly)
Evergreen tufted perennial, 30–80 cm high. Leaves narrow and channelled, tough and fibrous with minutely toothed margins. Flowers in white-woolly flat-topped panicles, mauve inside but white-woolly on the outside, 10 mm diameter.
Habitat: Clay and sandstone slopes.
Notes: Flowers mainly after fire.

Fynbos

Dilatris ixioides
BLOODROOT FAMILY
Common bloodroot (E), rooiwortel (A)
(Resembling the genus *Ixia*, not an accurate simile)

Rhizomatous perennial, 20–40 cm high. Leaves narrow and strap-like, in a narrow fan. Flowers crowded, in flat-topped panicles, mauve with two long stamens twice as long as tepals and one shorter stamen, 15 mm diameter.
Habitat: Rocky sandstone slopes in fynbos.
Notes: Flowers are either left- or right-handed depending on the direction in which the style is flexed.

Wachendorfia paniculata
BLOODROOT FAMILY
Common butterfly lily (E), rooikanol (A)
(Latin *paniculatus*, a branched inflorescence)

Rhizomatous perennial, mostly 20–70 cm high. Leaves narrow and pleated, usually hairy. Flowers in an open or dense panicle, buff to bright yellow, 30–35 mm diameter.
Habitat: Mainly sandy flats or sandstone slopes in fynbos.
Notes: Flowers are either left- or right-handed depending on the direction in which the style is flexed.

Wachendorfia thyrsiflora
BLOODROOT FAMILY
Royal butterfly lily (E), groot rooikanol (A)
(Latin *thyrsiflora*, with flowers arranged in the inflorescence type known as a thyrse)

Rhizomatous perennial, 1–2 m high. Leaves broad and pleated, hairless. Flowers in a crowded, cylindrical panicle, golden-yellow, 30 mm diameter.
Habitat: Permanent marshes and streams.
Notes: Flowers are either left- or right-handed depending on the direction in which the style is flexed. A wonderful garden plant for pondside plantings.

Fynbos

Cyanella lutea
CYANELLA FAMILY
Yellow lady's hand (E), geelraaptol (A)
(Latin *luteus*, golden-yellow)
Cormous perennial, 12–25 cm high. Leaves lance-shaped with wavy margins. Flowers in branched racemes, yellow or rarely pink, fragrant, with five upper and one larger lower stamens that are not joined.
Habitat: Mostly clay, or limestone flats.

Cyanella hyacinthoides
CYANELLA FAMILY
Blue lady's hand (E), blouraaptol (A)
(Hyacinth-like, particularly in flower colour)
Cormous perennial, 25–40 cm high. Leaves slender and often wavy on the margins, hairless or finely hairy. Flowers in branched racemes, mauve or rarely white, fragrant, with five upper and one larger lower stamens that are joined together at the base.
Habitat: Mostly clay and granite slopes, often in renosterveld.

Agapanthus africanus
AGAPANTHUS FAMILY
Cape agapanthus (E)
(Latin *africanus*, from Africa)
Evergreen perennial, 25–70 cm high. Leaves strap-shaped and channelled. Flowers on pedicels 15–50 mm long, broadly funnel-shaped and thick-textured with the stamens shorter than the petals, deep blue, 25–40 mm long.
Habitat: Rocky sandstone slopes.
Notes: Flowers best after fire. Much confused with *Agapanthus praecox* in the horticultural trade but not in cultivation at all.

Fynbos

Agapanthus praecox
AGAPANTHUS FAMILY
Agapanthus (E)
(Latin *praecox*, precocious, thus early flowering, not very appropriate)
Evergreen perennial, 50–100 cm high. Leaves strap-shaped and channelled. Flowers on pedicels 40–120 mm long, broadly funnel-shaped and thin-textured with the stamens mostly as long as the petals, white to medium blue, 30–70 mm long.
Habitat: Rocky slopes, often along bush margins.
Notes: A widely grown ornamental with many forms.

Tulbaghia violacea
ONION FAMILY
Wild garlic (E)
(Latin *violaceus*, violet-coloured)
Evergreen rhizomatous perennial smelling of garlic when bruised, 20–35 cm high. Leaves narrow and greyish. Flowers in rounded clusters, resembling minute daffodils in shape, mauve, lightly scented, 10–15 mm long.
Habitat: Forest margins and stream banks.
Notes: Widely cultivated. Traditionally used for fever and colds. Leaves may be eaten as a vegetable.

Amaryllis belladonna
AMARYLLIS FAMILY
March lily, belladonna (E)
(Italian *belladonna*, beautiful lady)
Bulbous perennial to 90 cm high. Leaves dry or absent at flowering, several, strap-shaped and channelled with a prominent midrib. Flowers trumpet-shaped, pink to nearly white and fragrant, 70–80 mm diameter.
Habitat: Seasonally damp, loamy soils in lowlands.
Notes: One of only two true species of *Amaryllis*; plants commonly cultivated under that name belong to the genus *Hippeastrum*.

Fynbos

Brunsvigia orientalis
AMARYLLIS FAMILY
King's candelabra (E), koningskandelaar (A)
(Latin *orientalis*, eastern, mistakenly thought to have come from the Far East)
Bulbous perennial, 40–50 cm high. Leaves dry at flowering, usually six, spreading flat on the ground, tongue-shaped and leathery with translucent margins. Flowers in a large, rounded cluster on long pedicels, red, trumpet-shaped with the petals rolled back, 50 mm long.
Habitat: Mainly sandy soils, usually coastal lowlands.
Notes: Pollinated by sunbirds.

Brunsvigia marginata
AMARYLLIS FAMILY
Scarlet candelabra (E)
(Latin *marginatus*, margined, referring to the leaves)
Bulbous perennial to 20 cm high. Leaves dry at flowering, four, spreading flat on the ground, elliptical and leathery with translucent margins. Flowers crowded in a round cluster, brilliant scarlet, star-shaped with a short tube and prominent stamens, 30 mm diameter.
Habitat: Rocky slopes in shale bands.
Notes: Pollinated by the Citrus swallowtail and Table Mountain beauty butterflies.

Haemanthus coccineus
AMARYLLIS FAMILY
April fool (E)
(Latin *coccineus*, deep red)
Bulbous perennial, 6–20 cm high. Leaves dry at flowering, two, tongue-shaped and glossy green above but usually speckled beneath and often minutely hairy on the margins. Flowers crowded in a dense, brush-like cluster on a spotted stalk, red, 40 mm long.
Habitat: Coastal scrub and rocky slopes, often in the lee of rocks.

Fynbos

Nerine sarniensis
AMARYLLIS FAMILY
Red nerina, Guernsey lily (E)
(Latin *sarniensis*, from Guernsey, from the mistaken belief that the species was native there)
Bulbous perennial, 25–45 cm high. Leaves dry at flowering, several, strap-shaped. Flowers star-shaped with a short tube and prominent stamens clustered together, scarlet or purplish with a golden sheen, 25–30 mm diameter.
Habitat: Stony slopes, often in the shelter of rocks.
Notes: Pollinated by the Table Mountain beauty butterfly, *Aeropetes tulbaghia*.

Ammocharis longifolia
AMARYLLIS FAMILY
(= *Cybistetes longifolia*)
Malgas lily (E), malgaslelie (A)
(Latin *longifolius*, long-leaved)
Bulbous perennial, 25–35 cm high. Leaves dry or green at flowering, several, sickle-shaped and spreading on the ground, with translucent margins. Flowers widely funnel-shaped, cream to pink turning reddish and very fragrant, 30–40 mm diameter.
Habitat: Sandy flats.

Cyrtanthus ventricosus
AMARYLLIS FAMILY
Fire lily (E), vuurlelie (A)
(Latin *ventricosus*, swollen, referring to the somewhat inflated flower tube)
Bulbous perennial, 10–25 cm high. Leaves dry at flowering, one to five, narrowly strap-shaped and channelled. Flowers two to ten per stalk, nodding and tubular to narrowly trumpet-shaped, bright shiny red but often with pink petals, 40–50 mm long.
Habitat: South-facing sandstone slopes in fynbos.
Notes: Flowering only after fire, appearing within 12 to 14 days after the burn.

Fynbos

Cyrtanthus elatus
AMARYLLIS FAMILY
George lily (E)
(Latin *elatus*, tall)

Bulbous geophyte to 60 cm high. Leaves strap-shaped and slightly channelled. Flowers two to nine per stalk, widely funnel-shaped, bright red or rarely pink, 70–100 mm long.
Habitat: Forest margins and moist mountain slopes.
Notes: Pollinated by the large brown butterfly, *Aeropetes tulbaghia*.

Nivenia stokoei
IRIS FAMILY
Stokoe's bush iris (E)
(Commemorating the Cape Town plant collector, Thomas Stokoe)

Evergreen shrub with woody stems to 60 cm high. Leaves sword-shaped, in flat fans at the branch tips. Flowers aggregated into loose, flat-topped clusters, pale to deep blue or rarely lilac, with a slender tube, 40–50 mm long.
Habitat: Rocky sandstone in fynbos.
Notes: The small Cape genera *Nivenia*, *Klattia* and *Witsenia* are the only members of this family to develop woody stems. They are all rather local and restricted to sandstone soils.

Aristea africana
IRIS FAMILY
Fringed aristea (E)
(Latin *africanus*, from Africa)

Evergreen rhizomatous perennial, mostly 10–15 cm high, with flattened, branched stems. Leaves narrow and fibrous. Flowers subtended by greenish bracts with wide membranous margins that are fringed and curled, blue, 15–20 mm diameter. Fruits short and three-winged.
Habitat: Sandy flats and mountain slopes.
Notes: Each flower lasts less than a day.

Fynbos

Aristea bakeri
IRIS FAMILY
(= *Aristea confusa*)
Aristea (E)
(Commemorates the English botanist, J.G. Baker)

Evergreen rhizomatous perennial to 1 m high, with cylindrical, usually well-branched stems. Leaves strap-like and fibrous. Flowers subtended by rust-brown bracts with transparent margins, blue, 20–25 mm diameter. Fruits three-winged.
Habitat: Stony sandstone slopes in fynbos.
Notes: Flowers mostly after fire and each flower lasts less than a day.

Aristea capitata
IRIS FAMILY
(= *Aristea major*)
Blue sceptre (E), blousuurkanol (A)
(Latin *capitatus*, with a knob-like head, referring to the crowded flowering stalks)

Evergreen rhizomatous perennial to 1,5 m high, with cylindrical stems that have short, crowded branches above. Leaves strap-like, fibrous. Flowers crowded and subtended by small dark bracts with papery margins, blue, 15–20 mm diameter. Fruits short, three-winged.
Habitat: Sheltered sandstone slopes in fynbos.
Notes: Better known under the name *Aristea major*. Flowers only after fire and each flower lasts less than a day.

Ferraria crispa
IRIS FAMILY
Sea spider iris (E), spinnekopblom (A)
(Latin *crispus*, crisped, referring to the petal margins)

Cormous perennial, 40–100 cm high, with branched, leafy stems. Leaves sword-shaped and slightly fleshy. Flowers brown or yellowish and speckled, with tightly crisped petal margins, acrid-smelling, 30 mm diameter.
Habitat: Mainly coastal, in sand or among rocks.

Fynbos

Bobartia indica
IRIS FAMILY
Greater rush iris (E), blombiesie (A)
(Latin *indicus*, from India, a mistake arising from the transport of the first specimens on board an East Indiaman returning to Europe from the East)
Evergreen rhizomatous perennial to 1 m or more high. Leaves cylindrical, longer than the stems and trailing. Flowers in a dense head on a slender leafless stalk, yellow, 20 mm diameter.
Habitat: Sandstone flats and slopes in fynbos.
Notes: Flowers mainly after fire.

Moraea miniata
IRIS FAMILY
(= *Homeria miniata*)
Common Cape tulip (E), tulp (A)
(Latin *miniatus*, flame-red)
Cormous perennial, 15–60 cm high. Leaves two or three, narrow and channelled, trailing. Flowers star-shaped, salmon-pink or rarely yellow or white, minutely speckled in the centre, the anthers held at the tip of a bulbous filament column, 20–30 mm diameter.
Habitat: Mainly clay slopes in renosterveld and karroid scrub.
Notes: Poisonous to stock.

Moraea flaccida
IRIS FAMILY
(= *Homeria flaccida*)
Red Cape tulip (E), rooitulp (A)
(Latin *flaccidus*, flaccid, referring to the rather limp leaf)
Cormous perennial, 35–60 cm high with the stem bent outwards above the leaf sheath. Leaf solitary, narrow and channelled. Flowers cup-shaped, salmon-pink with a yellow centre or entirely yellow, the anthers held beyond the cup on a thick filament column, 30–40 mm diameter.
Habitat: Seasonally wet sandstone and granitic soils.

Fynbos

Moraea collina
IRIS FAMILY
(= *Homeria collina*)
Yellow Cape tulip (E), geeltulp (A)
(Latin *collinus*, pertaining to hills, alluding to its habitat)

Cormous perennial, 20–50 cm high, stem bent outward above the leaf sheath. Leaf solitary, narrow, channelled. Flowers cup-shaped, yellow or salmon, lightly scented, the anthers held within the cup on a thick filament column.
Habitat: Lower mountain slopes and flats on sand or clay.
Notes: Common after fire.

Moraea fugacissima
IRIS FAMILY
(= *Galaxia fugacissima*)
Needle-leaved clockflower (E), horlosieblom (A)
(Latin *fugacissimus*, very fleeting, referring to the short-lived flowers)

Stemless cormous perennial, 3–6 cm high, often forming little cushions. Leaves narrow and grass-like or needle-like. Flowers yellow, sweetly scented, cup-shaped with a slender tube, 15–20 mm diameter.
Habitat: Wet sand and clay flats.
Notes: Each flower lasts only a single morning.

Moraea neglecta
IRIS FAMILY
Rush-leaved moraea (E)
(Latin *neglectus*, neglected, referring to the fact that the species was not recognised as distinct for many years)

Cormous perennial, 20–50 cm high with an unbranched stem that is sticky at the nodes. Leaf solitary, knitting needle-like. Flowers yellow with darkly stippled markings, fragrant, with the three inner petals smaller than the outer and lance-shaped, 50–70 mm diameter.
Habitat: Usually deep sandy soils.

Fynbos

Moraea fugax
IRIS FAMILY
Hottentot nut (E), soetuintjie, hottentotuintjie (A)
(Latin *fugax*, fleeting, referring to the short-lived flowers)

Cormous perennial, 12–80 cm high with the branches crowded together just above the leaves. Leaves one or two, inserted well above the ground, narrow or thread-like and channelled, often trailing. Flowers blue, white or yellow, fragrant, with the three inner petals lance-shaped, 40–50 mm diameter.
Habitat: Deep sands and rocky sandstone and granitic slopes.
Notes: Flowers open only in the mid-afternoon and each lasts less than one day. The corms were prized as food among early tribes.

Moraea gawleri
IRIS FAMILY
Wire-stemmed moraea (E)
(Commemorates the British botanist, Ker Gawler)

Loosely branched cormous perennial with wiry stems, 15–45 cm high. Leaves two or three, narrow with the margins usually wavy or crinkly. Flowers yellow, cream or brick-red, sometimes bicoloured, with the three inner petals lance-shaped, 15–20 mm diameter.
Habitat: Sandy or clay slopes, usually in renosterveld.

Moraea tripetala
IRIS FAMILY
Fleur-de-lys moraea (E), blou-uintjie (A)
(Latin *tripetalus*, three-petalled, due to the reduced or obsolete inner petals)

Slender cormous perennial, 20–45 cm high. Leaf solitary, narrow and channelled. Flowers blue to violet or rarely white or pink, the three inner tepals reduced to a minute thread or absent, 20–30 mm diameter.
Habitat: Rocky sandstone and clay soils in fynbos and renosterveld.

Fynbos

Moraea villosa
IRIS FAMILY

Peacock moraea (E), blouflappie (A)
(Latin *villosus*, shaggy, referring to the hairy leaves)

Cormous perennial, 30–40 cm high. Leaf solitary, narrow and channelled, hairy beneath. Flowers purple, blue, cream or orange with large, dark markings, the inner three petals three-lobed with a long, narrow central lobe, 45–60 mm diameter.
Habitat: Stony granite and clay slopes and flats in renosterveld.
Notes: Increasingly rare.

Moraea ramosissima
IRIS FAMILY

Vleiuintjie (A)
(Latin *ramosissimus*, highly branched)

Highly branched cormous perennial, 50–120 cm high. Leaves several in a fan and shiny green, narrow and channelled. Flowers yellow with darker yellow nectar guides on the outer tepals, the inner three tepals smaller than the others, 30 mm diameter.
Habitat: Damp sandy or stony flats and slopes, often along streams.
Notes: Flowering mostly after fire.

Dietes iridioides
IRIS FAMILY

Wood iris (E)
(*Iris*-like, referring to the flowers and rhizomatous habit)

Evergreen rhizomatous perennial to 60 cm high. Leaves sword-shaped in a tight fan. Flowers in tight clusters on an irrregularly branched stem, white with violet style arms, lasting only one day, 30–40 mm diameter.
Habitat: Evergreen forest and forest margins.

Fynbos

Ixia polystachya
IRIS FAMILY
Dark-eyed ixia (E), kalossie (A)
(Greek *polystachyos*, with many spikes, referring to the branched stems)
Slender cormous perennial, 40–80 cm high, the stem wiry with one to three short side-branches. Leaves narrow to sword-shaped. Flowers in a dense spike, white to pink or mauve or rarely yellow and usually with a darker centre, sometimes lightly fragrant, with a thread-like tube and small, translucent bracts, 10–15 mm diameter.
Habitat: Granite and sandstone slopes.

Ixia maculata
IRIS FAMILY
Black-eyed ixia (E), kalossie (A)
(Latin *maculatus*, blotched)
Cormous perennial, 25–60 cm high. Leaves narrowly sword-shaped. Flowers orange with a dark eye, with a thread-like tube and large rusty-spotted bracts, 20–25 mm diameter.
Habitat: Sandy flats and lower slopes.

Ixia dubia
IRIS FAMILY
Orange ixia (E), kalossie (A)
(Latin *dubius*, doubtful, reflecting the doubts regarding the true identity of the species)
Cormous perennial, 25–60 cm high. Leaves narrowly sword-shaped. Flowers orange to yellow and often dark in the centre, with a thread-like tube and small translucent bracts, 15–20 mm diameter.
Habitat: Sandstone and granite flats and slopes.

Fynbos

Ixia scillaris
IRIS FAMILY
Buzz ixia (E), pienk kalossie (A)
(Latin *scillaris*, pertaining to the genus *Scilla*, referring to the open spike of starry pinkish flowers)
Cormous perennial, 25–50 cm high. Leaves sword-shaped with the margins sometimes wavy or crisped. Flowers in an open spike, pale to deep pink, with a thread-like tube and the anthers nodding to one side, 10 mm diameter.
Habitat: Stony sandstone and granite flats and slopes.
Notes: The pollen is buzzed out of the flask-like anthers by visiting bees.

Hesperantha bachmannii
IRIS FAMILY
Ballerina hesperantha (E)
(Named after the nineteenth-century German naturalist, Frans Bachmann)
Cormous perennial, 15–30 cm high, with a rounded corm. Leaves narrowly sword-shaped. Flowers nodding on a slender curved tube, with the petals bent backwards, sweetly scented, opening in the late afternoon, 15–20 mm diameter.
Habitat: Mainly stony clay slopes in renosterveld.

Geissorhiza aspera
IRIS FAMILY
Blue satinflower (E), satynblom (A)
(Latin *asper*, rough, referring to the stems)
Cormous perennial with velvety stems, 10–35 cm high. Leaves sword-shaped with lightly thickened margins and midrib. Flowers blue-violet or rarely white, 10 mm diameter.
Habitat: Mainly sandy or granite flats and slopes.

Fynbos

Geissorhiza radians
IRIS FAMILY
Wine cup (E), kelkiewyn (A)
(Latin *radians*, radiating, referring to the rings of colour in the flowers)
Cormous perennial, 8–16 cm high. Leaves narrow and conspicuously ribbed. Flowers deep blue with a red centre surrounded by a white ring, with the stamens and style arching downward, 15–20 mm diameter.
Habitat: Seasonally wet sandy or granite soils.

Micranthus junceus
IRIS FAMILY
Marsh combflower (E), vleiblommetjie (A)
(Latin *junceus*, rush-like, referring to the leaves)
Cormous perennial, 25–45 cm high. Leaves slender, cylindrical and hollow. Flowers in a two-ranked spike, subtended by dry bracts with translucent margins, pale or dark blue or rarely white, 6 mm diameter.
Habitat: Seasonal seeps or stream sides on granite or sandstone.

Watsonia meriana
IRIS FAMILY
Wax-flowered watsonia (E), kanolpypie (A)
(Commemorating Maria Sybill Merian, the eighteenth-century painter of plants and animals)
Cormous perennial, 60–200 cm high, sometimes with cormlets at the stem nodes. Leaves sword-shaped. Flowers dull red, pink or mauve with a long tube, 60 mm long. Fruits oblong.
Habitat: Sandy or granitic soils, often in vleis and along streams.
Notes: The tubular flowers are visited by sunbirds.

Fynbos

Watsonia knysnana
IRIS FAMILY
Knysna watsonia (E)
(Latin *knysnana*, of Knysna)
Cormous perennial to 1,6 m high. Leaves sword-shaped. Flowers mostly pale pink to purple but rarely red with a long tube, 60 mm long. Fruits tapering upward.
Habitat: Sandstone slopes and grassy flats.
Notes: Hybridises extensively with both orange-flowered *Watsonia pillansii* and red-flowered *W. fourcadei* around Humansdorp.

Watsonia borbonica
IRIS FAMILY
Purple watsonia (E)
(Latin *borbonicus*, mistakenly thought to originate from Réunion (Île de Bourbon))
Robust cormous perennial to 2 m high, with branched, often purple stems. Leaves sword-shaped, bright green. Flowers purple-pink with a short tube and the stamens and style usually arching downward, 40–50 mm long. Fruits oblong.
Habitat: Mainly rocky sandstone slopes but also granite and clay.
Notes: Flowers best after fire.

Watsonia tabularis
IRIS FAMILY
Table Mountain watsonia (E)
(Latin *tabularis*, pertaining to Table Mountain, where the species is endemic)
Cormous perennial to 1,5 m high. Leaves sword-shaped with those on the stem swollen at the base. Flowers orange and pink with a long tube, 60–70 mm long. Fruits oblong with a blunt tip.
Habitat: Rocky sandstone slopes.
Notes: Endemic to the Cape Peninsula. The tubular flowers are pollinated by sugarbirds and sunbirds, especially the Malachite Sunbird.

Fynbos

Watsonia aletroides
IRIS FAMILY
Firecracker watsonia (E)
(Resembling species of *Aletris* in its spike of tubular flowers)
Cormous perennial to 45 cm high. Leaves sword-shaped. Flowers nodding and curved, red or purple to pink, tubular with very short petals, 35–45 mm long. Fruits very narrow and tapering to a pointed tip.
Habitat: Moist clay slopes, mainly in renosterveld.

Watsonia laccata
IRIS FAMILY
Overberg watsonia (E)
(Latin *laccatus*, lake-coloured, crimson)
Cormous perennial to 50 cm high. Leaves sword-shaped. Flowers funnel-shaped, pink to purple or orange with the stamens and style arching downward, 30–40 mm long. Fruits very narrow and tapering to a pointed tip.
Habitat: Moist clay slopes, mainly in renosterveld.

Tritoniopsis triticea
IRIS FAMILY
Summer snakeflower (E), somerpypie (A)
(Latin *triticeus*, of wheat, referring to the dry brown floral bracts)
Cormous perennial, 50–90 cm high. Leaves usually dry at flowering, the basal leaves spear-shaped with three equal veins, abruptly narrowed below into a slender petiole, the stem leaves thread-like and brown. Flowers tubular, scarlet with very small petals marked with black, 25–30 mm long.
Habitat: Rocky granite and sandstone slopes.
Notes: *Tritoniopsis burchellii* is very similar but has larger petals.

Fynbos

Tritoniopsis antholyza
IRIS FAMILY
(= *Anapalina nervosa*)
Common snakeflower (E)
(Greek *anthos-*, *-lyssa*, flower, rage, a poetical allusion to the open-mouthed (= snarling) flowers)
Cormous perennial to 90 cm high. Leaves sword- to strap-shaped with three to six equal veins. Flowers tubular and yellowish pink to red with the upper petals larger than the lower petals, 30–50 mm long.
Habitat: Rocky sandstone slopes.
Notes: Flowers best after a burn.

Tritoniopsis caffra
IRIS FAMILY
(= *Anapalina caffra*)
Outeniqua snakeflower (E)
(Latin *caffra*, from South Africa)
Cormous perennial to 80 cm high. Leaves sword-shaped with two to four equal veins. Flowers tubular with the lower petals smaller, bright red, 40 mm long.
Habitat: Sandstone slopes.
Notes: The odd-shaped flowers are pollinated by sunbirds.

Chasmanthe aethiopica
IRIS FAMILY
Lesser cobra lily (E), klein kapelpypie (A)
(Latin *aethiopicus*, from Africa, usually South Africa)
Cormous perennial with an unbranched stem, 40–65 cm high. Leaves in a tight fan, sword-shaped and thin-textured. Flowers in a single-ranked spike, orange-red and tubular with the tube flared and pouched near the base, 40–50 mm long.
Habitat: Coastal, in bush and forest margins.
Notes: The thinly fleshy, orange seeds are dispersed by fruit-eating birds.

Fynbos

Chasmanthe floribunda
IRIS FAMILY
Greater cobra lily (E), kapelpypie (A)
(Latin *floribundus*, flowering profusely)
Cormous perennial with one or two side branches, 45–100 cm high. Leaves in a tight fan, sword-shaped and thin-textured. Flowers in two ranks, orange-red or rarely yellow, with the tube flaring gradually near the base, 50–60 mm long.
Habitat: Coastal and montane on sandstone and granite in scrub.

Babiana ringens
IRIS FAMILY
(= *Antholyza ringens*)
Rat's tail babiana (E), rotstert (A)
(Latin *ringens*, gaping, a reference to the open mouth of the flowers)
Cormous perennial with the velvety main stem ending in a sterile point and the flowers borne on a short side branch near the ground, 15–40 cm high. Leaves narrow and pleated, smooth. Flowers tubular and strongly two-lipped, bright red with yellowish-green lower petals and spoon-shaped upper petal, 70 mm long.
Habitat: Sandy flats in open fynbos.
Notes: This unusual babiana was originally placed in the genus *Antholyza*. Its curious red flowers are pollinated by sunbirds which perch on the specially modified main stem.

Babiana patersoniae
IRIS FAMILY
Paterson's babiana (E)
(Named after Eastern Cape naturalist, Florence Paterson)
Cormous perennial, 15–25 cm high. Leaves narrowly lance-shaped, pleated and hairy. Flowers narrowly funnel-shaped with a slender tube 20–30 mm long, white to pale blue or mauve with yellow markings, fragrant, the inner floral bracts forked to the base.
Habitat: Clay slopes in renosterveld.

Fynbos

Babiana purpurea
IRIS FAMILY
Purple babiana (E)
(Latin *purpureus*, purple, referring to the flowers)
Slender cormous perennial, 10–15 cm high. Leaves lance-shaped, pleated and hairy. Flowers narrowly funnel-shaped with a slender tube 18–28 mm long, pink to purple with broad blackish anthers, fragrant, the inner bracts forked to the base.
Habitat: Clay flats and slopes in renosterveld.
Notes: Mostly restricted to road verges.

Babiana stricta
IRIS FAMILY
Breede Valley babiana (E)
(Latin *strictus*, very straight, referring to the upright stem)
Slender cormous geophyte, 10–20 cm high. Leaves narrowly lance-shaped, pleated and hairy. Flowers narrowly funnel-shaped with a slender tube 10–16 mm long, purple to blue, white or yellow, unscented or violet scented, the inner bracts forked to the base.
Habitat: Clay soils in renosterveld.

Babiana nana
IRIS FAMILY
Dwarf babiana (E), bobbejaantjie (A)
(Latin *nanus*, dwarf)
Cormous perennial with the stem mostly underground, 3–10 cm high. Leaves ovate to lance-shaped, soft-textured and only weakly pleated, softly hairy. Flowers two-lipped with a funnel-shaped tube 12–17 mm long, blue or purple with white markings, rose-violet scented, the inner bracts forked at the tips.
Habitat: Sandy coastal flats and dunes.

Fynbos

Babiana sambucina
IRIS FAMILY
Fragrant babiana (E)
(Latin *sambucinus*, pertaining to elderberry, *Sambucus*, the fruits of which were used to produce a blue dye, alluding to the flower colour)
Cormous perennial with the stem mostly underground, 5–15 cm high. Leaves strap- or narrowly lance-shaped, pleated and hairy. Flowers funnel-shaped with a long straight tube, 30–50 mm long, mauve to violet with white and sometimes red markings, fragrant, the inner bracts forked at the tips.
Habitat: Sandstone slopes and flats in fynbos and renosterveld.

Romulea flava
IRIS FAMILY
Yellow romulea (E), geelfroetang (A)
(Latin *flavus*, pale yellow)
Cormous perennial with a short or long stem, 5–30 cm high, the corm with a fringed U-shaped ridge along the base. Leaves one or two, needle-like with four narrow grooves along their length. Flowers cup-shaped, white or yellow, rarely blue or pinkish with a yellow cup, 15–20 mm diameter, the inner floral bract entirely papery.
Habitat: Seasonally moist sand and clay in fynbos or renosterveld.

Romulea rosea
IRIS FAMILY
Common romulea (E), froetang (A)
(Latin *roseus*, rose-pink)
Cormous perennial, 5–15 cm high, the corm rounded with curved teeth at the base. Leaves several, needle-like with four narrow longitudinal grooves. Flowers cup-shaped, pink to purple or rarely white with a yellow or white cup and the petals darkly striped on the underside, 10–25 mm diameter, the floral bracts with narrow membranous margins.
Habitat: Sandy and clay slopes and flats.

Fynbos

Romulea hirsuta
IRIS FAMILY
Pink romulea (E)
(Latin *hirsutus*, hairy, referring to the leaves)
Cormous perennial, 5–20 cm high, the corm bell-shaped with a circular rim of fibrils. Leaves several, needle-like with four narrow or wide longitudinal grooves and sometimes minutely hairy along the ridges. Flowers cup-shaped, pink to salmon or coppery orange with a yellow cup marked with dark blotches on the edges, 20–40 mm diameter, the floral bracts with membranous margins.
Habitat: Seasonally moist sandy flats and granite hills.

Romulea tabularis
IRIS FAMILY
Blue romulea (E)
(Latin *tabularis*, pertaining to Table Mountain, where it was first found)
Cormous perennial, 10–35 cm high, the corm with a fringed U-shaped ridge along the base. Leaves several, needle-like with four narrow longitudinal grooves. Flowers cup-shaped, white or pale blue with a yellow cup, sometimes fragrant, 15–20 mm diameter, the inner floral bract more or less membranous.
Habitat: Seasonally waterlogged coastal sands and limestone flats.
Notes: Often forms extensive colonies, especially between Hopefield and Velddrif.

Sparaxis grandiflora
IRIS FAMILY
Cape buttercup (E)
(Latin *grandiflorus*, large-flowered)
Cormous perennial, 10–25 cm high, unbranched. Leaves sword-shaped. Flowers cup-shaped with the stamens and style arched to one side, white or yellow to purple, 35–45 mm diameter, floral bracts dry and crinkly.
Habitat: Stony clay in renosterveld.
Notes: The yellow form occurs in the Olifants River Valley between Citrusdal and Clanwilliam.

Fynbos

Sparaxis bulbifera
IRIS FAMILY
Common Cape buttercup (E)
(Latin *bulbiferus*, bearing bulbils or, in this instance, cormlets)
Cormous perennial with branched stems bearing axillary cormlets after flowering, 15–45 cm high. Leaves sword-shaped. Flowers cup-shaped with the stamens and style arched to one side, white to cream but often purplish on the underside, 35–40 mm diameter, floral bracts dry and crinkly.
Habitat: Seasonally wet sandy or clay flats.

Sparaxis villosa
IRIS FAMILY
(= *Synnotia villosa*)
Purple bonnet (E)
(Latin *villosus*, with long hairs, a somewhat inappropriate allusion to the deep fringing of the floral bracts)
Cormous perennial, 12–35 cm high. Leaves sword-shaped and often rounded at the tips. Flowers two-lipped, purple and yellow, 20 mm long, floral bracts dry and crinkly
Habitat: Stony clay and granite in renosterveld.

Lapeirousia pyramidalis
IRIS FAMILY
Ballerina cabong (E)
(Latin *pyramidalis*, pyramid-shaped, referring to the young spikes in bud)
Cormous perennial, 5–10 cm high. Leaves narrow and ribbed. Flowers with a slender tube 20–40 mm long, cream or pale bluish and fragrant or dark purplish to magenta and scentless, the floral bracts broad and notched at the tips.
Habitat: Mainly stony shale in renosterveld.
Notes: The purple forms are pollinated by magnificent, long-proboscid flies.

Fynbos

Lapeirousia jacquinii
IRIS FAMILY

Harlequin cabong (E)

(Commemorating eighteenth-century botanist, Nikolaus van Jacquin)

Cormous perennial, 8–12 cm high. Leaves narrow and ribbed. Flowers with a slender tube 30–40 mm long, dark purple with cream and reddish streaks on the lower petals, the floral bracts two-keeled below and marked with white.

Habitat: Mainly sandy soils.

Lapeirousia anceps
IRIS FAMILY

Sandveld cabong (E), cabong (N)

(Latin *anceps*, two-edged, referring to the two-angled stems)

Cormous perennial, 10–30 cm high. Leaves narrow and ribbed. Flowers in short spikes with a slender tube 30–80 mm long and narrow petals, cream to pink with red markings on the lower petals, the floral bracts small.

Habitat: Deep sands or stony sandstone slopes in fynbos.

Freesia leichtlinii
IRIS FAMILY

Dune freesia (E), duine freesia (A)

(Named after horticulturist Max Leichtlin)

Cormous perennial, 8–20 cm high. Leaves sword-shaped, often inclined and sometimes prostrate. Flowers in a horizontal spike, broadly funnel-shaped, creamy yellow with broad yellow markings, sweetly scented, 15–25 mm long.

Habitat: Deep sands and limestone in coastal fynbos.

Fynbos

Gladiolus watsonius
IRIS FAMILY
(= *Homoglossum watsonium*)
Red afrikaner (E), rooi afrikaner (A)
(Latin *watsonius*, watsonia-like, alluding to the flowers)
Cormous perennial, 30–50 cm high. Leaves narrow with heavily thickened margins and midrib. Flowers long-tubed with nearly equal tepals, red to orange, 50–60 mm long.
Habitat: Clay and granite slopes in renosterveld.
Notes: Pollinated by sunbirds.

Gladiolus liliaceus
IRIS FAMILY
Large brown afrikaner (E),
groot bruinaandblom (A)
(Latin *liliaceus*, lily-like, alluding to the flowers)
Cormous perennial, 35–70 cm high. Leaves narrow with heavily thickened margins and midrib. Flowers narrowly funnel-shaped, brown to russet or beige but turning mauve in the evening and then fragrant, 60–70 mm long, the bracts long and tapering.
Habitat: Clay slopes, mainly in renosterveld.
Notes: The reversible change in colour of the flowers is most remarkable.

Gladiolus carneus
IRIS FAMILY
Painted lady (E), wit afrikaner (A)
(Latin *carneus*, flesh-coloured, thus pink)
Cormous perennial, 25–60 cm high. Leaves sword-shaped. Flowers funnel-shaped, pink or white, often with dark pink markings on the lower petals, 50–60 mm long.
Habitat: Damp sandstone slopes.
Notes: A well-loved species in the Cape.

Fynbos

Gladiolus alatus
IRIS FAMILY
Turkey-chick (E), kalkoentjie (A)
(Latin *alatus*, winged, referring to the flanged stems)
Cormous perennial with flanged stems, 8–25 cm high. Leaves sickle-shaped and ribbed. Flowers two-lipped with the upper petal straight, orange marked with yellow to greenish on the lower petals, scented, 40 mm diameter.
Habitat: Mainly sandy flats.
Notes: Similar species, *G. pulcherrimus* and *G. speciosus*, can be distinguished by their flat leaves.

Gladiolus venustus
IRIS FAMILY
Bright bonnet (E)
(Latin *venustus*, beautiful)
Cormous perennial, 20–60 cm high. Leaves narrow and grass-like. Flowers two-lipped with the lower petals pinched in and sharply bent near the base, purple to pink with yellow lower petals, fragrant, 30 mm diameter.
Habitat: Clay and sandstone slopes.
Notes: The bright pink form is found only in the Olifants River Valley.

Gladiolus carinatus
IRIS FAMILY
Blue afrikaner (E), sandpypie (A)
(Latin *carinatus*, keeled, referring to the prominent midrib on the leaves)
Cormous perennial, 30–60 cm high, with the base of the stem purple mottled with white. Leaves narrow and grass-like with a prominent midrib. Flowers two-lipped, blue to violet or yellow, rarely pink, strongly violet-scented, 30 mm diameter.
Habitat: Mainly deep coastal sands.
Notes: Favourite cut flower in earlier years, scenting drawing rooms and parlours.

Fynbos

Gladiolus rogersii
IRIS FAMILY
Riversdale bluebell (E)
(Commemorates the Rev. Moyle Rogers, who first collected the species)

Cormous perennial, 30–60 cm high. Leaves rather leathery and almost needle-like with the margins and midrib thickened. Flowers more or less bell-like, blue to purple with yellow or white markings on the lower petals, usually fragrant, 25–35 mm long.
Habitat: Sandstone and limestone slopes in fynbos.

Gladiolus gracilis
IRIS FAMILY
Blue pipe (E), bloupypie (A)
(Latin *gracilis*, slender, referring to the habit)

Cormous perennial, 30–60 cm high. Leaves narrow with the margins raised into wings that arch together over the leaf surface. Flowers two-lipped, blue to grey, rarely pink or yellow, with dark streaks on the lower petals, fragrant, 25 mm diameter.
Habitat: Mostly clay or granite in renosterveld.
Notes: Easily recognised by its leaves.

Gladiolus cunonius
IRIS FAMILY
(= *Anomalesia cunonia*)
Cockscomb gladiolus (E), lepelblom (A)
(Commemorating eighteenth-century Dutch botanist, J.C. Cuno)

Cormous perennial, 20–45 cm high, producing runners from the base. Leaves sword-shaped, thin-textured. Flowers tubular with the upper tepal long and spoon-shaped, bright red with small, greenish lower petals, 40 mm long.
Habitat: Coastal sands in scrub and fynbos.
Notes: The odd-shaped flowers are pollinated by sunbirds.

Fynbos

Disa ferruginea
ORCHID FAMILY
Cluster disa (E)
(Latin *ferrugineus*, rusty red)
Slender tuberous perennial to 45 cm high. Leaves dry at flowering, narrow and clustered at the base. Flowers crowded in a dense raceme, bright red to orange, deeply hooded with a slender pointed spur, 15 mm diameter.
Habitat: Rocky sandstone slopes in fynbos.
Notes: Does not secrete nectar but mimics the flowers of *Tritoniopsis triticea*, which do, thereby tricking its butterfly pollinator, *Aeropetes tulbaghia*, into visiting it.

Disa uniflora
ORCHID FAMILY
Red disa (E), rooi disa (A)
(Latin *uniflorus*, one-flowered, although often with more than a single bloom)
Erect or drooping tuberous perennial to 60 cm high. Leaves clustered towards the base, narrowly lance-shaped. Flowers one to few in a loose raceme, carmine red to orange, shallowly hooded with a short spur, 60–80 mm diameter.
Habitat: Wet cliffs, stream sides and seeps.
Notes: One of the most charismatic of the Cape plants and an icon for many organisations. Pollinated by the Table Mountain beauty, *Aeropetes tulbaghia*.

Disa racemosa
ORCHID FAMILY
Fire disa (E)
(Latin *racemosus*, in a raceme)
Slender tuberous perennial to 1 m high. Leaves in a basal cluster, narrowly lance-shaped. Flowers few in an open raceme, pale pink with darker veins, shallowly hooded with a short spur, 20–25 mm diameter.
Habitat: Sandstone seeps and marshes.
Notes: Flowers only after fire.

Fynbos

Disa graminifolia
ORCHID FAMILY
(= *Herschelia graminifolia*)
Blue disa (E)
(Latin *graminifolius*, grass-leaved)

Slender tuberous perennial to 60 cm high. Leaves dry at flowering, grass-like. Flowers few in a loose raceme, blue to violet-purple with the inner petals tipped with green and the lip dark purple, deeply hooded with a short club-shaped spur, 20–25 mm diameter.
Habitat: Sandstone slopes in fynbos.

Satyrium coriifolium
ORCHID FAMILY
Orange satyr orchid (E), ewwa trewwa (A)
(Latin *coriifolius*, leathery-leaved)

Stout tuberous perennial to 80 cm high. Leaves two to four, elliptical and leathery with purple spotting at the base, spreading. Flowers few to many in a dense raceme, narrowly hooded with paired spurs, bright yellow to bright orange, 15 mm diameter.
Habitat: Moist sandy and clay flats.
Notes: One of the few orchids pollinated by sunbirds.

Satyrium carneum
ORCHID FAMILY
Waxy satyr orchid (E), rooi trewwa (A)
(Latin *carneus*, flesh-coloured, thus pink)

Stout tuberous perennial to 80 cm high. Leaves two to four with the lowermost more or less spreading on the ground, thick and fleshy. Flowers in a dense raceme, broadly hooded with paired spurs, waxy, pale pink to rose, 20 mm diameter.
Habitat: Coastal flats and low slopes.
Notes: One of the few orchids pollinated by sunbirds.

Fynbos

Satyrium erectum
ORCHID FAMILY
Pink satyr orchid (E), pienk trewwa (A)
(Latin *erectus*, erect)
Tuberous perennial to 60 cm high. Leaves two, elliptical and spreading on the ground. Flowers in a dense raceme, narrowly hooded with paired spurs, pale to deep pink with darker tinges and spots on the petals, 15 mm diameter.
Habitat: Stony sandstone and clay flats in fynbos and karroid scrub.

Corycium orobanchoides
ORCHID FAMILY
Broomrape orchid (E), bastertrewwa (A)
(Resembling the broomrape, *Orobanche*)
Slender or robust tuberous perennial to 40 cm high. Leaves many, lance-shaped and keeled, banded with purple below. Flowers many in a dense raceme, yellow-green with purple tips, deeply hooded, strongly scented.
Habitat: Sandy coastal flats.
Notes: Pollinated by specialised oil-collecting bees.

Pterygodium catholicum
ORCHID FAMILY
Common bonnet orchid (E),
moederkappie (A)
(Latin *catholicus*, alluding to the flowers that recall the wimple of certain Catholic orders)
Slender tuberous perennial to 35 cm high. Leaves two or three, oblong. Flowers few in a loose raceme, yellowish but often flushed with red, shallowly hooded with an upright, triangular lip bearing a small, toothed tip, fragrant, 15–20 mm diameter.
Habitat: Mainly on clay and granite slopes in scrub.
Notes: Pollinated by specialised oil-collecting bees.

Fynbos

Euphorbia caput-medusae
EUPHORBIA FAMILY

Medusa's head (E), vingerpol (A)
(Latin *caput-medusae*, Medusa's head, one of the mythological Gorgons, whose head was covered with snakes and body with scales)
Succulent shrublet, mostly to 40 cm high, with a rosette of sprawling, knobbly branches 10–30 mm in diameter that ooze a milky sap when damaged. Leaves on knobs at the branch tips, narrow and fleshy but withering quickly. Flower heads surrounded by deeply fringed green and white glands resembling petals, 12–20 mm diameter.
Habitat: Sandy flats along the coast and stony slopes.

Euphorbia mauritanica
EUPHORBIA FAMILY

Golden spurge (E), geelmelkbos (A)
(Latin *mauritanicus*, from NW Africa, an incorrect belief)
Much-branched shrub to 2 m with bright green, cylindrical stems that ooze a milky sap when damaged. Leaves opposite, lance-shaped but withering and falling quickly. Flower heads surrounded by glossy yellow lobes resembling petals, 7–15 mm diameter.
Habitat: Sandy coastal flats and stony inland slopes.
Notes: Reputedly poisonous and largely avoided by stock.

Crassula natans
CRASSULA FAMILY

Water crassula (E)
(Latin *natans*, swimming or floating)
Erect or floating annual herb or sometimes a rhizomatous perennial, 2–25 cm high. Leaves opposite, narrow to broadly lance-shaped but the upper floating leaves often broader. Flowers one to three in the upper leaf axils, star-shaped, white or pinkish, 3–5 mm diameter.
Habitat: Moist depressions or pools, often along the margins.

Fynbos

Crassula dichotoma
CRASSULA FAMILY
Orange crassula (E)
(Latin *dichotomous*, branching in pairs, referring to the forked branches)
Annual herb with wiry stems to 20 cm high. Leaves opposite, narrow to lance-shaped. Flowers in a more or less flat-topped cluster, cup-shaped, yellow to orange and often marked with red in the throat, 8–12 mm diameter.
Habitat: Sandy and gravelly flats, often in damp places.

Crassula coccinea
CRASSULA FAMILY
Scarlet crassula (E), rooi crassula (A)
(Latin *coccineus*, deep red)
Succulent perennial with erect branches to 40 cm high. Leaves opposite, broadly lance-shaped to rounded with the margins usually lined with fine, recurved hairs. Flowers in flat-topped clusters, tubular, usually scarlet, 30–45 mm long.
Habitat: Sandstone outcrops.
Notes: Pollinated by the large brown butterfly, *Aeropetes tulbaghia*. Easily seen on Table Mountain.

Crassula rupestris
CRASSULA FAMILY
Concertina plant (E), sosaties (A)
(Latin *rupestris*, rock-dwelling)
Well-branched succulent shrublet to 50 cm high. Leaves opposite, greyish and rounded to lance-shaped with horny, red or yellowish margins. Flowers in rounded, stalked clusters, tubular, whitish tinged pink, 5 mm diameter.
Habitat: Dry stony slopes.
Notes: Common around Montagu.

Fynbos

Tylecodon paniculatus
CRASSULA FAMILY

Common butterbush (E), botterboom (A)
(Latin *paniculatus*, bearing the flowers in a branched raceme or panicle)

Succulent shrublet to 1,5 m high, with stout, fibrous and fleshy stems covered with yellowish, flaking bark. Leaves deciduous and usually withered at flowering, broadly rounded and fleshy, bright green. Flowers in reddish panicles, nodding and shortly tubular, greenish to orange or red, 20–25 mm long.
Habitat: Dry rocky slopes in scrub.
Notes: Seldom grazed by stock but sometimes eaten in summer, resulting in cramping and even death.

Tylecodon cacalioides
CRASSULA FAMILY

Sulphur butterbush, karkay cotyledon (E), nenta (A)
(Resembling sea rocket, *Cakile*, in its fleshy leaves)

Succulent shrublet with warty stems to 1 m high. Leaves dry at flowering and deciduous, narrowly paddle-shaped, fleshy. Flowers tubular, sulphur yellow, 17–25 mm long.
Habitat: Rocky sandstone slopes and flats.

Cotyledon orbiculata
CRASSULA FAMILY

Dog's ears (E), plakkie, hondeoor (A)
(Latin *orbiculatus*, circular, referring to the rounded leaves)

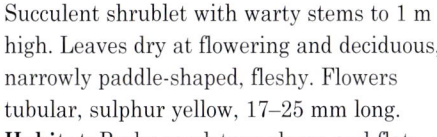
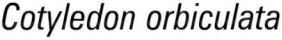

Brittle perennial shrublet to 1 m high, more or less covered with a powdery white bloom. Leaves opposite, succulent and very varied in shape from flat and rounded to almost finger-like, grey with a red or pale margin. Flowers pendulous, tubular with recurved lobes, red or orange, 25–30 mm long.
Habitat: Widespread in coastal and inland scrub on sandy or stony soils.
Notes: Flower stalks used by early hunters as a flute to mimic the call of a young klipspringer, luring the adults within arrow range.

Fynbos

Tetragonia namaquensis
MESEMB FAMILY
Namaqua dewbush (E), kinkelbossie (A)
(Latin *namaquensis*, from Namaqualand)
Sprawling perennial with sub-erect branches to 30 cm high. Leaves oblong and fleshy with the margins lightly rolled under. Flowers in clusters on short stalks, yellow, 6–8 mm diameter. Fruit with four soft wings.
Habitat: Stony shale soils.

Tetragonia herbacea
MESEMB FAMILY
Golden dewbush (E)
(Latin *herbaceus*, green and juicy, not woody or dry)
Tuberous perennial with sprawling stems to 50 cm high. Leaves oblong and fleshy. Flowers in clusters on long stalks arising from the same point or solitary in the upper leaf axils, bright yellow, 10 mm diameter. Fruit pear-shaped and smooth but ridged when dry.
Habitat: Mostly clay and granite slopes.

Tetragonia rosea
MESEMB FAMILY
Magenta dewbush (E)
(Latin *roseus*, reddish pink)
Sprawling perennial to 60 cm high. Leaves paddle- or diamond-shaped, fleshy. Flowers in small clusters, magenta, 10–15 mm diameter. Fruits four-winged with knobs between the wings.
Habitat: Sandstone slopes.
Notes: The vivid magenta flowers are a striking sight between Citrusdal and Clanwilliam.

Drosanthemum hispidum
MESEMB FAMILY
Roadside dewflower (E), douvygie (A)
(Latin *hispidus*, bristly, referring to the stems)

Erect or spreading shrublet to 60 cm high with red branches often covered with short, stiff hairs. Leaves sausage-shaped and covered with small bladder cells. Flowers solitary, magenta, 15 mm diameter. Fruits with five segments.
Habitat: Pioneer of disturbed, dry flats and lower slopes.

Drosanthemum speciosum
MESEMB FAMILY
Scarlet dewflower (E), rooi douvygie (A)
(Latin *speciosus*, showy)

Twiggy shrublets to 60 cm high with short, stiff hairs on the branches. Leaves sausage-shaped and covered with small bladder cells. Flowers in small clusters, orange to red with whitish centre fringed with small black petals, 30–40 mm diameter. Fruits with five segments.
Habitat: Dry shale hillsides in succulent scrub.
Notes: Locally common between Robertson and Montagu. Usually in colonies and spectacular when in flower.

Erepsia anceps
MESEMB FAMILY
Breede River erepsia (E)
(Latin *anceps*, two-edged, referring to the angled leaves)

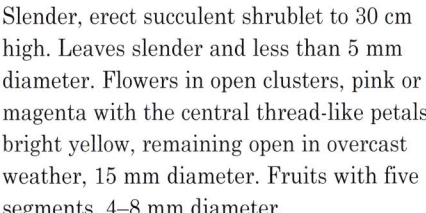

Slender, erect succulent shrublet to 30 cm high. Leaves slender and less than 5 mm diameter. Flowers in open clusters, pink or magenta with the central thread-like petals bright yellow, remaining open in overcast weather, 15 mm diameter. Fruits with five segments, 4–8 mm diameter.
Habitat: Sandstone slopes and flats.
Notes: Common in the Breede River Valley near Worcester.

Fynbos

Ruschia tumidula
MESEMB FAMILY
Brilliant ruschia (E)
(Latin *tumidulus*, highly swollen, referring to the succulent leaves)
Rounded succulent shrublet to 40 cm high, with reddish branches. Leaves fleshy and more or less cylindrical and slightly rough. Flowers in large clusters, with a central cone, white or pale to deep pink, 15 mm diameter. Fruits with five segments.
Habitat: Deep, mostly coastal sands.
Notes: Common near Bloubergstrand.

Ruschia tecta
MESEMB FAMILY
Sandveld ruschia (E)
(Latin *tectus*, covered or concealed, referring to the conical tuft of staminodes in the centre of the flower that conceals its inner parts)
Erect succulent shrublet to 1 m high. Leaves fleshy and arching with the leaf pairs united below into a swollen sheath. Flowers in dense, rounded clusters, with a central cone, purplish with a white centre, 15 mm diameter. Fruits with five segments.
Habitat: Sandy coastal flats.

Ruschia caroli
MESEMB FAMILY
Olifants River ruschia (E)
(Named for Dr Charles Juritz of Cape Town, who collected and grew the species)
Rounded succculent shrub to 1 m, with spreading, grey to reddish branches. Leaves succulent and three-angled with green dots. Flowers in clusters, magenta, with a central cone, 15 mm diameter. Fruit five-segmented.
Habitat: Stony slopes.
Notes: Common in dry fynbos in the Olifants River Valley, flowering in late spring.

Fynbos

Gibbaeum pubescens
MESEMB FAMILY
Visbekvygie (A)
(Latin *pubescens*, shortly hairy)
Succulent perennial forming compact cushions. Leaves in pairs and covered with white or silvery velvety hairs, unequal in size with a larger, somewhat cylindrical one 3 cm long and a smaller one about one-third as long. Flowers solitary, pale to deep purple, to 15 mm diameter. Fruits with six segments.
Habitat: White quartz flats.
Notes: Eaten by ostriches in times of drought.

Lampranthus bicolor
MESEMB FAMILY
Bi-coloured lampranthus (E), bont vygie (A)
(Latin *bicolor*, two-coloured)
Stiffly branched shrublet to 30 cm high. Leaves more or less cylindrical or weakly three-angled and green with a rough surface, 12–25 mm long. Flowers solitary or up to three in loose clusters, yellow with scarlet or copper on the reverse of the petals, 30 mm diameter.
Habitat: Sandy flats or slopes.
Notes: Readily seen at Silvermine.

Lampranthus aurantiacus
MESEMB FAMILY
Orange lampranthus (E), rooi vygie (A)
(Latin *aurantiacus*, orange)
Sparsely branched shrublet to 45 cm high. Leaves three-angled with a blunt tip and greyish bloom, 20–30 mm long. Flowers solitary on slender stalks, orange, 40–50 mm diameter.
Habitat: Sandy flats.
Notes: Relatively common near Langebaan.

Fynbos

Lampranthus amoenus
MESEMB FAMILY
Showy lampranthus (E)
(Latin *amoenus*, beautiful)
Succulent shrublet to 40 cm high. Leaves slightly spreading, cylindrical to three-angled with a short pointed tip, to 40 mm long. Flowers in clusters of three, magenta, 30 mm diameter. Fruits with five segments.
Habitat: Sandy flats.
Notes: Common along the West Coast.

Lampranthus watermeyeri
MESEMB FAMILY
Watermeyer's lampranthus
(Named after local resident E.B. Watermeyer who first collected the species)
Rounded succulent shrublet to 30 cm high. Leaves incurved and ± cylindrical, 20–35 x 6 mm. Flowers mostly solitary on long stalks, white or purple, 50–70 mm diameter. Fruits with five segments.
Habitat: Sandstone slopes in scrub.
Notes: Conspicuous along the road near Clanwilliam.

Oscularia deltoides
MESEMB FAMILY
Tooth-leaved rock vygie (E)
(Latin *deltoideus*, triangular, referring to the leaves)
Sprawling or rounded shrublet to 20 cm high, with shining reddish branches. Leaves with a greyish bloom, succulent and three-sided with teeth on the angles. Flowers in dense clusters, glistening pink, 15 mm diameter.
Habitat: Sandstone rocks.
Notes: Easily seen in Bain's Kloof.

Fynbos

Carpobrotus quadrifidus
MESEMB FAMILY
Dune sourfig (E)
(Latin *quadrifidus*, meaning split into four parts)

Succulent perennial with trailing stems. Leaves sickle-shaped and three-sided. Flowers brilliant purple, the base oblong or rounded and not tapering gradually into the pedicel, 60–70 mm diameter. Fruit fleshy.
Habitat: Coastal sands and granite outcrops.
Notes: Conspicuous on granite outcrops at Langebaan and Saldanha.

Carpobrotus edulis
MESEMB FAMILY
Hottentot sourfig (E), suurvy (A), gaukum (N)
(Latin *edulis*, edible, referring to the fruit)

Succulent perennial with trailing branches. Leaves straight or slightly curved and three-sided. Flowers yellow but fading to pink with age, the base top-shaped and tapering into the pedicel. Fruit fleshy.
Habitat: Coastal and inland slopes, often roadsides.
Notes: Leaf juice used as an antiseptic. Fruits used in jams and curries.

Conicosia pugioniformis
MESEMB FAMILY
Goslings (E), gansies (A)
(Latin *pugioniformis*, dagger-shaped, referring to the leaves)

Tufted succulent perennial to 40 cm high with a thick taproot. Leaves fleshy, slender and three-sided. Flowers solitary, yellow, 50–60 mm diameter. Fruits cone-shaped with 10–25 flaps, opening when dry.
Habitat: Sandy flats, mostly coastal.
Notes: One of very few mesembs with fruits that open when dry rather than when wet.

Fynbos

Jordaaniella dubia
MESEMB FAMILY
Mat vygie (E)
(Latin *dubius*, doubtful)
Mat-forming succulent with long trailing stems. Leaves slender and cylindrical. Flowers usually yellow, 30 mm diameter. Fruit with 10 to 15 segments.
Habitat: Coastal sands.
Notes: Conspicuous along the coast between Cape Town and Langebaan.

Dorotheanthus bellidiformis
MESEMB FAMILY
Common bokbaaivygie (E), bokbaaivygie (A)
(Resembling the daisy, *Bellis*, in its flowers)
Tufted annual herb to 10 cm high. Leaves mostly in a basal tuft, oblong to spatula-shaped and covered with small bladder cells. Flowers on slender stalks, red, yellow, salmon, mauve or white, 30–40 mm diameter. Fruit with five segments.
Habitat: Mostly on sandy coastal flats.
Notes: Widely cultivated as an ornamental, available in many colours.

Coleonema album
CITRUS FAMILY
White confetti bush (E)
(Latin *albus*, white)
Shrub to 2 m high, usually compact and densely leafy. Leaves needle-like and sweet-smelling when crushed. Flowers crowded at the branch tips, white, 8 mm diameter.
Habitat: Coastal sandstone or granite outcrops.
Notes: Readily seen in the Cape of Good Hope Nature Reserve.

Fynbos

Agathosma capensis
CITRUS FAMILY
Cape buchu (E)
(Latin *capensis*, from the Cape)
Multi-stemmed shrub to 90 cm high. Leaves needle-like to narrowly elliptical, sweetly spice-scented when crushed. Flowers in loose clusters, white or pink to purple, 8 mm diameter.
Habitat: Slopes and flats on shale, granite or coastal sands.

Agathosma thymifolia
CITRUS FAMILY
Thyme-leaved buchu (E)
(Latin *thymifolia*, thyme-leaved)
Single-stemmed, rounded shrub to over 1 m high, branching near ground level. Leaves narrowly elliptical and mildly aromatic when crushed. Flowers in loose clusters at the branch tips, pink or mauve, 8 mm diameter.
Habitat: Coastal sand and dunes on limestone.
Notes: Locally common near Langebaan.

Adenandra uniflora
CITRUS FAMILY
Chinaflower (E), porseleinblom (A)
(Latin *uniflorus*, solitary-flowered)
Sparsely branched shrublet to 50 cm high. Leaves oblong to lance-shaped with the margins rolled under, aromatic when crushed. Flowers usually solitary and almost stalkless, glistening white to pink, 15 mm diameter.
Habitat: Sandstone slopes in fynbos.

Fynbos

Silene undulata
CARNATION FAMILY
Cape campion (E)
(Latin *undulatus*, wavy, referring to the leaf margins)
Erect perennial to 60 cm high, covered with minute glandular hairs. Leaves oblong. Flowers in loose clusters, white or pink to crimson with two-lobed petals, 20 mm diameter.
Habitat: Sandy flats and slopes.
Notes: Similar to *Silene undulata* but calyx *c.*20 mm long vs 25–30 mm long. The flowers open in the evening and are pollinated by moths.

Drosera cistiflora
SUNDEW FAMILY
Rose-flowered sundew (E), snotrosie (A)
(Latin *cistiflora*, resembling the rockrose, *Cistus*, in its flowers)
Slender perennial to 40 cm high, covered with long, sticky hairs. Leaves of two kinds or uniform, the upper scattered along the stem and narrow. Flowers large, few in a more or less flat-topped cluster, mostly mauve to purple or white but sometimes yellow or red and often with a darker centre, 25–35 mm diameter.
Habitat: Seasonally wet sandy flats.
Notes: Carnivorous, trapping and digesting insects with its sticky hairs.

Grielum grandiflorum
DUIKER-ROOT FAMILY
Green-eyed duiker-root (E), platdoring (A)
(Latin *grandiflorus*, large-flowered)
Sprawling white-woolly perennial forming mats. Leaves deeply divided into narrow to thread-like segments, each with a small pointed tip and covered with silvery hairs. Flowers glossy yellow, usually greenish in the centre, 35–50 mm diameter.
Habitat: Sandy and stony coastal flats.

Fynbos

Oxalis pes-caprae
OXALIS FAMILY
Common sorrel (E), suring (A)
(Latin *pes-caprae*, goat's foot, alluding to the leaflet shape)

Stemless or stalked cormous perennial to 25 cm high. Leaves usually all at the base, divided into three wedge- to heart-shaped leaflets that are notched at the tips and hairy beneath. Flowers 3 to 20 per stalk, yellow, 15 mm diameter.
Habitat: Widespread on sandy and clay soils.
Notes: Leaves have a pleasantly sour taste.

Oxalis luteola
OXALIS FAMILY
Golden sorrel (E)
(Latin *luteolus*, yellowish)

Dwarf tufted cormous perennial to 10 cm high. Leaves divided into three broadly wedge-shaped to rounded leaflets that are notched at the tips and usually hairy on the margins, often purple beneath. Flowers solitary on slender stalks that bear a pair of minute scales at a joint near the middle, yellow, 15 mm diameter.
Habitat: Mainly sandy flats and lower slopes.
Notes: An early-flowering species.

Oxalis obtusa
OXALIS FAMILY
Yellow-eyed sorrel (E), geeloogsuring (A)
(Latin *obtusus*, blunt, referring to the leaflets)

Tufted cormous perennial to 10 cm high. Leaves divided into three broad, hairy or hairless leaflets that are deeply notched at the tips. Flowers solitary on slender stalks that bear a pair of minute scales at a joint near the middle, pink, brick-red or pale yellow with a yellow eye and usually with reddish veining on the petals, 20 mm diameter.
Habitat: Common and widespread on sandy, gravelly or clay soils, often in the shelter of rocks.

Fynbos

Oxalis purpurea
OXALIS FAMILY
Grand duchess sorrel (E)
(Latin *purpureus*, purple)
Stemless cormous perennial to 5 cm high. Leaves divided into three heart-shaped leaflets that are hairy on the margins and purple beneath but streaked with black when dry. Flowers solitary, pink, purple, yellow or white with a yellow cup, 20–25 mm diameter.
Habitat: Sandy and gravelly flats and lower slopes.
Notes: A showy species cultivated in Europe and North America.

Oxalis versicolor
OXALIS FAMILY
Sugarstick sorrel (E)
(Latin *versicolor*, variously coloured, referring to the contrasting margins of the petals)
Cormous perennial with a partly leafy stem to 20 cm high, sometimes branched. Leaves mostly crowded at the top of the stem, divided into three narrow leaflets that are folded in the midline. Flowers solitary, white with a yellow cup but the petals with broad reddish margins beneath, 15 mm diameter.
Habitat: Clay flats and lower slopes.

Heliophila africana
CABBAGE FAMILY
Common sunflax (E), sporrie (A)
(Latin *africanus*, from Africa)
Almost hairless or hairy annual to 1 m high. Leaves lance-shaped or sometimes toothed above. Flowers blue or mauve, 10 mm diameter. Fruit slender and not beaded.
Habitat: Sandy flats.
Notes: Distinguished from *Heliophila coronopifolia* by its smaller flowers and smooth fruits.

Fynbos

Heliophila coronopifolia
CABBAGE FAMILY
Showy sunflax (E), sporrie (A)
(Latin *coronopifolia*, with leaves like swine-cress, *Coronopus*)
Annual to 60 cm high, with the stem roughly hairy below. Leaves narrow but sometimes lobed. Flowers blue with a white or greenish centre, 15 mm diameter. Fruit slender and beaded, 30–90 mm long.
Habitat: Gravelly and sandy flats and lower slopes.
Notes: A very showy species.

Heliophila juncea
CABBAGE FAMILY
(= *Brachycarpaea juncea*)
Wild stock (E), bergviool (A)
(Latin *junceus*, rush-like, alluding to the rod-like stems)
Low shrub to 1 m high, with willowy branches. Leaves narrow to oblong. Flowers crowded along the stem, white to pink to purple, 15 mm diameter. Fruit rounded and slightly rough.
Habitat: Rocky slopes in fynbos.
Notes: Flowers especially well after fire.

Anisodontea scabrosa
HIBISCUS FAMILY
Sandrose (E), sandroos (A)
(Latin *scabrosus*, distinctly rough, alluding to the scurfy leaves and stems)
Shrub to 2 m high, with more or less glandular-hairy stems and leaves. Leaves mostly obscurely three-lobed or oblong and toothed. Flowers solitary or few in the leaf axils on slender stalks, pink, 25 mm diameter.
Habitat: Coastal sands and granite outcrops.

Fynbos

Hibiscus aethiopicus
HIBISCUS FAMILY
Cape hibiscus (E)
(Latin *aethiopicus*, from Africa, especially South Africa)
Roughly hairy shrublet to 30 cm high, with stems produced from a woody underground base. Leaves oblong and toothed above with three to five prominent veins from the base, nearly hairless above. Flowers cream to yellow, often with dark centre, 30–40 mm diameter.
Habitat: Stony sandstone or clay slopes.

Hermannia pinnata
HIBISCUS FAMILY
Magic carpet (E)
(Latin *pinnatus*, divided into narrow segments like a feather, referring to the stipules)
Mat-forming, almost hairless shrublet to 15 cm high with long creeping stems. Leaves often appearing as if in rings, narrow and sometimes three-lobed above, with the stipules divided into two or three narrow lobes. Flowers on slender stalks, yellow but orange on the reverse, fragrant, 10 mm diameter.
Habitat: Sandy coastal flats and dunes.
Notes: Common on the West Coast.

Hermannia althaeifolia
HIBISCUS FAMILY
Furry doll's rose (E), poprosie (A)
(Latin *althaeifolius*, with leaves like mallow, *Althaea*)
Softly hairy and mealy, grey-green shrublet to 50 cm high, mostly with sprawling branches. Leaves on long petioles, oblong and toothed with crinkly margins, subtended by broad, leafy stipules. Flowers in loose clusters, yellow, the calyx balloon-like and reddish but fading to cream, 7 mm diameter.
Habitat: Clay, granite and limestone slopes.

Fynbos

Hermannia scabra
HIBISCUS FAMILY
Gold cups (E), poprosie (A)
(Latin *scabrus*, rough)
Sprawling, roughly hairy shrublet to 60 cm high. Leaves shortly stalked, wedge-shaped to narrow and coarsely toothed above with the terminal tooth curving back. Flowers in small clusters along elongate, raceme-like branches, yellow, 7 mm diameter.
Habitat: Mostly sandstone slopes, rarely granite or limestone.

Hermannia alnifolia
HIBISCUS FAMILY
Golden bells (E), poprosie (A)
(Latin *alnifolius*, with leaves like alder, *Alnus*)
Rounded, grey-mealy shrub with hairy branches to 1 m high. Leaves wedge-shaped to oblong and toothed above, pale mealy beneath. Flowers small, in many-flowered, elongate terminal clusters, yellow, 5 mm diameter.
Habitat: Shale or rocky slopes.

Phylica plumosa
JUJUBE FAMILY
Plumed phylica (E)
(Latin *plumosus*, feathery)
Sparsely branched shrublet to 60 cm high. Leaves narrowly lance-shaped and rough with the margins rolled under. Flowers in dense spikes surrounded by feathery bracts longer than the leaves.
Habitat: Mainly clay and granite soils in renosterveld.
Notes: *Phylica pubescens* is a showier species with the flowers in feathery heads 40–50 mm in diameter.

Fynbos

Roepera foetida
ZYGOPHYLLUM FAMILY
(= *Zygophyllum foetidum; Z. meyeri*)
Scrambling twinleaf (E), spekbos (A)
(Latin *foetidus*, stinking)

Sprawling or climbing shrub to 2 m or more high, foetid-smelling when crushed. Leaves somewhat fleshy and divided into two oblique, broad leaflets. Flowers deep yellow with red markings, 20 mm diameter. Fruit roundish when fresh but five-lobed with prominent bony ribs when dry.
Habitat: Slopes, flats and stream banks.

Roepera flexuousa
ZYGOPHYLLUM FAMILY
(= *Zygophyllum flexuosum*)
Coastal twinleaf (E)
(Latin *flexuosus*, zigzag, referring to the stems)

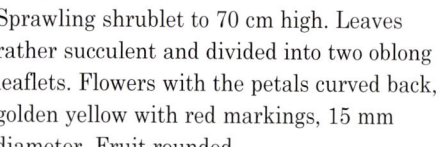

Sprawling shrublet to 70 cm high. Leaves rather succulent and divided into two oblong leaflets. Flowers with the petals curved back, golden yellow with red markings, 15 mm diameter. Fruit rounded.
Habitat: Coastal sands and limestone.

Monsonia speciosa
GERANIUM FAMILY
Cape parasol-flower (E), sambreeltjie (A)
(Latin *speciosus*, showy)
Sprawling perennial with annual stems from a woody base. Leaves rounded to deeply lobed and nearly hairless. Flowers solitary on long, stout stalks, the petals rather creased and toothed at the tips, white to pink but deep pink beneath, 50–60 mm diameter.
Habitat: Clay and granite slopes and flats, mostly in renosterveld.

Fynbos

Geranium incanum
GERANIUM FAMILY
Cape geranium, carpet geranium (E)
(Latin *incanus*, white with age, referring to the underside of the leaves)
Sprawling perennial with a thickened taproot. Leaves on long petioles and finely divided into narrow segments that are nearly hairless or sparsely hairy above but densely white-hairy beneath. Flowers one or two on slender stalks, white to pink or mauve with dark veins, 15–30 mm diameter.
Habitat: Mainly coastal forelands.
Notes: Wonderful garden plant.

Pelargonium scabrum
GERANIUM FAMILY
Sandpaper-leaved stork's bill (E)
(Latin *scabrus*, rough or gritty, referring to the leaves)
Shrub to 1,2 m high. Leaves firm, deeply lobed and roughly hairy, lemon-scented when crushed. Flowers up to six in short clusters, white to purplish, 15 mm diameter.
Habitat: Rocky sandstone slopes in fynbos.

Pelargonium capitatum
GERANIUM FAMILY
Seaside stork's bill (E), kusmalva (A)
(Latin *capitatus*, with a knob-like head, referring to the flower head)
Sprawling shrublet to 50 cm high. Leaves heart-shaped, with lobed, crinkly margins, softly velvety and aromatic when crushed. Flowers many in a rounded cluster on stout stalks, pink and purple, 15–20 mm diameter.
Habitat: Coastal dunes and sandy flats.
Notes: Leaves a source of Oil of Geranium.

Fynbos

Pelargonium cucullatum
GERANIUM FAMILY
Cape mallow (E), wildemalva (A)
(Latin *cucullatus*, hooded, referring to the rather cupped leaves)

Shrub to 2 m high. Leaves stiff, more or less rounded and cupped with toothed margins. Flowers several in loose clusters, pinkish purple, 25 mm diameter.
Habitat: Sandy and granite slopes along coast.
Notes: One of the parents of the regal pelargonium hybrids. Common on the slopes of Lion's Head and Table Mountain.

Pelargonium magenteum
GERANIUM FAMILY
Magenta stork's bill (E)
(Latin *magenteus*, magenta, referring to the flowers)

Rounded, twiggy shrub to 1 m high. Leaves broadly heart-shaped and shallowly lobed, velvety. Flowers several in clusters, magenta with purple marks, 15 mm diameter.
Habitat: Dry sandstone slopes and rock outcrops in arid fynbos.

Pelargonium fulgidum
GERANIUM FAMILY
Scarlet stork's bill (E), rooimalva (A)
(Latin *fulgens*, shining or brightly coloured, referring to the flowers)

Succulent-stemmed shrublet to 40 cm high. Leaves shallowly to deeply lobed and densely silky hairy, often greyish and soft textured. Flowers few in stalked clusters, red, 15 mm diameter.
Habitat: Rocky slopes, often coastal on granite.
Notes: Pollinated by sunbirds.

Fynbos

Pelargonium elongatum
GERANIUM FAMILY
Lesser stork's bill (E)
(Latin *elongatus*, elongate, referring to the long floral tube)
Soft shrublet to 25 cm high. Leaves heart-shaped and toothed, roughly hairy and often with a reddish circular or zonal marking. Flowers few in stalked clusters, creamy white to pale yellow, 15 mm diameter.
Habitat: Rocky slopes.

Pelargonium triste
GERANIUM FAMILY
Clove-scented stork's bill (E), kaneeltjie (A)
(Latin *tristis*, sad or dull-coloured as in mourning garb)
Perennial with a large, woody tuber. Leaves spreading on the ground, finely divided like those of a carrot into narrow, softly hairy lobes. Flowers in radiating clusters on long stalks, pale yellow with more or less extensive dark maroon to black markings, clove-scented at night, 15 mm diameter.
Habitat: Sandy flats and slopes, often coastal.
Notes: One of several species that are alike in their flowers and distinguished by details of the leaves and habitat preferences.

Cysticapnos vesicaria
FUMITORY FAMILY
Crackerpod (E), klappertjie (A)
(Latin *vesicarius*, swollen and bladder-like, referring to the fruits)
Climbing or trailing annual to 1 m high. Leaves deeply lobed and bearing tendrils, with a greyish bloom. Flowers in short racemes, two-lipped with broadly winged petals, pink, 10 mm diameter. Fruit bladder-like, nodding.
Habitat: Sandy flats and slopes, especially coastal.

Fynbos

Melianthus elongatus
MELIANTHUS FAMILY
(= *Melianthus minor*)
Crested turkeybush (E), kalkoentjiebos (A)
(Latin *elongatus*, elongate, referring to the flower spikes)

Shrub to 2 m high. Leaves divided into toothed leaflets with the margins rolled under, thinly white-felted beneath. Flowers in whorls of two to four in erect racemes among the leaves, with petals that are red in bud but brown at maturity, 20–25 mm long. Fruits with four velvety wings.
Habitat: Sandstone or granite slopes and flats.
Notes: *Melianthus comosus* is very similar but has flat leaflets and solitary flowers arranged in short, pendulous racemes.

Melianthus major
MELIANTHUS FAMILY
Greater turkeybush (E),
kruidjie-roer-my-nie (A)
(Latin *major*, greater)

Foetid-smelling shrub to 2 m high, with sprawling, often dark purplish, branches. Leaves large and with a grey bloom, divided into toothed leaflets. Flowers in whorls of two to four in large racemes on long stems, with petals smaller than the large maroon or greenish sepals, 30–40 mm long. Fruits with four wings.
Habitat: Moist places, often along streams.

Muraltia spinosa
BUTTERFLY-BUSH FAMILY
(= *Nylandtia spinosa*)
Spiny tortoise berry (E), skilpadbessie (A)
(Latin *spinosus*, spiny)

Rounded, thorny shrub to 1 m high, with short lateral branchlets. Leaves oblong, with very short stalks. Flowers solitary in the leaf axils, purplish or pink and white,
6 mm diameter. Fruit reddish and fleshy to yellow and leathery, edible when ripe.
Habitat: Sandy or stony flats and slopes.

Muraltia heisteria
BUTTERFLY-BUSH FAMILY
Spiny purple gorse (E), skilpadbos (A)
(Honouring the eighteenth-century German botanist, Lorenz Heister)

Loosely branched shrub with more or less upright stems to 1 m high. Leaves in tufts, stiff and lance-shaped, tapering to a spiny tip, often with finely hairy margins. Flowers crowded in the leaf axils, pinkish purple and white, 5 mm diameter.
Habitat: Rocky slopes, mainly on sandstone.

Polygala ericaefolia
BUTTERFLY-BUSH FAMILY
Heath-leaved butterfly bush (E)
(Latin *ericaefolius*, heath-leaved)

Leafy perennial with slender stems to 40 cm high. Leaves erect, narrow and channelled, sparsely hairy beneath. Flowers in short, flat-topped racemes, purple, 10 mm diameter.
Habitat: Sandy coastal slopes and flats.

Polygala myrtifolia
BUTTERFLY-BUSH FAMILY
September butterfly bush (E), septemberbos (A)
(Latin *myrtifolius*, with leaves like myrtle, *Myrtus*)

Sprawling or erect shrub to 2 m high, often velvety on the young parts. Leaves varying from narrow with the margins lightly rolled under to oblong and flat. Flowers in short racemes at the branch tips, purplish, 15 mm diameter.
Habitat: Rocky slopes.

Fynbos

Polygala virgata
BUTTERFLY-BUSH FAMILY
Willowy butterfly bush (E)
(Latin *virgatus*, slender and rod-like)
Slender-stemmed shrub to
2 m high, with wand-like stems that are only branched and leafy above. Leaves mostly narrowly elliptical, sometimes shed before flowering. Flowers in arching racemes at the branch tips, purple, 10 mm diameter.
Habitat: Stony slopes, often along forest margins.

Aspalathus chenopoda
PEA FAMILY
Hiker's horror (E)
(Greek *chenopoda*, goose-foot, alluding presumably to the three-forked leaves)
Stiff shrub, 1–2 m high. Leaves divided into three, sharply pointed, needle-like leaflets that are sparsely and softly hairy. Flowers in head-like clusters at the branch tips, bright yellow, the calyx densely woolly and with needle-like lobes, 8 mm diameter.
Habitat: Stony slopes in mountain fynbos.
Notes: Pioneer colonising recently burned slopes, sometimes forming impenetrable bush.

Aspalathus cordata
PEA FAMILY
Heart-leaved gorse (E)
(Latin *cordatus*, heart-shaped, of the leaves)
Stiff shrub to 1 m high. Leaves hard and broadly lance-shaped, more or less clasping the stem, sharply pointed at the tips with 11 to 21 veins from the base. Flowers crowded at the branch tips, bright yellow fading to bright red, the calyx white-hairy, 10 mm diameter.
Habitat: Stony slopes in mountain fynbos.

Fynbos

Aspalathus capensis
PEA FAMILY
Table Mountain gorse (E)
(Latin *capensis*, from the Cape)
Well-branched shrub, 0,6–2,5 m high. Leaves divided into three sausage-shaped leaflets. Flowers in small clusters at the branch tips or scattered, bright yellow, the calyx fleshy with rounded lobes and mostly hairless, 10 mm diameter.
Habitat: Sandstone slopes in lowland fynbos.

Aspalathus ericifolia
PEA FAMILY
Heather-leaved gorse (E)
(Latin *ericifolius*, with leaves like an *Erica*)
Erect or sprawling shrublet, 20–60 cm high. Leaves divided into three needle-like leaflets that are smooth or hairy. Flowers scattered, pale or bright yellow, the calyx lobes narrow to thread-like, 8 mm diameter.
Habitat: Rocky slopes in fynbos.

Aspalathus cephalotes
PEA FAMILY
Mauve gorse (E)
(Greek *cephalotus*, head-like, referring to the flower spikes)
Greyish shrub, 0,3–2 m high. Leaves divided into cylindrical or slightly flattened leaflets that are thinly hairy. Flowers in a spike or head-like cluster, pale violet or rose to almost white, the calyx silky with needle-like lobes, 8 mm diameter.
Habitat: Stony slopes in mountain fynbos.

Fynbos

Indigofera incana
PEA FAMILY
Swartland indigo (E), pienk lewertjie (A)
(Latin *incanus*, frosted, referring to the silvery hairs on the leaves)
Sprawling or prostrate shrublet, 30–60 cm high. Leaves divided into three oblong leaflets that are sparsely hairy above. Flowers in racemes on robust stalks, rose to pink, 10 mm diameter.
Habitat: Renosterveld, often on roadside banks.

Indigofera brachystachya
PEA FAMILY
Powderpuff indigo (E)
(Greek *brachystachyos*, short-spiked, referring to the flower spike)
Dense shrub to 1,5 m high, with thickly greyish hairy stems, mass flowering. Leaves divided into five to seven narrow leaflets that are shortly hairy above and densely grey-hairy beneath with the margins rolled under. Flowers in dense racemes on short or long stalks, mauve to pink, 8 mm diameter. Pods hairy.
Habitat: Coastal sandstone or limestone in fynbos.

Indigofera filifolia
PEA FAMILY
Thread-leaved indigo (E)
(Latin *filifolius*, thread-leaved)
Resprouting, almost leaf-less shrub with wand-like branches to 3 m high. Leaves mostly on younger plants or new growth, divided into a mix of scale-like and elliptical leaflets that are sparsely hairy beneath. Flowers in racemes on short stalks, white to pink or purple, 10 mm diameter. Pods hairless.
Habitat: Stream sides in fynbos.
Notes: Conspicuous after a burn.

Fynbos

Rafnia angulata
PEA FAMILY
Common widow pea (E)
(Latin *angulatus*, angled, referring to the stems)

Willowy or more or less trailing shrub to 2 m high. Leaves alternate or sometimes opposite on the flowering branches, narrow to more or less diamond-shaped, greyish and leathery. Flowers solitary or up to six in false racemes, yellow but turning black on drying, 10 mm diameter.
Habitat: Stony slopes in fynbos.

Lebeckia plukenetiana
PEA FAMILY
Cat's tail ganna (E)
(Honouring seventeenth-century British botanist, Leonard Plukenet)

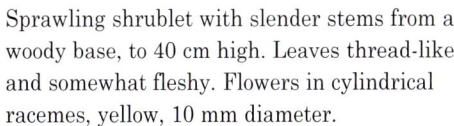

Sprawling shrublet with slender stems from a woody base, to 40 cm high. Leaves thread-like and somewhat fleshy. Flowers in cylindrical racemes, yellow, 10 mm diameter.
Habitat: Sandy coastal flats and lower slopes.
Notes: Flowering profusely after a burn.

Lebeckia cytisoides
PEA FAMILY
Bush ganna (E), ganna (A)
(Resembling broom, *Cytisus*)

Silvery shrub or small tree to 2 m high. Leaves divided into three elliptical grey leaflets. Flowers in short racemes, bright yellow, wistaria-scented, 10–15 mm diameter.
Habitat: Stony flats in scrub and fynbos, often along roadsides.
Notes: Distinguished from *Lebeckia sericea* by the smooth, hairless calyx.

Fynbos

Lebeckia sericea
PEA FAMILY
Silver ganna (E), blou fluitjiebos (A), t'aibie (N)
(Latin *sericeus*, covered with silky hairs pressed flat against the surface)

Shrub to 1,5 m high. Leaves divided into three narrow leaflets thinly or more thickly covered with silvery silky hairs. Flowers in dense or open racemes, cream to bright yellow, 10 mm diameter.
Habitat: Gravelly slopes, often along roadsides.

Wiborgia mucronata
PEA FAMILY
Spiny pennypod (E)
(Latin *mucronatus*, abruptly tapered to a point, referring to the leaves)

Erect or spreading, somewhat thorny shrub to 1,5 m high, with smooth, reddish or yellow branches. Leaves greyish and somewhat leathery, divided into three elliptical leaflets. Flowers in slender racemes, pale greenish yellow, 10 mm long. Pods almost circular and flattened with a strongly veined surface and a small wing along the upper edge.
Habitat: Stony soil in fynbos or renosterveld-fynbos scrub.

Xiphotheca fruticosa
PEA FAMILY
(= *Priestleya villosa*)
Silver pea (E), vaalertjie (A)
(Latin *fruticosus*, shrubby)

Slender-stemmed shrub to 2 m high. Leaves elliptical and densely silvery silky. Flowers crowded in head-like clusters nested among the leaves at the branch tips, yellow, 10 mm diameter.
Habitat: Sandstone slopes in fynbos.

Fynbos

Liparia splendens
PEA FAMILY
Mountain dahlia (E)
(Latin *splendens*, brilliant)

Slender-stemmed shrub to 1 m high, resprouting from a woody base. Leaves elliptical and leathery, overlapping one another. Flowers crowded in nodding heads, orange and red, 40 mm long.
Habitat: Rocky sandstone slopes in fynbos.
Notes: The showy flowers are pollinated by sunbirds.

Lessertia frutescens
PEA FAMILY
(= *Sutherlandia frutescens*)
Scarlet balloon pea (E), kankerbos, kalkoentjiebos (A)
(Latin *frutescens*, becoming shrubby)

Erect or sprawling shrublet to 1 m high. Leaves divided into many small oblong leaflets that are rounded at the tips, greyish green and mostly thinly hairy above. Flowers in short racemes, bright red, 20–40 mm long. Pods large and balloon-like with smooth papery walls.
Habitat: Widespread on a variety of soils but usually along roads.
Notes: Very variable in stature and in the size of its flowers and fruit. Enjoys a high repute for the treatment of cancer but there is no evidence in support of this belief.

Dipogon lignosus
PEA FAMILY
Cape sweet pea (E), bosklimop (A)
(Latin *lignosus*, woody, referring to the stems)

Trailing vine climbing through bush, with stems that are woody below. Leaves divided into three diamond-shaped leaflets that are greyish beneath. Flowers in long-stalked racemes, magenta or pink, 15 mm diameter.
Habitat: Scrub or coastal forest.

Psoralea pinnata
PEA FAMILY
Fountain bush (E), bloukeurtjie (A)
(Latin *pinnatus*, divided into narrow segments like a feather, referring to the leaves)

Willowy tree to 4 m high. Leaves divided into seven to nine thread-like leaflets that are dotted with glands. Flowers in dense clusters at the branch tips, blue, sweetly scented, 10 mm diameter.
Habitat: Mountain fynbos on forest margins or riverbeds.

Psoralea aphylla
PEA FAMILY
Slender fountain bush (E), fonteinbos (A)
(Latin *aphyllus*, leafless, not actually true but appearing so)

Willowy or broom-like shrub to 4 m high. Leaves narrow and very small. Flowers clustered at the branch tips, blue and white, 10 mm diameter.
Habitat: Stream banks in fynbos.

Psoralea fleta
PEA FAMILY
Blue willow pea (E)
(Latin *fletus*, weeping, alluding to the willowy habit of the trees)

Willowy tree to 6 m with drooping branches. Leaves divided into one to three thread-like leaflets or leafless and with a greyish bloom. Flowers in slender drooping racemes, blue to pale mauve, fragrant, 10 mm diameter.
Habitat: Mountain fynbos at 660–1 000 m.
Notes: Perfumes the mountain sides when in flower. Conspicuous in Bain's Kloof.

Fynbos

Podalyria sericea
PEA FAMILY
Lesser bush sweet pea (E), keurtjie (A)
(Latin *sericeus*, silky, referring to the leaves)
Single-stemmed shrub to 1 m high. Leaves oblong to rounded and silvery silky. Flowers in the leaf axils, pink and white with lance-shaped bracts, 10 mm diameter.
Habitat: Sandstone and granite outcrops near the coast.

Podalyria calyptrata
PEA FAMILY
Tree sweet pea (E), keurtjie (A)
(Latin *calyptratus*, bearing a cap-like covering, referring to the flower bracts)
Small tree to 5 m high. Leaves elliptical and silky. Flowers crowded at the branch tips, bright pink and white with very broad bracts that are united to form a loose cap over the bud, 25 mm diameter.
Habitat: Sandstone slopes in damper gullies in fynbos.
Notes: Very conspicuous when in flower. Easily seen at Silvermine.

Hypocalyptus sophoroides
PEA FAMILY
Pagoda pea (E)
(Resembling the pagoda tree, *Sophora*)
Shrub or small tree to 6 m high. Leaves divided into three more or less triangular leaflets. Flowers crowded into dense racemes at the branch tips, magenta with a yellow nectar guide, the calyx smooth and hairless. Pods narrow and almost segmented between the seeds.
Habitat: Sandstone slopes along streams in fynbos.

Fynbos

Cyclopia genistoides
PEA FAMILY
Honeybush tea (E), heuningtee (A)
(Latin *genistoides*, resembling the broom-like genus *Genista*)

Erect, somewhat willowy shrub to 2 m high. Leaves divided into three very narrow leaflets with the margins strongly rolled under. Flowers clustered at the branch tips, yellow, 10 mm diameter.
Habitat: Lowland fynbos, often in moist places.
Notes: The dried leaves are used as a very palatable tea known locally as *heuningtee* or honeybush tea.

Moquiniella rubra
FLOWERING MISTLETOE FAMILY
Matchstickflower (E), vuurhoutjies (A)
(Latin *ruber*, red, referring to the flowers)
Twiggy stem-parasite to 1 m high. Leaves elliptical. Flowers in clusters among the leaves, tubular with five petals and a swelling at the base, mostly orange but red below and with a black tip, 30–35 mm long.
Habitat: A stem-parasite on various trees, including *Acacia* and *Rhus*.

Septulina glauca
FLOWERING MISTLETOE FAMILY
Candles (E), kersies (A)
(Latin *glaucus*, with a greyish bloom)
Twiggy stem-parasite to 50 cm high. Leaves oblong and covered with grey, star-like hairs. Flowers in small clusters among the leaves, tubular with four short petals and a slight swelling at the base, greyish green flushed red, 30–40 mm long.
Habitat: A stem-parasite on various shrubs, often *Lycium*.

Fynbos

Lachnaea grandiflora
DAPHNE FAMILY
Greater mountain carnation (E),
bergangelier (A)
(Latin *grandiflorus*, large-flowered)

Rounded, usually compact shrublet, mostly to 60 cm high. Leaves more or less pressed to the stems, narrowly oblong to lance-shaped. Flowers solitary at the branch tips, pink or white and silky on the outside, 12 mm diameter.
Habitat: Sandy flats and lower slopes in fynbos.

Struthiola ciliata
DAPHNE FAMILY
Whip-stemmed featherhead (E),
katstertjie (A)
(Latin *ciliatus*, fringed with hairs, referring to the leaves)

Wiry shrub to 1,5 m high. Leaves opposite, lance- or almost needle-shaped with fine hairs on the margins. Flowers narrowly tubular with eight small scales in the mouth of the tube, cream, pink or reddish, scented in the evening, 5 mm diameter.
Habitat: Sandy flats and slopes in fynbos.

Struthiola argentea
DAPHNE FAMILY
Silvery featherhead (E), aandgonna (A)
(Latin *argenteus*, silvery, referring to the leaves)

Willowy shrub to 2 m high. Leaves opposite and overlapping, elliptical and leathery with a silvery sheen and conspicuous white hairs fringing the margins. Flowers narrowly tubular with 12 small scales in the mouth of the tube, yellow or sometimes reddish orange, 5–7 mm diameter.
Habitat: Coastal flats or slopes.

Fynbos

Stilbe ericoides
STILBE FAMILY
Pink stilbe (E)
(Resembling a heath, *Erica*)
Erect or straggling shrublet to 80 cm high. Leaves overlapping, in rings of four and needle-like with two grooves beneath. Flowers in cylindrical spikes, pink or mauve, 6 mm diameter.
Habitat: Sandy flats or limestone hills near the coast.
Notes: The commonest member of this small endemic Cape family.

Erica cubica
HEATH FAMILY
Lampshade heath (E)
(Latin *cubicus*, cubic, referring to the square lower half of the flowers)
Erect shrublet to 45 cm high. Leaves needle-like. Flowers in round clusters at the branch tips, nodding on slender, hairy stalks, flaring, pink or reddish, 3–6 mm long.
Habitat: Marshy southern slopes in fynbos.

Erica corifolia
HEATH FAMILY
(Latin *corifolius*, leathery-leaved)
Erect shrublet to 1 m high. Leaves pressed to the stems, small and needle-like. Flowers in clusters at the branch tips, nodding on slender stalks, flaring, pink but soon turning brown at the tips.
Habitat: Sandy flats and slopes in fynbos.
Notes: Common in Cape of Good Hope Nature Reserve.

Fynbos

Erica pulchella
HEATH FAMILY
Pink rattle heath (E)
(Latin *pulchellus*, small and beautiful)
Erect shrublet to 60 cm high. Leaves needle-like. Flowers in dense, cylindrical spikes, urn- to cup-shaped, pink to dark red, 3–4 mm long.
Habitat: Sandy coastal flats and lower slopes in fynbos.
Notes: Common in Cape of Good Hope Nature Reserve.

Erica multumbellifera
HEATH FAMILY
Bead heath (E)
(Latin *multumbelliferus*, bearing many umbels, referring to the many flower clusters)
Erect shrublet to 40 cm high. Leaves needle-like. Flowers in small heads, urn-shaped or almost bead-like and slightly sticky, purple to red, musky-scented, 4 mm long.
Habitat: Sandy flats and mountains in fynbos.
Notes: Especially common on the southern Cape Peninsula.

Erica hirtiflora
HEATH FAMILY
Table Mountain hairy heath (E)
(Latin *hirtiflorus*, hairy-flowered)
Erect, loosely branched shrublet to 1 m high. Leaves needle-like. Flowers in loose clusters, egg-shaped and hairy, mauve-pink, 3–4 mm long.
Habitat: Sandy flats and slopes in fynbos.
Notes: Forms sheets of pink on mountain sides.

Fynbos

Erica glomiflora
HEATH FAMILY

(Latin *glomiflorus*, with flowers resembling a ball of yarn)

Erect shrublet to 1 m high. Leaves needle-like. Flowers in dense cylindrical spikes, urn-shaped and slightly sticky, white to deep pink, 6–13 mm long.
Habitat: Sandy flats and slopes in fynbos.

Erica daphniflora
HEATH FAMILY

Daphne-flowered heath (E)

(Latin *daphniflorus*, with flowers resembling those of the genus *Daphne*)

Erect shrublet to 1 m high. Leaves needle-like. Flowers in dense spikes, urn-shaped with flaring petals, white, yellow, pink or red, 6–14 mm long.
Habitat: Sandy flats and slopes in fynbos, often beside water.

Erica sessiliflora
HEATH FAMILY

Bottlebrush heath (E)

(Latin *sessiliflorus*, with sessile or stalkless flowers)

Erect shrub to 2 m high. Leaves needle-like. Flowers in short, dense spikes near the branch tips, tubular, light green, 16–30 mm long, developing into distinctive reddish, nut-like fruits that persist on the older branches.
Habitat: Moist sandstone slopes and seeps in fynbos.
Notes: Unique and highly distinctive in its fruits.

Fynbos

Erica viscaria subsp. *longifolia*
HEATH FAMILY
Varicoloured heath (E)
(Latin *longifolius*, long-leaved)
Erect shrublet to 1 m high.
Leaves long and needle-like. Flowers in spreading clusters at the branch tips, tubular and usually hairy and slightly sticky, white,
yellow, orange, red, purple, greenish or sometimes bicoloured, 12–22 mm long.
Habitat: Sandy or stony slopes in fynbos.
Notes: Common near Grabouw. Very variable in flower colour.

Erica abietina
HEATH FAMILY
(= *Erica phylicifolia* and *E. grandiflora*)
Table Mountain red heath (E)
(Resembling a fir tree, *Abies*, in its leaves)
Erect shrublet to 1 m high. Leaves needle-like. Flowers in spreading clusters at the branch tips, tubular, bright red to magenta, 10–25 mm long.
Habitat: Rocky sandstone slopes in fynbos.
Notes: This species now includes several others, such as *Erica grandiflora*.

Erica pinea
HEATH FAMILY
Pine-leaved heath (E)
(Latin *pineus*, pine-like, referring to the leaves)
Erect shrublet to 1,5 m high. Leaves needle-like. Flowers in short spikes, tubular and flaring at the mouth, white or yellow with white tips, 20–24 mm long.
Habitat: Moist sandstone slopes in fynbos.

Fynbos

Erica curviflora
HEATH FAMILY
Water heath (E), waterbos (A)
(Latin *curviflorus*, with curved flowers)
Erect soft to stout shrub to
1,6 m high. Leaves needle-like, hairy. Flowers in long spikes, tubular and curved, orange, red or yellow, hairy or smooth, 20–30 mm long.
Habitat: Widespread in damp or wet areas in fynbos.

Erica densifolia
HEATH FAMILY
Harlequin heath (E)
(Latin *densifolius*, densely leafy)
Erect shrub to 1,5 m high.
Leaves needle-like, often in tufts. Flowers in short, spreading spikes, curved, tubular and hairy, red with greenish-yellow tips, 24–30 mm long.
Habitat: Sandstone flats and slopes in fynbos.

Erica discolor
HEATH FAMILY
Bicoloured heath (E)
(Latin *discolorus*, variegated, referring to the two-toned flowers)
Dense resprouting shrublet to 1 m high. Leaves needle-like. Flowers in small clusters at the branch tips, tubular, pink to dark red with pale tips, 18–24 mm long.
Habitat: Sandy coastal flats and lower slopes in fynbos.

Fynbos

Erica perspicua
HEATH FAMILY
Prince of Wales heath (E), veerheide (A)
(Latin *perspicuus*, transparent, referring to the translucent flowers)
Erect shrub to 2 m high. Leaves needle-like, often in clusters. Flowers in elongate spikes, tubular and hairy, white to pink with white tips, 10–20 mm long.
Habitat: Marshy lower slopes and coastal flats in fynbos.
Notes: Common between Hangklip and Hermanus.

Erica mammosa
HEATH FAMILY
Ninepin heath (E)
(Latin *mammosus*, with breasts, alluding to the resemblance of the flowers to a cow's teats)
Erect shrub to 1,5 m high. Leaves needle-like. Flowers in dense clusters, flask-shaped with four furrows at the base, orange to red or pink, 25 mm long.
Habitat: Sandy flats and rocky slopes in fynbos.
Notes: Easily recognised by the little furrows at the base of the flowers.

Erica cerinthoides
HEATH FAMILY
Fire heath (E), rooihaartjie (A)
(Resembling the honeywort, *Cerinthe,* in its flowers)
Resprouting shrublet, mostly compact but sometimes with a few slender branches reaching to 1,2 m high. Leaves needle-like and glandular-hairy. Flowers in round clusters at the branch tips, flask-shaped and glandular-hairy, orange-red, 25–35 mm long.
Habitat: Sandy flats and slopes in fynbos, especially after fire.

Fynbos

Erica plukenetii
HEATH FAMILY
Coat-hanger heath (E)
(Honouring seventeenth-century British botanist, Leonard Plukenet)

Erect shrublet to 1,5 m high. Leaves long and needle-like. Flowers in short spikes, nodding, flask-shaped with the anthers protruding well beyond the tube, pink to red or rarely white to yellowish or green and often with brown or yellowish tips, 13–18 mm long.
Habitat: Widespread on sandy flats and rocky slopes in fynbos.

Erica coccinea
HEATH FAMILY
Crimson heath (E)
(Latin *coccineus*, deep red)

Erect, stiffly branched shrub to 1,2 m high. Leaves needle-like, usually in small clusters. Flowers in short spikes, nodding, tubular with the anthers protruding well beyond the tube, yellow, orange or red and often with brown tips, 6–17 mm long.
Habitat: Common on sandy flats and rocky slopes in fynbos.
Notes: Distinguished from similar species by the sepal-like bracts attached to the calyx.

Erica patersonia
HEATH FAMILY
Mealie heath (E), mielieheide (A)
(Honouring the eighteenth-century collector, Lt William Paterson)

Erect sparsely branched shrublet to 1 m high. Leaves needle-like. Flowers in dense, cylindrical spikes near the branch tips, tubular, yellow, 14–18 mm long.
Habitat: Marshy coastal flats.
Notes: Common around Betty's Bay.

Fynbos

Saltera sarcocolla
PENAEA FAMILY
Cape fellwort (E), vlieëbos (A)
(Greek *sarco-*, *colla*, fleshy + glue, referring to the sticky, leathery bracts)
Sparsely branched shrub to 1,5 m high, resprouting from a woody base. Leaves more or less pressed to the stems and overlapping, rounded and leathery. Flowers crowded in head-like spikes surrounded by broad, sticky bracts, glistening pink and waxy in texture, 20 mm diameter.
Habitat: Rocky sandstone slopes.
Notes: Pollinated by sunbirds.

Lycium ferocissimum
POTATO FAMILY
Snake berry (E), slangbessie (A)
(Latin *ferocissimus*, extremely fierce, referring to the thorns)
Stiffly branched, thorny shrub to 2 m high. Leaves in tufts on short shoots, leathery and more or less oblong. Flowers bell-shaped, white to mauve, 20 mm long. Berries bright red.
Habitat: Dry stony flats.

Solanum guineense
POTATO FAMILY
Sea nightshade (E)
(Latin *guineense*, from Guinea, a misnomer due to confusion about the origin of the species)
Erect or sprawling shrub to 1,5 m high. Leaves softly leathery and oblong, mostly broader towards the tips. Flowers one to few among the leaves, mauve to light blue, 20 mm diameter. Berries yellow to red.
Habitat: Coastal dunes, slopes and river banks.
Notes: *Solanum africanum* is similar but has clusters of flowers and black berries.

Fynbos

Convolvulus capensis
MORNING GLORY FAMILY
Cape bindweed (E)
(Latin *capensis*, from the Cape)
Thinly hairy perennial climber to 2 m high. Leaves broadly spear-shaped or lobed and often toothed. Flowers white to pink, 30 mm diameter.
Habitat: Stony slopes.
Notes: Common along roadsides in the fringing shubbery.

Limonium peregrinum
PLUMBAGO FAMILY
Dune sea pink (E), strandroos, papierblom (A)
(Latin *peregrinus*, foreign, in relation to the European species)
Shrub to 1 m high, with the branches leafy at the tips. Leaves more or less spatula-shaped, rough and sometimes pitted. Flowers in flat-topped clusters on long stalks, pink with a conspicuous papery calyx, 15 mm diameter.
Habitat: Coastal dunes.

Limonium capense
PLUMBAGO FAMILY
Saldanha sea pink (E)
(Latin *capensis*, from the Cape)
Rounded shrublet to 60 cm high. Leaves elliptical and greyish, rough and minutely pitted. Flowers in short spikes at the branch tips, pink with a conspicuous papery calyx, 10 mm diameter.
Habitat: Coastal limestone flats between Saldanha and Paternoster.
Notes: Locally common around Saldanha.

Fynbos

Limonium scabrum
PLUMBAGO FAMILY
Creeping sea pink (E)
(Latin *scabrus*, rough, referring to the branches)

Tufted dwarf perennial to 25 cm high. Leaves in a basal tuft, lance-shaped. Flowers in dense, erect or spreading, flat-topped panicles with the lower branchlets often sterile and roughly scurfy, mauve, 5 mm diameter.
Habitat: Coastal dunes and estuaries.

Microloma sagittatum
MILKWEED FAMILY
Firecracker vine (E), melktou (A)
(Latin *sagittatus*, shaped like an arrowhead, referring to the leaves)

Slender climber to 1 m or more high. Leaves opposite, narrow and leathery with a central groove. Flowers in small clusters, cylindrical with the petals twisted together at the tips, pinkish to red with greenish tips, 15 mm long.
Habitat: Stony slopes or sandy flats in scrub.
Notes: Pollinated by sunbirds.

Microloma tenuifolium
MILKWEED FAMILY
Fairy pitcher (E)
(Latin *tenuifolius*, narrow-leaved)

Slender deciduous climber to 1-m high. Leaves opposite, long and narrow, almost thread-like, drooping. Flowers in small clusters, urn-shaped, shiny orange to red, 10 mm long.
Habitat: Stony slopes, usually in renosterveld.
Notes: Pollinated by sunbirds. *Microloma namaquense* from around Springbok is similar but has shorter, erect leaves.

Fynbos

Orbea variegata
MILKWEED FAMILY
Cape carrion flower (E), aasblom (A)
(Latin *variegatus*, variegated, for the mottled flowers)

Leafless, mat-forming succulent with the stems bearing conical knobs arranged loosely into four rows. Flowers leathery and wrinkled, cream to yellow variously speckled with purple-brown, with a raised central ring forming a shallow bowl, unpleasantly scented, 50–80 mm diameter.
Habitat: Mainly coastal on north-facing rocks.

Chironia baccifera
GENTIAN FAMILY
Christmas berry (E), aambeibossie (A)
(Latin *bacciferus*, berry-bearing)
Rounded shrublet to 1 m high, with angular twigs. Leaves opposite, narrow and spreading. Flowers glossy pink with a short tube that is pinched above the ovary, 15 mm diameter. Fruit a red, fleshy berry.
Habitat: Sandy or rocky flats and slopes, often in light bush.
Notes: Traditionally used as a purgative and blood purifier but potentially toxic.

Chironia linoides
GENTIAN FAMILY
Narrow-leaved centaury (E)
(Resembling flax, *Linum*)
Shrublet to 50 cm high. Leaves opposite, narrow and erect or spreading. Flowers pink with a short tube, 15–20 mm diameter.
Habitat: Sandy or marshy flats and slopes.

Fynbos

Orphium frutescens
GENTIAN FAMILY
Sea rose (E), teringbos (A)
(Latin *frutescens*, becoming shrubby)
Erect shrublet to 80 cm high.
Leaves opposite, oblong and finely hairy with the margins rolled under. Flowers one or two at the branch tips and among the upper leaves, glossy deep pink with twisted anthers that open through pores, 30 mm diameter.
Habitat: Seasonally waterlogged coastal sands and pans.
Notes: The flowers are buzzed by carpenter bees to release the pollen from the tube-like anthers.

Sebaea exacoides
GENTIAN FAMILY
Painted yellowwort (E), naeltjieblom (A)
(Resembling the Arabian violet, *Exacum*)
Delicate annual herb to 30 cm high. Leaves opposite, oblong to lance-shaped. Flowers in a flat-topped cluster, yellow or cream with orange streaks in the throat, 10–20 mm diameter.
Habitat: Seasonally wet sandy flats and slopes.
Notes: Easily recognised by the orange streaks around the throat.

Lobostemon argenteus
FORGET-ME-NOT FAMILY
Blue rocket (E)
(Latin *argenteus*, silvery, referring to the leaves)
Roughly hairy shrublet to 1 m high. Leaves lance-shaped with the margins rolled under, silvery hairy. Flowers in spikes, funnel-shaped and hairless outside except for the mid-vein and margins, deep blue, 20 mm long.
Habitat: Shale slopes in renosterveld.
Notes: Easily recognised by the spike-like inflorescences.

Fynbos

Lobostemon glaucophyllus
FORGET-ME-NOT FAMILY
Smooth-leaved bush bugloss (E)
(Latin *glaucophyllus*, greyish leaved)
Shrublet to 1 m high, with the young branches hairless. Leaves elliptical and leathery, smooth apart from some hairs on the midrib and tip. Flowers in short clusters at the branch tips, funnel-shaped and hairless outside, blue or pink, 20 mm long.
Habitat: Sandy flats and slopes.

Lobostemon fruticosus
FORGET-ME-NOT FAMILY
Pyjama bush (E), agtdaegeneesbos (A)
(Latin *fruticosus*, shrubby)
Roughly hairy shrublet to 80 cm high. Leaves lance-shaped to oblong, roughly hairy. Flowers in branched clusters, funnel-shaped and hairy outside, blue or pink, 20 mm long.
Habitat: Sandy or gritty flats.
Notes: Readily seen around Darling.

Wahlenbergia androsacea
BELLFLOWER FAMILY
Lesser bellflower (E), blouklokkie (A)
(Recalling the genus *Androsace* in the primula family)
Tufted annual herb to 40 cm high. Leaves mostly in a basal tuft, elliptical and roughly hairy with wavy margins. Flowers on long slender stalks, cup-shaped, white to pale blue, 10–15 mm diameter.
Habitat: Sandy flats and lower slopes.
Notes: Similar to *W. annularis*, which has larger, shallower flowers.

Wahlenbergia capensis
BELLFLOWER FAMILY
Cape bellflower (E)
(Latin *capensis*, from the Cape)
Erect annual herb to 50 cm high with roughly hairy stems. Leaves sometimes clustered towards the base, narrowly elliptical and roughly hairy with wavy or toothed margins. Flowers on long stalks, bowl-shaped, blue with a darker centre, 10–16 mm diameter.
Habitat: Sandstone slopes and flats.
Notes: The hairy, black centre is distinctive.

Roella incurva
BELLFLOWER FAMILY
White-eyed roella (E)
(Latin *incurvus*, curved inwards, probably from the leaves)
Shrublet to 40 cm high. Leaves stiff and narrow and curved inwards with a sharp tip, finely hairy and often prickly-toothed in the upper part, often with tufts of smaller leaves in the axils. Flowers one to three at the branch tips, white or blue but rarely pink or red and mostly with dark blotches on the petals, 20–30 mm diameter, surrounded by long bracts with prickly margins.
Habitat: Sandy lower slopes.

Monopsis debilis
BELLFLOWER FAMILY
Pansy lobelia (E)
(Latin *debilis*, weak, referring to the slender stems)
Slender annual herb to 25 cm high. Leaves small and lance-shaped with lightly toothed margins. Flowers purple with a darker centre and rounded petals, 10 mm diameter.
Habitat: Damp, sandy or gravelly places.

Fynbos

Lobelia tomentosa
BELLFLOWER FAMILY
Summer swifts (E)
(Latin *tomentosus*, thickly hairy, referring to the stems)

Shrublet to 40 cm high, with roughly hairy stems branching from a woody base. Leaves narrow with the margins more or less deeply lobed or toothed. Flowers few on long, wiry stalks, dark blue to pinkish, 20 mm long, with the anthers not protruding between the upper petals which are minutely hairy at the tips.
Habitat: Stony lower slopes.

Lobelia coronopifolia
BELLFLOWER FAMILY
Summer swallows (E)
(Latin *coronopifolia*, with leaves like swine-cress, *Coronopus*)

Tufted shrublet to 30 cm high, with roughly hairy stems branching from a woody base. Leaves narrow with the margins more or less deeply lobed or toothed. Flowers few on long, wiry stalks, dark blue to pinkish, 25–30 mm long, with the anthers protruding between the upper petals which are completely hairless.
Habitat: Sandstone flats and lower slopes.

Lobelia pinifolia
BELLFLOWER FAMILY
Pine-leaved lobelia (E)
(Latin *pinifolius*, with leaves like the pine, *Pinus*)

Erect shrublet to 50 cm high, with the stems densely leafy in the upper parts. Leaves closely overlapping one another, narrow and stiff. Flowers on short wiry stalks, blue, 10–15 mm long, finely hairy on the outside.
Habitat: Rocky slopes and flats.

Fynbos

Cyphia volubilis
BELLFLOWER FAMILY
Twining baroe (E), baroe (N)
(Latin *volubilis*, twining)

Twining tuberous perennial to 60 cm high. Leaves narrow to lance-shaped with the margins toothed or deeply lobed. Flowers in the axils of the upper leaves, white to purple, 15–20 mm long, with the stamens less than half as long as the floral tube.
Habitat: Stony flats and slopes in scrub.
Notes: Tubers eaten by early tribes, with a sweet but watery taste.

Cyphia bulbosa
BELLFLOWER FAMILY
Larkspur baroe (E), baroe (N)
(Latin *bulbosus*, bulbous, referring to the root)

Erect tuberous perennial to 30 cm high. Leaves mostly towards the base of the plant but grading into the floral bracts, deeply divided with the margins lightly rolled under, paler beneath. Flowers in racemes, white to mauve, 20 mm long.
Habitat: Sandy and stony flats and slopes.

Salvia africana-caerulea
MINT FAMILY
Soft blue sage (E), bloublomsalie (A)
(Latin *africanus*, *caeruleus*, African, sky-blue)

Grey-hairy shrub to 2 m high. Leaves elliptical and sometimes toothed. Flowers in whorls in racemes, mauve to blue or pink with darker spots, 20 mm long, with a silky calyx.
Habitat: Sandy flats and slopes.
Notes: *Salvia chamelaeagnea*, the rough blue sage, is similar but the calyx is shortly and roughly hairy.

Fynbos

Salvia lanceolata
MINT FAMILY
Rusty sage (E)
(Latin *lanceolatus*, lance- or spear-shaped, referring to the leaves)

Aromatic grey shrub to 2 m high. Leaves opposite, elliptical and sometimes obscurely toothed, greyish. Flowers mostly in pairs in short spikes, dull rosy red to greyish blue, 25–35 mm long with the upper lip *c.*17 mm long, the calyx shortly hairy and dotted with glands.
Habitat: Mainly coastal sands and rocky outcrops.

Salvia africana-lutea
MINT FAMILY
Brown sage (E), bruinsalie, strandsalie (A)
(Latin *africanus*, *luteus*, African, golden-yellow)

Aromatic grey shrub to 2 m high. Leaves leathery and broadly elliptical, greyish and sometimes toothed. Flowers mostly in pairs in short spikes, golden brown, 30–35 mm long with the upper lip 25 mm long, with a large greenish or maroon calyx that is shortly hairy.
Habitat: Coastal dunes and lower slopes.
Notes: Leaves can be used to flavour fish dishes.

Leonotis leonurus
MINT FAMILY
Wild dagga (E), wildedagga (A)
(Greek *leonurus*, lion-tailed, a fanciful allusion to the inflorescences)

Roughly hairy shrub to 1,5 m high. Leaves narrowly lance-shaped and toothed. Flowers in well-spaced spherical clusters, velvety orange, 40–55 mm long.
Habitat: Forest margins, stony grassland and coastal bush often along roads.
Notes: An important plant in traditional pharmacopoeia. The leaves were smoked as a substitute for tobacco. Decoctions are used externally for skin problems and internally to treat coughs, colds, fever, headaches and high blood pressure.

Fynbos

Plectranthus fruticosus
MINT FAMILY
Common forest sage (E)
(Latin *fruticosus*, shrubby)
Soft shrub to 2 m high, with purplish branches. Leaves opposite, broadly elliptical and toothed, more or less hairy and the underside usually suffused with purple. Flowers in branched panicles, two-lipped with a small sac at the base, mauve, blue or pink with darker speckling, 6–13 mm long.
Habitat: Forests and shaded rocky places.

Ballota africana
MINT FAMILY
Horehound (E), kattekrui (A)
(Latin *africanus*, from Africa)
Aromatic, soft, greyish shrublet to 1,2 m high. Leaves opposite, softly hairy, heart-shaped with toothed margins. Flowers in a dense whorl above each pair of leaves, pink to purple, two-lipped and 6–8 mm diameter, calyx densely hairy with 10 to 20 spreading teeth.
Habitat: Rocky or disturbed places.
Notes: An infusion of the leaves, often mixed with leaves of salvias, was used by Khoi and Nama tribes to treat fevers. Brandy tinctures were used for colds, headaches and other ailments.

Hyobanche sanguinea
BROOMRAPE FAMILY
Red broomrape (E), katnaels (A)
(Latin *sanguineus*, blood-red)
Fleshy root parasite to 10 cm high with scale-like leaves. Flowers crimson red or pink and densely hairy, tubular and hooded with the stamens hidden in the tube, 30–40 mm long.
Habitat: Sandy slopes and flats, parasitic on the roots of various shrubs, especially daisies.
Notes: *Hyobanche glabrata* has thinly hairy flowers with the stamens protruding from the tube.

Fynbos

Diascia capensis
SUTERA FAMILY
Hook-spur diascia (E), gesiggie (A)
(Latin *capensis*, from the Cape)
Annual herb to 35 cm high.
Leaves mostly basal, narrow, with the margins lobed or deeply divided. Flowers solitary on slender pedicels, greyish violet with a dark magenta and yellow centre, 16 mm diameter, with a pair of short spurs 2–5,5 mm long and strongly arching stamens and style.
Habitat: Mainly coastal sandveld.

Diascia longicornis
SUTERA FAMILY
Long-spurred diascia (E)
(Latin *longicornis*, long-horned, referring to the two spurs)
Annual herb to 32 cm high, branching from the base. Leaves mostly basal, narrowly elliptical and often lobed. Flowers solitary on slender stalks, reddish or white with a deep magenta centre and a large and small yellow spot below each upper lobe, 15 mm diameter, with a pair of slender spurs 5–18 mm long either turned upwards or extending downwards.
Habitat: Loamy clay in renosterveld.

Hemimeris racemosa
SUTERA FAMILY
Common yellowfaces (E), bobbejaangesiggies (A)
(Latin *racemosus*, with the flowers in a raceme)
Annual herb, 35–44 cm high, branching from the base. Leaves opposite, ovate with the margins toothed or lobed. Flowers on slender stalks in the upper leaf axils, yellow, *c.*7,5–13 mm long with two spurs 1,5–3 mm long.
Habitat: Shaded and moist places, often among rocks.

Nemesia bicornis
SUTERA FAMILY
Lilac mist (E)
(Latin *bicornis*, two-horned, referring to the spurs)

Diffuse annual herb to 80 cm high, branching above. Leaves opposite, narrowly lance-shaped and toothed or lobed. Flowers in branched racemes, pale lilac with grey veins, 10 mm diameter, the upper four petals narrow or oblong and the lower lip with four velvety bumps in the mouth and a swollen spur about 4 mm long.
Habitat: Deep coastal sands.

Nemesia affinis
SUTERA FAMILY
Sandveld nemesia (E),
sandveldleeubekkie (A)
(Latin *affinis*, related to, alluding to its close resemblance to some other species)

Annual herb to 30 cm high. Leaves opposite, lance-shaped and toothed. Flowers in racemes, usually yellow but sometimes white or blue, 15 mm diameter, the upper four petals oblong and the lower lip bulging with two velvety bumps in the mouth and a spur 3–5 mm long.
Habitat: Sandy and granite slopes and flats.

Nemesia strumosa
SUTERA FAMILY
Nemesia (E), leeubekkie (A)
(Latin *strumosus*, with a swelling, referring to the sac-like lower lip)

Annual herb to 40 cm high. Leaves opposite, narrow or lance-shaped and lightly toothed. Flowers clustered in short racemes, white, cream, pink, mauve or red with brown mottling in the throat, 20 mm diameter, the upper four petals rounded and the lower lip sac-like and coarsely hairy in the mouth.
Habitat: Sandy flats, often in sandveld.
Notes: Introduced into cultivation from seed sent to Suttons in 1891 by Hildagonda Duckitt of Darling and now widely grown.

Fynbos

Nemesia cheiranthus
SUTERA FAMILY
Long-horned nemesia (E),
langoorleeubekkie (A)
(Greek *cheiranthus*, graceful flower)
Slender annual herb to 20 cm high. Leaves opposite, elliptical and lightly toothed. Flowers in loose racemes, two-lipped with the lower lip yellow and the upper lip white with purple at the base, 18–22 mm diameter, the upper four petals narrow and the lower lip bulging and velvety with a short spur 3–5 mm long.
Habitat: Stony sandstone slopes.

Nemesia barbata
SUTERA FAMILY
Bearded nemesia (E)
(Latin *barbatus*, bearded, alluding to the dark, hairy lower lip of the flowers)
Annual herb to 30 cm high. Leaves opposite, broadly elliptical and toothed. Flowers in short racemes, white to cream with a blue to blackish lower lip, 10–15 mm diameter, the upper four petals small and rounded and the lower lip bulging and velvety with a blunt sac-like spur 2 mm long.
Habitat: Sandy flats and slopes, often after fire.

Polycarena lilacina
SUTERA FAMILY
Common Cape phlox (E)
(Latin *lilacinus*, lilac)
Well-branched annual herb to 28 cm high. Leaves narrow and often toothed, shortly glandular-hairy. Flowers in flat-topped clusters, white or pale mauve with a yellow patch at the base of the upper lip, 7 mm diameter with a slender tube.
Habitat: Sandy flats near the coast.

Zaluzianskya villosa
SUTERA FAMILY
Purple drumstick-flower (E)
(Latin *villosus*, shaggy, referring to the leaves and bracts)

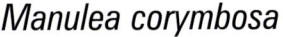

Hairy annual herb to 30 cm high. Leaves more or less elliptical and hairy. Flowers in crowded spikes that elongate in fruit, white to mauve with a yellow or reddish eye and Y-shaped petals, 10 mm diameter with a slender tube 10–25 mm long.
Habitat: Sandy flats and slopes, often along the coast.
Notes: Replaced in the north by the less hairy *Z. affinis*. In both species the yellow eye in the flower turns red after pollination.

Manulea corymbosa
SUTERA FAMILY
Common fingerphlox (E), vingertjies (A)
(Latin *corymbosus*, with flowers in a rounded cluster)

Glandular-hairy annual herb to 45 cm high. Leaves crowded at the base, narrow and toothed. Flowers crowded in round, head-like racemes on slender stalks with the mouth of the floral tube circular, creamy white with an orange centre, 8 mm diameter.
Habitat: Sandy soils near the coast.

Hebenstretia dentata
SUTERA FAMILY
Common slugwort (E), slakblom (A)
(Latin *dentatus*, toothed, referring to the leaves)

Erect, sparsely hairy annual herb to 40 cm high. Leaves narrow and toothed with long hairs on the margins towards the base. Flowers in cylindrical spikes, white with orange marks, 5 mm diameter, with a slit along the lower side.
Habitat: Rocky sandstone and granite slopes.

Fynbos

Pseudoselago serrata
SUTERA FAMILY
(= *Selago dentata*)
Purple powderpuff (E)
(Latin *serratus*, saw-edged, referring to the leaves)
Stout, leafy perennial to 40 cm high, with tapering wings down the stems. Leaves overlapping one another, broad and leathery with the tips curved back and the margins sparsely toothed. Flowers crowded in flat-topped panicles, mauve with an orange patch and a narrow tube, 5 mm diameter.
Habitat: Stony sandstone slopes.

Teedia lucida
SUTERA FAMILY
Blue lazybush (E), bergsukkelbossie (A)
(Latin *lucidus*, shining)
Sprawling shrublet to 1 m high, often dwarfed. Leaves elliptical and finely toothed with winged petioles. Flowers in clusters in the axils of the upper leaves, mauve, 8 mm diameter. Berries glossy black, 6 mm diameter.
Habitat: Montane, in cracks and crevices among rocks.
Notes: *Teedia pubescens* is very similar but has shortly hairy stems.

Oftia africana
SUTERA FAMILY
Mountain lazybush (E), sukkelbossie (A)
(Latin *africanus*, from Africa)
Sprawling, roughly hairy shrublet with trailing branches to 1 m high. Leaves elliptical and toothed, stiff and roughly hairy. Flowers in the axils of the upper leaves, white, fragrant, 8 mm diameter.
Habitat: Rocky sandstone and granite slopes.
Notes: *Oftia glabra* from the Little Karoo is completely hairless.

Arctopus monacanthus

CARROT FAMILY

Paperfruit sandholly (E), platdoring (A)
(Greek *monacanthus*, one-spined, referring to the fruit bracts)

Stemless perennial with a taproot. Leaves large, broad or almost circular and deeply lobed or irregularly toothed with bristly margins. Flowers in tight clusters between the leaves with the sexes on different plants, cream to yellow, 5 mm diameter. Fruit enclosed in large, rounded papery bracts with a spiny tip.
Habitat: Sandstone and clay slopes and flats.
Notes: *Arctopus echinatus* is very similar but the fruits are enclosed in small, spiny bracts.

Hermas villosa

CARROT FAMILY

True tinderleaf (E), tontelblaar (A)
(Latin *villosus*, shaggy, referring to the leaves and bracts)

Single- or few-stemmed shrub to 1 m high. Leaves stalkless or shortly stalked, oblong to elliptical with the margins rolled under and toothed, leathery, hairless above and white-felted beneath. Flowers crowded in head-like clusters, cream, 5 mm diameter.
Habitat: Rocky sandstone slopes in fynbos.

Berzelia abrotanoides

BRUNIA FAMILY

Redleg buttonbush (E)
(Resembling wormwood, *Artemisia abrotonum*, in its small flower heads)

Densely leafy shrub to 1,5 m high, resprouting from a woody base. Leaves overlapping one another and needle-like. Flowers crowded in tight, rounded clusters borne on red, often swollen and fleshy stalks and aggregated into flat-topped groups, cream, 5 mm diameter.
Habitat: Rocky sandstone slopes in fynbos.

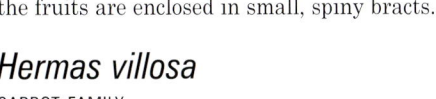

Fynbos

Berzelia lanuginosa
BRUNIA FAMILY
Common buttonbush (E)
(Latin *lanuginosus*, woolly, referring to the fine hairs often present on the young branchlets)
Finely and densely leafy shrub to 2 m high. Leaves more or less curved upwards and needle-like. Flowers crowded in tight, rounded clusters often grouped together at the branch tips, cream, 5 mm diameter.
Habitat: Damp sandstone slopes, seeps and stream banks in fynbos.

Brunia laevis
BRUNIA FAMILY
Grey snowbush (E)
(Latin *laevis*, smooth, an obscure reference to the leaves, which are actually hairy)
Densely leafy, rounded shrub to 1,5 m high, resprouting from a woody base. Leaves oblong and pressed to the stems, closely overlapping one another and curved inward at the tips, minutely hairy and greyish. Flowers crowded in dense, rounded clusters, cream, 5 mm diameter.
Habitat: Rocky sandstone and limestone slopes in fynbos.

Brunia noduliflora
BRUNIA FAMILY
(= *Brunia nodiflora*)
Common snowbush (E), fonteinbos (A)
(Latin *noduliflorus*, bearing flowers in nodules)
Rounded shrub resembling a cypress, to 1,5 m high, resprouting from a woody base. Leaves almost scale-like, triangular and pressed to the branches. Flowers crowded in dense, rounded clusters loosely grouped together, white, 5 mm diameter.
Habitat: Rocky sandstone slopes in fynbos.

Fynbos

Male

Female

Leucadendron rubrum
PROTEA FAMILY
Spinning top (E), tolletjiesbos (A)
(Latin *ruber*, red, referring to the purplish bracts around the female cones)
Shrub to 2,5 m high, with sexes on separate plants. Leaves elliptical and almost hairless, to 34 mm long on male plants and to 70 mm long on female plants. Male flower heads clustered, ±5 mm diameter, female heads ±20 mm diameter.
Habitat: Sandstone slopes in fynbos.

Male

Female

Leucadendron conicum
PROTEA FAMILY
Garden route conebush (E), vaaltolbos (A)
(Latin *conicus*, conical, referring to the shape of the flower heads)
Shrub or tree to 6 m high, with sexes on separate plants. Leaves narrowly elliptical, 40–50 mm long, those beneath the cones spreading and reddish. Male flower heads ±15 mm diameter, female heads ±12 mm diameter, slightly fruit-scented.
Habitat: Sandstone slopes near streams.

Fynbos

Male

Female

Leucadendron pubescens
PROTEA FAMILY
Grey conebush (E)
(Latin *pubescens*, shortly hairy)
Shrub to 2,5 m high, with sexes on separate plants. Leaves elliptical and hairless or with silvery hairs pressed to the surface, 16–28 mm long on male plants and 25–57 mm long on female plants. Male flower heads 9–18 mm diameter and female heads 10–20 mm diameter, sweetly or yeast-scented.
Habitat: Sandstone slopes in fynbos.

Male

Female

Leucadendron uliginosum
PROTEA FAMILY
Outeniqua conebush (E), silwerbos (A)
(Latin *uliginosus*, growing in marshes)
Single-stemmed shrub to 4 m high but bushy below, with sexes on separate plants. Leaves oblong and almost hairless or covered with silvery silky hairs pressed to the surface, 20–35 mm long but those beneath the cones longer and ivory to pale yellow. Male flower heads ±15 mm diameter and female heads ±12 mm diameter, slightly scented.
Habitat: Sandstone slopes in fynbos.
Notes: Occurs in dense stands.

Fynbos

Male

Female

Leucadendron loranthifolium
PROTEA FAMILY
Green-flowered conebush (E)
(Latin *loranthifolius*, with leaves like a flowering mistletoe, *Loranthus*)
Shrub to 2 m high, with sexes on separate plants. Leaves elliptical and bluish green, 38–70 mm long. Male flower heads 20–40 mm diameter and female heads ±15 mm in diameter, foetid.
Habitat: Sandstone slopes in fynbos.

Male

Female

Leucadendron album
PROTEA FAMILY
Silver conebush (E)
(Latin *albus*, white, referring to the silvery appearance)
Shrub to 2 m high, with sexes on separate plants. Leaves narrowly elliptical and covered with silvery hairs pressed to the surface, 28–42 mm long in the male plants and 45–59 mm long in the female plants, but those beneath the cones larger. Male flower heads ±15 mm diameter and female heads ±26 mm diameter, slightly scented.
Habitat: Sandstone slopes in fynbos.

Fynbos

Male

Female

Leucadendron argenteum
PROTEA FAMILY
Silver tree (E), silwerboom (A)
(Latin *argenteus*, silver, referring to the leaves)
Tree to 10 m high, with sexes on separate plants. Leaves lance-shaped, covered with silvery hairs pressed to the surface and with the margins fringed, to 150 mm long. Male flower heads ±50 mm diameter and female heads 40 mm diameter.
Habitat: Granite and clay slopes.
Notes: Almost restricted to the middle slopes of Lion's Head and Devil's Peak.

Male

Female

Leucadendron salignum
PROTEA FAMILY
Sunshine conebush (E)
(Latin *salignus*, willow-like, referring to the slender leaves)
Sprawling or erect shrub to 2 m high resprouting from a woody base, with sexes on separate plants. Leaves narrow, 20–47 mm long on male plants and 48–58 mm long on female plants, the upper leaves on male plants slightly longer and yellow or red and on female plants larger and ivory or red. Male flower heads 10–14 mm diameter and female heads 9–12 mm diameter, sweet or yeast-scented.
Habitat: Sandy and clay slopes and flats.

Fynbos

Male

Female

Leucadendron eucalyptifolium
PROTEA FAMILY
Gum-leaved conebush (E), grootgeelbos (A)
(Latin *eucalyptifolius*, with leaves like a gum tree, *Eucalyptus*)
Shrub or tree to 5 m high, with sexes on separate plants. Leaves narrow and almost hairless, to 105 mm long, with those beneath the cones longer and yellow. Male flower heads ±16 mm diameter and female heads ±12 mm diameter, fruit-scented, surrounded by conspicuous yellow bracts.
Habitat: Forest margins and open sandstone slopes in fynbos.

Male

Female

Leucadendron xanthoconus
PROTEA FAMILY
Sickle-leaved conebush (E)
(Greek *xanthoconus*, yellow-coned)
Shrub to 2 m high, with sexes on separate plants. Leaves narrowly sickle-shaped and almost hairless, to 65 mm long with those beneath the cones larger and yellow. Flower heads similar in both sexes, 10–11 mm diameter.
Habitat: Sandstone slopes in fynbos.

Fynbos

Male

Female

Leucadendron meridianum
PROTEA FAMILY
Limestone conebush (E)
(Latin *meridianus*, south, alluding to its distribution near Cape Agulhas)
Densely branched shrub to 2 m high, with sexes on separate plants. Leaves narrowly elliptical and hairless or silky, ±40 mm long but those beneath the cones longer and yellow. Flower heads ±12 m diameter, slightly scented.
Habitat: Limestone flats in fynbos.

Male

Female

Leucadendron microcephalum
PROTEA FAMILY
Oilbract conebush (E)
(Latin *microcephalus*, small-headed, referring to the flower heads or cones)
Shrub to 2 m high, with sexes on separate plants. Leaves oblong, to 90 mm long with those beneath the cones yellow. Male flower heads ±18 mm diameter and female heads ±11 mm diameter, surrounded by conspicuous oily brown bracts.
Habitat: Sandstone slopes in fynbos.

Fynbos

Male

Female

Leucadendron gandogeri
PROTEA FAMILY

Gandoger's conebush (E), berggeelbos (A)

(Honouring French botanist, Michel Gandoger)

Rounded shrub to 1,6 m high, with sexes on separate plants. Leaves elliptical and almost hairless, 42–85 mm long in male plants and 60–105 mm long in female plants but those beneath the cones larger and yellow tinged with red. Male flower heads ±24 mm diameter and female heads ±18 mm diameter, fruit-scented.

Habitat: Rocky sandstone slopes in fynbos.

Male

Female

Leucadendron laureolum
PROTEA FAMILY

Golden conebush (E)

(Latin *laureolus*, laurel-like, referring to the leaves)

Rounded shrub to 2 m high, with sexes on separate plants. Leaves oblong and almost hairless, to 75 mm long on male plants and to 95 mm long on female plants, the upper leaves larger and yellow and hiding the young heads. Male flower heads ±20 mm diameter and female heads ±14 mm diameter, lightly fruit-scented.

Habitat: Sandstone slopes in fynbos.

Fynbos

Male

Female

Leucadendron sessile
PROTEA FAMILY
Western sunbush (E)
(Latin *sessilis*, stalkless, referring to the leaves)

Shrub to 1,5 m high, with sexes on separate plants. Leaves narrowly elliptical, to 64 mm long on male plants and to 80 mm long on female plants with those beneath the cones yellow turning red. Male flower heads ±35 mm diameter and female heads 14–18 mm diameter, lemon-scented.
Habitat: Granite slopes and flats.
Notes: Common on Sir Lowry's Pass.

Male

Female

Leucadendron tinctum
PROTEA FAMILY
Toffee-apple (E)
(Latin *tinctus*, dyed, referring to the coloured leaves around the cones)

Rounded shrub to 1,3 m high, with sexes on separate plants. Leaves elliptical with the lower ones curved upwards, to 90 mm long on male plants and to 115 mm long on female plants, with those beneath the cones larger and yellow turning red. Male flower heads ± 35 mm diameter, female heads ±27 mm diameter, spicy scented, surrounded by oily bracts that are bent down at the tips.
Habitat: Sandstone slopes in fynbos.

Fynbos

Serruria decipiens
PROTEA FAMILY
Sandveld spiderhead (E)
(Latin *decipiens*, deceiving, referring to its similarity to other species)
Rounded shrub to 1 m high. Leaves finely divided into thread-like segments, almost hairless. Flower heads in clusters 20–25 mm across, without surrounding bracts, creamy-white and fragrant with styles 8–9 mm long.
Habitat: Sandy flats and slopes, mainly coastal.

Serruria fasciflora
PROTEA FAMILY
Pinleaf spiderhead (E)
(Latin *fasciflorus*, with flowers in clusters)
Sprawling to erect shrublet to 1 m high. Leaves finely divided into thread-like segments, sparsely hairy. Flower heads in clusters 15–50 mm across, surrounded by lance-shaped bracts, silvery pink and sweetly scented with styles 5–7 mm long.
Habitat: Sandy flats and lower slopes.

Serruria elongata
PROTEA FAMILY
Long-stalked spiderhead (E)
(Latin *elongatus*, elongated, referring to the flower stalk)
Erect shrub to 1,5 m high. Leaves in whorls, finely divided into thread-like segments. Flower heads several on a long stalk, silvery pink and fragrant with styles 7–11 mm long.
Habitat: Sandy flats and slopes.

Fynbos

Serruria villosa
PROTEA FAMILY
Golden spiderhead (E)
(Latin *villosus*, shaggy, referring to the silky leaves)
Compact rounded shrublet to 80 cm high. Leaves finely divided into silky, thread-like segments. Flower heads solitary and nested among the upper leaves, 20–25 mm diameter, yellow, fragrant, with styles ±10 mm long.
Habitat: Sandy flats and slopes.
Notes: Common in the Cape of Good Hope Nature Reserve.

Leucospermum rodolentum
PROTEA FAMILY
Sandveld pincushion (E), beesbos (A)
(Latin *rodolentum*, compound of nibbled and tough, alluding to the leathery leaves that look as though they have been gnawed at the ends)
Erect or spreading shrub to 3 m high. Leaves elliptical to triangular and blunt with three to six teeth at the tips, densely grey-velvety. Flowers in rounded heads 30–35 mm diameter, bright yellow, with the styles 15–25 mm long.
Habitat: Sandy flats, mainly coastal.

Leucospermum hypophyllocarpodendron
PROTEA FAMILY
Creeping pincushion (E)
(Greek *hypophyllocarpodendron*, fruit-bearing tree growing beneath its leaves)
Sprawling to prostrate shrublet with trailing stems. Leaves all pointing upwards, narrowly elliptical with two to four teeth at the tips, smooth or grey-felted. Flowers in rounded heads 30–40 mm diameter, yellow, with styles 20–26 mm long.
Habitat: Sandy flats, often coastal.

Fynbos

Leucospermum calligerum
PROTEA FAMILY
Strawberry pincushion (E), pienk luisiesbos (A)
(Greek *calligerus*, beauty-bearing)
Shrub to 2 m high. Leaves elliptical with one or rarely two or three teeth at the tips, grey-hairy. Flowers in round heads 20–35 mm diameter, cream-coloured fading dull red, with styles 21–25 mm long.
Habitat: Dry sandy or stony slopes.

Leucospermum oleifolium
PROTEA FAMILY
Overberg pincushion (E)
(Latin *oleifolius*, with leaves like an olive tree, *Olea*)
Rounded shrub to 1 m high. Leaves elliptical with one to five teeth at the tips, smooth or hairy. Flowers in flat-topped heads 25–40 mm diameter, yellow-green fading red, with styles 25–30 mm long.
Habitat: Sandstone slopes in fynbos.

Leucospermum cuneiforme
PROTEA FAMILY
Warty-stemmed pincushion (E), gewoneluisiesbos (A)
(Latin *cuneiformis*, wedge-shaped, referring to the leaves)
Many-stemmed shrub to 2 m high, resprouting from a woody base with the stems warty below. Leaves more or less wedge-shaped with three to ten teeth at the tips. Flowers in rounded heads 50–90 mm diameter, yellow fading to red, with styles 38–55 mm long.
Habitat: Sandstone slopes and flats in fynbos.

Fynbos

Leucospermum conocarpodendron
PROTEA FAMILY

Cripplewood (E), kreupelhout (A)
(Greek *conocarpodendron*, cone-fruited tree)
Rounded shrub or tree to 5 m high, with thickly hairy branches. Leaves wedge-shaped with three to ten teeth at the tips, leathery and sometimes felted. Flowers in rounded heads 70–90 mm diameter, yellow, with styles 45–55 mm long.
Habitat: Dry rocky sandstone slopes in fynbos.

Leucospermum tottum
PROTEA FAMILY

Ribbon pincushion (E)
(Derived from the word Hottentot, alluding to its provenance)
Rounded shrub to 1,3 m high, with spreading branches. Leaves elliptical with one to three teeth at the tips. Flowers in rounded heads 90–150 mm diameter, pink, with styles ±50 mm long.
Habitat: Rocky sandstone slopes in fynbos.

Leucospermum vestitum
PROTEA FAMILY

Cedarberg pincushion (E)
(Latin *vestitus*, clothed, referring to the silky hairs on the flowers)
Rounded shrub to 2,5 m high. Leaves elliptical with two to four teeth at the tips. Flowers in round heads 70–90 mm diameter, orange to scarlet, with curved styles 50–60 mm long.
Habitat: Rocky sandstone slopes in fynbos.
Notes: *Leucospermum cordifolium* from further south has flower heads 100–120 mm diameter.

Fynbos

Male

Female

Aulax pallasia
PROTEA FAMILY
Coppicing featherbush (E)
(Possibly from *palla*, an overmantle held by brooches and worn by Roman women, alluding to the brooch-like female flower heads)
Sparsely branched shrub to 2 m high, coppicing from a woody rootstock, with the sexes on different plants. Leaves needle-like. Flowers in racemes crowded into flat-topped clusters, yellow, the female flowers surrounded by feathery branchlets.
Habitat: Sandstone slopes in fynbos.

Male

Female

Aulax umbellata
PROTEA FAMILY
Featherbush (E), kanariebos (A)
(Latin *umbellatus*, like an umbrella, referring to the clustered flower heads)
Single-stemmed shrub to 2,5 m high, with the sexes on different plants. Leaves narrow. Flowers in racemes crowded into flat-topped clusters, yellow, the female flowers surrounded by feathery branchlets.
Habitat: Sandstone slopes and flats.
Notes: *Aulax cancellata* is similar but has needle-like leaves.

Fynbos

Paranomus sceptrum-gustavianus
PROTEA FAMILY

King Gustave's sceptre (E),
septerpluimbos (A)

(Latin *sceptrum-gustavianum*, an allusion by the Swedish naturalist Sparrmann to the sceptre of the King of Sweden)
Shrub to 1,8 m high. Leaves of two types, the lower ones finely divided and the upper ones spoon- or diamond-shaped. Flowers in small heads 16–22 mm long, clustered in cylindrical spikes, cream-coloured and strongly scented.
Habitat: Damp, sandstone mountain slopes in fynbos.

Mimetes pauciflorus
PROTEA FAMILY

Outeniqua flame (E), vlambos (A)

(Latin *pauciflorus*, few-flowered, referring to the individual flower heads)
Single-stemmed shrub, 2–4 m high. Leaves elliptical and held upright, hairy when young. Flower heads in narrow spikes surrounded by orange-yellow bracts, cream-coloured with orange styles tipped with red.
Habitat: Moist sandstone slopes in fynbos.

Mimetes hirtus
PROTEA FAMILY

Marsh pagoda (E), vleistompie (A)

(Latin *hirtus*, hairy, referring to the flowers)
Slender, single-stemmed shrub to 2 m high. Leaves elliptical and more or less hairless. Flower heads in spikes among yellow bracts with red tips, white with red styles.
Habitat: Peaty marshes.
Notes: Good stands can be seen in the Cape of Good Hope Nature Reserve.

Fynbos

Mimetes cucullatus
PROTEA FAMILY
Red-crested pagoda (E), rooistompie (A)
(Latin *cucullatus*, hooded, referring to the spoon-shaped inflorescence leaves)
Many-stemmed shrub to 1,4 m high. Leaves oblong to elliptical with those among the flowers spoon-shaped and red. Flower heads in spikes, white with red styles.
Habitat: Sandstone slopes and flats.
Notes: Resprouts rapidly after fire.

Mimetes fimbriifolius
PROTEA FAMILY
Tree pagoda (E), maanhaarstompie (A)
(Latin *fimbriifolius*, fringe-leaved, referring to the hairy leaf margins)
Single-stemmed tree to 4 m high. Leaves oblong to elliptical with hairy margins, those among the flowers spoon-shaped and dull red. Flower heads in spikes, white with yellow styles tipped with red.
Habitat: Rocky slopes.
Notes: Endemic to the Cape Peninsula. Easily distinguished by its tree-like growth.

Protea eximia
PROTEA FAMILY
Broad-leaved sugarbush (E)
(Latin *eximius*, distinguished)
Large shrub to 4 m high.
Leaves egg-shaped and lobed at the base. Flowers in conical heads, 90–120 × 50–80 mm, surrounded by cream-coloured to red bracts, the inner ones spoon-shaped, the individual flowers tipped with black and with styles ±65 mm long.
Habitat: Sandstone slopes in fynbos.

Fynbos

Protea compacta
PROTEA FAMILY
Bot River protea (E)
(Latin *compactus*, pressed together, referring to the dense leaves)
Large shrub to 4 m high. Leaves oblong and lobed at the base. Flowers in conical heads, 90–120 × 50–80 mm, surrounded by cream-coloured to red bracts, the inner ones spoon-shaped, with styles ±65 mm long.
Habitat: Coastal slopes and flats.

Protea aurea
PROTEA FAMILY
Shuttlecock sugarbush (E)
(Latin *aureus*, golden, an inappropriate reference to the bracts which appear yellowish when dry)
Shrub or tree to 5 m high. Leaves oblong. Flowers in shuttlecock-shaped heads 90–120 mm long, surrounded by silky pink to creamy green bracts, with styles 85–105 mm long.
Habitat: Cool sandstone slopes in fynbos.

Protea nitida
PROTEA FAMILY
Waboom (A)
(Latin *nitidus*, shining, referring to the leaves)
Tree 5–10 m high. Leaves elliptical with a greyish bloom. Flowers in cup-shaped heads 80–160 mm diameter, surrounded by short, silver-grey and sometimes silky bracts, with styles 60–80 mm long.
Habitat: Drier sandstone slopes in fynbos.
Notes: The wood was used for wagon wheels.

Fynbos

Protea glabra
PROTEA FAMILY
Chestnut sugarbush (E)
(Latin *glabrus*, smooth or hairless, referring to the stems and leaves)
Shrub or tree to 5 m high, coppicing from a woody rootstock. Leaves elliptical. Flowers in rounded heads 70–120 mm diameter, surrounded by short, dull brownish bracts that are smooth or velvety, with styles 40–50 mm long.
Habitat: Dry sandstone slopes and plateaus in arid fynbos.

Protea punctata
PROTEA FAMILY
(Latin *punctatus*, marked with dots, referring to the stomata on the leaves)
Shrub to 4 m high. Leaves broadly elliptical and almost hairless with a grey bloom. Flowers in bowl-shaped heads 20–25 mm diameter, surrounded by silky pink or white bracts with fringed margins, with styles ±50 mm long.
Habitat: Rocky sandstone slopes in fynbos.

Protea scabra
PROTEA FAMILY
Sandpaper-leaved sugarbush (E)
(Latin *scabrus*, rough)
Mat-forming shrublet with sprawling stems coppicing from a woody rootstock. Leaves tufted and needle-like to narrow and channelled with a sandpapery surface. Flowers in cup-shaped heads 50–80 mm diameter, surrounded by silky brown and cream-coloured bracts, with styles 30–35 mm long.
Habitat: Sandstone slopes in fynbos.

Fynbos

Protea repens
PROTEA FAMILY
Sugarbush (E), suikerbos (A)
(Latin *repens*, creeping, a misnomer based on an illustration)
Shrub or tree to 4,5 m high. Leaves narrow. Flowers in narrowly conical heads, 100–160 × 70–90 mm, surrounded by sticky cream-coloured to red bracts, with styles 70–90 mm long.
Habitat: Sandstone and clay flats and slopes.
Notes: The copious nectar was commonly collected in the nineteenth century and boiled down to make a syrup known as *bossiestroop*.

Protea cynaroides
PROTEA FAMILY
King protea (E)
(Resembling the globe artichoke, *Cynara*, in its flower heads)
Shrub to 3 m high, coppicing from a woody base. Leaves with long petioles and an elliptical to rounded blade. Flowers in large conical to cup-shaped heads 120–300 mm diameter, surrounded by pale or deep pink and often silky bracts, with styles 80–95 mm long.
Habitat: Moist sandstone slopes in fynbos.

Protea laurifolia
PROTEA FAMILY
Grey-leaved bearded protea (E)
(Latin *laurifolius*, with leaves like a laurel)
Small tree to 8 m high. Leaves narrow and with a greyish bloom. Flowers in oblong heads, 100–130 × 40–60 mm, surrounded by silky, cream-coloured to pink bracts, the inner ones with a dense blackish beard and the outer with brown horny margins, with styles 65–70 mm long.
Habitat: Sandstone slopes in fynbos.
Notes: *Protea neriifolia* is similar but has distinctly green leaves.

Fynbos

Protea speciosa
PROTEA FAMILY
Brown-bearded sugarbush (E)
(Latin *speciosus*, showy)
Shrub to 1,2 m high, coppicing from a woody base. Leaves elliptical. Flowers in oblong heads on short, hairy stems, 90–140 × ±70 mm, surrounded by silky, greenish to pink bracts with a heavy brown or sometimes white beard, with styles 65–75 mm long.
Habitat: Sandstone flats and slopes in fynbos.

Scabiosa africana
SCABIOUS FAMILY
Cape scabious (E)
(Latin *africanus*, from Africa)
Straggling shrublet to 1 m high. Leaves elliptical and toothed or deeply divided, softly velvety. Flowers in button-shaped heads on slender stalks, mauve, 5 mm diameter.
Habitat: Sheltered sandstone slopes.
Notes: *Scabiosa columbaria* is a tufted perennial with hairless leaves and white or mauve flower heads.

Stoebe alopecuroides
DAISY FAMILY
Cattail snakebush (E), katstertslangbos (A)
(Resembling the fox-tail grass, *Alopecurus*, in its flower spikes)
Grey shrub to 1 m high. Leaves stiffly needle-like with the margins rolled in, spreading and twisted. Flower heads massed in elongate spikes, without ray florets, white, surrounded by several series of brown papery bracts.
Habitat: Forest margins and fynbos.

Fynbos

Metalasia densa
DAISY FAMILY
Common flowerbush (E), blombos (A)
(Latin *densus*, dense)
Rounded shrub with white-woolly branches, mostly to 2,5 m high. Leaves often arching downward, lance-shaped and stiff with a sharp point, twisted and with the margins rolled over. Flower heads in flat-topped clusters at the branch tips, without ray florets, 5 mm diameter, surrounded by several series of bracts with the inner petal-like at the tips and white or sometimes brown.
Habitat: Sandy or stony flats and slopes.

Eriocephalus africanus
DAISY FAMILY
Wild rosemary (E)
(Latin *africanus*, from Africa)
Twiggy shrub to 1 m high.
Leaves in tufts, thread-like or three-forked. Flower heads in flat-topped clusters at the branch tips, purple with a few white ray florets, 8 mm diameter, surrounded by several series of pointed bracts.
Habitat: Mostly clay or granite slopes.
Notes: Used medicinally for dropsy and stomach ache.

Eriocephalus racemosus
DAISY FAMILY
Sandveld rosemary (E), kapkoppie (A)
(Latin *racemosus*, bearing flower heads in a raceme)
Erect, silky shrublet to 1,5 m high. Leaves cylindrical and often somewhat fleshy. Flower heads solitary in the leaf axils and forming long racemes, apparently without ray florets, 3 mm diameter, surrounded by several series of bracts.
Habitat: Coastal dunes and sandy flats.
Notes: Conspicuous in fruit. The fluffy seeds are used by many birds to line their nests.

Fynbos

Helichrysum pandurifolium
DAISY FAMILY
Fiddle-leaved strawflower (E)
(Latin *pandurifolius*, with leaves shaped like a fiddle)

Straggling, grey-woolly shrublet or shrub. Leaves paddle-shaped and narrowed below with ear-like expansions at the base and crinkly margins. Flower heads few to many in flat-topped clusters at the end of leafless branches, bell-shaped, cream-coloured without ray florets, 5 mm diameter, surrounded by several series of pointed papery bracts.
Habitat: Sandy flats and slopes.

Helichrysum dasyanthum
DAISY FAMILY
Brown-tipped strawflower (E)
(Greek *dasyanthus*, with shaggy flowers, referring to the woolly bases of the flower heads)

Straggling shrub to 1,5 m high. Leaves spreading, narrow with the margins often wavy and lightly rolled under, grey-woolly. Flower heads crowded in flat-topped clusters, without ray florets and straw-yellow, 6 mm diameter, surrounded by several series of papery bracts with brown tips.
Habitat: Sandy flats and slopes.

Helichrysum retortum
DAISY FAMILY
Sea strawflower (E)
(Latin *retortus*, bent back, referring to the leaves)

Straggling, closely leafy, silvery shrublet to 50 cm high. Leaves overlapping, spreading or the upper ones curved back, oblong and folded with hooked tips, silvery-silky with tissue-paper-like hairs. Flower heads solitary and nested in the leaves at the branch tips, top-shaped and without ray florets, 15 mm diameter, surrounded by several series of glossy white papery bracts that are often flushed with pink and brown.
Habitat: Coastal sands and cliffs.

Fynbos

Edmondia sesamoides
DAISY FAMILY
Common paperflower (E), sewejaartjie (A)
(Resembling sesame, *Sesamum*, an obscure allusion)

Sparsely branched shrublet to 30 cm high. Leaves of two kinds, the stem leaves spreading and narrow with the margins rolled upward but those on the flower stalks short and pressed against the stem. Flower heads solitary on long stalks, yellow and without ray florets, 20 mm diameter, surrounded by several series of papery bracts, mostly glistening white to yellow.
Habitat: Sandstone slopes in fynbos.

Syncarpha paniculata
DAISY FAMILY
(= *Helichrysum paniculatum*)
Narrow-leaved everlasting (E), sewejaartjie (A)
(Latin *paniculatus*, a branched inflorescence)

Erect, densely leafy shrublet to 60 cm high. Leaves narrow and pointed, silvery felted. Flower heads few to several in clusters, without ray florets, ±10 mm diameter, surrounded by several series of pointed papery bracts that are yellow or pink in bud but turn white.
Habitat: Coastal and lower sandstone slopes in fynbos.

Syncarpha speciosissima
DAISY FAMILY
(= *Helipterum speciosissimus*)
Cape everlasting (E)
(Latin *speciosissimus*, most showy)

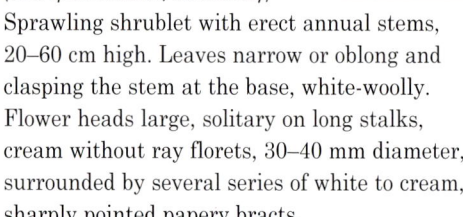

Sprawling shrublet with erect annual stems, 20–60 cm high. Leaves narrow or oblong and clasping the stem at the base, white-woolly. Flower heads large, solitary on long stalks, cream without ray florets, 30–40 mm diameter, surrounded by several series of white to cream, sharply pointed papery bracts.
Habitat: Sandstone slopes in fynbos.

Fynbos

Syncarpha vestita
DAISY FAMILY
(= *Helichrysum vestitum*)
Cape snow (E)
(Latin *vestitus*, clothed, referring to the woolly hairs on the leaves)

Densely leafy shrublet to 1 m high. Leaves slightly broader at the tips and grey-woolly. Flower heads large, few to several in loose clusters nested in the leaves, white without ray florets, 35–40 mm diameter, surrounded by several series of pointed, white papery bracts.
Habitat: Sandstone slopes and flats in fynbos.
Notes: Common in the Cape of Good Hope Nature Reserve.

Syncarpha eximia
DAISY FAMILY
(= *Helipterum eximium*)
Strawberry everlasting (E)
(Latin *eximius*, distinguished)

Mostly single-stemmed, robust, closely leafy shrub to 40 cm high. Leaves elliptical and overlapping one another, silvery felted. Flower heads large and crowded in dense, flat-topped clusters nested in the leaves, without ray florets, 20–25 mm diameter, surrounded by several series of blunt, bright red papery bracts.
Habitat: Cool sandstone slopes in fynbos.

Syncarpha canescens
DAISY FAMILY
(= *Helipterum canescens*)
Pink everlasting (E), pienksewejaartjie (A)
(Latin *canescens*, greyish)

Sparsely branched, closely leafy shrublet to 50 cm high. Leaves small and overlapping, elliptical and grey-felted. Flower heads mostly solitary at the branch tips, without ray florets, conical and 25–35 mm diameter, surrounded by several series of pointed papery bracts that are pink to red.
Habitat: Rocky sandstone slopes in fynbos.

Fynbos

Phaenocoma prolifera
DAISY FAMILY
Red everlasting (E)
(Latin *prolifer*, producing offsets, referring to the many short branchlets)
Stiffly branched, white-stemmed shrublet to 60 cm high with short branchlets. Leaves minute and overlapping. Flower heads large and solitary without ray florets, 30–40 mm diameter, surrounded by several series of sharp papery bracts that are pink shading to red.
Habitat: Sandstone slopes in fynbos.

Leysera gnaphalodes
DAISY FAMILY
Shrubby wireweed (E), skilpadteebossie (A)
(Resembling the genus *Gnaphalium*)
Slender shrublet to 40 cm high, branching from the base. Leaves grey and hairy, narrow and thread-like. Flower heads loosely clustered at the ends of the branches on wiry stalks, yellow with yellow rays, 15–18 mm diameter, surrounded by several series of stiff bracts that are papery at the tips.
Habitat: Sandy flats.
Notes: *Leysera tenella* (page 326) is similar but is an annual herb to 20 cm high and the bristles on the seeds are feathery only in the upper part.

Pteronia divaricata
DAISY FAMILY
Round-leaved gumbush (E), geelgombos (A)
(Latin *divaricatus*, spreading widely, referring to the branches)
Rounded leafy shrub to 2 m high. Leaves broadly elliptical, shortly and often roughly hairy. Flower heads in dense, flat-topped clusters, without ray florets, yellow or whitish, 5 mm diameter, surrounded by several series of narrow green bracts.
Habitat: Sandy and stony slopes and flats.

Fynbos

Athanasia trifurcata
DAISY FAMILY
Common klaaslouw bush (E), kouterbos (A)
(Latin *trifurcatus*, three-forked, referring to the leaves)

Hairless or grey-velvety shrub to 1,5 m high. Leaves triangular with three to five teeth at the tips. Flower heads in flat-topped clusters, without ray florets, yellow, 6 mm diameter, surrounded by several series of blunt bracts.
Habitat: Flats and rocky slopes.
Notes: Common along roads and in fallow lands.

Cotula turbinata
DAISY FAMILY
Common button daisy (E), ganskos (A)
(Latin *turbinatus*, top-shaped, referring to the swollen tips of the fruiting stalks)

Softly hairy annual herb 5–30 cm high. Leaves twice- or thrice-divided into narrow or thread-like segments. Flower heads solitary on slender, naked peduncles which are swollen and hollow above in fruit, yellow or white with short white ray florets, 5–10 mm diameter, surrounded by two series of small scale-like bracts.
Habitat: Sandy or disturbed areas.
Notes: *Cotula duckittiae* has larger yellow to orange flower heads.

Chrysocoma ciliata
DAISY FAMILY
(= *Chrysocoma tenuifolia*)
Bitter cowcud (E), bitterbos (A)
(Latin *ciliatus*, fringed with fine hairs, referring to the leaves)

Slender-stemmed, closely leafy shrublet to 60 cm high. Leaves narrow or needle-like with minute stiff hairs on the margins, sub-erect. Flower heads solitary at the branch tips, without ray florets, yellow, 6–8 mm diameter, surrounded by several series of narrow bracts.
Habitat: Rocky slopes and stony flats.

Fynbos

Chrysocoma coma-aurea
DAISY FAMILY

Golden cowcud (E), beesbos (A)

(Latin *coma*, tuft or crown, *aureus*, golden yellow, referring to the flower heads)

Densely leafy shrublet to 50 cm high. Leaves narrow with minute stiff hairs on the margins, spreading or curved back. Flower heads solitary, without ray florets, yellow, 8–10 mm diameter, surrounded by several series of narrow bracts.

Habitat: Sandstone and granite slopes.

Cullumia squarrosa
DAISY FAMILY

Coastal bush thistle (E), steekhaarbos (A)

(Latin *squarrosus*, rough with scales or bracts spreading sharply outwards)

Sprawling shrublet to 50 cm high, cobwebby on the young parts. Leaves bent down, narrowly lance-shaped and spine-tipped with the margins strongly rolled under and bristly. Flower heads yellow with yellow ray florets, 20 mm diameter, surrounded by several series of sharp bracts but the inner bracts unlike the outer and without spines or bristles.

Habitat: Coastal bush on sandstone.

Oncosiphon suffruticosum
DAISY FAMILY

(= *Pentzia suffruticosa*)

Cluster stinkweed (E), stinkkruid, wurmbossie (A)

(Latin *suffruticosus*, somewhat woody only at the base)

Much-branched annual herb to 50 cm high, highly aromatic when bruised. Leaves twice- or thrice-divided into narrow segments. Flower heads many in dense, flat-topped clusters, without ray florets, yellow, 6 mm diameter, surrounded by several series of narrow bracts with papery margins.

Habitat: Sandy flats and slopes, often coastal.

Notes: Common in disturbed sites, often forming dense stands.

Fynbos

Foveolina tenella
DAISY FAMILY
Lazy daisy (E)
(Latin *tenellus*, delicate)

Sprawling, thinly hairy annual herb to 25 cm high, aromatic when bruised. Leaves twice-divided into thread-like segments. Flower heads solitary on long naked stalks, yellow with a few white ray florets that bend down at night, 15–20 mm diameter, surrounded by several series of blunt bracts with papery margins.
Habitat: Sandy flats, mostly coastal.

Cineraria geifolia
DAISY FAMILY
Coastal cineraria (E)
(Latin *geifolius*, with leaves like avens, *Geum*)

Roughly hairy perennial to 60 cm high. Leaves kidney-shaped and lobed and toothed, the slender petioles with large ear-like lobes at the base. Flower heads in flat-topped clusters, yellow with yellow ray florets, 10 mm diameter, surrounded by a single series of narrow bracts.
Habitat: Mainly coastal bush.

Senecio burchellii
DAISY FAMILY
Poison ragwort (E)
(Honouring the nineteenth-century naturalist, William Burchell)

Softly woody shrublet to 40 cm high, sometimes roughly hairy below. Leaves narrow with the margins rolled under and sometimes toothed, usually with additional tufts of leaves in the axils. Flower heads in loose, flat-topped clusters, yellow with yellow ray florets, 10 mm diameter, surrounded by a single series of narrow bracts.
Habitat: Sandy and stony slopes.
Notes: One of many *Senecio* species that are poisonous to stock, especially horses. The danger is highest in spring when the young plants are cropped along with grass.

Fynbos

Senecio littoreus
DAISY FAMILY
Coastal ragwort (E), geelhongerblom (A)
(Latin *littoreus*, of the seashore)
Hairless or shortly hairy annual herb to 40 cm high. Leaves elliptical and toothed or lobed, sometimes eared at the base. Flower heads in loose, flat-topped clusters, yellow with yellow ray florets, 10 mm diameter, surrounded by a single series of narrow bracts.
Habitat: Mainly coastal sands, often along roadsides.

Senecio arenarius
DAISY FAMILY
Lesser purple ragwort (E), pershongerblom (A)
(Latin *arenarius*, growing in sand)
Glandular-hairy annual herb to 40 cm high. Leaves toothed to lobed with the margins sometimes rolled under. Flower heads several in branching, flat-topped clusters, yellow with mauve or rarely white ray florets, 20 mm diameter, surrounded by a single series of narrow, sticky bracts forming a cylinder.
Habitat: Sandy flats, often coastal.

Senecio elegans
DAISY FAMILY
Greater purple ragwort (E)
(Latin *elegans*, elegant)
Densely glandular-hairy annual to 1 m high. Leaves fleshy and cut or deeply lobed with the margins rolled under. Flower heads numerous in dense, flat-topped clusters, yellow with mauve ray florets, 20 mm diameter, surrounded by a single series of narrow bracts with black tips that form a globular involucre.
Habitat: Coastal sands.

Fynbos

Senecio umbellatus
DAISY FAMILY
Purple mountain groundsel (E)
(Latin *umbellatus*, like an umbrella, referring to the clustered flower heads)
Finely leafy perennial to 80 cm high, with the stems sometimes sparsely hairy near the base. Leaves thread-like or deeply divided into narrow to thread-like segments with the margins rolled under and minutely toothed. Flower heads in loosely branched, flat-topped clusters, yellow with magenta to pink or rarely white ray florets, 15 mm diameter, surrounded by a single series of narrow bracts.
Habitat: Sandstone flats and slopes.

Amellus tenuifolius
DAISY FAMILY
Grey-leaved wild aster (E), astertjie (A)
(Latin *tenuifolius*, narrow-leaved)
Grey-silky, much-branched perennial or shrublet to 50 cm high. Leaves narrow to lance-shaped. Flower heads solitary at the branch tips, yellow with mauve ray florets, 15–20 mm diameter, surrounded by several series of narrow, pointed bracts.
Habitat: Sandy flats, often near the coast.

Felicia fruticosa
DAISY FAMILY
Bush felicia (E)
(Latin *fruticosus*, shrubby)
Well-branched shrub to 1 m high. Leaves in tufts, small and fleshy, elliptical and lightly gland-dotted. Flower heads solitary at the branch tips, yellow with blue to mauve ray florets, 15 mm diameter, surrounded by three series of narrow, pointed bracts.
Habitat: Rocky lower slopes.
Notes: *Felicia filifolia* (page 323) has needle-like leaves.

Fynbos

Felicia aethiopica
DAISY FAMILY
Garden felicia (E)
(Latin *aethiopicus*, from Africa, usually South Africa)

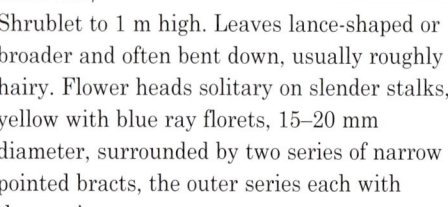

Shrublet to 1 m high. Leaves lance-shaped or broader and often bent down, usually roughly hairy. Flower heads solitary on slender stalks, yellow with blue ray florets, 15–20 mm diameter, surrounded by two series of narrow pointed bracts, the outer series each with three veins.
Habitat: Rocky sandstone flats and slopes.
Notes: *Felicia amelloides* is very similar but the bracts have only a single vein each.

Felicia tenella
DAISY FAMILY
Dainty felicia (E)
(Latin *tenellus*, delicate)
Thinly hairy annual herb 5–25 cm high. Leaves narrow with rough hairs on the margins. Flower heads solitary on wiry stalks, yellow with blue, violet or white ray florets, 15–20 mm diameter, surrounded by three series of narrow, pointed bracts.
Habitat: Seasonally moist sandy soils and coastal dunes.

Euryops abrotanifolius
DAISY FAMILY
Common rosinbush (E)
(Latin *abrotanifolius*, with leaves like *Artemisia abrotonum*)

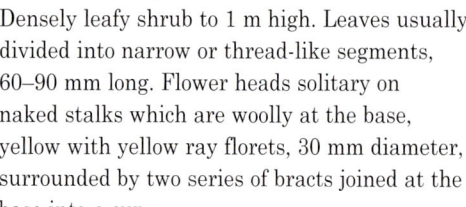

Densely leafy shrub to 1 m high. Leaves usually divided into narrow or thread-like segments, 60–90 mm long. Flower heads solitary on naked stalks which are woolly at the base, yellow with yellow ray florets, 30 mm diameter, surrounded by two series of bracts joined at the base into a cup.
Habitat: Sandstone slopes in fynbos.
Notes: Readily seen on the slopes of Lion's Head.

Fynbos

Euryops speciosissimus
DAISY FAMILY
Giant rosinbush (E), grootharpuisbos (A)
(Latin *speciosissimus*, extremely showy)
Slender or willowy shrub to over 2 m high. Leaves rather fleshy and divided into drooping needle-like or thread-like segments, 60–200 mm long. Flower heads solitary on thick naked stalks, yellow with straggling yellow ray florets, 50–60 mm diameter, surrounded by two series of bracts that are joined below into a cup.
Habitat: Drier, rocky sandstone slopes in fynbos.

Euryops tenuissimus
DAISY FAMILY
Rosinbush (E), harpuisbos (A)
(Latin *tenuissimus*, extremely narrow, referring to the leaves)
Shrub to 2,5 m high, often mealy on the young parts. Leaves needle-like and sometimes three-lobed, 15–150 mm long. Flower heads clustered among the leaves on short, wiry stalks, yellow or orange with yellow ray florets, 10–12 mm diameter, surrounded by two series of bracts joined at the base into a cup.
Habitat: Stony karroid slopes.
Notes: *Euryops thunbergii* has shorter leaves 10–50 mm long.

Euryops virgineus
DAISY FAMILY
Outeniqua rosinbush (E), rivierharpuisbos (A)
(Latin *virgineus*, pure white, an inexplicable choice for the name)
Densely leafy shrub to 3 m high, with stiffly erect stems. Leaves ascending, elliptical and narrowly lobed to toothed above, 5–12 mm long. Flower heads solitary on short wiry stalks among the upper leaves, yellow with yellow ray florets, 10 mm diameter, surrounded by two series of bracts joined at the base into a cup.
Habitat: Sandstone slopes in fynbos.

Fynbos

Gymnodiscus capillaris
DAISY FAMILY
Yellowweed (E), geelkruid (A)
(Latin *capillaris*, thread-like, referring to the flower stalks)

Tufted annual herb to 20 cm high. Leaves in a basal rosette and somewhat succulent, lance-shaped to lyre-shaped and usually lobed below. Flower heads in small clusters on slender branched stalks, yellow with yellow ray florets, 6–8 mm diameter, surrounded by a single series of broad bracts.
Habitat: Sandy flats and lower slopes.

Othonna cylindrica
DAISY FAMILY
Common babooncress (E), bobbejaankool (A)
(Latin *cylindricus*, cylindrical, referring to the leaves)

Brittle-stemmed succulent shrub to 1 m high. Leaves clustered at the branch tips, more or less cylindrical and fleshy. Flower heads few in loose, flat-topped clusters on slender stalks, yellow with yellow ray florets, 20 mm diameter, surrounded by a single series of bracts.
Habitat: Sandy and stony flats and rocks, often coastal.

Othonna quinquedentata
DAISY FAMILY
(= *Othonna parviflora*)
Mountain babooncress (E)
(Latin *quinquedentatus*, five-toothed, referring to the leaves)

Shrub with several slender, erect stems to 1 m high. Leaves crowded toward the bottom of the stems, leathery and lance-shaped or broad and often toothed above. Flower heads many in loose, flat-topped clusters on wand-like stalks, yellow with yellow ray florets, 5 mm diameter, surrounded by a single series of bracts.
Habitat: Rocky sandstone slopes in fynbos, often in damp places.

Fynbos

Osteospermum clandestinum
DAISY FAMILY
(= *Tripteris clandestina*)
Sticky windowseed (E), trekkertjie (A)
(Latin *clandestinus*, hidden, possibly a reference to the relatively inconspicuous ray florets)
Glandular-hairy, aromatic annual herb to 40 cm high, often with purplish stems. Leaves elliptical and toothed to lobed. Flower heads purplish with pale yellow ray florets that are brown at the base, 20 mm diameter, surrounded by two series of narrow bracts, nodding in seed. Seeds large and three-winged, papery.
Habitat: Sandy and gravelly flats, often in disturbed places along roadsides or in lands.

Osteospermum oppositifolium
DAISY FAMILY
(= *Tripteris oppositifolia*)
Winter windowseed (E), stinkskaapbos (A)
(Latin *oppositifolius*, opposite-leaved)
Rounded, brittle-stemmed shrub to 1 m high, foetid-smelling. Leaves opposite, narrow and obscurely toothed, leathery with a grey bloom. Flower heads black with pale to golden yellow ray florets, 30–40 mm diameter, drooping in seed, surrounded by two series of narrow bracts. Seeds three-winged and papery.
Habitat: Dry sandstone or granite outcrops among rocks.

Osteospermum moniliferum
DAISY FAMILY
(= *Chrysanthemoides monilifera*)
Common tickberry (E), bietou, bosluisbessie (A)
(Latin *moniliferus*, bead-carrying, referring to the round seeds)
Rounded shrub to over 1,5 m high, thinly woolly on the young parts. Leaves leathery, oblong to elliptical with coarsely toothed margins. Flower heads in clusters, yellow with yellow ray florets, 20 mm diameter, surrounded by several rows of pointed bracts. Seeds round and glossy black.
Habitat: Sandstone and limestone slopes and flats.

Fynbos

Dimorphotheca pluvialis
DAISY FAMILY

Rain daisy (E), reënblommetjie (A)
(Latin *pluvialis*, relating to rain, referring to the growth of the plants in the wet season)

Erect to sprawling, glandular-hairy annual herb to 30 cm high. Leaves lance-shaped and lobed or toothed. Flower heads solitary and nodding in fruit, purple with white ray florets which have a purple band at the base and a darker underside, and which close at night, 30–45 mm diameter, surrounded by a single row of narrow pointed bracts forming a shallow cup. Seeds disc-like.
Habitat: Sandy and clay flats and slopes.

Ursinia cakilefolia
DAISY FAMILY

Glossy-eyed parachute-daisy (E)
(Latin *cakilefolius*, with leaves like the sea rocket, *Cakile maritima*)

Sprawling annual herb to 45 cm high. Leaves mostly twice-divided into narrow segments. Flower heads solitary on long stalks, glossy blackish with yellow or orange ray florets, the inner florets covered with shiny scales in bud to form the glossy eye, 30–35 mm diameter, surrounded by many series of overlapping bracts, the innermost with large, papery tips. Seeds with five white, papery scale-like wings.
Habitat: Sandy flats and slopes.

Ursinia anthemoides
DAISY FAMILY

Common parachute-daisy (E)
(Resembling chamomile, *Anthemis*)
Annual herb to 50 cm high.
Leaves divided or twice-divided into narrow segments. Flower heads solitary at the branch tips, dull blackish with yellow or orange ray florets with a dark underside and sometimes a dark band at the base, 30–35 mm diameter, surrounded by many series of overlapping bracts, the innermost with large, papery tips. Seeds with five white, papery scale-like wings.
Habitat: Sandy and gravel slopes and flats.

Ursinia paleacea
DAISY FAMILY
Shrubby parachute-daisy (E), geelmagriet (A)
(Latin *paleaceus*, chaffy, referring to the papery scales among the florets)

Short-lived shrublet to 90 cm high, single-stemmed at the base. Leaves divided into narrow segments. Flower heads solitary on long stalks, yellow with yellow ray florets, 20–50 mm diameter, surrounded by many series of overlapping bracts, the innermost with large, papery tips. Seeds with five white, papery scale-like wings.
Habitat: Sandstone slopes after fire.

Berkheya armata
DAISY FAMILY
Greater berkheya (E), grootdissel (A)
(Latin *armatus*, armed, referring to the spines)

Tufted perennial to 40 cm high, sprouting from a woody rootstock. Leaves crowded at the base of the stem, broad, with the margins lightly rolled under and toothed and spiny, hairless above and white-felted beneath. Flower heads loosely clustered, yellow with yellow ray florets, 40–50 mm diameter, surrounded by several series of spiny bracts, the innermost smooth on the margins.
Habitat: Clay and granite slopes after fire.

Berkheya barbata
DAISY FAMILY
Holly-leaved berkheya (E)
(Latin *barbatus*, bearded, alluding to the copious prickles on the bracts)

Shrublet with grey-felted branches to 60 cm high, sprouting from a woody rootstock. Leaves opposite, elliptical, with the margins rolled under and lightly toothed and spiny, leathery, hairless above and white-felted beneath. Flower heads solitary, yellow with yellow ray florets, 40–50 mm diameter, surrounded by several series of bracts with long spines on the margins.
Habitat: Rocky sandstone slopes after fire.

Fynbos

Didelta spinosa
DAISY FAMILY
Namaqua salad thistle (E), slaaibos (A)
(Latin *spinosus*, spiny, referring to the leaves)

Shrub to 2 m high. Leaves opposite, glossy, elliptical and spine-tipped, lobed at the base with the margins lightly rolled under and sometimes prickly. Flower heads yellow with yellow ray florets, 40–50 mm diameter, surrounded by two rows of bracts, the outer four bracts large and leafy and the inner narrow with prickly teeth.
Habitat: Dry granite and sandstone slopes.
Notes: Highly palatable, especially the dry leaves in summer.

Didelta carnosa
DAISY FAMILY
Dune salad thistle (E), kusslaaibos (A)
(Latin *carnosus*, fleshy, referring to the leaves)

Rounded shrublet to 1 m high. Leaves fleshy and lance-shaped with the margins usually rolled under, thinly or densely cobwebby. Flower heads yellow with yellow ray florets, 40–50 mm diameter, surrounded by two rows of bracts, the outer four bracts large and leafy and the inner narrow with prickly teeth.
Habitat: Coastal dunes and sandy flats.

Fynbos

Gazania rigens
DAISY FAMILY
Strand gazania (E), strandgazania (A)
(Latin *rigens*, stiff, referring to the leaves)

Sprawling, mat-forming perennial to 20 cm high. Leaves usually narrowly elliptical with the margins rolled under but sometimes divided into narrow lobes, smooth above but white-felted below with smooth petioles. Flower heads yellow with yellow ray florets, 30–40 mm diameter, surrounded by several series of partially white-woolly bracts that are joined into a cup, the inner bracts pointed.
Habitat: Coastal dunes, rocks and sandy flats.

Gazania pectinata
DAISY FAMILY
Comb-leaved gazania (E)
(Latin *pectinatus*, with narrow divisions like a comb, referring to the leaves)
Tufted annual herb to 20 cm high. Leaves mostly divided into narrow segments with the margins rolled under, sometimes rough above but white-felted beneath. Flower heads blackish with yellow or orange ray florets marked with a dark band at the base, 40–50 mm diameter, surrounded by several series of bracts that are joined into a cup, the inner bracts gradually tapering.
Habitat: Coastal flats and sandy lower slopes.

Osmitopsis asteriscoides
DAISY FAMILY
Marsh daisy (E), belskruie (A)
(Resembling the genus *Asteriscus*)
Sparsely branched shrub to 2 m high with erect stems which are densely leafy at the ends. Leaves lance-shaped and smooth or felted, aromatic when bruised. Flower heads in flat-topped clusters at the branch tips, yellow with white ray florets, 20 mm diameter, surrounded by several series of bracts.
Habitat: Marshes and seeps on sandstone.
Notes: Brandy tinctures (*belsbrandewyn*) traditionally used for chest and stomach ailments.

Fynbos

Arctotheca calendula
DAISY FAMILY
Cape weed (E)
(Referring to the marigold, *Calendula*)
Tufted to sprawling annual herb to 20 cm high. Leaves mostly in a basal tuft, lyre-shaped or divided into oblong, toothed segments, rough above and woolly beneath. Flower heads blackish with pale yellow ray florets usually with darker yellow or blackish bands at the base, 30–35 mm diameter, surrounded by several series of bracts with papery margins. Fruits woolly.
Habitat: Coastal areas or disturbed soil.

Arctotheca populifolia
DAISY FAMILY
Sea pumpkin (E)
(Latin *populifolius*, with leaves resembling those of a poplar, *Populus*)
Creeping, mat-forming perennial to 10 cm high. Leaves stalked and heart-shaped or rarely lobed with the margins sparsely toothed, white-felted. Flower heads yellow with yellow ray florets, 30 mm diameter, surrounded by several series of woolly bracts with papery margins. Fruits woolly.
Habitat: Seashore.

Arctotis hirsuta
DAISY FAMILY
Common arctotis (E), gousblom (A)
(Latin *hirsutus*, covered with coarse hairs)
Slightly fleshy, often robust annual herb to 45 cm high. Leaves lyre-shaped and divided, often with ear-like lobes at the base, sparsely hairy. Flower heads blackish with yellow, cream or orange ray florets marked with a dark band at the base, 40–50 mm diameter, surrounded by several series of bracts with papery margins, the inner with large papery tips.
Habitat: Sandy slopes and coastal flats.

Fynbos

Arctotis acaulis
DAISY FAMILY

Tufted arctotis (E), renostergousblom (A)
(Latin *acaulis*, stemless)

Stemless perennial to 20 cm high. Leaves lyre-shaped and divided or broad and toothed, rough above and grey-felted beneath. Flower heads blackish with orange, yellow or cream ray florets marked with a dark band at the base, 40–50 mm diameter, surrounded by several series of bracts with papery margins, the inner with large papery tips.
Habitat: Clay, granite and limestone flats.

Arctotis angustifolia
DAISY FAMILY

Sandveld arctotis (E)
(Latin *angustifolius*, narrow-leaved)

Creeping perennial to 40 cm high, with stems arising from a diffuse underground system. Leaves broadly to narrowly elliptical and toothed or divided with the margins weakly rolled under, thinly white-woolly and usually paler beneath. Flower heads blackish with white or yellow ray florets that are reddish reverse beneath, 35–45 mm diameter, surrounded by several series of thinly woolly bracts with papery margins, the inner with large papery tips.
Habitat: Sandy slopes and flats.

Arctotis stoechadifolia
DAISY FAMILY

Silver arctotis (E)
(With leaves resembling those of French lavender, *Lavandula stoechas*)

Sprawling perennial with erect shoots to 35 cm high. Leaves lance-shaped or divided and silvery-felted. Flower heads blackish with cream ray florets that are reddish beneath, 40–50 mm diameter, surrounded by several series of thinly woolly bracts with papery margins, the inner with large papery tips.
Habitat: Dunes and sandy flats, mostly coastal.

Namaqualand

The area known as Namaqualand is a narrow stretch of country along the south-west coast, extending for 200 km in a band little more than 80 km wide, from the mouth of the Olifants River in the south to the mouth of the Orange or Gariep River in the north. This arid strip is home to a unique assemblage of plants that is without equal elsewhere in the world. Packed into an area of around 50 000 km² are about 3 000 different species of wildflowers in a concentration that is at least four times richer than that found in comparable winter-rainfall desert areas. Furthermore, about 50% of these do not occur outside of the area, a staggering proportion in the context of its desert climate. Around one third of all the plants in the region are succulents, a number that encompasses one tenth of all the succulents in the world! They come in a great variety of sizes, around a quarter of them minuscule plants little more than 1 cm high. At the other extreme are the towering quiver trees that reach 9 m in height. The majority, however, are small, succulent-leaved shrublets less than 50 cm high that fall between these extremes. The most common succulents by far are members of the Mesemb family. Like the Cape Region to the south, Namaqualand also has a wonderfully rich bulb flora. With almost 500 different species, representing about 16% of the flora, it has five to ten times the number of bulbs typically found in other winter-rainfall deserts. Namaqualand has been well described as a succulent desert, enriched by a large and beautiful bulb flora.

Rainfall in the region is strictly confined to the winter months, between April and August, but sea fogs are an invaluable source of moisture for many plants. The cold Benguela current, which is responsible for the condensation of these fogs, also ensures that temperatures near the coast never soar to blistering levels in the summer. The dominant vegetation in Namaqualand is a low shrubland dominated by dwarf shrubs with succulent leaves, known as Succulent Karoo. Along the coastal plain and on the highest peaks of the Kamiesberg and Richtersveld mountains are patches of depauperate fynbos, but these are relatively unimportant. Although it may scarcely cover the ground and appear threadbare in comparison with the lush grasslands and thickets to the east, Succulent Karoo deserves our highest admiration. Not only does it support between four and six times as many species as are found in other winter-rainfall deserts around the world

Namaqualand

but the large numbers of leaf succulents and bulbs that occur in it are completely lacking in these areas. Finally, the reliable rains mean that prolonged droughts are not a feature of Namaqualand, allowing this unique assemblage of plants to thrive.

Namaqualand is famous for its brilliant displays of spring annuals. A really fine flower season, however, occurs only once every eight to ten years. In these years the landscape is transformed into a kaleidoscope of dazzling colours by great swathes of annuals that cover the fallow fields and line the roadsides. Less disturbed veld is often covered in a haze of yellow cotula with pools of pale blue *Felicia merxmuelleri*. Unfortunately these massed displays, remarkable though they may be, are artefacts of cultivation, often obscuring the true glory that the countryside has to offer to the more discerning visitor.

Namaqualand's flower season is the shortest of the three floral areas, with the main spring displays lasting for little more than a month and peaking for a few brief weeks in August. Flowering usually starts earlier in the north and on the coast, which are often best in late July or early August. The flats near Port Nolloth can be carpeted with annuals in July, including the pale yellow *Grielum humifusum*, although this is considered to be early in the season. The coastal strip can be golden with *Didelta carnosa*. At this time, too, the lovely apricot *Jordaaniella cuprea* and the brilliant white *Osteospermum scullyi* are also conspicuous. By August, however, these same coastal flats are often already dry and brown, although the succulent *Cephalophyllum spongiosum*, with its lusciously coloured purple and orange flowers, is a spectacular exception. The higher country between Steinkopf and Garies is best a little later, during the second half of August, when several types of glorious flowering shrubs dot the rocky slopes. Among the most spectacular are the golden mounds of *Osteospermum oppositifolium*, and several gorgeous

Spring annuals, like Cleretum papulosum, *blanket fallow lands near Kamieskroon*

Namaqualand

magenta pelargoniums, among which the rather rare *P. sericifolium* stands out for the brilliance of its colouring. At this time it is well worth wandering among the granite domes around Springbok or Kamieskroon. Tucked between the coppery boulders and contorted quiver trees are numerous flowering shrubs, annuals and bulbs. Among the shrubs, the most conspicuous are the silvery-leaved bushes of *Lebeckia sericea*, bearing trusses of pale creamy yellow flowers. A variety of orange annual daisies occur in these outcrops and careful examination is necessary to distinguish between *Osteospermum hyoseroides*, *O. amplectens*, *Dimorphotheca sinuata*, *Ursinia calenduliflora*, *Arctotis fastuosa* and *Gorteria diffusa*, among others. Later than elsewhere, the top of the Kamiesberg only comes into full bloom in early or mid September, when it becomes a wonderland of brightly coloured bulbs. The mountain passes that wend onto the coastal plains are often very rewarding. They include the Spektakel Pass east of Steinkopf and the Anenous Pass east of Springbok. The main wildflower reserves, the Namaqua National Park and Skilpad in the south near Kamieskroon and Goegap further north outside Springbok, are almost always rewarding for the easy access that they provide to visitors walking among the flowers themselves. Because the rains are often local and the flowers go over so rapidly it is always advisable to check with local sources for the best sites before visiting.

In the southern part of Namaqualand, there is a similar relationship between altitude and flowering time, with the Knersvlakte at its best early in the season and the Hantam, 600 m higher up on the Bokkeveld Escarpment, only coming into full bloom in early September. The Knersvlakte is famous among succulent enthusiasts for its unique

The sculptural Aloe dichotoma

flora of dwarf succulents. This arid basin is characterised by glittering stretches of quartz fields that sparkle over its gently undulating plains. These quartz fields are home to a bewildering array of minute succulents, each beautifully adapted to these highly unusual habitats. They cannot be seen from a vehicle and a hands-and-knees approach is the only way to appreciate these miniature jewels. Among the larger, cushion-forming species, *Argyroderma fissum*, with magenta flowers, and *Cephalophyllum spissum*, with delicate salmon-pink flowers, are common but the real gems must be searched for. Here, concealed among pebbles, and often stepped on in ignorance, are thousands of cryptic little silver bodies belonging to various species of *Argyroderma*, *Conophytum* and *Oophytum*. The first two genera flower in early winter and only their strange leaf pairs are discernible in spring.

Namaqualand

Overlooking these flats in the east are the ramparts of the Bokkeveld Mountains, on which lies the settlement of Nieuwoudtville. It is no idle boast that this village has dubbed itself the Bulb Capital of the World. Incredibly, researchers have excavated well over 20 000 bulbs, corms and other forms of underground roots in a square metre of soil near the village! It comes as no surprise, then, that Nieuwoudtville can produce swathes of colourful bulbs that rival the daisies of Namaqualand in their sheer abundance. Among the jewels of the region are the large red romuleas or satinflowers, with their enormous poppy-like blooms, several species of *Bulbinella* with their poker-like spikes of flowers and the three species of *Sparaxis* that are the parents of cultivated sparaxis hybrids that brighten gardens the world over. The staggering profligacy of individual plants is not, however, the whole tale of the Hantam's glory. The secret to its botanical riches lies in the confluence, around Nieuwoudtville itself, of several very different types of soils, each supporting its own distinctive suite of species. Here it is common for pairs of closely related species to occur, one on the sticky red soils derived from the dolerite intrusions and another on the lighter soils from either the shales of the Karoo or the tillites deposited by ancient glaciers.

One of the features of the flowers of many Namaqualand annuals is that they close at night and in cool or wet weather. This means that an early start in winter or spring is not recommended, as the flowers will not be open until the day warms up. The display is characterised by a distinctive combination of magenta and orange colours that is not found elsewhere. The orange is due to an almost bewildering array of daisies, mainly annuals but also shrubs. The cerise, magenta or purple is provided by a range of bulbs, particularly the Springbok painted petals, *Lapeirousia silenoides*, and the T'neitjie, *Pelargonium incrassatum*. Altogether, an impressive total of 20 different species of iris and pelargonium produce similar magenta or purple, long-tubed flowers. This extraordinary floral convergence is due to the occurrence in Namaqualand of two highly specialised flower-visiting flies that survive by sucking nectar from flowers. These flies have developed long, straw-like mouth parts that are ideal for reaching the nectar held at the base of long floral tubes. They are the main or only pollinators of these plants and the existence of some of Namaqualand's most characteristic flowers is thus due to the activities of these marvellous insects.

Although Namaqualand is known for its spring wildflower displays, there are other times of the year during which the countryside bursts into bloom. For a brief few weeks in autumn the dry, barren ground is transformed by a flowering that is even more remarkable than the spring season. Responding to the cooling temperatures of autumn and the first rains of the season, the dramatic flower spikes of numerous species of amaryllid burst through the soil. Pink brunsvigias and scarlet haemanthus appear almost overnight, to be followed by a range of smaller species in the early winter. The flowering of stone plants also enlivens the quartz patches of the Knersvlakte, while the flats around Nieuwoudtville become a shifting tapestry of colour as several species of oxalis carpet the ground. Unfortunately the exact timing of this floral spectacle is highly dependent on rains and is impossible to predict far in advance. This is one show for which tickets must be bought on the night but it is one that is well worth seeing.

Namaqualand

Aloe dichotoma
ALOE FAMILY
Quiver tree (E), kokerboom (A), choje (N)
(Latin *dichotomous*, branching in pairs, a reference to the repeatedly forked branches)
Sturdy tree to 9 m high. Leaves bluish green, tapering with inconspicuous teeth along the margins. Flowers in short, branched racemes among the leaves, yellow, urn-shaped with conspicuous reddish stamens protruding from the mouth, 30 mm long.
Habitat: Dry rocky slopes.
Notes: The hollow branches were used as quivers by the San people. In a few localities the plants grow in dense stands of thousands, the famous Quiver Tree forests.

Aloe pearsonii
ALOE FAMILY
Pearson's aloe (E)
(Named after Prof. Harold Pearson, the first director of the National Botanical Gardens)
Large shrub with erect stems to 2 m high bearing leaves along their length. Leaves dull bluish but turning red in times of drought, curved downwards and neatly arranged in vertical rows, triangular with toothed margins. Flowers in head-shaped racemes, red to yellow with the stamens shortly protruding from the mouth, 30 mm long.
Habitat: Arid stony slopes.

Aloe microstigma
ALOE FAMILY
(= *Aloe framesii, A. khamiesensis*)
Cape speckled aloe (E)
(Greek *microstigma*, little spot, referring to the white speckling on the leaves)
Single-stemmed or clump-forming succulent to 3 m high. Leaves tapering, often reddish and usually with small white spots, the margins with sharp, reddish-brown teeth. Flowers nodding in conical racemes, usually red in bud but opening yellow, 20–30 mm long.
Habitat: Stony slopes and granite outcrops among scrub.

Namaqualand

Aloe falcata
ALOE FAMILY
Sickle-leaved aloe (E)
(Latin *falcatus*, sickle-shaped, a reference to the curved leaves)

Stemless or short-stemmed succulent, usually growing in clumps with the rosettes pointing outwards. Leaves greyish green, lance-shaped and curved inwards with a rough, sandpapery surface and coarsely toothed margins. Flowers in conical, branched racemes, nodding, red or yellow with green tips, tubular with the stamens protruding from the mouth, 40 mm long.
Habitat: Dry sandy flats.

Aloe variegata
ALOE FAMILY
Partridge aloe (E), kanniedood (A)
(Latin *variegatus*, variegated, for the conspicuously mottled leaves)

Stemless succulent to 50 cm high. Leaves in compact, three-ranked rosettes, keeled, green to brown and boldly mottled with white, the margins horny and white with minute teeth. Flowers in conical racemes, nodding, pink to red, tubular with the stamens not protruding from the mouth, 40 mm long.
Habitat: In the shelter of bushes on stony flats.
Notes: This beautiful species is widely grown and in some parts of the Karoo is planted on graves.

Kniphofia sarmentosa
ALOE FAMILY
Karoo poker (E), vuurpyl (A)
(Latin *sarmentosus*, producing long runners, although this species actually produces numerous short rhizomes)

Rhizomatous perennial to 60 cm high. Leaves greyish, strap-shaped, channelled and V-shaped in cross section. Flowers in dense, ovoid to cylindrical racemes, nodding, tubular, pinkish red in bud but tipped with buff when open, 20–25 mm long.
Habitat: Along mountain streams and in moist hollows, often in dense colonies.

Namaqualand

Bulbinella latifolia
ALOE FAMILY
Broad-leaved bulbinella (E), rooikatstert, rooidirk (A)

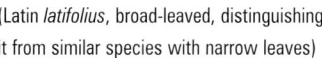

(Latin *latifolius*, broad-leaved, distinguishing it from similar species with narrow leaves)
Sturdy tufted perennial to 1 m high. Leaves broadly strap-shaped and tapering. Flowers in dense, cylindrical racemes, yellow, cream or orange, 6–8 mm diameter.
Habitat: Seasonally damp soils.
Notes: Varies in flower colour and soil preference. The striking orange-flowered subspecies occurs only around Nieuwoudtville.

Bulbinella eburniflora
ALOE FAMILY
Scented bulbinella (E), bleekkatstert (A)
(Latin *eburniflora*, with ivory-coloured flowers)
Tufted perennial to 75 cm high. Leaves slender and channelled with finely toothed margins. Flowers in dense, conical racemes, creamy white with a musty odour, 6–8 mm diameter.
Habitat: Gravelly clay soils in renosterveld.
Notes: The strong, musty odour of the flowers is distinctive.

Namaqualand

Bulbinella nutans
ALOE FAMILY

Marsh bulbinella (E), waterkatstert (A)
(Latin *nutans*, nodding, an exaggerated reference to the slight curvature evident in young flower spikes)

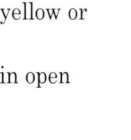

Sturdy tufted perennial to 80 cm high. Leaves narrowly strap-shaped and channelled. Flowers in dense, conical racemes, yellow or cream, 6–8 mm diameter.
Habitat: Damp clay or peaty soils in open scrub, often forming colonies.

Bulbine praemorsa
ALOE FAMILY

Common bulbine (E)
(Latin *praemorsus*, as if bitten off, for the abruptly truncated base of the tuberous root)

Deciduous perennial with a tuberous root, 40–60 cm high. Leaves narrow and channelled, thick and fleshy with slimy sap, surrounded at the base by a short fibrous collar. Flowers in a loose raceme, yellow to salmon, 10 mm diameter, lasting a day.
Habitat: Stony slopes in open scrub.
Notes: The soothing, gel-like sap of *Bulbine* species is widely used as an emollient to treat skin abrasions.

Trachyandra falcata
ALOE FAMILY

Namaqua starlily (E), Namakwakool (A)
(Latin *falcatus*, sickle-shaped, a reference to the curved leaves)

Robust tufted perennial to 60 cm high. Leaves leathery, flat and curving with a grey bloom. Flowers in a dense, few-branched raceme with the lowest bract forming a collar around the flower stalk, white or pinkish, only a few open each afternoon, 10 mm diameter, lasting a day.
Habitat: Common on sandy soils, often near the coast.
Notes: The young flower shoots can be cooked and eaten as a vegetable, much like asparagus.

Chlorophytum undulatum
ANTHERICUM FAMILY
Namaqua grasslily (E), namakwagifkool (A)
(Latin *undulatus*, wavy, a reference to the unnaturally limp leaves in the cultivated specimen from which the species was originally described)
Tufted perennial to 50 cm high, with numerous slender, wiry roots and sometimes additional small tubers. Leaves strap-shaped, narrow or broader with finely hairy margins. Flowers in loose racemes with several flowers in each bract, white with brown keels, each lasting a single day, 15 mm diameter.
Habitat: Stony clay or loamy flats.
Notes: Species of grasslily, *Chlorophytum*, like *Trachyandra*, have short-lived flowers and the two are often confused but grasslilies have fibrous, not succulent leaves, more than one flower in each bract and distinctly three-winged fruits.

Ornithogalum pruinosum
HYACINTH FAMILY
Grey-leaved chincherinchee (E)
(Latin *pruinosus*, covered with a whitish bloom, a reference to the leaves)
Bulbous perennial, 10–50 cm high. Leaves three to six, oblong and firm-textured with a greyish bloom and the margins sometimes wavy. Flowers in a short, dense raceme, white and fragrant with rather shiny petals, 20–25 mm diameter.
Habitat: Stony slopes in open scrub.

Albuca consanguinea
HYACINTH FAMILY
(= *Ornithogalum polyphyllum*)
Large striped chincherinchee (E)
(Latin *consanguineus*, similar to another species)
Bulbous perennial, 25–35 cm high. Leaves many, grass-like and channelled with the tips sometimes dry and coiled. Flowers in a cylindrical raceme on long stalks, white or pale yellow with green keels, fragrant, 20–30 mm diameter.
Habitat: Gravelly clay flats in open scrub.

Namaqualand

Ornithogalum xanthochlorum
HYACINTH FAMILY
Slangkop (A)
(Greek *xantho-*, *chloro-*, yellow-green, for the greenish flowers)
Stout bulbous perennial to 60 cm. Leaves 9 to 14 in a spreading tuft, strap-shaped. Flowers in a dense, cylindrical raceme, waxy, green with white stamens, scented, 25 mm diameter.
Habitat: Open sandy or gravelly flats and low hills in open scrub.
Notes: Plants are poisonous.

Albuca canadensis
HYACINTH FAMILY
(= *Albuca altissima, A. maxima*)
Greater slime lily (E), wittamarak (A)
(Latin *maximus*, greatest, for its large size)

Stout bulbous perennial, usually 1–2 m high, the bulb tunics slightly fibrous at the top. Leaves several, channelled and clasping the stem below, fleshy and oozing a slimy sap when torn. Flowers in racemes that elongate markedly in fruit, nodding, white with green keels, the inner tepals with a hinged flap at the tip, 25–30 mm diameter.
Habitat: Rocky outcrops.
Notes: Can form dense colonies along roadsides.

Albuca cooperi
HYACINTH FAMILY
Warty slime lily (E), geldbeursie (A)
(Named after Thomas Cooper, a Victorian plant collector)

Bulbous perennial to 40 cm high, the bulb tunics becoming fibrous at the top. Leaves two or three, slender and grooved above, distinctly warty at the base just above the bulb, oozing a slimy sap when torn. Flowers in loose racemes, nodding, yellow with green keels, the inner three petals with a hinged flap at the tip, lightly scented, 20–25 mm diameter.
Habitat: Sandy and rocky soils in open scrub.
Notes: Distinguished from other slime lilies by the conspicuous warts at the base of the stem.

Namaqualand

Lachenalia framesii
HYACINTH FAMILY
Frames' lachenalia (E)
(Named after Percy Ross Frames, a keen grower of succulents, who first collected the species)

Bulbous perennial to 15 cm high. Leaves one or two, narrow and plain green with wavy margins. Flowers in narrow spikes, without pedicels, urn-shaped with the anthers enclosed within the flower, the outer petals yellowish green but the inner whitish with spreading bright purple or magenta tips, 8–10 mm long.
Habitat: Sandy flats, often in large colonies.
Notes: A dainty species especially common on the Knersvlakte just north of Vanrhynsdorp.

Lachenalia elegans
HYACINTH FAMILY
Elegant lachenalia (E), fraaiviooltjie (A)
(Latin *elegans*, elegant)

Bulbous perennial to 20 cm high. Leaves one or two, ovate, often with green or maroon spots. Flowers in narrow spikes, without pedicels, urn-shaped with the anthers enclosed within the flower, in shades or combinations of yellow, blue, mauve or purple, with white tips, 8–10 mm long.
Habitat: Sandstone outcrops and gravelly clay, often in large colonies.

Lachenalia carnosa
HYACINTH FAMILY
Fleshy-leaved lachenalia (E)
(Latin *carnosus*, fleshy or succulent, for the leaves)

Bulbous perennial to 25 cm high. Leaves two, ovate and fleshy with parallel grooves on the upper surface and sometimes also green or brownish warts. Flowers in dense spikes, without pedicels, urn-shaped with the anthers enclosed within the flower, whitish with the inner petals broadly tipped with purple or magenta, 8–10 mm long.
Habitat: Rocky outcrops in gravelly soil.

Namaqualand

Lachenalia violacea
HYACINTH FAMILY
Karoo lachenalia (E), karooviooltjie (A)
(Latin *violaceus*, violet, for the flowers)
Bulbous perennial to 20 cm high. Leaves one or two, lanceolate, plain green or variously spotted or banded, with smooth or wavy margins. Flowers in a cylindrical raceme on distinct pedicels, goblet-shaped with the anthers conspicuously protruding, green or brownish with purple tips and violet stamens, scented of coconut, 10–12 mm long.
Habitat: Gravelly soils in open scrub.

Veltheimia capensis
HYACINTH FAMILY
Winter veltheimia (E), sandlelie (A)
(Latin *capensis*, from the Cape)
Robust bulbous perennial to 40 cm high. Leaves several in a spreading tuft, bluish green with a grey bloom, tapering with the margins more or less wavy or crisped. Flowers in a dense conical raceme, drooping, pink with darker speckling and green tips, tubular, 25–30 mm long.
Habitat: Sandy or gravelly flats and rocky outcrops, often in the shelter of shrubs.
Notes: The flowers, which resemble those of an aloe or red hot poker, give way to attractive papery, three-winged fruits.

Massonia bifolia
HYACINTH FAMILY
Pagoda lily (E)
(= *Whiteheadia bifolia*)
(Latin *bifolius*, two-leaved)
Bulbous perennial, 8–12 cm high. Leaves two, spreading on the ground, fleshy and fragile in texture. Flowers in a dense, cylindrical spike topped with a tuft of leaf-like bracts, creamy, 20 mm diameter.
Habitat: Mostly in the lee of rocks.
Notes: Pollinated by rodents.

Namaqualand

Daubenya aurea
HYACINTH FAMILY
Jewel of the desert (E)
(Latin *aureus*, golden yellow, after the yellow form which was discovered first)

Bulbous perennial, 5–8 cm high. Leaves two, spreading on the ground, ovate and leathery with longitudinal grooves. Flowers crowded between the leaves, the outer flowers with much larger petals than the inner, usually red but some populations yellow, the flower head 30–50 mm diameter.
Habitat: Red doleritic clays.
Notes: Restricted to a few populations near the village of Middelpos. Bulbs of both colour forms are available commercially.

Spiloxene serrata
STARGRASS FAMILY
Common Cape star (E), sterretjie (A)
(Latin *serratus*, saw-edged, referring to the toothed leaf margins)

Cormous perennial, 6–20 cm high. Leaves several, grass-like and channelled with the margins minutely toothed. Flowers one per flowering stalk, subtended by two narrow bracts, yellow, orange or white with the petals green on the reverse, 15–25 mm diameter.
Habitat: Seasonally moist stony clay flats and lower slopes in open scrub.

Empodium flexile
STARGRASS FAMILY
Fragrant autumn star (E), klipsterretjie (A)
(Latin *flexilis*, flexible, referring to the slender appendages at the tips of the anthers)

Cormous perennial to 10 cm high. Leaves three and usually not developed at flowering, lance-shaped and pleated. Flowers solitary on a three-angled stalk, pale to bright yellow and lemon-scented, 30 mm diameter, the stamens tipped with slender orange appendages.
Habitat: Stony or sandy flats.

Namaqualand

Ornithoglossum vulgare
COLCHICUM FAMILY
Common snakelily (E), slangkop (A)
(Latin *vulgaris,* common or ordinary)

Cormous perennial, 6–30 cm high. Leaves narrow and tapering with the margins usually wavy, greyish. Flowers nodding on long, spreading pedicels, the petals green with maroon margins or red to brown, 10–15 mm diameter.
Habitat: Stony flats or gentle slopes in open scrub.
Notes: Like all members of this family these plants are poisonous.

Cyanella alba
CYANELLA FAMILY
Hooded lady's hand (E)
(Latin *albus*, white)

Cormous perennial, 12–25 cm high. Leaves several in a tuft, thread-like, round in cross section. Flowers one or two on long stalks, white to pink or yellow, fragrant, with five smaller stamens clustered together above one larger stamen.
Habitat: Stony clay and sandstone flats.

Cyanella orchidiformis
CYANELLA FAMILY
Orchid-flowered lady's hand (E)
(Latin *orchidiformis*, orchid-shaped, a reference to the exotic flowers)

Cormous perennial, 30–40 cm high. Leaves lance-shaped and tapering, soft-textured and often with wavy margins. Flowers in branched racemes, mauve with a darker purplish centre, fragrant, with three smaller stamens clustered above three larger ones.
Habitat: Seasonally moist rocky flats and lower slopes.

Namaqualand

Colchicum capense
COLCHICUM FAMILY
(= *Androcymbium capense*)
White cup-and-saucer (E)
(Latin *capensis*, from the Cape)
Cormous perennial, 5–8 cm high. Leaves two, spreading on the ground and lance-shaped with finely hairy margins. Flowers clustered between the leaves and enclosed in large, white bracts sometimes striped with green, the flower head 30–50 mm diameter.
Habitat: Clay or loamy flats.

Colchicum coloratum
COLCHICUM FAMILY
(= *Androcymbium latifolium*)
Red cup-and-saucer (E)
(Latin *coloratus*, colourful)
Cormous perennial, 5–8 cm high. Leaves two, spreading on the ground and lance-shaped with finely hairy margins. Flowers clustered between the leaves and enclosed in large, red to purple bracts, the flower head 30–50 mm diameter.
Habitat: Clay flats, usually in red doleritic clay.

Strumaria truncata
AMARYLLIS FAMILY
Namaqua snowdrop (E)
(Latin *truncatus*, abruptly cut off, a reference to the blunt sheath that encircles the bases of the leaves)
Slender bulbous perennial to 40 cm high. Leaves just emerging at flowering, two to four in a basal fan, strap-shaped and twisted, enclosed at the base in a swollen purple sheath. Flowers nodding on a slender peduncle, funnel-shaped, white to pink, 8–10 mm long.
Habitat: Seasonally moist stony and gravelly flats.

Namaqualand

Haemanthus barkerae
AMARYLLIS FAMILY
Bokkeveld paintbrush lily (E)
(Commemorating Cape Town botanist, Miss W.F. Barker)
Bulbous geophyte, 10–15 cm high, often growing in clumps. Leaves withered at flowering, two, narrow and smooth or shortly hairy, barred with maroon at the base on the underside. Flowers in a loose head surrounded by four to six pointed bracts, usually pink but rarely reddish, the flower head 30–40 mm diameter.
Habitat: Dolerite and shale flats.
Notes: Common around Nieuwoudtville.

Haemanthus crispus
AMARYLLIS FAMILY
Crispy-leaved paintbrush lily (E)
(Latin *crispus*, crisped or wavy, a reference to the leaf margins)
Bulbous geophyte, 4–10 cm high, often growing in clumps. Leaves withered at flowering, two, narrow and channelled with wavy or crisped margins and speckled with purple at the base on the underside. Flowers in a small, compact head surrounded by four or five blunt, waxy bracts, usually red but rarely pink, the flower head 20–30 mm diameter.
Habitat: Gravelly flats and lower slopes.
Notes: Common on the granite flats around Springbok and Garies.

Crossyne flava
AMARYLLIS FAMILY
(= *Boophone flava*)
Yellow parasol lily (E), geelsambreelblom (A)
(Latin *flavus*, pale yellow)
Bulbous perennial to 30 cm high. Leaves withered at flowering, four to six, spreading flat on the ground, oblong and leathery with coarsely bristly margins. Flowers in large round heads on long pedicels, pale yellow, lightly scented, 12–15 mm diameter.
Habitat: Gravelly flats and lower slopes.

Namaqualand

Crinum variabile
AMARYLLIS FAMILY
Groen River lily (E), turflelie (A)
(Latin *variabilis*, varying in colour)
Robust bulbous perennial to
1 m high. Leaves withered or just emerging at flowering, several, strap-shaped and channelled with minutely toothed margins. Flowers large and trumpet-shaped, nodding, pale to deep pink, 60–80 mm diameter.
Habitat: Stream sides and riverbeds among rocks.
Notes: Pollinated by hawk moths at dusk.

Brunsvigia bosmaniae
AMARYLLIS FAMILY
Scented candelabra (E), soet kandelaar (A)
(Named after a Mrs Bosman who collected the first plant on her farm near Kuils River between Cape Town and Stellenbosch)
Bulbous perennial to 20 cm high. Leaves dry at flowering, five or six, spreading flat on the ground, tongue-shaped with firm translucent margins. Flowers crowded in a large round head, the tepals broadly oblong and pink with darker veins, 30–40 mm diameter.
Habitat: Clay or gravelly flats.
Notes: In good seasons can flower in the thousands, covering the autumn veld with its pink balloons. There are especially large colonies between Klawer and Nieuwoudtville.

Ammocharis longifolia
AMARYLLIS FAMILY
(= *Cybistetes longifolia*)
Malgas lily (E)
(Latin *longifolia*, long-leaved)
Bulbous perennial, 25–35 cm
high. Leaves dry or green at flowering, sickle-shaped and spreading on the ground with translucent margins. Flowers in a large round head, widely funnel-shaped, cream to pink and wonderfully fragrant, 40–60 mm diameter.
Habitat: Open sandy flats.
Notes: Flowering occurs within one or two weeks after a summer shower.

Namaqualand

Ferraria variabilis
IRIS FAMILY

Yellow spider iris (E), geelspinnekopblom (A)
(Latin *variabilis*, variable, referring to the colour)

Cormous perennial, 6–20 cm high, the stem often much-branched. Leaves sword-shaped with thickened margins. Flowers yellowish to brown with dark streaks and blotches and finely ruffled margins, foetid-smelling, 30–35 mm diameter, each lasting one day.
Habitat: Sandy and shale flats and rock outcrops.

Moraea tripetala
IRIS FAMILY

Fleur-de-lys moraea (E), blou-uintjie (A)
(Latin *tripetalus*, three-petalled, a reference to the suppression or loss of three of the six petals that is characteristic of this species)

Slender cormous perennial, 20–45 cm high. Leaf solitary, narrow and channelled. Flowers blue to violet or rarely white or pink, with three large petals on narrow stalks alternating with three thread-like petals or these absent, 30–35 mm diameter.
Habitat: Stony sandstone and clay soils in open scrub.

Moraea serpentina
IRIS FAMILY

Serpentine moraea (E)
(Latin *serpentinus*, snake-like, a reference to the wavy or coiled leaves)

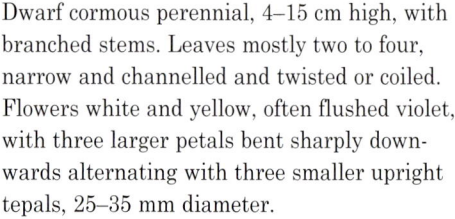

Dwarf cormous perennial, 4–15 cm high, with branched stems. Leaves mostly two to four, narrow and channelled and twisted or coiled. Flowers white and yellow, often flushed violet, with three larger petals bent sharply downwards alternating with three smaller upright tepals, 25–35 mm diameter.
Habitat: Dry stony flats.

Namaqualand

Moraea ciliata
IRIS FAMILY
Velvet-leaved moraea (E)
(Latin *ciliatus*, fringed with fine hairs)
Stemless cormous perennial, 5–10(–20) cm high. Leaves three to five, narrow, usually greyish in colour and sparsely to densely hairy. Flowers blue or yellow, rarely white, spicy-fragrant with the inner three tepals lance-shaped, 30–40 mm diameter.
Habitat: Sandy and clay slopes.

Moraea falcifolia
IRIS FAMILY
Pouooguintjie (A)
(Latin *falcifolius*, sickle-leaved)
Stemless, dwarf cormous perennial to 5 cm high. Leaves narrow and channelled. Flowers white with yellow and lilac to purple markings in the centre, with three larger, spreading petals alternating with three smaller, somewhat upcurved petals, foetid-smelling, lasting a single day, 25–30 mm diameter.
Habitat: Seasonally damp stony clay flats.

Moraea bifida
IRIS FAMILY
(= *Homeria bifida*)
Pink Cape tulip (E), pienktulp (A)
(Latin *bifidus*, two-cleft, referring to the forked style branches)
Cormous perennial to 50 cm high. Leaf solitary, fairly broad below and clasping the lower half of the stem, channelled. Flowers star-shaped, yellow or pink, minutely speckled in the centre, the anthers held at the tip of a bulbous filament column, 25–30 mm diameter.
Habitat: Clay soils in renosterveld.
Notes: Most Cape tulips are poisonous to stock and proliferate in overgrazed veld.

Namaqualand

Moraea schlechteri
IRIS FAMILY
(= *Homeria schlechteri*)
Schlechter's homeria (E)
(Named after the German botanist, Rudolf Schlechter, who first collected the species)
Cormous perennial to 60 cm high, the stem usually well-branched. Leaves several, strap-shaped and channelled. Flowers pale yellow with six spreading petals marked with dark blotches at the base, 30–35 mm diameter, each lasting only a single morning and withering at around 1.00 pm.
Habitat: Stony or gravelly flats in open scrub.

Ixia rapunculoides
IRIS FAMILY
Blue ixia (E), bloukalossie (A)
(Resembling a rampion, or campanula, in its flowers)
Slender cormous perennial, 15–70 cm high, often with side branches. Leaves narrowly sword-shaped. Flowers funnel-shaped, blue or mauve, 10–15 mm diameter.
Habitat: Mainly clay soils in renosterveld.

Romulea tortuosa
IRIS FAMILY
Golden romulea (E)
(Latin *tortuosus*, twisted, referring to the leaves)
Cormous perennial to 5 cm high, often in large colonies, the corm flattened and fan-like. Leaves several, needle-like with a narrow groove along the top and twisted or coiled. Flowers cup-shaped, bright yellow with or without dark markings in the throat, lightly scented, 15–25 mm diameter, the floral bracts mostly papery and translucent and the fruits carried on coiled stalks.
Habitat: Seasonally wet gravelly or clay flats or seeps.

Namaqualand

Romulea citrina
IRIS FAMILY
Lemon romulea (E)
(Latin *citrinus*, lemon yellow)
Cormous perennial to 12 cm high, the corm with a fringed U-shaped ridge along the base. Leaves several, needle-like with four narrow grooves along their length. Flowers pale to deep yellow, 20–25 mm diameter, the floral bracts with narrow membranous margins.
Habitat: Seasonal seeps or washes in gravelly soils.

Romulea namaquensis
IRIS FAMILY
Namaqua romulea (E)
(Latin *namaquensis*, from Namaqualand)
Cormous perennial to 20 cm high, the corm with a fringed U-shaped ridge along the base. Leaves several, needle-like with four narrow grooves along their length. Flowers pink to coppery orange or rarely white and usually with dark markings in the pale greenish throat, 20–30 mm diameter, the floral bracts with narrow membranous margins.
Habitat: Seasonally moist gravelly seeps on granite outcrops.

Romulea subfistulosa
IRIS FAMILY
Thick-leaved romulea (E)
(Latin *subfistulosus*, somewhat hollow and pipe-like, referring to the spongy leaves)
Cormous perennial to 10 cm high, the corm rounded with curved teeth at the base. Leaves several, curved and somewhat spongy with four broad grooves along their length. Flowers magenta to deep pink with dark blotches around the yellow cup, 20–40 mm diameter, the floral bracts with brown-spotted membranous margins and a prominent membranous tip and the fruits carried on slightly arched stalks.
Habitat: Seasonally moist dolerite clay soils, often among rocks, near Sutherland.

Namaqualand

Romulea sabulosa
IRIS FAMILY
Bokkeveld crocus (E)
(Latin *sabulosus*, sand-loving, a misnomer as the species prefers clay soils)
Cormous perennial to 10 cm high, the corm rounded with curved teeth at the base. Leaves several, needle-like with four narrow grooves along their length. Flowers dark red or rarely pink with black blotches at the edge of a creamy green cup, 30–50 mm diameter, the floral bracts with narrow membranous margins.
Habitat: Seasonally moist clay flats in open renosterveld.
Notes: *Romulea monadelpha* has black filaments.

Hesperantha cucullata
IRIS FAMILY
Bokkeveld hesperantha (E), bokkeveldaandblom (A)
(Latin *cucullatus*, hooded, a reference to the cupped petals)
Cormous perennial, 15–30 cm high, with a rounded corm. Leaves sword-shaped. Flowers upright with cupped petals, white inside but red to brown on the outside, fragrant, opening in the late afternoon, 18–22 mm diameter.
Habitat: Mainly seasonally moist shale flats in renosterveld.

Hesperantha bachmannii
IRIS FAMILY
Ballerina hesperantha (E)
(Named after the nineteenth-century German naturalist, Frans Bachmann)
Cormous perennial, 15–30 cm high, with a rounded corm. Leaves narrowly sword-shaped. Flowers nodding on a slender, curved tube with the petals bent backwards, sweetly scented, opening in the late afternoon, 15–20 mm diameter.
Habitat: Mainly stony clay slopes in renosterveld.

Namaqualand

Hesperantha vaginata
IRIS FAMILY

Harlequin hesperantha (E), perdeblom (A)
(Latin *vaginatus*, sheathed, referring to the leaves that clasp the stem in the lower part)
Cormous perennial, 12–18 cm high, with a rounded corm. Leaves sword-shaped. Flowers large, cup-shaped, yellow often marked with dark brown, opening in the early afternoon, 25–35 mm diameter.
Habitat: Heavy clay soils usually derived from dolerite.

Hesperantha pauciflora
IRIS FAMILY

Pink hesperantha (E)
(Latin *pauciflorus*, few-flowered)
Cormous perennial to 10 cm high, with corms that have spiny teeth radiating from a flat base. Flowers deep pink to purple, rarely yellow, fragrant, opening in mid-afternoon, 20–25 mm diameter.
Habitat: Seasonally moist clay or gravelly flats in renosterveld.

Geissorhiza splendidissima
IRIS FAMILY

Bokkeveld pride (E)
(Latin *splendidissimus*, most brilliant, referring to the flowers)
Cormous perennial with velvety stems, 8–20 cm high. Leaves narrow and X-shaped in section. Flowers glossy blue-violet with small greenish centres surrounded by prominent black marks and with reddish-brown anthers, 20–25 mm diameter.
Habitat: Stony clay soils in renosterveld.
Notes: Restricted to patches of renosterveld around Nieuwoudtville.

Namaqualand

Sparaxis tricolor
IRIS FAMILY
Harlequin flower (E), fluweeltjie (A)
(Latin *tricolor*, three-coloured)
Cormous perennial, 10–30 cm high. Leaves sword-shaped. Flowers orange with a large yellow and black cup and yellow anthers, 35–40 mm diameter.
Habitat: Seasonally moist stony clay flats in renosterveld, often along streams.
Notes: This and the following species, along with *Sparaxis pillansii*, were used in the breeding programmes that have given us the commercially grown sparaxis hybrids. All three of these species are found in the wild only around Nieuwoudtville.

Sparaxis elegans
IRIS FAMILY
Streptanthera, pale harlequin flower (E), spogfluweeltjie (A)
(Latin *elegans*, elegant)
Cormous perennial, 10–20 cm high. Leaves sword-shaped. Flowers salmon pink or white with a purple cup edged in black and yellow and with coiled, purple anthers, 40–50 mm diameter.
Habitat: Clay flats in renosterveld.

Babiana curviscapa
IRIS FAMILY
(Latin *curviscapus*, with a curved flowering stem)
Dwarf cormous perennial to 10 cm high. Leaves lance-shaped and stiffly pleated, velvety. Flowers on short horizontal stems, with a slender tube sharply bent near the top and usually about twice as long as the petals, brilliant purple or cerise with white markings towards the centre, 20–30 mm diameter.
Habitat: Sandy and gravelly flats in open scrub.
Notes: Usually purple-flowered but cerise in colour around Springbok.

Namaqualand

Babiana attenuata
IRIS FAMILY

Showy babiana (E)

(Latin *attenuatus*, drawn gradually into a sharp point, referring to the petals)

Dwarf cormous perennial to 10 cm high. Leaves lance-shaped and stiffly pleated, velvety. Flowers on short horizontal stems, with a slender, slightly curved tube usually about as long as the petals, brilliant purple or magenta with white markings towards the centre, fragrant, 30–50 mm diameter.
Habitat: Seasonally moist sandy and gravelly flats in open scrub.

Babiana vanzyliae
IRIS FAMILY

Yellow babiana (E), stinkbobbejaantjie (A)

(Named after Mrs Van Zyl, who grew the species in her Cape Town garden)

Dwarf cormous perennial to 12 cm high. Leaves lance-shaped and stiffly pleated, velvety. Flowers with a slender tube somewhat longer than the petals, yellow to mauve, fragrant, 30–50 mm diameter.
Habitat: Stony sandstone in fynbos and renosterveld.

Babiana hirsuta
IRIS FAMILY

(= *Babiana thunbergii*)

Cockscomb (E)

(Latin *hirsutus*, hairy, referring to the branches)

Cormous perennial 40–70 cm high, with short, velvety, horizontal branches. Leaves lance-shaped and stiffly pleated, hairless. Flowers bright red with greenish-yellow and black markings on some of the petals, tubular with the tube curved upwards, 25–35 mm long.
Habitat: Coastal sandy flats and dunes.
Notes: The curious red flowers are pollinated by sunbirds.

Namaqualand

Gladiolus saccatus
IRIS FAMILY

(= *Anomalesia saccata*)

Suikerkannetjie (A)

(Latin *saccatus*, spurred or pouched, a reference to the little spur on the underside of the flowers)

Slender, usually branched cormous perennial, 20–100 cm high, the base of the stems purplish with paler mottling. Leaves narrow and usually with two ribs along their length, often greyish. Flowers facing upwards along the inclined stems, brilliant red with a large, stalked upper petal and five greenish scale-like lower petals, 45–60 mm long.

Habitat: Along shale slopes.

Notes: The curious flowers are adapted to pollination by sunbirds.

Gladiolus scullyi
IRIS FAMILY

Partridge gladiolus (E), patryspypie (A)

(Named after William Scully, Magistrate of Namaqualand in the 1890s)

Cormous perennial, 20–60 cm high. Leaves narrowly sword-shaped. Flowers two-lipped, dull mauve or yellowish grey, strongly scented of violets, 25–30 mm diameter.

Habitat: Stony clay soils in open scrub.

Gladiolus watermeyeri
IRIS FAMILY

Soetkalkoentjie (A)

(Named after Mr E.B. Watermeyer, farmer and surveyor)

Cormous perennial, 10–30 cm high. Leaves narrow and strongly ribbed along their length. Flowers with the upper petal deeply hooded and translucent, the side petals conspicuously veined with brown and the lower tepals yellowish towards the base, strongly scented of violets, 30–40 mm diameter.

Habitat: Rocky sandstone soils in open scrub.

Notes: Marvellously fragrant but very cryptic and more often located first by its smell.

Namaqualand

Gladiolus equitans
IRIS FAMILY
Namaqua kalkoentjie (E), groot rooikalkoentjie (A)
(Latin *equitans*, riding astride, alluding to the successively overlapping leaves)
Cormous perennial, 15–30 cm high. Leaves rather broadly oblong and leathery with thickened reddish margins. Flowers orange to scarlet with the lower tepals yellowish in the lower half, the upper petals broadest and the lower two narrow, 30–35 mm diameter.
Habitat: Granite hills, usually wedged in rock cracks.

Melasphaerula ramosa
IRIS FAMILY
Fairybells (E), feëklokkie, baardmannetjie (A)
(Latin *ramosus*, branched)
Cormous perennial, 30–60 cm high. Leaves sword-shaped and soft-textured. Flowers on slender, wiry branches, small and two-lipped, cream to pale yellow with the lower petals streaked with reddish brown, 10 mm diameter.
Habitat: Rocky slopes, usually sheltered by rocks or shrubs.

Lapeirousia silenoides
IRIS FAMILY
Springbok painted petals (E), cabong (N)
(Resembling the genus *Silene* in its flowers)
Tufted, dwarf cormous perennial, 5–12 cm high. Leaves narrow and conspicuously ribbed along their length, the lowermost longest and arching. Flowers crowded, with long slender tubes 30–50 mm long, magenta to cerise with cream-coloured markings in the centre, 15–20 mm diameter.
Habitat: Seasonally moist gravelly granite-derived soils.
Notes: Common along the roadsides near Kamieskroon. Pollinated by long-proboscid flies.

Namaqualand

Lapeirousia arenicola
IRIS FAMILY

(Latin *arenicola,* sand-dwelling, alluding to its favoured habitat)

Tufted, dwarf cormous perennial, 10–12 cm high. Leaves narrow and conspicuously ribbed along their length, the lowermost longest and arching. Flowers crowded, with slender tubes 10–30 mm long, cream to pink with red spots at the base of the lower three petals, 10–15 mm diameter.
Habitat: Deep sandy flats towards the coast.
Notes: Most commonly seen on the sandy flats north-west of Vanrhynsdorp.

Euphorbia dregeana
EUPHORBIA FAMILY

Dikloot-melkbos (A)

(One of many species commemorating the plant collector J.F. Drége)

Rounded succulent shrub to 2 m high, with straight, cane-like branches that are 8–12 mm diameter, pale greyish with prominent leaf scars and exuding a milky sap when damaged. Leaves reduced to scales and soon deciduous. Flower heads in loose flat-topped clusters at the branch tips, yellowish, 6–8 mm diameter.
Habitat: Dry rocky slopes.

Euphorbia hamata
EUPHORBIA FAMILY

Beesmelkbos, beeskrag (A)

(Latin *hamatus,* hooked, referring to the prong-like tubercles on the stems)

Bushy succulent shrublet to 45 cm high, with somewhat three-angled branches 6–13 mm diameter, covered with prominent spreading or curved tubercles, exuding a milky sap when damaged. Leaves elliptical but soon deciduous. Flower heads unisexual, solitary at the branch tips and surrounded by three prominent, often pinkish leaf-like bracts, yellowish, honey-scented, 5–7 mm diameter.
Habitat: Dry stony slopes.

Namaqualand

Crassula columnaris
CRASSULA FAMILY
Khakibutton (E), sentkannetjie, bergkoesnaatjie (A)
(Latin *columnaris*, columnar, alluding to the shape of the plant)
Dwarf perennial or biennial succulent to 10 cm high, sometimes branched at the base. Leaves opposite, succulent, scale-like with minutely hairy margins, closely overlapping in four rows to form a column. Flowers in a round head, tubular, white to yellow or tinged reddish, fragrant, 7–13 mm long.
Habitat: Rock pavements and quartz patches.

Crassula brevifolia
CRASSULA FAMILY
(Latin *brevifolius*, short-leaved)
Twiggy shrublets to 50 cm high. Leaves opposite, succulent and clustered towards the ends of the branches, boat-shaped with hard, translucent margins and covered with a grey bloom. Flowers in clusters on slender stalks at the branch tips, yellowish or white tinged pink, cup-shaped, 3–5 mm diameter.
Habitat: In crevices on granite or quartzite outcrops.

Tylecodon wallichii
CRASSULA FAMILY
Yellow butterbush (E), kokerbos, kandelaarbos (A)
(Named after the nineteenth-century Danish botanist, Nathaniel Wallich)
Succulent shrublet to 1 m high, with fibrous stems that are covered with short, blunt protuberances formed from the leaf bases. Leaves dry or shed at flowering, lance-shaped to rounded. Flowers in a spreading panicle, urn-shaped, nodding, greenish yellow, 10–15 mm long.
Habitat: Dry stony soils among scrub.

Namaqualand

Tylecodon paniculatus
CRASSULA FAMILY
Common butterbush (E), botterboom (A)
(Latin *paniculatus*, bearing the flowers in a branched raceme or panicle)

Succulent shrublet to 1,5 m high. Leaves deciduous and usually withered at flowering, broadly rounded and fleshy, bright green. Flowers in reddish panicles, nodding and shortly tubular, greenish to orange or red, 20–25 mm long.
Habitat: Dry rocky slopes in scrub.
Notes: Seldom grazed by stock but sometimes eaten in summer, causing cramping or death.

Cotyledon orbiculata
CRASSULA FAMILY
Dog's ears (E), plakkie, hondeoor (A)
(Latin *orbiculatus*, circular, referring to the rounded leaves)

Brittle perennial shrublet to 1 m high, more or less covered with a powdery white bloom. Leaves opposite, succulent and very varied in shape, grey with a red or pale margin. Flowers pendulous, tubular with recurved lobes, red or orange, 25–30 mm long.
Habitat: Widespread in coastal and inland scrub on sandy or stony soils.
Notes: Flower stalks used by early hunters as a flute to mimic the call of a young klipspringer, luring the adults within arrow range.

Tetragonia fruticosa
MESEMB FAMILY
Klimopkinkelbossie, waterslaaibos (A)
(Latin *fruticosus*, shrubby)

Erect or sprawling shrub to 1 m high, often with long trailing branches. Leaves somewhat diamond-shaped, fleshy with the margins rolled under and covered with glistening papillae. Flowers in small groups towards the ends of the branches, yellow, 3–4 mm diameter. Fruits broadly four-winged, with knobs between the wings.
Habitat: Gravelly and sandy soils, especially along the coast.

Namaqualand

Mesembryanthemum guerichianum
MESEMB FAMILY
Ice plant (E), brakvy (A), kama, nuta (N)
(Named for Georg Gürich, a German geologist, who collected the species)

Trailing or sprawling succulent annual or biennial to 60 cm high with four-angled stems. Leaves in a basal tuft and along the stems, ovate and folded, covered with large, glistening bladder cells and often flushed reddish, to 25 × 10 cm. Flowers in branched clusters, pink with a white or greenish centre, 25–55 mm diameter. Fruits five-segmented.
Habitat: Sandy flats, often along roadsides.

Mesembryanthemum barklyi
MESEMB FAMILY
Giant ice plant, elephant's toilet paper (E), olifantslaai (A), kama, nuta (N)
(Named for Sir H. Barkly, who first collected the species)

Trailing or sprawling succulent annual or biennial to 1 m with four-angled stems. Leaves in a basal tuft and along the stems, ovate, covered with glistening bladder cells, to 40 × 25 cm. Flowers in branched clusters, pink or white, 25–55 mm diameter. Fruits five-segmented.
Habitat: Sandy plains.
Notes: May form large fields.

Cleretum papulosum
MESEMB FAMILY
(Latin *papulosus*, with nipple-like pustules, referring to the leaves)

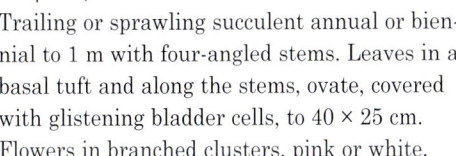

Tufted annual herb to 5 cm high. Leaves mostly in a basal tuft, elliptical and lightly channelled, covered with large bladder cells. Flowers solitary on short stalks, yellow, 10–40 mm diameter. Fruits five-segmented.
Habitat: Sandy or gravelly flats.
Notes: Occurs in two forms, an early blooming, small-flowered form (subspecies *papulosum*) that is self-fertilised and a later blooming, large-flowered form (subspecies *schlechteri*) that is cross-fertilised.

Namaqualand

Dorotheanthus maughanii
MESEMB FAMILY
Karoo snow (E)
(Named after Dr Maughan Brown, resident in Calvinia, who first collected the species)
Tufted annual herb to 5 cm high. Leaves mostly in a basal tuft, spade-shaped, covered with large bladder cells. Flowers solitary on slender stalks, white with a red centre, with prominent, glistening, knob-like stigmas, 50–60 mm diameter. Fruits five-segmented.
Habitat: Dry gravelly clay in karroid scrub.
Notes: Common near Calvinia.

Dorotheanthus rourkei
MESEMB FAMILY
(Named after Cape Town botanist, John Rourke)
Tufted annual herb to 5 cm high. Leaves mostly in a basal tuft, narrowly paddle-shaped, covered with large bladder cells. Flowers solitary on slender stalks, white, yellow, orange or pinkish to red, 20–40 mm diameter. Fruits five-segmented.
Habitat: Deep red sands.
Notes: Common on the sandy flats north of Vanrhynsdorp.

Mesembryanthemum brevicarpum
MESEMB FAMILY
(= *Aridaria brevicarpa*)
Day-blooming donkeybush (E)
(Greek *brevicarpus*, short-fruited, referring to the almost globular capsules)
Twiggy shrub to 1 m high. Leaves succulent and cylindrical, to 30 × 4 mm. Flowers white to pale pink, closing at dusk, 25 mm diameter. Fruits subglobose, remaining open when dry.
Habitat: Sandy and gravelly slopes.

Namaqualand

Lampranthus watermeyeri
MESEMB FAMILY
Watermeyer's lampranthus (E)
(Named after local resident E.B. Watermeyer, who first collected the species)
Rounded succulent shrublet to 30 cm high. Leaves incurved and ± cylindrical, 20–35 × 6 mm. Flowers mostly solitary on long stalks, white or rarely purple, 50–70 mm diameter. Fruits five-segmented.
Habitat: Stony flats in low scrub.

Lampranthus hoerleinianus
MESEMB FAMILY
Hörlein's lampranthus (E)
(Named after a Mr Hörlein, probably of Consolidated Diamond Mines, who facilitated the expedition on which the species was first collected)
Succulent shrublet to 70 cm high. Leaves spreading and ± three-sided, 25–30 × 9 mm. Flowers on very short stalks, purple, 30–40 mm diameter. Fruits five-segmented.
Habitat: Sandy places among rocks.

Ruschia goodiae
MESEMB FAMILY
Namaqua cushion ruschia (E)
(Named for a Mrs Good who first collected the species)
Rounded succulent shrub to 60 cm high, with erect, yellowish branches. Leaves three-angled and succulent. Flowers in clusters, pinkish magenta, 20–25 mm diameter. Fruits five-segmented, top-shaped.
Habitat: Gravelly granite slopes.

Namaqualand

Ruschia extensa
MESEMB FAMILY
Namaqua bush ruschia (E)
(Latin *extensus*, stretched out, referring to the long internodes)
Rounded shrub to 1 m high, with spreading, reddish branches. Leaves succulent and almost cylindrical. Flowers in clusters, with a central cone of staminodes, magenta, 15 mm diameter.
Habitat: Gravelly granite slopes.

Drosanthemum hispidum
MESEMB FAMILY
Roadside dew vygie (E)
(Latin *hispidus*, bristly, referring to the branches)
Erect or spreading shrublet to 60 cm high, with red branches covered in short, stiff hairs. Leaves sausage-shaped, bending downwards, rounded at the tips and densely covered with small bladder cells. Flowers solitary, magenta, 20 mm diameter. Fruits 4–6-segmented.
Habitat: Pioneer of disturbed, dry flats and roadsides.

Malephora crocea
MESEMB FAMILY
Saffron finger kanna (E), rooivinger-kanna (A)
(Latin *croceus*, saffron yellow)
Erect succulent shrublet to 20 cm high. Leaves crowded on short shoots, finger-like and three-sided. Flowers solitary on short stalks at the branch tips, orange to red, 25–30 mm diameter. Fruits 8–12-segmented.
Habitat: Dry sandy flats.

Namaqualand

Cheiridopsis namaquensis
MESEMB FAMILY
(= *Cheiridopsis cigarettifera*)
Cigarettes (E)
(Latin *namaquensis*, from Namaqualand)

Compact, cushion-forming succulent perennial to 5 cm high. Leaves of two sizes, three-sided and pincer-like, slightly warty on the keels, drying to form a cylindrical papery sheath. Flowers yellow fading red, 30–45 mm diameter. Fruits with ±10 segments.
Habitat: Stony slopes and rock crevices.

Cheiridopsis denticulata
MESEMB FAMILY
T'noutsiama (N)
(Latin *denticulatus*, finely toothed, referring to the leaf keels)

Compact, cushion-forming succulent perennial to 10 cm high. Leaves three-sided, warty and usually with some teeth on the keels, drying to form a cylindrical papery sheath. Flowers cream to yellow and often purplish towards the edges, 60–70 mm diameter. Fruits with 17–19 segments.
Habitat: Sandy and gravelly flats, often in seasonal washes.

Conicosia elongata
MESEMB FAMILY
Goslings (E), gansies, varkslaai (A)
(Latin *elongatus*, elongate, referring to the slender leaves)

Sprawling succulent perennial with a tuber, 10–20 cm high. Leaves slender and tapering, cylindrical to half-cylindrical. Flowers solitary, white or yellow, 50–60 mm diameter. Fruits cone-shaped with 10–25 flaps, opening when dry.
Habitat: Sandy flats, often coastal.
Notes: One of very few mesembs with fruits that open when dry rather than when wet.

Namaqualand

Jordaaniella cuprea
MESEMB FAMILY
Copper mat vygie (E)
(Latin *cupreus*, coppery, referring to the flower colour)

Creeping succulent perennial forming compact mats. Leaves finger-shaped, 5–10 cm long. Flowers solitary on short side branches, yellow to salmon-coloured with orange to pink edging, 30–100 mm diameter. Fruits on horizontal stalks, 14–20-segmented.
Habitat: Coastal sands.
Notes: Common near Port Nolloth.

Cephalophyllum pillansii
MESEMB FAMILY
Namaqua creeping vygie (E)
(Named for Cape Town botanist, N.S. Pillans, who first collected the species)

Compact succulent shrublet to 10 cm high, with creeping, annual branches. Leaves erect, cylindrical and succulent, greyish. Flowers solitary on slender stalks, pale yellow with a red centre, 60 mm diameter. Fruits 10–15-segmented.
Habitat: Loamy granite flats, often a pioneer along road banks.

Cephalophyllum spongiosum
MESEMB FAMILY
Giant mat vygie (E), volstruisvygie (A)
(Latin *spongiosus*, spongy and succulent, referring to the leaves)

Sprawling or trailing succulent perennial. Leaves large and finger-shaped, ±10 cm long. Flowers solitary on short side branches, red with an orange centre, 70–100 mm diameter. Fruits on erect stalks, 18–28-segmented.
Habitat: Coastal sands in scrub.

Namaqualand

Cephalophyllum spissum
MESEMB FAMILY
(Latin *spissus*, compact, dense, alluding to the plant form)
Compact, cushion-forming succulent perennial to 10 cm high. Leaves finger-shaped and three-sided. Flowers solitary or few on short stalks, purple to pink with a paler centre, 30–40 mm diameter. Fruits 11–15-segmented.
Habitat: Quartz patches.

Monilaria moniliformis
MESEMB FAMILY
White beaded vygie (E), ertjievygie (A)
(Latin *moniliformis*, like a string of beads, referring to the curious stems)
Cushion-forming succulent shrublet to 12 cm high, with the branches pinched like a string of barrel-shaped beads. Leaves finger-like, fleshy, covered with glistening bladder cells. Flowers solitary on long stalks, white, 35–40 mm diameter. Fruits 5–7-segmented.
Habitat: Quartz patches and stony quartzite slopes.

Mesembryanthemum digitatum
MESEMB FAMILY
(= *Dactylopsis digitata*)
Hitchhiker plant (E),
vingertjie-en-duimpie (A)
(Latin *digitatus*, with the leaves arranged like fingers)
Compact succulent perennial to 20 cm high. Leaves very succulent and cylindrical, the first short and stubby and the second emerging at an angle and longer, thus resembling a thumb and finger. Flowers white to cream, 10–20 mm diameter, remaining open day and night. Fruits five-segmented.
Habitat: Gravelly quartz patches.

Namaqualand

Argyroderma fissum
MESEMB FAMILY
False stoneflower (E)
(Latin *fissus*, cleft or split, referring to the distinct leaf pairs)

Tufted succulent to 15 cm high, usually forming clumps. Leaves reduced to a single pair, finger-like but often flattened on the upper side, firm and highly succulent. Flowers solitary, protruding from between the leaves, purple with a white centre, 30–40 mm diameter. Fruits 14–18-segmented.
Habitat: Patches of gravelly white quartz on the Knersvlakte.

Argyroderma delaetii
MESEMB FAMILY
Silver stoneflower (E), bababoudjies, jakkalsniertjie (A)
(Named after the succulent grower, Mr de Laet-Contich, in whose collection the species was first noticed)

Dwarf succulents to 5 cm high, solitary or forming clumps. Leaves reduced to a single pair, almost globular, smooth, silver-skinned, firm and highly succulent. Flowers solitary, protruding from between the leaves, white to purple or yellow, 30–40 mm diameter. Fruits 14–18-segmented.
Habitat: Patches of gravelly white quartz on the Knersvlakte north of Vanrhynsdorp.

Conophytum subfenestratum
MESEMB FAMILY
Fenestrate coneflower (E)
(Latin *sub-, fenestratus*, somewhat windowed, referring to the transparent patches on the leaves)

Dwarf succulent perennial to 5 cm high, usually solitary. Leaves reduced to a single pair joined together into a rounded body with more or less transparent patches or windows at the top, 20–25 mm long. Flowers solitary with the petals joined into a slender tube protruding from the mouth of the leaf-body, pink, 15–20 mm diameter.
Habitat: Gravelly quartz fields.

Namaqualand

Conophytum minutum
MESEMB FAMILY
Common coneflower (E), toontjies (A)
(Latin *minutus*, very small, minute)
Dwarf succulent perennial to
5 cm high, forming clumps. Leaves reduced to
a single pair joined together into a cone-like
body, spotted, 15–20 mm long. Flowers solitary
with the petals joined into a slender tube
protruding from the mouth of the leaf-body,
magenta to pink, 10–15 mm diameter.
Habitat: Rock sheets or quartzite outcrops.

Oophytum nanum
MESEMB FAMILY
Pebbleflower (E)
(Latin *nanus*, dwarf)
Dwarf succulent perennial to
5 cm high, forming clumps. Leaves reduced to
two pairs joined together into a small globular
body, 10 mm long. Flowers solitary and protruding from the mouth of the leaf-body, pink
with a paler centre, 20–25 mm diameter.
Habitat: Gravelly quartz fields.

Hypertelis salsoloides
MOLLUGO FAMILY
Braksuring (A)
(Resembling the genus *Salsola* or saltwort)
Dwarf, tufted shrublet to 30 cm
high, often much-grazed. Leaves cylindrical
and fleshy, greyish. Flowers in umbels on slender, glandular pedicels which bend down after
flowering, white to pink with the sepals folded
back, 10–12 mm diameter.
Habitat: Dry, often limey or saline soils.

Namaqualand

Augea capensis
ZYGOPHYLLUM FAMILY
Elandslaai, boesmandruiwe (A)
(Latin *capensis*, from the Cape)

Brittle succulent annual or
short-lived perennial to 40 cm high. Leaves
opposite and cylindrical or club-shaped, very
succulent. Flowers in small clusters, whitish
with the petals three-toothed at the ends,
15 mm diameter. Fruits large and egg-shaped
with woolly seeds.
Habitat: Dry sandy flats.

Roepera morgsana
ZYGOPHYLLUM FAMILY
(= *Zygophyllum morgsana*)
Four-winged twinleaf (E), slaaibos (A)
(Named for the similarity of the leaves to
those of a Syrian species, *Z. fabago*, locally
known as 'morgsani')

Rounded shrub with grey stems to 1,5 m high.
Leaves opposite and shortly stalked, fleshy and
divided into two broad leaflets with an unpleasant smell when crushed. Flowers in pairs
between the leaves, with four petals that are
pale yellow with a purple blotch just above
the base, 20 mm diameter. Fruits rounded
with four large wings.
Habitat: Sandy flats, often coastal.
Notes: Leaves and seeds are poisonous.

Roepera cordifolia
ZYGOPHYLLUM FAMILY
(= *Zygophyllum cordifolium*)
Penny-leaved twinleaf (E), sjielingbos,
geldjiesbos (A)
(Latin *cordifolius*, heart-shaped with two lobes,
alluding to the paired, rounded leaves)

Greyish shrublet to 70 cm high. Leaves opposite and not stalked, fleshy and almost circular.
Flowers in pairs between the leaves with five
petals that are pale yellow with a prominent
red blotch near the base, 20 mm diameter.
Fruits egg-shaped with five narrow wings.
Habitat: Sandy or gravelly flats, often coastal.

Namaqualand

Tribulus cristatus
ZYGOPHYLLUM FAMILY

(Latin *cristatus*, crested, referring to the winged fruits)

Prostrate annual with stems radiating from a crown. Leaves opposite and unequal in size, divided into numerous oblong, silky leaflets. Flowers solitary in the leaf axils, bright yellow, 20 mm diameter. Fruits with four crested wings.
Habitat: Sandy flats and roadsides.
Notes: A similar species, *T. zeyheri*, has small, spiny fruits that fragment into four segments.

Grielum humifusum
DUIKER-ROOT FAMILY

White-eyed duiker-root (E), duikerwortel (A), t'koeibee (N)

(Latin *humifusus*, spreading on the ground)

Prostrate, thinly white-woolly annual often forming mats. Leaves lobed to deeply divided into flat segments that are rounded at the tips and nearly hairless above. Flowers yellow, usually with a pale eye, 20–30 mm in diameter.
Habitat: Sandy lower slopes and flats.
Notes: Fleshy roots are edible although slimy. Common along roadsides and in fallow lands.

Grielum grandiflorum
DUIKER-ROOT FAMILY

Green-eyed duiker-root (E), platdoring (A)

(Latin *grandiflorus*, large-flowered)

Sprawling white-woolly perennial forming mats. Leaves deeply divided into narrow to thread-like segments, each with a small pointed tip and covered with silvery hairs. Flowers yellow, usually greenish in the centre, 35–50 mm diameter.
Habitat: Sandy and stony coastal flats.

Namaqualand

Monsonia parvifolia
GERANIUM FAMILY
Desert parasol-flower (E)
(Latin *parvifolius*, small-leaved)
Mat-forming perennial to 1 m diameter with the branches covered in glandular hairs. Leaves broadly ovate with irregularly toothed margins. Flowers few on slender stalks in the leaf axils, yellow or white to pink, 25–35 mm diameter.
Habitat: Dry sandy flats.

Monsonia crassicaule
GERANIUM FAMILY
(= *Sarcocaulon crassicaule*)
Bushman's candle (E), boesmanskers (A), noerap (N)
(Latin *crassicaulis*, thick-stemmed)
Spiny shrublet to 50 cm high, with succulent branches thicker than 10 mm diameter. Leaves ovate and irregularly divided with the margins toothed, usually hairy. Flowers pale to bright yellow, to 55 mm diameter with the sepals each bearing a sharp point at the tips longer than 2 mm.
Habitat: Dry rocky or stony slopes.
Notes: *Monsonia ciliata* has the petals fringed with fine hairs. *Monsonia spinosa* has notched leaves with smooth margins.

Pelargonium echinatum
GERANIUM FAMILY
Hedgehog stork's bill (E), krimpvarkmalva (A)
(Latin *echinatus*, armed with prickles or spines like a hedgehog)
Fleshy shrublet to 50 cm high, with gnarled, dark grey, prickly stems. Leaves rounded and shallowly three- to seven-lobed, grey-powdery beneath. Flowers in clusters on prominent stalks, white or pale pink to brilliant magenta with dark red streaks and blotches on the upper petals, 18–25 mm diameter.
Habitat: Rocky slopes in scrub.

Namaqualand

Pelargonium crithmifolium
GERANIUM FAMILY
Dikbasmalva (A)
(Latin *crithmifolium*, with leaves like a *Crithmum* or samphire)

Fleshy shrublet to 1 m high, with smooth, swollen, pale greenish stems. Leaves fleshy and deeply divided into narrow, toothed lobes. Flowers in branched clusters, pale pink with reddish flecks on the upper petals, 15–20 mm diameter, the old pedicels becoming stiff and thorny.
Habitat: Dry stony soils.

Pelargonium sericifolium
GERANIUM FAMILY
Silver-leaved stork's bill (E)
(Latin *sericifolium*, leaves with silky hairs pressed to the surface)

Closely branched shrublet to 20 cm high, with the remains of the leaf bases persisting on the branches. Leaves deeply divided into narrow segments covered with silvery silky hairs. Flowers in pairs at the branch tips on slender pedicels, brilliant magenta with darker streaks on the three lower petals, 20 mm diameter.
Habitat: Rocky or stony granite slopes near Springbok.

Pelargonium incrassatum
GERANIUM FAMILY
T'neitjie (N)
(Latin *incrassatus*, thickened, a mistaken reference to the leaves which are not evidently leathery or succulent)

Tufted tuberous perennial to 50 cm high, with a large tuber covered with flaking brown bark. Leaves in a tuft, irregularly lobed and soft and silky with a silvery sheen. Flowers in dense rounded clusters on long stalks, brilliant magenta with the three lower petals very much smaller than the upper, 15 mm diameter.
Habitat: Gravelly soils.
Notes: Easily the most outstanding pelargonium in Namaqualand. The tubers were a traditional food source.

Namaqualand

Pelargonium praemorsum
GERANIUM FAMILY
Engeltjiemalva (A)
(Latin *praemorsus*, much bitten, alluding to the distinctly toothed leaves that appear to have been bitten off at the ends)
Twiggy shrublet to 1 m high, with jointed, brown stems. Leaves fleshy and deeply divided with five toothed lobes. Flowers mostly solitary, white with red veining on the two upper petals and with only two, smaller lower petals, 25–35 mm diameter.
Habitat: Rocky slopes in open scrub.

Montinia caryophyllacea
MONTINIA FAMILY
Peperbos (A), t'iena (N)
(Latin *caryophyllaceus*, resembling certain members of the carnation family Caryophyllaceae in its flowers)
Erect greyish shrub to 1,5 m high. Leaves elliptical, leathery and sometimes in tufts. Flowers at the branch tips with the sexes on separate plants, the male flowers in small clusters and the female flowers solitary or in pairs, white, 8 mm diameter.
Habitat: Stony or rocky slopes in scrub.
Notes: The hard stems were used by the Khoisan as digging sticks.

Solanum giftbergense
POTATO FAMILY
Gifappeltjie (A)
(Latin *giftbergensis*, from the Gifberg near Klawer)
Shrub to 1,5 m high, with mealy stems armed with slender, yellow or reddish-brown spines to 12 mm long. Leaves ovate and conspicuously lobed, spiny on the veins. Flowers in clusters of one to four, mauve to purple, to 10 mm diameter. Berries orange to red and 10 mm diameter.
Habitat: Rocky slopes.
Notes: The berries of all solanums should be regarded as poisonous.

Namaqualand

Gomphocarpus cancellatus
MILKWEED FAMILY
(= *Asclepias cancellata*)
Milkweed (E), katoenbos (A)
(Latin *cancellatus*, latticed, alluding to the lacy appearance of the flower heads)

Shrub to 1,5 m high, with hairy branches oozing a milky sap when damaged. Leaves opposite, elliptical and leathery with wavy margins. Flowers cream-coloured and green, 10 mm diameter. Fruits swollen and teardrop-shaped with fleshy spines.
Habitat: Stony slopes.
Notes: All milkweeds should be regarded as toxic. Powdered roots used as a snuff.

Hoodia gordonii
MILKWEED FAMILY
Hoodia (E), wolweghaap (A), ghaap (N)
(Commemorates Col. Robert Gordon, commander of the garrison at the Cape, who collected the species in 1779)

Leafless succulent producing clumps of 11–17-ridged stems closely covered with spine-tipped warts. Flowers saucer-shaped, pinkish to maroon and foul-smelling, 40–100 mm diameter.
Habitat: Dry stony slopes and flats.
Notes: Used traditionally by the San as an appetite suppressant. Now exploited commercially for appetite suppressants.

Pachypodium namaquanum
MILKWEED FAMILY
Halfmens (A)
(Latin *namaquensis*, from Namaqualand)

Usually single-stemmed succulent trees to 3 m high, with a tapering, swollen stem covered with spine-tipped warts. Leaves elliptical and densely velvety with wavy margins. Flowers clustered among the leaves, tubular, yellowish green outside and reddish inside, *c*.50 mm long.
Habitat: Very arid rocky slopes.
Notes: Stems tilted towards the north, probably as protection from overheating in the summer sun.

Namaqualand

Oxalis comosa
OXALIS FAMILY
Rock sorrel (E)
(Latin *comosus*, bearing a tuft of leaves)
Erect and often branched cormous perennial to 80 cm high. Leaves crowded at the tips of the stems and branches, divided into three triangular leaflets that are deeply notched at the tips and either hairless or sparsely hairy beneath. Flowers solitary on slender stalks from the leaf clusters, pale pink with a yellow cup, 15 mm diameter.
Habitat: Rocky granite outcrops, often in the shade of boulders.
Notes: Common in the Kamiesberg.

Oxalis namaquana
OXALIS FAMILY
Namaqua sorrel (E), namakwasuring (A)
(Latin *namaquensis*, from Namaqualand)
Tufted cormous perennial to 10 cm high. Leaves divided into three hairless oblong leaflets that are shortly notched at the tips. Flowers solitary on slender stalks, bright yellow, 20 mm diameter.
Habitat: Along seasonal streams and in seeps on granite outcrops.

Oxalis obtusa
OXALIS FAMILY
Yellow-eyed sorrel (E), geeloogsuring (A)
(Latin *obtusus*, blunt, referring to the leaflets)
Tufted cormous perennial to 10 cm high. Leaves divided into three broad, hairy or hairless leaflets that are deeply notched at the tips. Flowers solitary on slender stalks that bear a pair of minute scales at a joint near the middle, pink, brick-red or pale yellow with a yellow eye and usually with reddish veining on the petals, 20 mm diameter.
Habitat: Common and widespread on sandy, gravelly or clay soils, often in the shelter of rocks.

Namaqualand

Oxalis callosa
OXALIS FAMILY
Red-eyed sorrel (E)
(Latin *callosus*, bearing a callus or wart, a reference to the orange calli on the sepals, a common feature in oxalis)
Small cormous perennial to 10 cm high. Leaves on hairy petioles and divided into three elliptical leaflets that are lightly notched at the tips and hairy beneath. Flowers solitary on slender hairy stalks, pink with a yellow tube ringed with purple at the mouth, 20 mm across.
Habitat: Clay flats.
Notes: Common between Nieuwoudtville and Calvinia.

Oxalis pulchella
OXALIS FAMILY
Large sorrel (E), grootsuring (A)
(Latin *pulchellus*, beautiful and little)
Tufted cormous perennial to 15 cm high. Leaves divided into three oblong leaflets that are shortly notched at the tips and sparsely hairy beneath. Flowers solitary on slender stalks, pale lilac with a broad yellow cup, 20–30 mm diameter.
Habitat: Sheltered spots on granite outcrops.

Wahlenbergia annularis
BELLFLOWER FAMILY
Greater bellflower (E), pronkblouklokkie (A)
(Latin *annularis*, ring-shaped, referring to the often ring-shaped gland below the stigma)
Tufted annual herb to 40 cm high. Leaves mostly in a basal tuft, elliptical and roughly hairy with wavy margins. Flowers on long slender stalks, bowl-shaped, white to pale blue, 15–20 mm diameter.
Habitat: Sandy flats and lower slopes.
Notes: Similar to *W. androsacea*, which has smaller, deeper flowers.

Namaqualand

Heliophila coronopifolia
CABBAGE FAMILY
Showy sunflax (E), sporrie (A)
(Latin *coronopifolius*, with leaves like swine-cress, *Coronopus*)
Annual herb to 60 cm high with the stem roughly hairy below. Leaves narrow but sometimes lobed. Flowers blue with a white or greenish centre, 15 mm diameter. Fruits slender and beaded, 30–90 mm long.
Habitat: Gravelly and sandy flats and lower slopes.

Heliophila variabilis
CABBAGE FAMILY
Sporrie (A)
(Latin *variabilis*, varying in colour, a reference to the flowers which open white but turn pink with age)
Erect or spreading annual herb to 35 cm high, with minutely hairy stems and leaves. Leaves divided into three to seven thread-like segments. Flowers white turning pinkish with age, 10 mm diameter. Fruits narrow and weakly beaded, 20–40 mm long.
Habitat: Dry sandy or gravelly flats.

Pharnaceum aurantium
MOLLUGO FAMILY
Karoosneeuvygie (A)
(Latin *aurantius*, orange, referring to the colour of the flowers in the original specimens seen)
Sprawling or erect shrublet to 80 cm high. Leaves scattered along the stems, small and needle-like with membranous, fringed stipules at the base. Flowers on long wiry pedicels that flex down in fruit, white to yellow or rarely orange, 5 mm diameter.
Habitat: Stony or gravelly slopes in open scrub.
Notes: Flowers are usually white but populations near Garies have wonderful orange flowers.

Namaqualand

Hermannia trifurca
MALLOW FAMILY
Koerhassie, koerasie (N)
(Latin *trifurcatus*, three-forked, alluding to the leaves)

Twiggy shrublet to 1 m high. Leaves oblong, often blunt and three-toothed at the tips, leathery with a greyish powdery surface. Flowers nodding on slender, arching, one-sided racemes, pinkish mauve, slightly sour smelling, 10–12 mm long.
Habitat: Rocky slopes in scrub.

Hermannia stricta
MALLOW FAMILY
Desert rose (E)

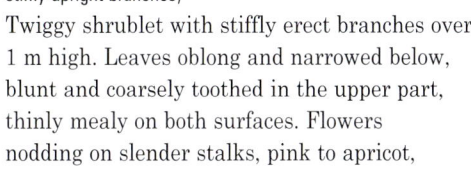

(Latin *strictus*, very straight, referring to the stiffly upright branches)
Twiggy shrublet with stiffly erect branches over 1 m high. Leaves oblong and narrowed below, blunt and coarsely toothed in the upper part, thinly mealy on both surfaces. Flowers nodding on slender stalks, pink to apricot, 15–25 mm diameter.
Habitat: Dry stony slopes.
Notes: May become covered in charming, lantern-shaped flowers.

Hermannia disermifolia
MALLOW FAMILY
Jeukbos (A)
(Greek, origin obscure, possibly suggesting with leaves like *Salvia disermas*)
Twiggy shrublet to 1 m high, with mealy branches. Leaves oblong and stiffly leathery with crisped margins, densely mealy on both surfaces. Flowers nodding on slender stalks, yellow, 10 mm diameter.
Habitat: Granite outcrops.

Namaqualand

Melianthus pectinatus
MELIANTHUS FAMILY

Namaqua turkeybush (E)

(Latin *pectinatus*, with narrow divisions like a comb, referring to the leaves)

Shrub to 2 m high. Leaves divided into narrow, often toothed leaflets with the margins rolled under, hairless above but hairy beneath. Flowers in whorls of two to four in erect racemes among the leaves, with red petals in bud that turn brown at maturity, 20–25 mm long. Fruits with four large wings.

Habitat: Rocky granite outcrops.

Notes: The curiously shaped flowers, that appear withered when they are in fact in full bloom, are pollinated by nectar-feeding birds.

Lebeckia sericea
PEA FAMILY

Silver ganna (E), blou fluitjiebos (A), t'aibie (N)

(Latin *sericeus,* covered with silky hairs pressed flat against the surface)

Shrub to 1,5 m high. Leaves divided into three narrow leaflets thinly or more thickly covered with silvery silky hairs. Flowers in dense or open racemes, cream to bright yellow, 10 mm diameter.

Habitat: Gravelly slopes, often along roadsides.

Lessertia brachypus
PEA FAMILY

Namaqualand balloon pea (E)

(Greek *brachypus*, short-footed, alluding to the very shortly stalked racemes)

Erect shrublet to 60 cm high. Leaves divided into several elliptical leaflets. Flowers in very short racemes that are much shorter than the leaves, purplish, 6 mm diameter. Pods swollen and balloon-like with smooth papery walls.

Habitat: Gravelly slopes.

Namaqualand

Lessertia frutescens
PEA FAMILY
(= *Sutherlandia frutescens*)
Scarlet balloon pea (E), kankerbos, kalkoentjiebos (A)
(Latin *frutescens*, becoming shrubby)

Erect or sprawling shrublet to 1 m high. Leaves divided into many small oblong leaflets that are rounded at the tips, greyish green and mostly thinly hairy above. Flowers in short racemes, bright red, 20–40 mm long. Pods large and balloon-like with smooth papery walls.
Habitat: Widespread on a variety of soils but usually along roads.
Notes: Very variable in stature and in the size of its flowers and fruit. It is palatable to stock and although it enjoys high repute for the treatment of cancer there is no evidence in support of this belief.

Dyerophytum africanum
PLUMBAGO FAMILY
(Latin *africanus*, from Africa)

Straggling shrub to 1 m high, with slender greyish branches. Leaves leathery and broadly spoon-shaped with a pointed tip, covered with mealy granules. Flowers crowded in narrow spikes, with the calyx papery and apparently five-winged, creamy with pink tinges, 8–10 mm long.
Habitat: Dry stony slopes.
Notes: Very palatable to stock.

Codon royenii
FORGET-ME-NOT FAMILY
Suikerkelk (A)
(Named after the eighteenth-century Dutch botanist, Adriaan van Royen)

Roughly hairy shrublet to 1,5 m high, covered with white prickles. Leaves elliptical and covered with straight white prickles. Flowers large and bell-shaped, cream to yellow with purple stripes, 25 mm long.
Habitat: Dry stony slopes.

Namaqualand

Peliostomum virgatum
SUTERA FAMILY

(Latin *virgatus*, with slender rod-like stems)
Loosely branched shrublet to 30 cm high, with slender wand-like branches. Leaves elliptical and covered with glandular hairs. Flowers violet with purple and white marks in the throat, 20 mm long.
Habitat: Stony slopes and flats.

Aptosimum indivisum
SUTERA FAMILY

Karoo violet (E), karooviooltjie (A)
(Latin *indivisus*, undivided, referring to the leaves)
Cushion-forming dwarf shrublet to 7 cm high, with a woody taproot. Leaves spatula-shaped and leathery. Flowers violet with purple marks around the white throat, 15 mm diameter.
Habitat: Rocky flats in open scrub.

Jamesbrittenia fruticosa
SUTERA FAMILY

(= *Sutera fruticosa*)
(Latin *fruticosus*, shrubby)
Aromatic, twiggy shrublet to 1 m high, with glandular hairs on the new growth. Leaves elliptical and sparsely hairy. Flowers crowded towards the tips of the branches, mauve to purple with a dark purple eye, 15–20 mm diameter with a tube 16–26 mm long.
Habitat: Sandy and stony flats in open scrub.
Notes: Often along roads and at the base of rock outcrops.

Namaqualand

Jamesbrittenia racemosa
SUTERA FAMILY
(= *Sutera tomentosa*)
(Latin *racemosus*, with the flowers in a raceme)

Aromatic annual herb to 50 cm high, covered with glandular hairs. Leaves ovate and coarsely toothed. Flowers in the axils of the upper leaves, white to pale lilac with a star-like purple eye and notched petals, 12–24 mm diameter with a tube 15–18 mm long.
Habitat: Usually granite outcrops in the shelter of boulders or crevices but also gravelly watercourses.

Jamesbrittenia glutinosa
SUTERA FAMILY
(= *Sutera glutinosa*)
(Latin *glutinosus*, glutinous or gooey)

Aromatic annual or possibly short-lived perennial herb to 50 cm high, covered with glandular hairs. Leaves ovate with toothed margins, covered with glistening glandular hairs. Flowers in the axils of the leaves almost from the base, mauve to lilac with a pale yellow eye, 15–18 mm diameter with a tube 16–24 mm long.
Habitat: Usually granite outcrops in the shelter of boulders or crevices but also gravelly watercourses.

Zaluzianskya affinis
SUTERA FAMILY
Purple drumstick-flower (E)
(Latin *affinis*, related to, alluding to its close resemblance to *Z. villosa*)

Hairy annual herb to 30 cm high. Leaves more or less elliptical and sparsely hairy. Flowers in crowded spikes that elongate in fruit, white to mauve with a yellow or reddish eye and Y-shaped petals, 10 mm diameter with a slender tube 10–25 mm long.
Habitat: Sandy flats and slopes, often along the coast.
Notes: Replaced in the south by the more hairy *Zaluzianskya villosa*.

Namaqualand

Manulea silenoides
SUTERA FAMILY
Mauve fingerphlox (E)
(Resembling the genus *Silene* in its flowers)
Annual herb branching from the base, to 15 cm high. Leaves in a basal tuft, more or less elliptical and sparsely hairy. Flowers in crowded spikes, mauve with a yellow eye and Y-shaped petals, 6–12 mm diameter with a tube 3,5–5,5 mm long.
Habitat: Sandy granite soils.

Manulea altissima
SUTERA FAMILY
Keyhole fingerphlox (E), vingertjies (A)
(Latin *altissimus*, tallest, alluding to the unusually long flowering stalks)
Short-lived perennial herb to 1 m high, covered with foetid glandular hairs. Leaves in a basal tuft, elliptical and obscurely toothed. Flowers crowded in head-like racemes on slender stalks, with the mouth of the floral tube keyhole-shaped, white to pale yellow with a dark yellowish centre, scented, 10 mm diameter.
Habitat: Deep sandy soils, mainly coastal.

Colpias mollis
SUTERA FAMILY
Rock snapdragon (E), klipblom (A)
(Latin *mollis*, soft, alluding to the soft hairs)
Tufted shrublet to 20 cm high, usually softly hairy but sometimes hairless. Leaves ovate with toothed margins. Flowers on slender stalks in the leaf axils, funnel-shaped with a pair of small pouches beneath, yellow to white, scented, 20–30 mm diameter.
Habitat: Shaded, south-facing rock crevices, mostly in granite.

Namaqualand

Nemesia leipoldtii
SUTERA FAMILY
Karoo nemesia (E), karooleeubekkie (A)
(Named after the famous South African poet and naturalist, C.L. Leipoldt)

Annual herb to 30 cm high. Leaves opposite, ovate with toothed margins. Flowers in racemes, two-lipped and white to mauve with a yellow patch on the lower lip, the upper four petals oblong and the lower lip pouched beneath.
Habitat: Clay flats in open scrub, often along roadsides.

Nemesia anisocarpa
SUTERA FAMILY
Namaqua nemesia (E), geelbekkie (A)
(Greek, *anisocarpus*, unequal fruit, a misnomer based on malformed fruit)

Annual herb to 20 cm high. Leaves opposite, elliptical with lightly toothed margins. Flowers in racemes, two-lipped with a white upper lip and a yellow lower lip, the upper four petals oblong and the lower lip with a straight spur 3–5 mm long.
Habitat: Mainly sandy flats and lower slopes.

Nemesia affinis
SUTERA FAMILY
Sandveld nemesia (E), sandveldleeubekkie (A)
(Latin *affinis*, related to, alluding to its close resemblance to some other species)

Annual herb to 30 cm high. Leaves opposite, lance-shaped and toothed. Flowers in racemes, usually yellow but sometimes white or blue, 15 mm diameter, the upper four petals oblong and the lower lip bulging with two velvety bumps in the mouth and a spur 3–5 mm long.
Habitat: Sandy and granite slopes and flats.

Namaqualand

Hemimeris racemosa
SUTERA FAMILY
Common yellowfaces (E), bobbejaan-gesiggies (A)
(Latin *racemosus*, with the flowers in a raceme)

Annual herb, 3,5–40 cm high. Leaves opposite, ovate with the margins toothed or lobed. Flowers on slender pedicels in the upper leaf axils, yellow, *c.*7,5–13 mm long with two spurs 1,5–3 mm long.
Habitat: Shaded and moist places, often among rocks.

Diascia rudolphii
SUTERA FAMILY
Schlechter's diascia (E)
(Named after the German botanist, Rudolph Schlechter)

Annual herb, 5–50 cm high. Leaves mostly basal, elliptical with toothed or scalloped margins. Flowers solitary on long, slender pedicels, orange to salmon with a yellow cup edged with maroon, bowl-shaped with two shallow pockets, 15–20 mm diameter.
Habitat: Seasonally moist gravelly soils, often in the shelter of boulders or along stream lines.

Diascia tanyceras
SUTERA FAMILY
Long-horned diascia (E), bokhorinkies (A)
(Greek *tanyceras*, long-horned, alluding to the long spurs on the flowers)

Annual herb, 10–50 cm high. Leaves mostly basal, elliptical with toothed or deeply lobed margins. Flowers solitary on long stalks, reddish purple with a pair of elliptical spots at the base of each of the upper two petals, two-lipped, 15 mm diameter with a pair of spreading spurs ± 20 mm long.
Habitat: Gravelly loam soils, often in fallow lands.
Notes: *D. namaquensis* has a single large yellow spot stretching from the base of each upper petal onto the base of the adjacent side petal.

Namaqualand

Acanthopsis disperma
ACANTHUS FAMILY
(Greek *dispermus*, two-seeded, alluding to the generic character of only one or two seeds per ovary chamber)
Spiny dwarf perennial to 10 cm high. Leaves in a basal tuft, narrowly elliptical with coarsely toothed and spiny margins. Flowers in dense spikes among spiny bracts, one-lipped, blue or rarely white, 20 mm long.
Habitat: Dry stony slopes and flats.

Paranomus bracteolaris
PROTEA FAMILY
Bokkeveldpoppiesbos (A)
(Latin *bracteolaris*, with small bracts)
Single-stemmed shrub to 2 m high. Leaves finely divided into needle-like segments, hairy when young. Flowers in small clusters arranged in spikes at the branch tips, purple-pink, lightly scented, 20–25 mm long.
Habitat: Drier sandstone slopes.

Vexatorella alpina
PROTEA FAMILY
Kamiesberg vexatorella (E)
(Latin *alpinus*, literally growing in the alpine zone but in this case in the mountains)
Dense shrub to 2 m high, forming large stands. Leaves narrowly elliptical, leathery and greyish green. Flowers in rounded heads 20–25 mm diameter, cream-coloured and fragrant.
Habitat: Granite soils at high altitude.
Notes: Restricted to the upper slopes in the Kamiesberg.

Namaqualand

Male

Female

Leucadendron remotum
PROTEA FAMILY
Bokkeveld conebush (E)
(Latin *remotus*, scattered or remote, an allusion to the fact that this species occurs at the extremity of the range of the genus)
Single-stemmed, densely leafy shrub to 1,5 m high, branching from near the base. Leaves narrowly elliptical and rounded at the tips, greyish and thinly silky when young. Flowers very small, in rounded heads 15–20 mm across that are surrounded by dark brown bracts; the sexes are on separate plants, with the male flower heads in clusters at the branch tips and the female flower heads solitary and nested in the upper leaves.
Habitat: Sandy soils on sandstone in dry fynbos.
Notes: Common on the Bokkeveld escarpment near Nieuwoudtville.

Protea glabra
PROTEA FAMILY
Chestnut protea (E), kaiingbos (A)
(Latin *glabrus*, hairless, referring to the leaves or bracts)
Small tree to 5 m high, branching from the base. Leaves elliptical, leathery and grey. Flowers crowded in pincushion-like heads surrounded by spreading, brown bracts, the heads 70–90 mm diameter.
Habitat: Dry sandstone slopes and plateaus in arid fynbos.

Namaqualand

Pteronia incana
DAISY FAMILY
Karoo gumbush (E), gombos (A), t'kaibe (N)
(Latin *incanus,* hoary, alluding to the grey-woolly leaves)
Stiffly branched, grey-leaved shrub to 1 m high. Leaves narrow, opposite, grey-woolly. Flower heads solitary at the branch tips, without ray florets, yellow, surrounded by several series of hairless bracts.
Habitat: Dry stony places on sand or clay.

Eriocephalus punctulatus
DAISY FAMILY
Kapokbossie (A)
(Latin *punctulatus,* minutely dotted, referring to the oil glands on the leaves)
Greyish shrublet to 1 m high. Leaves in clusters on short side branches, leathery and needle-like. Flower heads in small clusters above the leaves, purple with a few white ray florets, 6–8 mm diameter, surrounded by four or five elliptical bracts with membranous margins. Seeds silky.
Habitat: Rocky slopes in scrub.

Pentzia incana
DAISY FAMILY
Skaapkaroo, alsbossie (A)
(Latin *incanus,* hoary, alluding to the grey-woolly leaves)
Aromatic, twiggy shrub to 1 m high, with white-woolly stems. Leaves divided into narrow or thread-like lobes, grey-woolly. Flower heads solitary on long, sometimes leafy stalks, without ray florets, yellow, 7–10 mm diameter, surrounded by several rows of blunt bracts with membranous margins.
Habitat: Dry stony flats in scrub.

Namaqualand

Cotula leptalea
DAISY FAMILY
Namaqua buttons (E),
namakwaganskos (A)
(Greek *leptaleus*, also slender, alluding
to the resemblance to other species)

Slender annual herb to 15 cm high. Leaves mostly towards the base of the stem, finely once- or twice-divided and silky. Flower heads solitary on wiry stalks, without ray florets, yellow with the outermost florets female, 5–10 mm diameter, surrounded by two series of elliptical bracts with brown-edged membranous margins.
Habitat: Gravelly slopes.

Cotula barbata
DAISY FAMILY
Buttons (E), kleinganskos (A)
(Latin *barbatus*, bearded, alluding to the hairy leaves)

Slender annual herb to 15 cm high. Leaves crowded in a basal tuft, finely once- or twice-divided and softly hairy. Flower heads solitary on wiry stalks, without ray florets, yellow or white with all the florets bisexual, 10 mm diameter, surrounded by two series of almost round bracts with membranous margins.
Habitat: Gravelly slopes.

Felicia brevifolia
DAISY FAMILY
Grey-leaved felicia (E)
(Latin *brevifolius*, short-leaved)
Well-branched shrub to 1 m high. Leaves variously toothed or lobed, greyish. Flower heads solitary on short stalks, yellow with blue to mauve ray florets, 15–30 mm diameter, surrounded by three series of narrow, pointed bracts.
Habitat: Stony flats and slopes in scrub.

Namaqualand

Felicia filifolia
DAISY FAMILY

Needle-leaved felicia, fine-leaved felicia (E), draaibos (A)

(Latin *filifolius*, thread-leaved)

Well-branched shrub to 1 m high. Leaves in tufts, needle-like, lightly dotted with glands. Flower heads solitary on slender stalks, yellow with blue to mauve ray florets, 15–20 mm diameter, surrounded by three series of narrow, pointed bracts.
Habitat: Stony flats and slopes in scrub.

Felicia merxmuelleri
DAISY FAMILY

Namaqualand felicia (E), Namakwa-sambreeltjies (A)

(Honouring German botanist, Hermann Merxmüller)

Shortly hairy annual herb to 25 cm high. Leaves spatula-shaped and covered with short, coarse hairs. Flower heads solitary on slender stalks, yellow with blue ray florets, 15–30 mm diameter, the ray florets without bristles, surrounded by two series of narrow, pointed bracts.
Habitat: Granite outcrops and gravelly slopes.

Felicia australis
DAISY FAMILY

Common felicia (E), sambreeltjies (A)

(Latin *australis*, southern)

Thinly hairy, sprawling annual herb, 5–25 cm high. Leaves very narrow and sometimes lightly toothed with hairs along the margins. Flower heads solitary on slender stalks, yellow with blue to mauve ray florets, 15–18 mm diameter, surrounded by three series of narrow, pointed bracts.
Habitat: Sandy or clay flats.

Namaqualand

Senecio arenarius
DAISY FAMILY
(= *Senecio cakilefolius*)
Lesser purple ragwort (E),
pershongerblom (A)
(Latin *arenarius*, growing in sand)

Glandular-hairy annual herb to 40 cm high. Leaves toothed to lobed with the margins sometimes rolled under. Flower heads several in branching, flat-topped clusters, yellow with mauve or rarely white ray florets, 20 mm diameter, surrounded by a single series of narrow, sticky bracts forming a cylinder.
Habitat: Sandy flats, often coastal.

Senecio cardaminifolius
DAISY FAMILY
Namaqua groundsel (E)
(Latin *cardaminifolius*, with leaves like bitter-cress, *Cardamine*)

Hairless annual herb, 15–40 cm high. Leaves more or less deeply lobed. Flower heads several in branched clusters, yellow with yellow ray florets, 10–15 mm diameter, surrounded by a single series of narrow bracts.
Habitat: Gravelly and sandy slopes, often in disturbed places.

Senecio erosus
DAISY FAMILY
Sticky-leaved groundsel (E)
(Latin *erosus*, with the margins irregularly toothed as if gnawed)

Tufted perennial to 60 cm high, with smooth or roughly hairy stems issuing from a woolly crown. Leaves mostly in a basal tuft, petiolate and narrowly elliptical with irregularly toothed or lobed margins. Flower heads solitary or few on sparsely leafy stems, yellow with yellow ray florets, 18–20 mm diameter, surrounded by a single series of narrow bracts.
Habitat: Seasonally moist gravelly or clay flats.

Namaqualand

Senecio junceus
DAISY FAMILY
Sjambokbos (A)
(Latin *junceus*, rush-like, alluding to the rod-like stems)

Apparently leafless, succulent-stemmed shrub to 90 cm high, with rod-like stems from a woody rootstock. Leaves scale-like, dry. Flower heads in clusters at the branch tips, yellow with ± five short yellow ray florets, 10 mm diameter, surrounded by a single series of narrow bracts.
Habitat: Dry rocky lower slopes.

Senecio corymbiferus
DAISY FAMILY
Grey-leaved bush senecio (E)
(Latin *corymbiferus*, bearing the flower heads in flat-topped clusters known as corymbs)

Succulent shrublet with smooth, greyish stems to 60 cm high. Leaves clustered near the tips, succulent and finger-like with a grey bloom and tapering, pointed tips. Flower heads in clusters at the branch tips, yellow with yellow ray florets, 10 mm diameter, surrounded by a single series of narrow bracts.
Habitat: Dry rocky slopes.

Othonna cylindrica
DAISY FAMILY
Common babooncress (E), ossierapuisbos (A)
(Latin *cylindricus*, cylindrical, referring to the leaves)

Succulent shrub to 1 m high, with pale grey, brittle stems. Leaves clustered at the branch tips, cylindrical and succulent and covered with a white bloom. Flower heads few in open, branched clusters on long stalks, yellow with yellow ray florets, 15–20 mm diameter, surrounded by a single series of smooth, broad bracts.
Habitat: Sandy and stony flats and rocks, often coastal.

Namaqualand

Othonna sedifolia
DAISY FAMILY
Namaqua babooncress (E), karoorapuis (A)
(Latin *sedifolius*, with leaves like a houseleek, *Sedum*)

Succulent shrublet to 60 cm high, with pale grey, brittle stems. Leaves clustered at the branch tips, ovoid or spherical and succulent and covered with a white bloom. Flower heads one to few on long stalks, yellow with yellow ray florets, 15–20 mm diameter, surrounded by a single series of smooth, broad bracts.
Habitat: Stony slopes and banks.

Leysera tenella
DAISY FAMILY
Common wireweed (E), skilpadteebossie (A)
(Latin *tenellus*, delicate)
Annual herb to 20 cm high, branching from the base. Leaves grey and hairy, narrow and thread-like. Flower heads loosely clustered at the ends of the branches, yellow with yellow rays, 15–18 mm diameter, surrounded by several series of stiff bracts that are papery at the tips.
Habitat: Sandy flats.
Notes: *Leysera gnaphalodes* (page 246) is similar but is a shrublet to 40 cm high and the bristles on the seeds are feathery from the base rather than just in the upper part.

Rhynchopsidium pumilum
DAISY FAMILY
Yellow snow (E), geelsneeu (A)
(Latin *pumilus*, dwarf, alluding to the small stature)
Spreading, thinly cobwebby annual herb to 10 cm high, often forming carpets. Leaves narrow or thread-like and hairy. Flower heads solitary on short, slender stalks, yellow with yellow ray florets, 12–15 mm diameter, surrounded by several rows of firm bracts with papery tips.
Habitat: Sandy or gravelly flats.

Namaqualand

Dimorphotheca cuneata
DAISY FAMILY
Bosmagriet (A)
(Latin *cuneatus*, wedge-shaped, referring to the leaves)

Rounded, glandular-hairy and sticky shrublet to 50 cm high. Leaves elliptical and toothed to lobed. Flower heads on short peduncles, yellow with white, salmon or orange ray florets that are purplish beneath, 40–50 mm diameter, surrounded by two series of narrow bracts.
Habitat: Stony and shale ridges and flats.
Notes: When in bloom may give the landscape the appearance of a snow-covered field.

Dimorphotheca tragus
DAISY FAMILY
(= *Castalis tragus*)
Geelmagriet, jakkalsbos (A)
(Latin *tragus*, the goat-like smell of the armpits, a picturesque but obscure reference)

Cushion-like, tufted perennial to 25 cm high, sprouting from a woody base. Leaves narrow and coarsely toothed, rough. Flower heads on long peduncles, blackish with orange to salmon-coloured ray florets, 40–50 mm diameter, surrounded by two series of narrow bracts, nodding in seed. Seeds disc-like and papery.
Habitat: Stony or rocky places in scrub.

Dimorphotheca sinuata
DAISY FAMILY
Namaqualand daisy (E),
Namakwalandmadeliefie, jakkalsblom (A)
(Latin *sinuatus*, sinuate or strongly waved, referring to the leaf margins)

Sprawling, roughly hairy annual herb to 30 cm high. Leaves narrowly elliptical and shallowly lobed or toothed. Flower heads on elongate peduncles, black with pale orange to biscuit-coloured ray florets, 40–50 mm diameter, surrounded by one series of narrow bracts. Seeds disc-like and papery.
Habitat: Sandy and gravelly slopes.

Namaqualand

Osteospermum microcarpum
DAISY FAMILY
(= *Tripteris microcarpa*)
(Greek *microcarpus*, small-fruited)
Glandular-hairy, sticky annual or short-lived perennial to 60 cm high. Leaves glandular-hairy and deeply lobed. Flower heads on slender stalks, yellow with yellow ray florets, 15–20 mm diameter surrounded by ± one series of narrow bracts.
Habitat: Arid sandy or gravelly flats, often along seasonal washes.

Osteospermum sinuatum
DAISY FAMILY
(= *Tripteris sinuata*)
Golden windowseed (E), skaapbos (A)
(Latin *sinuatus*, waved, referring to the toothed leaves)
Rounded, brittle-stemmed shrub to 60 cm high, foetid-smelling. Leaves opposite, narrow and conspicuously toothed, leathery with a grey bloom. Flower heads several on branching stems, yellow with golden yellow ray florets, 30–40 mm diameter, drooping in seed, surrounded by two series of narrow bracts. Seeds three-winged, translucent and papery.
Habitat: Dry sandstone or granite outcrops among rocks.

Osteospermum oppositifolium
DAISY FAMILY
(= *Tripteris oppositifolia*)
Dark-eyed windowseed (E), stinkskaapbos (A)
(Latin *oppositifolius*, opposite-leaved)
Rounded, brittle-stemmed shrub to 1 m high, foetid-smelling. Leaves opposite, narrow and obscurely toothed, leathery with a grey bloom. Flower heads several on branching stems, black with pale to golden yellow ray florets, 30–40 mm diameter, drooping in seed, surrounded by two series of narrow bracts. Seeds three-winged, translucent and papery.
Habitat: Dry sandstone or granite outcrops among rocks.

Namaqualand

Osteospermum amplectens
DAISY FAMILY
(= *Tripteris amplectens*)
Springbok windowseed (E),
dassiegousblom (A)
(Latin *amplectens*, clasping, alluding to the leaf bases)
Glandular-hairy, aromatic annual herb to 50 cm high. Leaves elliptical and irregularly toothed. Flower heads dark purplish with yellow ray florets, 30–40 mm diameter, surrounded by two series of narrow bracts with membranous margins narrower than the central green portion, nodding in seed. Seeds three-winged, 4–5 mm long.
Habitat: Rock outcrops and gravelly flats, often along roadsides.
Notes: Common around Springbok.

Osteospermum hyoseroides
DAISY FAMILY
(= *Tripteris hyoseroides*)
Namaqua windowseed (E),
dassiegousblom (A)
(Resembling the Mediterranean daisy, *Hyoseris*)
Glandular-hairy, aromatic annual herb to 50 cm high. Leaves elliptical and irregularly toothed. Flower heads dark purplish with orange ray florets, 30–50 mm diameter, surrounded by two series of bracts with membranous margins broader than the central green portion, nodding in seed. Seeds three-winged, 7–8 mm long.
Habitat: Stony flats.

Dimorphotheca pinnata
DAISY FAMILY
(= *Osteospermum pinnatum*)
Satin boneseed (E), jakkalsbos (A)
(Latin *pinnatus*, divided into narrow segments like a feather, referring to the leaves)
Sprawling, hairy annual herb to 5 cm high. Leaves divided to the base into narrow or thread-like lobes. Flower heads orange with glistening cream to biscuit ray florets that are dark at the base, 40–50 mm diameter, surrounded by one series of narrow bracts. Seeds warty.
Habitat: Dry gravelly or sandy slopes and flats.

Namaqualand

Ursinia calenduliflora
DAISY FAMILY
Namaqua parachute-daisy (E),
berggousblom (A)
(Latin *calenduliflorus*, with flowers like a *Calendula*)
Annual herb to 35 cm high. Leaves divided into narrow lobes. Flower heads dull black with orange ray florets that have a dark band at the base, 30–60 mm diameter, surrounded by many series of overlapping bracts, the innermost with large, papery tips. Seeds with five white, papery scale-like wings.
Habitat: Gravelly slopes and flats.

Ursinia chrysanthemoides
DAISY FAMILY
Red parachute-daisy (E), rooibergmagriet (A)
(Resembling a chrysanthemum)
Sprawling annual or perennial herb to 45 cm high with the stems more or less woody below. Leaves mostly twice-divided into narrow lobes. Flower heads glossy black with orange to reddish ray florets with dark reverse, 35–50 mm diameter, surrounded by many series of overlapping bracts, the innermost with large, papery tips. Seeds with five white, papery scale-like wings plus five whiskers.
Habitat: Gravelly slopes and flats.

Hirpicium alienatum
DAISY FAMILY
Haarbos (A)
(Latin *alienus*, incongruous or foreign, a reference to its anomalous appearance when it was first described in the genus *Oedera*)
Twiggy shrub to 1 m high, with stiff blackish branchlets. Leaves in tufts, narrow with the margins rolled under, bristly above and white-felted beneath. Flower heads yellow with pale or deep yellow ray florets, 20–30 mm diameter, surrounded by several series of spreading, spine-like bracts that are joined at the base.
Habitat: Stony shale slopes in scrub.

Namaqualand

Berkheya fruticosa
DAISY FAMILY
Large wild thistle (E), vaaldissel (A)
(Latin *fruticosus*, shrubby or bushy)

Shrub with white-woolly stems to 1,5 m high. Leaves elliptical and lightly toothed with spiny margins, dark green and ± hairless above but white-woolly beneath. Flower heads in clusters at the branch tips, yellow with yellow ray florets, 40–50 mm diameter, surrounded by several series of spine-tipped bracts.
Habitat: Dry rocky slopes in scrub.

Didelta spinosa
DAISY FAMILY
Namaqua salad thistle (E), slaaibos (A)
(Latin *spinosus*, spiny, referring to the leaves)

Shrub to 2 m high. Leaves opposite, glossy, elliptical and spine-tipped, lobed at the base with the margins lightly rolled under and sometimes prickly. Flower heads solitary, yellow with yellow ray florets, 40–50 mm diameter, surrounded by two rows of bracts, the outer four bracts large and leafy and the inner narrow with prickly teeth.
Habitat: Dry granite and sandstone slopes.
Notes: Highly palatable, especially the dry leaves in summer.

Didelta carnosa
DAISY FAMILY
Dune salad thistle (E), kusslaaibos (A)
(Latin *carnosus*, fleshy, referring to the leaves)

Rounded shrublet to 1 m high. Leaves fleshy and lance-shaped with the margins usually rolled under, thinly or densely cobwebby. Flower heads yellow with yellow ray florets, 40–50 mm diameter, surrounded by two rows of bracts, the outer four bracts large and leafy and the inner narrow with prickly teeth.
Habitat: Coastal dunes and sandy flats.

Namaqualand

Gorteria diffusa
DAISY FAMILY
Beetle daisy (E)
(Latin *diffusus*, diffuse or loosely branched)
Sprawling annual herb to 10 cm high. Leaves narrowly elliptical and sometimes lobed with the margins rolled under, roughly hairy above and white-felted beneath. Flower heads black with orange ray florets, some or all with beetle-like markings at the base, 25–35 mm diameter, surrounded by several series of spine-like bracts.
Habitat: Stony clay or gravelly granitic flats.

Gazania lichtensteinii
DAISY FAMILY
Yellow gazania (E), geelgazania, kougoed (A)
(Named after the nineteenth-century German doctor and naturalist, Martin Lichtenstein)
Annual herb to 20 cm high. Leaves elliptical and toothed with the margins lightly rolled under, leathery and ± hairless above but woolly beneath. Flower heads yellow with yellow to orange ray florets that are marked with small green blotches at the base, 25–35 mm diameter, the bracts joined into a smooth cup that is pushed in at the bottom like a champagne bottle.
Habitat: Arid gravelly and sandy flats, often in washes.

Gazania rigida
DAISY FAMILY
Karoo gazania (E), karoogazania (A)
(Latin *rigidus*, rigid or stiff, alluding to the rather firm-textured leaves)
Tufted stemless perennial herb to 25 cm high. Leaves usually deeply lobed, rarely strap-like with the margins rolled under, thinly hairy above and white-woolly beneath. Flower heads yellow with yellow or orange ray florets usually banded with dark marks at the base, 50–60 mm diameter, the bracts joined into a roughly hairy cup that is rounded at the base.
Habitat: Stony flats and lower slopes.

Namaqualand

Gazania krebsiana
DAISY FAMILY
Red gazania (E), rooigazania (A)
(Named after an eighteenth-century Eastern Cape farmer, George Krebs)

Tufted stemless perennial herb to 20 cm high. Leaves strap-like or lobed with margins rolled under, thinly hairy above and white-felted beneath. Flower heads yellow with yellow to orange ray florets variously marked at the base, 50–60 mm diameter, the bracts joined into a smooth cup that is rounded at the base.
Habitat: Stony flats, often along roadsides.

Arctotheca calendula
DAISY FAMILY
Cape weed (E)
(Named for the purported resemblance to the marigold genus, *Calendula*)

Tufted to sprawling annual herb to 20 cm high. Leaves mostly in a basal tuft, paddle-shaped to deeply lobed or even twice-lobed, roughly hairy above and white-woolly beneath. Flower heads black with yellow ray florets that are paler towards the base or marked with a dark band, 30–40 mm diameter, surrounded by several series of bracts, the outer with their tips bent back. Seeds woolly.
Habitat: Coastal sands and disturbed places along roads or in lands.

Arctotis fastuosa
DAISY FAMILY
Namaqualand arctotis (E), namakwa-gousblom (A)
(Latin *fastuosus*, proud or haughty)

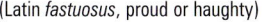

Slightly fleshy, often robust annual herb to 45 cm high. Leaves elliptical and deeply lobed, often eared at the base and softly white-woolly. Flower heads solitary, blackish with orange ray florets that are marked with a dark band at the base, 60–80 mm diameter, surrounded by several series of bracts, the outer with short tails and the inner with rounded, papery tips.
Habitat: Sandy and gravel slopes in drier areas, often along washes.

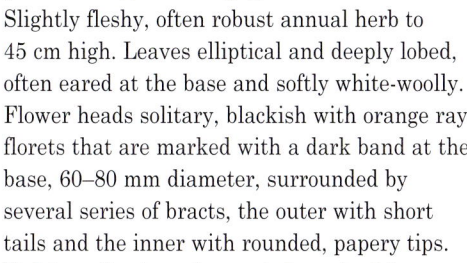

Namaqualand

Arctotis campanulata
DAISY FAMILY
Kamiesberg arctotis (E)
(Latin *campanulatus*, bell-shaped, referring to the flower heads)

Stemless perennial to 40 cm high. Leaves divided into elliptical lobes with crisped margins, thickly silvery-cobwebby on both sides. Flower heads black with orange ray florets that are marked with a dark band at the base, 50–70 mm diameter, surrounded by several series of bracts, the outer with slender woolly tips and the inner with rounded, papery tips.
Habitat: Seasonally damp granitic flats.

Arctotis acaulis
DAISY FAMILY
Tufted arctotis (E), renostergousblom (A)
(Latin *acaulis*, stemless)

Stemless perennial to 40 cm high. Leaves lanceolate to paddle-shaped and often lobed with obscurely toothed margins, roughly hairy above and grey-felted beneath. Flower heads black with orange, yellow or cream-coloured ray florets that are marked with dark bands at the base, 50–70 mm diameter, surrounded by several series of bracts, the outer with slender woolly tips and the inner with rounded, papery tips.
Habitat: Clay, granitic or limestone flats.

Arctotis scullyi
DAISY FAMILY
(= *Arctotis merxmuelleri*)
Wit-sôe (A), sôe (N)
(Named after William Charles Scully, Magistrate of Namaqualand in the 1890s)

Perennial herb to 40 cm high. Leaves lance-shaped and shallowly lobed or toothed, very roughly hairy. Flowers black with white ray florets that are banded with black at the base, 40–60 mm diameter, surrounded by several series of bracts, the outer with long dark tails and the inner with rounded, papery tips.
Habitat: Coastal sands in scrub.

Index of scientific names

Acanthopsis disperma 319
Acridocarpus natalitius 66
Adenandra uniflora 175
Adenium multiflorum 83
   A. oleifolium 83
Adhatoda densiflora 94
Agapanthus africanus 137
   A. campanulatus 48
   A. inapertus 48
   A. praecox 138
Agathosma capensis 175
   A. thymifolia 175
Ajuga ophrydis 96
Albuca abyssinica 26
   A. altissima see Albuca canadensis
   A. bracteata 26
   A. canadensis 133, 272
   A. consanguinea 271
   A. cooperi 272
   A. flaccida 132
   A. grandis 132
   A. humilis 26
   A. maxima see Albuca canadensis
   A. nelsonii 27
   A. suaveolens 133
   A. virens 25
Aloe arborescens 129
   A. castanea 40
   A. chabaudii 39
   A. ciliaris 40
   A. comptonii see Aloe perfoliata
   A. cooperi 38
   A. cryptopoda 39
   A. dichotoma 267
   A. ecklonis 38
   A. falcata 268
   A. ferox 130
   A. framesii see Aloe microstigma
   A. greatheadii 39
   A. khamiesensis see Aloe microstigma
   A. kniphofioides 37
   A. maculata 38
   A. marlothii 40
   A. microstigma 129, 267
   A. mitriformis see Aloe perfoliata
   A. pearsonii 267
   A. perfoliata 128
   A. plicatilis 129
   A. variegata 268

Amaryllis belladonna 138
Amellus tenuifolius 251
Ammocharis coranica 47
   A. longifolia 140, 279
Anapalina caffra see Tritoniopsis caffra
   A. nervosa see Tritoniopsis antholyza
Androcymbium capense see Colchicum capense
   A. latifolium see Colchicum coloratum
   A. melanthioides see Colchicum melanthioides
Aneilema aequinoctiale 31
Anemone fanninii 64
   A. transvaalensis 63
Anisodontea scabrosa 179
Anomalesia cunonia see Gladiolus cunonius
   A. saccata see Gladiolus saccatus
Anomatheca laxa see Freesia laxa
   A. ringens see Babiana ringens
Aponogeton distachyos 125
Aptosimum indivisum 314
Arctopus monacanthus 221
Arctotheca calendula 260, 333
   A. populifolia 260
Arctotis acaulis 261, 334
   A. angustifolia 261
   A. campanulata 334
   A. fastuosa 333
   A. hirsuta 260
   A. leiocarpa 119
   A. merxmuelleri see Arctotis scullyi
   A. scullyi 334
   A. stoechadifolia 261
Argyroderma delaetii 300
   A. fissum 300
Argyrolobium robustum 78
   A. sandersonii 78
Aridaria brevicarpa see Mesembryanthemum brevicarpum
Aristea africana 141
   A. angolensis 49
   A. bakeri 142
   A. capitata 142
   A. confusa see Aristea bakeri
   A. major see Aristea capitata
Asclepias cancellata see Gomphocarpus cancellatus
   A. cucullata 84

Aspalathus capensis 189
   A. cephalotes 189
   A. chenopoda 188
   A. cordata 188
   A. ericifolia 189
Asparagus capensis 125
Aster bakerianus 116
Athanasia trifurcata 247
Augea capensis 302
Aulax pallasia 235
   A. umbellata 235

Babiana attenuata 287
   B. curviscapa 286
   B. hirsuta 287
   B. nana 154
   B. patersoniae 153
   B. purpurea 154
   B. ringens 153
   B. sambucina 155
   B. stricta 154
   B. thunbergii see Babiana hirsuta
   B. vanzyliae 287
Ballota africana 215
Bauhinia galpinii 74
Becium obovatum see Ocimum obovatum
Begonia sutherlandii 70
Berkheya armata 257
   B. barbata 257
   B. cirsiifolia 112
   B. fruticosa 331
   B. multijuga 113
   B. purpurea 112
   B. rosulata 111
   B. speciosa 111
   B. subulata 111
   B. umbellata 110
Berzelia abrotanoides 221
   B. lanuginosa 222
Bobartia indica 143
Boophone disticha 47
   B. flava see Crossyne flava
Brachycarpaea juncea see Heliophila juncea
Brownleea macroceras 60
Brunia laevis 222
   B. nodiflora see Brunia noduliflora
   B. noduliflora 222
Brunsvigia bosmaniae 279
   B. grandiflora 48
   B. marginata 139

Index of scientific names

B. natalensis 47
B. orientalis 139
Bulbine annua 127
　B. capitata 34
　B. narcissifolia 34
　B. praemorsa 270
Bulbinella caudafelis 127
　B. eburniflora 269
　B. latifolia 269
　B. nutans 270

Cadaba aphylla 73
Callilepis laureola 116
Canavalia rosea 80
Carpobrotus dimidiatus 61
　C. edulis 173
　C. quadrifidus 173
Castalis tragus see Dimorphotheca tragus
Cephalophyllum pillansii 298
　C. spissum 299
　C. spongiosum 298
Ceratotheca triloba 98
Ceropegia ampliata 86
Chamaecrista comosa 74
Chascanum latifolium 90
Chasmanthe aethiopica 152
　C. floribunda 153
Cheiridopsis cigarettifera see Cheiridopsis namaquensis
　C. denticulata 297
　C. namaquensis 297
Chironia baccifera 208
　C. linoides 208
　C. palustris 91
Chlorophytum bowkeri 24
　C. triflorum 126
　C. undulatum 271
Chrysanthemoides monilifera see Osteospermum moniliferum
Chrysocoma ciliata 247
　C. coma-aurea 248
　C. tenuifolia see Chrysocoma ciliata
Cineraria geifolia 249
Citrullus lanatus 82
Clematis brachiata 63
Cleome angustifolia 73
　C. gynandra 73
Cleretum papulosum 293
Clerodendrum hirsutum see Rotheca hirsuta
　C. triphyllum see Rotheca hirsuta
Clivia caulescens 43
　C. miniata 43
Codon royenii 313
Colchicum capense 277
　C. coloratum 277
　C. melanthioides 42
Coleonema album 174
Colpias mollis 316
Conicosia elongata 297
　C. pugioniformis 173
Conophytum minutum 301
　C. subfenestratum 300
Conostomium natalense 91
Convolvulus capensis 206
Corycium orobanchoides 164
Cotula barbata 322
　C. leptalea 322
　C. turbinata 247
Cotyledon orbiculata 62, 167, 292
Crassula brevifolia 291
　C. coccinea 166
　C. columnaris 291
　C. dichotoma 166
　C. natans 165
　C. rupestris 166
　C. sarcocaulis 61
　C. vaginata 62
Crinum bulbispermum 45
　C. macowanii 45
　C. moorei 46
　C. variabile 279
Crocosmia aurea 54
　C. paniculata 54
Crossandra greenstockii 94
Crossyne flava 278
Crotalaria globifera 77
Cucumis africanus 82
Cullumia squarrosa 248
Cyanella alba 276
　C. hyacinthoides 137
　C. lutea 137
　C. orchidiformis 276
Cyanotis speciosa 31
Cybistetes longifolia see Ammocharis longifolia
Cyclopia genistoides 196
Cycnium adonense 100
　C. racemosum 99
　C. tubulosum 99
Cyphia bulbosa 213
　C. volubilis 213
Cyrtanthus breviflorus 44
C. elatus 141
C. mackenii 45
C. sanguineus 44
C. tuckii 44
C. ventricosus 140
Cysticapnos vesicaria 185
Dactylopsis digitata see Mesembryanthemum digitatum
Daubenya aurea 275
Delosperma obtusum 60
Dianthus basuticus 65
Diascia anastrepta 103
　D. capensis 216
　D. longicornis 216
　D. rudolphii 318
　D. tanyceras 318
Didelta carnosa 258, 331
　D. spinosa 258, 331
Dierama floriferum 51
　D. luteoalbidum 51
Dietes iridioides 49, 146
Dilatris ixioides 136
Dimorphotheca cuneata 327
　D. fruticosa 115
　D. jucunda 115
　D. pinnata 329
　D. pluvialis 256
　D. sinuata 327
　D. tragus 327
Dipogon lignosus 193
Disa ferruginea 162
　D. graminifolia 163
　D. racemosa 162
　D. uniflora 162
Disperis stenoplectron 60
Dissotis canescens 70
Dorotheanthus bellidiformis 174
　D. maughanii 294
　D. rourkei 294
Drimia altissima 24
　D. macrocentra 25
Drosanthemum hispidum 169, 296
　D. speciosum 169
Drosera cistiflora 176
Dyerophytum africanum 313

Edmondia sesamoides 244
Empodium flexile 275
　E. plicatum 134
Erepsia anceps 169
Erica abietina 201
　E. algida 88
　E. cerinthoides 203

Index of scientific names

E. coccinea 204
E. corifolia 198
E. cubica 198
E. curviflora 202
E. daphniflora 200
E. densifolia 202
E. discolor 202
E. glomiflora 200
E. grandiflora see *Erica abietina*
E. hirtiflora 199
E. mammosa 203
E. multumbellifera 199
E. oatesii 88
E. patersonia 204
E. perspicua 203
E. phylicifolia see *Erica abietina*
E. pinea 201
E. plukenetii 204
E. pulchella 199
E. sessiliflora 200
E. viscaria subsp. *longifolia* 201
Eriocephalus africanus 242
E. punctulatus 321
E. racemosus 242
Eriosema cordatum 76
E. distinctum 75
E. kraussianum 76
E. salignum 76
Erythrina zeyheri 75
Eucomis autumnalis 28
E. bicolor 29
E. pallidiflora 28
Eulophia angolensis 59
E. clavicornis 58
E. ensata 58
E. foliosa 58
E. speciosa 59
E. streptopetala 59
Euphorbia caput-medusae 165
E. dregeana 290
E. hamata 290
E. mauritanica 165
Euryops abrotanifolius 252
E. speciosissimus 253
E. tenuissimus 253
E. tysonii 113
E. virgineus 253

Felicia aethiopica 252
F. australis 323
F. brevifolia 322
F. filifolia 110, 323

F. fruticosa 251
F. merxmuelleri 323
F. tenella 252
Ferraria crispa 142
F. variabilis 280
Foveolina tenella 249
Freesia laxa 52
F. leichtlinii 158

Galaxia fugacissima see *Moraea fugacissima*
Galtonia candicans see *Ornithogalum candicans*
G. regalis see *Ornithogalum regale*
Gazania krebsiana 119, 333
G. lichtensteinii 332
G. pectinata 259
G. rigens 259
G. rigida 332
Geissorhiza aspera 148
G. radians 149
G. splendidissima 285
Geranium incanum 183
G. pulchrum 71
G. wakkerstroomianum 71
Gerbera ambigua 117
G. aurantiaca 118
G. jamesonii 118
G. piloselloides 117
G. viridifolia 117
Gethyllis afra 135
Gibbaeum pubescens 171
Gladiolus alatus 160
G. carinatus 160
G. carneus 159
G. crassifolius 55
G. cunonius 161
G. dalenii 57
G. ecklonii 56
G. equitans 289
G. gracilis 161
G. liliaceus 159
G. longicollis 55
G. oppositiflorus 56
G. papilio 55
G. rogersii 161
G. saccatus 288
G. saundersii 57
G. scullyi 288
G. sericeovillosus 56
G. venustus 160
G. watermeyeri 288
G. watsonius 159

G. woodii 54
Gloriosa modesta 41
G. superba 41
Glumicalyx goseloides 89
Gnidia capitata see *Lasiosiphon capitatus*
G. compacta 88
G. kraussiana see *Lasiosiphon kraussiana*
Gomphocarpus cancellatus 307
Gorteria diffusa 332
Grielum grandiflorum 176, 303
Gymnanthemum myrianthum 109
G. humifusum 303
Gymnodiscus capillaris 254

Haemanthus barkerae 278
H. coccineus 139
H. crispus 278
H. humilis 42
Haplocarpha scaposa 116
Harpagophytum procumbens 98
Harveya speciosa 100
Hebenstretia dentata 219
Helichrysum adenocarpum 108
H. aureum 108
H. cymosum 106
H. dasyanthum 243
H. ecklonis 108
H. glomeratum 106
H. nudifolium 107
H. pallidum 107
H. pandurifolium 243
H. paniculatum see *Syncarpha paniculata*
H. retortum 243
H. ruderale 107
H. splendidum 106
H. vestitum see *Syncarpha vestita*
Heliophila africana 178
H. coronopifolia 179, 310
H. juncea 179
H. variabilis 310
Helipterum canescens see *Syncarpha canescens*
H. eximium see *Syncarpha eximia*
H. speciosissimum see *Syncarpha speciosissima*
Hemimeris racemosa 216, 318
Hermannia alnifolia 181
H. althaeifolia 180
H. cristata 68

Index of scientific names

H. disermifolia 311
H. pinnata 180
H. scabra 181
H. stricta 311
H. trifurca 311
Hermas villosa 221
Herschelia graminifolia see *Disa graminifolia*
Hesperantha bachmannii 148, 284
  H. baurii 52
  H. coccinea 52
  H. cucullata 284
  H. pauciflora 285
  H. vaginata 285
Hibiscus aethiopicus 69, 180
  H. calyphyllus 70
  H. cannabinus 68
  H. diversifolius 69
  H. trionum 69
Hilliardiella aristata 109
  H. hirsuta 109
Hirpicium alienatum 330
  H. armerioides 119
Homeria bifida see *Moraea bifida*
  H. collina see *Moraea collina*
  H. flaccida see *Moraea flaccida*
  H. miniata see *Moraea miniata*
  H. schlechteri see *Moraea schlechteri*
Homoglossum watsonium see *Gladiolus watsonius*
Hoodia gordonii 307
Hybanthus enneaspermus 95
Hyobanche sanguinea 215
Hypericum aethiopicum 65
  H. revolutum 66
Hypertelis salsoloides 301
Hypocalyptus sophoroides 195
Hypoxis costata 33
  H. hemerocallidea 33
  H. rigidula 33

Impatiens hochstetteri 81
  I. sylvicola 81
Indigofera brachystachya 190
  I. filifolia 190
  I. hilaris 79
  I. incana 190
  I. oxytropis 79
Ipomoea cairica 87
  I. crassipes 86
  I. oblongata 87
  I. obscura 86
Ixia dubia 147

I. maculata 147
I. polystachya 147
I. rapunculoides 282
I. scillaris 148

Jamesbrittenia breviflora 103
  J. fruticosa 314
  J. glutinosa 315
  J. racemosa 315
Jordaaniella cuprea 298
  J. dubia 174
Kalanchoe thyrsiflora 62
Kniphofia caulescens 37
  K. ensifolia 36
  K. ichopensis 35
  K. laxiflora 34
  K. northiae 37
  K. ritualis 36
  K. sarmentosa 268
  K. thodei 35
  K. triangularis 35
  K. tysonii 36
  K. uvaria 130
Knowltonia transvaalensis see *Anemone transvaalensis*

Lachenalia aloides 131
  L. bulbifera 130
  L. carnosa 273
  L. elegans 273
  L. framesii 273
  L. mutabilis 131
  L. pustulata 131
  L. violacea 274
Lachnaea grandiflora 197
Lampranthus amoenus 172
  L. aurantiacus 171
  L. bicolor 171
  L. hoerleinianus 295
  L. watermeyeri 172, 295
Lanaria lanata 135
Lapeirousia anceps 158
  L. arenicola 290
  L. jacquinii 158
  L. pyramidalis 157
  L. silenoides 289
Lasiosiphon capitatus 89
  L. kraussiana 89
Lebeckia cytisoides 191
  L. plukenetiana 191
  L. sericea 192, 312
Ledebouria cooperi 30
  L. floribunda 30
  L. revoluta 30

Leonotis leonurus 214
  L. ocymifolia 95
Lessertia brachypus 312
  L. frutescens 75, 193, 313
Leucadendron album 225
  L. argenteum 226
  L. conicum 223
  L. eucalyptifolium 227
  L. gandogeri 229
  L. laureolum 229
  L. loranthifolium 225
  L. meridianum 228
  L. microcephalum 228
  L. pubescens 224
  L. remotum 320
  L. rubrum 223
  L. salignum 226
  L. sessile 230
  L. tinctum 230
  L. uliginosum 224
  L. xanthoconus 227
Leucospermum calligerum 233
  L. conocarpodendron 234
  L. cuneiforme 233
  L. hypophyllocarpodendron 232
  L. oleifolium 233
  L. rodolentum 232
  L. tottum 234
  L. vestitum 234
Leysera gnaphalodes 246
  L. tenella 326
Limonium capense 206
  L. peregrinum 206
  L. scabrum 207
Liparia splendens 193
Littonia modesta see *Gloriosa modesta*
Lobelia coronopifolia 212
  L. pinifolia 212
  L. tomentosa 212
Lobostemon argenteus 209
  L. fruticosus 210
  L. glaucophyllus 210
Lotononis corymbosa 77
Lycium ferocissimum 205

Malephora crocea 296
Manulea altissima 316
  M. corymbosa 219
  M. silenoides 316
Massonia bifolia 274
  M. depressa 132
Melasphaerula ramosa 289
Melhania prostrata 67

Index of scientific names

Melianthus elongatus 186
   M. major 186
   M. minor see *Melianthus elongatus*
   M. pectinatus 312
Merwilla natalensis 31
Mesembryanthemum barklyi 293
   M. brevicarpum 294
   M. digitatum 299
   M. guerichianum 293
Metalasia densa 242
Micranthus junceus 149
Microloma sagittatum 207
   M. tenuifolium 207
Mimetes cucullatus 237
   M. fimbriifolius 237
   M. hirtus 236
   M. pauciflorus 236
Monilaria moniliformis 299
Monopsis debilis 211
   M. decipiens 96
Monsonia attenuata 71
   M. crassicaule 304
   M. parvifolia 304
   M. speciosa 182
Montinia caryophyllacea 306
Moquiniella rubra 196
Moraea bifida 281
   M. brevistyla 49
   M. ciliata 281
   M. collina 144
   M. falcifolia 281
   M. flaccida 143
   M. fugacissima 144
   M. fugax 145
   M. gawleri 145
   M. inclinata 50
   M. miniata 143
   M. muddii 50
   M. neglecta 144
   M. polystachya 50
   M. ramosissima 146
   M. schlechteri 282
   M. serpentina 280
   M. spathulata 51
   M. tripetala 145, 280
   M. villosa 146
Muraltia heisteria 187
   M. spinosa 186

Nemesia affinis 217, 317
   N. anisocarpa 317
   N. barbata 218
   N. bicornis 217

   N. cheiranthus 218
   N. denticulata 103
   N. leipoldtii 317
   N. strumosa 217
Nerine angustifolia 46
   N. bowdenii 46
   N. sarniensis 140
Nivenia stokoei 141
Nylandtia spinosa see *Muraltia spinosa*
Nymphaea caerulea see *Nymphaea nouchali*
   N. nouchali 63
Ocimum obovatum 96
Oftia africana 220
Oncosiphon suffruticosum 248
Onixotis stricta see *Wurmbea stricta*
Oophytum nanum 301
Orbea variegata 208
Ornithogalum candicans 27
   O. dubium 134
   O. longibracteatum see *Albuca bracteata*
   O. polyphyllum see *Albuca consanguinea*
   O. pruinosum 271
   O. regale 28
   O. saundersiae 27
   O. suaveolens see *Albuca suaveolens*
   O. tenuifolium see *Albuca virens*
   O. thyrsoides 133
   O. xanthochlorum 272
Ornithoglossum undulatum 126
   O. vulgare 276
Orphium frutescens 209
Oscularia deltoides 172
Osmitopsis asteriscoides 259
Osteospermum amplectens 329
   O. clandestinum 255
   O. fruticosum see *Dimorphotheca fruticosa*
   O. hyoseroides 329
   O. jucundum see *Dimorphotheca jucunda*
   O. microcarpum 328
   O. moniliferum 255
   O. oppositifolium 255, 328
   O. pinnatum see *Dimorphotheca pinnata*
   O. sinuatum 328
Othonna cylindrica 254, 325
   O. parviflora see *Othonna quinquedentata*
   O. quinquedentata 254
   O. sedifolia 326
Oxalis callosa 309
   O. comosa 308
   O. luteola 177
   O. namaquana 308
   O. obliquifolia 65
   O. obtusa 177, 308
   O. pes-caprae 177
   O. pulchella 309
   O. purpurea 178
   O. versicolor 178
Pachycarpus campanulatus 85
   P. concolor 85
   P. schinzianus 85
Pachypodium namaquanum 307
   P. saundersii 83
Papaver aculeatum 66
Paranomus bracteolaris 319
   P. sceptrum-gustavianus 236
Pelargonium capitatum 183
   P. crithmifolium 305
   P. cucullatum 184
   P. echinatum 304
   P. elongatum 185
   P. fulgidum 184
   P. incrassatum 305
   P. luridum 72
   P. magenteum 184
   P. praemorsum 306
   P. scabrum 183
   P. schizopetalum 72
   P. schlechteri 72
   P. sericifolium 305
   P. triste 185
Peliostomum virgatum 314
Pentanisia prunelloides 91
Pentzia incana 321
   P. suffruticosa see *Oncosiphon suffruticosum*
Phaenocoma prolifera 246
Pharnaceum aurantium 310
Phygelius aequalis 102
   P. capensis 102
Phylica plumosa 181
Plectranthus fruticosus 215
   P. saccatus 97
Plumbago auriculata 90
Podalyria calyptrata 195
   P. sericea 195
Polycarena lilacina 218
Polygala ericaefolia 187
   P. myrtifolia 187

Index of scientific names

P. *virgata* 81, 188
Portulacaria afra 61
Priestleya villosa see *Xiphotheca fruticosa*
Protea aurea 238
   P. *caffra* 104
   P. *compacta* 238
   P. *cynaroides* 240
   P. *dracomontana* 104
   P. *eximia* 237
   P. *gaguedi* 104
   P. *glabra* 239, 320
   P. *laurifolia* 240
   P. *nitida* 238
   P. *punctata* 239
   P. *repens* 240
   P. *roupelliae* 105
   P. *scabra* 239
   P. *speciosa* 241
   P. *subvestita* 105
   P. *welwitschii* 105
Pseudarthria hookeri 78
Pseudogaltonia clavata 29
Pseudoselago serrata 220
Psoralea aphylla 194
   P. *fleta* 194
   P. *pinnata* 194
Pteronia divaricata 246
   P. *incana* 321
Pterygodium catholicum 164

Radyera urens 68
Rafnia angulata 191
Ranunculus baurii 64
   R. *multifidus* 64
Raphionacme hirsuta 84
Rhigozum obovatum 92
   R. *trichotomum* 92
Rhodohypoxis baurii 32
Rhynchopsidium pumilum 326
Rhynchosia cooperi 77
Roella incurva 211
Roepera cordifolia 302
   R. *flexuousa* 182
   R. *foetida* 182
   R. *morgsana* 302
Romulea citrina 283
   R. *flava* 155
   R. *hirsuta* 156
   R. *namaquensis* 283
   R. *rosea* 155
   R. *sabulosa* 284
   R. *subfistulosa* 283
   R. *tabularis* 156

R. *tortuosa* 282
Rotheca hirsuta 95
Ruschia caroli 170
   R. *extensa* 296
   R. *goodiae* 295
   R. *tecta* 170
   R. *tumidula* 170

Saltera sarcocolla 205
Salvia africana-caerulea 213
   S. *africana-lutea* 214
   S. *disermas* 97
   S. *lanceolata* 214
Sandersonia aurantiaca 41
Sarcocaulon crassicaule see *Monsonia crassicaule*
Satyrium carneum 163
   S. *coriifolium* 163
   S. *erectum* 164
Scabiosa africana 241
Scadoxus multiflorus 43
   S. *puniceus* 42
Scaevola plumieri 102
Schizocarphus nervosus 25
Schizostylis coccinea see *Hesperantha coccinea*
Scilla natalensis see *Merwilla natalensis*
   S. *nervosa* see *Schizocarphus nervosus*
Sebaea exacoides 209
   S. *natalensis* 92
Selago dentata see *Pseudoselago serrata*
Senecio arenarius 250, 324
   S. *barbatus* 110
   S. *bupleuroides* 114
   S. *burchellii* 249
   S. *cakilefolius* see *Senecio arenarius*
   S. *cardaminifolius* 324
   S. *corymbiferus* 325
   S. *elegans* 250
   S. *erosus* 324
   S. *junceus* 325
   S. *littoreus* 250
   S. *macrospermus* 114
   S. *microglossus* 113
   S. *polyanthemoides* 114
   S. *speciosus* 115
   S. *umbellatus* 251
Senna italica 74
Septulina glauca 196
Serruria decipiens 231

S. *elongata* 231
S. *fasciflora* 231
S. *villosa* 232
Sesamum triphyllum 98
Silene undulata 176
Solanum giftbergense 306
   S. *guineense* 205
Sopubia cana 99
Sparaxis bulbifera 157
   S. *elegans* 286
   S. *grandiflora* 156
   S. *tricolor* 286
   S. *villosa* 157
Spiloxene aquatica 135
   S. *capensis* 134
   S. *serrata* 275
Stilbe ericoides 198
Stoebe alopecuroides 241
Strelitzia reginae 57
Streptocarpus dunnii 101
   S. *formosus* 101
   S. *grandis* 100
   S. *rexii* 101
Strumaria truncata 277
Struthiola argentea 197
   S. *ciliata* 197
Stylochaeton natalensis 23
Sutera breviflora see *Jamesbrittenia breviflora*
   S. *fruticosa* see *Jamesbrittenia fruticosa*
   S. *glutinosa* see *Jamesbrittenia glutinosa*
   S. *tomentosa* see *Jamesbrittenia racemosa*
Sutherlandia frutescens see *Lessertia frutescens*
Syncarpha canescens 245
   S. *eximia* 245
   S. *paniculata* 244
   S. *speciosissima* 244
   S. *vestita* 245
Syncolostemon densiflorus 97
Synnotia villosa see *Sparaxis villosa*

Tecoma capensis 94
Tecomaria capensis see *Tecoma capensis*
Teedia lucida 220
Tephrosia grandiflora 79
   T. *macropoda* 80
Tetragonia fruticosa 292
   T. *herbacea* 168

Index of scientific names

T. namaquensis 168
T. rosea 168
Thunbergia alata 93
   T. atriplicifolia 93
   T. natalensis 93
Trachyandra divaricata 128
   T. falcata 270
   T. muricata 128
Tribulus cristatus 303
Trichodesma physaloides 82
Tricliceras longipedunculatum 67
Tripteris amplectens see Osteospermum amplectens
   T. clandestina see Osteospermum clandestinum
   T. hyoseroides see Osteospermum hyoseroides
   T. microcarpa see Osteospermum microcarpum
   T. oppositifolia see Osteospermum oppositifolium
   T. sinuata see Osteospermum sinuatum
Tritoniopsis antholyza 152
   T. caffra 152
   T. triticea 151
Triumfetta welwitschii 67
Tulbaghia violacea 138
Turbina oblongata see Ipomoea oblongata
Tylecodon cacalioides 167

T. paniculatus 167, 292
T. wallichii 291

Ursinia paleacea 257
   U. anthemoides 256
   U. cakilefolia 256
   U. calenduliflora 330
   U. chrysanthemoides 330

Veltheimia bracteata 29
   V. capensis 274
Vernonia hirsuta see Hilliardiella hirsuta 109
   V. myriantha see Gymnanthemum myrianthum
   V. natalensis see Hilliardiella aristata
Vexatorella alpina 319
Vigna vexillata 80

Wachendorfia paniculata 136
   W. thyrsiflora 136
Wahlenbergia androsacea 210
   W. annularis 309
   W. capensis 211
   W. grandiflora 87
Watsonia aletroides 151
   W. borbonica 150
   W. densiflora 53
   W. knysnana 150
   W. laccata 151

W. lepida 53
W. meriana 149
W. pillansii 53
W. tabularis 150
Whiteheadia bifolia see Massonia bifolia
Wiborgia mucronata 192
Wurmbea stricta 126
   W. variabilis 127
Xerophyta retinervis 32
   X. viscosa 32
Xiphotheca fruticosa 192
Xysmalobium undulatum 84

Zaluzianskya affinis 315
   Z. goseloides see Glumicalyx goseloides
   Z. microsiphon 90
   Z. villosa 219
Zantedeschia aethiopica 125
   Z. albomaculata 23
   Z. pentlandii 24
   Z. rehmannii 23
Zygophyllum cordifolium see Roepera cordifolia
   Z. flexuosum see Roepera flexuousa
   Z. foetidum see Roepera foetida
   Z. meyeri see Roepera foetida
   Z. morgsana see Roepera morgsana

Index of vernacular names

Aalwyn, berg- 40
  bitter- 130
  bont- 38
  geel- 39
  katstert- 40
  krans- 128, 129
  Transvaal- 39
  waaier- 129
Aambeibossie 208
Aandblom 55
  bokkeveld- 284
  groot bruin- 159
Aandgonna 197
Aasblom 208
Adhatoda 94
Afrikaner, blue 160
  large brown 159
  red 159
  rooi 159
  wit 159
Agapanthus 138
  bell 48
  Cape 137
  drooping 48
Agtdaegeneesbos 210
Agurkie 82
utywAla bentaka 62
utywAla benyoni 62
Aloe, bitter 130
  bushveld 39
  Cape speckled 129, 267
  cat's-tail 40
  Chabaud's 39
  cliff 128
  common rambling 40
  common soap 38
  Cooper's grass 38
  Ecklon's grass 38
  fan 129
  Greathead's 39
  krans 129
  Marloth's mountain 40
  mitre 128
  partridge 268
  Pearson's 267
  poker 37
  sickle-leaved 268
Alsbossie 321
Ammocharis 47
Aneilema, clinging 31
Anemone, giant 64
Anemoon, groot 64
April fool 139
Arctotis, common 260
  Kamiesberg 334
  Karoo 119

Namaqualand 333
  sandveld 261
  silver 261
  tufted 261, 334
Aristea 142
  common branched 49
  fringed 141
Arum, bushveld 23
Arum lily 125
  dwarf 23
  spotted-leaved 23
  yellow 24
Asparagus, thorny 125
Astertjie 251
Astral-bell 85
Aunt-Eliza 54
Autumn star, common 134
  fragrant 275

Baardmannetjie 289
Bababoudjies 300
umBabaza 26
Babiana, Breede Valley 154
  dwarf 154
  fragrant 155
  Paterson's 153
  purple 154
  rat's tail 153
  showy 287
  yellow 287
Babooncress, common 254, 325
  mountain 254
  Namaqua 326
Balloon pea, Namaqualand 312
  scarlet 75, 193, 313
uBangalala olukhulu 75
uBani 75
Barberton daisy 118
Baroe 213
  larkspur 213
  twining 213
Beesbos 232, 248
Beeskrag 290
Beetle daisy 332
Begonia, orange 70
umBejo 55
amaBelejongosi 59
Belladonna 138
Bellflower, Cape 211
  Drakensberg 87
  greater 309
  lesser 210
Belskruie 259
uBendle 119
Berg lily, royal 28
  white 27

Bergangelier 197
Bergbietou 115
Berggeelbos 229
Bergkoesnaatjie 291
Berglelie 27, 28
Bergsukkelbossie 220
Bergviool 179
Berkheya, Drakensberg 111
  greater 257
  holly-leaved 257
  lesser thistle-leaved 112
  mop-headed 110
  purple 112
  showy 111
  Transvaal grass 111
Bietou 255
Bitterbos 247
Bitterwortel 84, 85, 91
Black storm 73
Black-eyed Susan 93
Black-stick lily, large 32
  small 32
Blistering leaves, Transvaal 63
Blombiesie 143
Blombos 242
Blood lily 42
Bloodroot, common 136
Blouflappie 146
Bloukappies 81
Bloukeurtjie 194
Blouklokkie 210
  pronk- 309
Bloulelie 48
Bloupypie 161
Blousuurkanol 142
Blousyselbos 90
Blue bugle 96
Blue pipe 161
Blue rocket 209
Blue sceptre 142
Blue willow pea 194
Bluebell, Riversdale 161
Bobbejaanboek 132
Bobbejaangesiggies 216, 318
Bobbejaankloue 98
Bobbejaankool 254
Bobbejaanoor 42
Bobbejaanstert 32
Bobbejaantjie 154
  stink- 287
Boesmandruiwe 302
Boesmanskers 304
Boesmanspyp 86
Bokbaaivygie 174
  common 174
Bokhorinkies 318

Index of vernacular names

Bokkeveld pride 285
umBola 29
Boneseed, satin 329
Bonsai bush 61
umBophe 91
uBoqo 86
Bosklimop 193
Boslelie 43, 46
Bosluisbessie 255
Bosmagriet 327
Bospaletblaar 52
Bosui 25
Botterboom 167, 292
Braksuring 301
Brakvy 293
Brandblaar 63
Brandlelie 44
Brandogie 98
Bright bonnet 160
Broomrape, red 215
Buchu, Cape 175
   thyme-leaved 175
Bug-catcher 78
Bulbine, annual 127
   common 270
   narrow-leaved 34
   strap-leaved 34
Bulbinella, broad-leaved 269
   cat's tail 127
   marsh 270
   scented 269
Bush bugloss, smooth-leaved 210
Bush iris, Stokoe's 141
Bush lily 43
Bush pea, pink 79
Bush sweet pea, lesser 195
Bush thistle, coastal 248
Bush violet 95
Bushman's candle 304
Bushman's pipe 86
iButha 55
Butterbush, common 167, 292
   sulphur 167
   yellow 291
Buttercup, common 64
   nasturtium-leaved 64
Butterfly bush, heath-leaved 187
   September 187
   willowy 188
Butterfly lily, common 136
   royal 136
Button daisy, common 247
Buttonbush, common 222
   redleg 221
Buttons 322
   Namaqua 322

uCabazane 117
Cabong 158, 289
   ballerina 157
   harlequin 158
   sandveld 158
iCacane 34
iCakatha 94
Calla lily, common 125
Canavalia, beach-bean 80
Candelabra, common 47
   giant 48
   king's 139
   scarlet 139
   scented 279
Candles 196
Cape bindweed 206
Cape buttercup 156
   common 157
Cape campion 176
Cape cowslip 131
Cape fellwort 205
Cape gold 106
Cape honeysuckle 94
Cape mallow 184
Cape phlox, common 218
Cape primrose 101
Cape snow 245
Cape star, common 275
Cape sweet pea 193
Cape tulip, common 143
   pink 281
   red 143
   yellow 144
Cape weed 260, 333
Carnation, Lesotho 65
Carrion flower, Cape 208
Cassia, trailing dwarf 74
Cat's whiskers 96
Catherine wheel 43
inCembuzane 53
Centaury, narrow-leaved 208
Cerise stars 91
Chascanum, broad-leaved 90
Chinaflower 175
Chincherinchee 133
   grey-leaved 271
   large striped 271
   striped 133
   varicoloured 134
Chironia, marsh 91
Chlorophytum, Bowker's 24
Chocolate bells 82
Choje 267
iCholocholo 107
Christmas bells 41
Christmas berry 208

isiChwe 48
Cigarettes 297
Cineraria, coastal 249
iCishamlilo 91
iCitha 31
Cleome, spider-wisp 73
   yellow 73
Clivia 43
   Transvaal 43
Clockflower, needle-leaved 144
Cobra lily, greater 153
   lesser 152
Cockscomb 287
Combflower, marsh 149
Concertina plant 166
Conebush, bokkeveld 320
   Gandoger's 229
   Garden Route 223
   golden 229
   green-flowered 225
   grey 224
   gum-leaved 227
   limestone 228
   oilbract 228
   Outeniqua 224
   sickle-leaved 227
   silver 225
   sunshine 226
Coneflower, common 301
   fenestrate 300
Confetti bush, white 174
Cotyledon, karkay 167
Cowcud, bitter 247
   golden 248
Crackerpod 185
Crane flower 57
Crassula, orange 166
   rooi 166
   scarlet 166
   water 165
   yellow 62
Creeping vygie, Namaqua 298
Cripplewood 234
Crocosmia, zigzag 54
Crocus, bokkeveld 284
Crossandra, bushveld 94
iCubudwana 30
Cup-and-saucer, red 277
   white 277
Curry bush 66
inCwadi 47

inDabula-luvalo 114
iDada 96
isiDala somkhuhlane 96
iDambiso 115

Index of vernacular names

iDangabane elikhulu 31
Dark-eyed bell 85
inDawo yehlati 49
uDekane 68
Desert rose 311
Devil's claw 98
Devil's onion 26
Dew vygie, roadside 296
Dewbush, golden 168
   magenta 168
   Namaqua 168
Dewflower, roadside 169
   scarlet 169
Diascia, hook-spur 216
   long-horned 318
   long-spurred 216
   Schlechter's 318
Dietes 49
isiDikili 89
Disa, blue 163
   cluster 162
   fire 162
   red 162
   rooi 162
Dissel, vaal- 331
Disseldoring, blou- 112
   skraal- 111
Dissotis, marsh 70
isiDiya 47
uDlatshana 116
isiDleke senqomfi 97
uDodo 94
Dog's ears 167, 292
Doll's powderpuff 31
Doll's rose, furry 180
   scarlet 68
Donkeybush, day-blooming 294
uDonqa 98
Douvygie 169
   rooi 169
Draaibos 110, 323
Driedoring 92
Drumstick-flower, diurnal 90
   gooseneck 89
   purple 219, 315
Duiker-root, green-eyed 176, 303
   white-eyed 303
Duikerwortel 303
umDumbukane 62
isiDwa 52, 56
iDwarane 114
uDwendweni 54
isiDwi esibomvu 57

Edible pond blossom 125
Elandsertjie 74

Elandslaai 302
Elephant bush 61
Elephant's toilet paper 293
Erepsia, Breede River 169
Eriosema, heart-leaved 76
   narrow-leaved 76
   pale 76
   scarlet 75
Eulophia, early fire 58
   green cluster 58
   yellow cluster 58
   yellow marsh 59
Everlasting, Cape 244
   Ecklon's pink 108
   narrow-leaved 244
   pink 108, 245
   red 246
   straggling 106
   strawberry 245
   weedy 107
   yellow 108

Fairy bell 85
Fairy pitcher 207
Fairybells 289
Falling stars 54
False disa, large 60
False gentian 84
False gerbera 116
False violet 95
umFana-kamacejane 23
umFana-nkomo 23
umFazi onengxolo 101
Featherbush 235
   coppicing 235
Featherhead, silvery 197
   whip-stemmed 197
Feëklokkie 289
Felicia, bush 251
   common 323
   dainty 252
   fine-leaved 110, 323
   garden 252
   grey-leaved 322
   Namaqualand 323
   needle-leaved 110, 323
imFeyamasele eluhlaza 58
imFeyenkala 70
Finger kanna, saffron 296
Fingerphlox, common 219
   keyhole 316
   mauve 316
Fire lily 140
   green-tipped 44
   yellow 44
Fireball lily 43

Firecracker vine 207
Flame lily 41
Flowerbush, common 242
Fluitjiebos, blou 192, 312
Fluweelboon 78
Fluweeltjie 286
   spog- 286
Fonteinbos 194, 222
Fountain bush 194
   slender 194
Freesia, duine 158
   small forest 52
Froetang 155
   geel- 155

Ganna 191
   bush 191
   cat's tail 191
   silver 192, 312
Gansies 173, 297
Ganskos 247
   klein- 322
   Namakwa- 322
Gaukum 61, 173
Gazania, comb-leaved 259
   common 119
   geel- 332
   Karoo 332
   red 333
   rooi- 333
   strand 259
   strand- 259
   yellow 332
uGebeleweni 48
Geel piesang 57
Geelbekkie 317
Geelgombos 246
Geelklokkie 41
Geelkruid 254
Geelmagriet 257, 327
Geelmelkbos 165
Geelsneeu 326
Geldbeursie 272
Geldjiesbos 302
George lily 141
Geranium, Cape 183
   carpet 183
   silver 71
   white 71
Gerbera, common 117
   mountain 119
   pink 117
   small 117
Gesiggie 216
Ghaap 307
   wolwe- 307

Index of vernacular names

Ghamaghoe 98
Gifappeltjie 306
Gifbossie 89
Gifkool, Namakwa- 271
Gladiolus, butterfly 55
   cockscomb 161
   large pink 56
   large speckled 56
   moth 55
   partridge 288
   Saunder's 57
   speckled 56
   thick-leaved 55
   Wood's 54
Gold cups 181
Golden bells 181
Gombos 321
Gorse, heart-leaved 188
   heather-leaved 189
   mauve 189
   Table Mountain 189
Goslings 173, 297
Gousblom 260
   berg- 330
   bruin- 119
   dassie- 329
   Karoo- 119
   Namakwa- 333
   renoster- 261, 334
iGqokisi 79
Grapplethorn 98
Grasslily, Namaqua 271
   wire-root 126
Greater two-day cure 113
Griekwatee 117
Groen River lily 279
Grootdissel 257
Grootgeelbos 227
Groundsel, great alpine 114
   magenta 115
   Namaqua 324
   purple mountain 251
   sticky-leaved 324
   sticky-plume 110
isiGubengubu 83
Guernsey lily 140
umGulube 24
iGulusha 55
Gumbush, Karoo 321
   round-leaved 246

Haarbos 330
Hairbell, large white 51
   tufted 51
Halfmens 307
Handkerchief flower 100

Harlequin flower 286
   pale 286
Harlequin orchid, bushveld 59
   yellow 59
Harpuisbos 253
   groot- 253
   rivier- 253
Heath, alpine 88
   bead 199
   bicoloured 202
   bottlebrush 200
   coat-hanger 204
   crimson 204
   daphne-flowered 200
   fire 203
   harlequin 202
   lampshade 198
   mealie 204
   ninepin 203
   Oates' 88
   pine-leaved 201
   pink rattle 199
   Prince of Wales 203
   Table Mountain hairy 199
   Table Mountain red 201
   varicoloured 201
   water 202
Hedgehog lily, common 132
Heide, mielie- 204
   veer- 203
Hesperantha, ballerina 148, 284
   bokkeveld 284
   common 52
   harlequin 285
   pink 285
Hibiscus, bladder 69
   Cape 69, 180
   dwarf 69
   hemp-leaved 68
   large yellow 70
   prickly-leaved 69
Hiker's horror 188
Hilton daisy 118
Hitchhiker plant 299
umHlaba 40
uHlabahlangane 99
umHlakanye 68
amaHlala 38
iHlambe 87
iHlamvu 41, 116
iHlamvu lehlathi 41
iHlamvu lentaba 51
Hlapi 64
inHlazi 129
isiHlele 83
Hlokoa-la-tsela 65

iHlonzo lezinduli 63
iHlozane 79, 80
iHlula 81
isiHlungu sedobo 95
Homeria, Schlechter's 282
Hondeoor 167, 292
Hongerblom, geel- 250
   Namakwa- 324
   pers- 250
Hoodia 307
Horehound 215
Horlosieblom 144
Hottentot nut 145
Hottentot's tea 107
   silver 107
Hottentotstee 107
Hyacinth, desert 29

Ice plant 293
   giant 293
Ifafa lily 45
Ifafalelie 45
Impala lily 83
   tufted 83
Impalalelie 83
Impatiens, Transvaal 81
   wild 81
Inanda lily 44
Indigo, keeled 79
   powderpuff 190
   red bush 79
   Swartland 190
   thread-leaved 190
Inkblom, groot- 100
   pienk- 99
   wit- 100
Inkflower, great white 100
Ipomoea, common 87
   leafy-flowered 86
   yellow 86
Ixia, black-eyed 147
   blue 282
   buzz 148
   dark-eyed 147
   orange 147

Jaagsiekte-bossie 77
Jakkalsblom 327
Jakkalsbos 327, 329
Jakkalsniertjie 300
inJanga 99
Jeukbol 24
Jeukbos 311
Jewel of the desert 275
inJoba 25

Index of vernacular names

Kaiingbos 320
inKalane 39
Kalkoentjie 160
   groot rooi- 289
   Namaqua 289
   soet- 288
Kalkoentjiebos 186, 193, 313
Kalossie 147
   blou- 282
   pienk- 148
Kama 293
Kanariebos 235
Kandelaar 48
   konings- 139
   soet 279
Kandelaarbos 291
Kaneeltjie 185
Kankerbos 75, 193, 313
Kanniedood 268
Kanolpypie 149
Kapelpypie 153
   klein 152
Kapkoppie 242
Kapok lily 135
Kapokbossie 321
Karkoer 82
Karoo iris 50
Karoo pumpkin 68
Karoo snow 294
Karoo violet 314
Katdoring 125
Katnaels 215
Katoenbos 307
Katsnor 96
Katstert 127
   bleek- 269
   rooi- 269
   water- 270
Katstertjie 197
Kattekrui 215
Kei lily 44
Kelkiewyn 149
Kerriebos 66
Kersies 196
Keurtjie 195
Khadiwortel 84
Khahla 53, 56
Khahla-enyenyane 52
Khahlana 52
iKhakhasana elincane 110
Khakibutton 290
Khala ea maloti 57
iKhala 130
Khala-e-kholo 57
Khala-enyenyane 55
isiKhali 116

iKhambi lenyongo 109
Khara 42
Kharatsa 33
Kherere 31
Khopa 95
isiKhwali 80
King Gustave's sceptre 236
Kinkelbossie 168
   klimop- 292
Klaaslouw bush, common 247
Klappertjie 185
Klipblom 316
Klipdagga 95
Klipsterretjie 134, 275
Klossiedissel 110
Koedoelelie 83
Koekemakranka 135
Koerasie 311
Koerhassie 311
Kokerboom 267
Kokerbos 291
inKomfe 33
Komo-ea-balisa 34
Kool, Namakwa- 270
Kougoed 332
Kouterbos 247
Kreupelhout 234
Kruidjie-roer-my-nie 186
Kudu lily 83
Kukumakranka 135

Lachenalia, elegant 273
   fleshy-leaved 273
   Frames' 273
   Karoo 274
   red 130
   tasselled 131
   warty 131
Lady's hand, blue 137
   hooded 276
   orchid-flowered 276
   yellow 137
Lady's slipper, pink 95
Lampranthus, bi-coloured 171
   Hörlein's 295
   orange 171
   showy 172
   Watermeyer's 172, 295
ubuLawu 117
isiLawu esimhlope 44
Lazy daisy 249
Lazybush, blue 220
   mountain 220
Leabane 108
Ledebouria, common 30
   Cooper's 30

   green 30
Leeubekkie 103, 217
   Karoo- 317
   langoor- 218
   sandveld- 217, 317
Lefiroane 32
Leilane 99
Lekholela 58
iLeleva 109
Leloele 37
Leloele-la-loti 37
Leloele-le-lenye 35
Lelutla 45
Lematla 47
Lematlana 46
Lemoenbloeisels 63
Lepelblom 161
Lesapho 76
Lesotho lily 57
Letapiso 107
Lewertjie, pienk 190
Lilac mist 217
Lion's eye 67
Liquorice bean, common 78
   large 78
Littonia 41
Lobelia, pansy 211
   pine-leaved 212
Lotononis, pincushion 77
Luisiesbos, gewone- 233
   pienk 233
umLunge 54
umLunge omhlope 59

Maagbossie 67
uMabopha 66
uMabophe 90
uMadinsane 61
Mafifi-matso 102
MaGagana 25
Magic carpet 180
uMagobongwana 41
uMagoswana 31
uMakotigoyile 31
Malgas lily 140, 279
Malgaslelie 140
Malva, dikbas- 305
   engeltjie- 306
   krimpvark- 304
   kus- 183
   rooi- 184
uManzamnyama 64
uMaphola 111
March lily 138
Marsh daisy 259
uMasigcolo-nkonekazi 115

Index of vernacular names

Matchstickflower 196
uMathanjana 95
Mauve daisy 115
Maxabana 26
uMayime 43
Meadow-star, hooded 84
Medusa's head 165
Meelplakkie 62
Melhania, common 67
Melkbos, bees- 290
   dikloot- 290
Melktou 207
Milkweed 307
Minaret flower, broad-leaved 95
isiMiselo 41
Misryblom 47
Moarubetso 116, 117
Moederkappie 60, 164
Mohata-o-mosoeu 112
Mohatollo 113
Mohlatsisa 84
Monopsis, butterfly 96
Monsonia, narrow-leaved 71
Montbretia, forest 54
Moonyane 96
Moraea, common blue 50
   early yellow 50
   fleur-de-lys 145, 280
   large yellow 51
   partridge 49
   peacock 146
   rush-leaved 144
   serpentine 280
   velvet-leaved 281
   wire-stemmed 145
Morarana-oa-mafehlo 63
Moth-fruit 66
Mountain carnation, greater 197
Mountain dahlia 193
Mouse-whiskers, white 73
mouse-whiskers, yellow 73
Muishondbossie 72
iMunyane 95
Mushroom-flower, large pink 99
   small pink 99
   white 100

Naeltjieblom 209
isiNama 100
Namakwalandmadeliefie 327
Namaqua snowdrop 277
Namaqualand daisy 327
Natal bluebell 93
Natal primrose 101

Natal primrose 93
iNcini 77
iNdlolothi 51
umNduze 45, 46
Nemesia 217
   bearded 218
   Karoo 317
   long-horned 218
   Namaqua 317
   Natal 103
   sandveld 217, 317
Nenta 167
Nerina, great 46
   red 140
   ribbon-leaved 46
iNgcolo 25
uNgcolosi 91
Noerap 304
umNsinsana 75
Nuta 293
iNyonkulu 72

Olifantslaai 293
Oorpynpeultjie 73
Orange River lily 45
Orchid, broomrape 164
   common bonnet 164
   orange satyr 163
   pink satyr 164
   waxy satyr 163
Ornithogalum, common 25
   giant white 27
Ossierapuisbos 325
Ouhiep 83
Outeniqua flame 236
Oxbane 47
Ox-eye daisy 116
Pagoda lily 274
Pagoda pea 195
Pagoda, marsh 236
   red-crested 237
   tree 237
Paintbrush lily, bokkeveld 278
   common 42
   crispy-leaved 278
Painted lady 159
Pampoenbossie 68
Papawer, doring- 66
Paperflower, common 244
Papierblom 206
Parachute-daisy, common 256
   glossy-eyed 256
   Namaqua 330
   red 330
   shrubby 257

Parasol lily, yellow 278
Parasol-flower, Cape 182
   desert 304
Parrot lily 57
Patrysblom 42
Patryspypie 288
Peacockflower, painted 134
Pebbleflower 301
Pelargonium, fringed 72
   starburst 71
   two-tiered 72
imPengu 74
Pennypod, spiny 192
Pentanisia 91
Peperbos 306
imPepho 106
Perdeblom 285
Perdevy 61
Peultjiesbos 73
iPhamba lentaba 58
uPhandosi 78
iPhewula 62
isiPhompo 42, 43
isiPhondo esikhulu 93
isiPhondo esincane 93
isiPhukutwane 38
Phylica, plumed 181
Pig lily 125
Pig's ears 62
Pincushion, Cedarberg 234
   creeping 232
   Overberg 233
   ribbon 234
   sandveld 232
   strawberry 233
   warty-stemmed 233
Pineapple lily, bicoloured 29
   common 28
   giant 28
Pink plume 97
Plakkie 167, 292
Platdoring 176, 221, 303
Ploegbreker 75
Ploughbreaker 75
Plumbago 90
Poker, Cape 130
   Ixopo 35
   Karoo 268
   Lesotho 36
   mandarin 35
   Marianne North's 37
   pale 36
   ritual 36
   slender 34
   Thode's 35
   Tyson's 36

Index of vernacular names

Poppiesbos, bokkeveld- 319
Poppy, orange 66
Poprosie 180, 181
Porch jacaranda 97
Porseleinblom 175
Poublom 134
Pregnant onion 26
Pride-of-de Kaap 74
Protea, Bot River 238
   chestnut 320
   grey-leaved bearded 240
   king 240
Purple bonnet 157
Purple broom 81
Purple fountain 100
Purple gorse, spiny 187
Purple granny's bonnet 60
Purple powderpuff 220
Pyjama bush 210
Pyjama flower 52
Pylgif 83
Pynappellelie, bont- 29

uQamamawene 70
umQhapphu 102
umQhele-wenkuzi 48
Qojoana 64
uQonsi 76
Quiver tree 267
inQwebebane 30

Raaptol, blou- 137
   geel- 137
Rabbit's ears 42
Ragwort, coastal 250
   greater purple 250
   lesser purple 250
   poison 249
   weedy 114
Rain daisy 256
Rankmargriet 115
Rapuis, Karoo- 326
Rattle bush, round-pod 77
Red star 32
Reënblommetjie 256
Rhigozum, Karoo 91
   pale 92
Rhynchosia, common creeping 77
River bell, northern 102
   southern 102
River lily, MacOwan's 45
   Moore's 46
   scarlet 52
Rivierklokkie 102
Rivierlelie 45
Rock snapdragon 316

Roella, white-eyed 211
Romulea, blue 156
   common 155
   golden 282
   lemon 283
   Namaqua 283
   pink 156
   thick-leaved 283
   yellow 155
Rooibergmagriet 330
Rooiblom 94
Rooidirk 269
Rooihaartjie 203
Rooikanol 136
   groot 136
Rooikwas 42
Rooinaeltjie 130
Rooisterretjie 32
Rooiwortel 136
Rosemary, sandveld 242
   wild 242
Rosinbush 253
   common 252
   giant 253
   Outeniqua 253
   Tyson's 113
Rotstert 153
Ruschia, brilliant 170
   Namaqua bush 296
   Namaqua cushion 295
   Olifants River 170
   sandveld 170
Rush iris, greater 143
Rysblommetjie 126
Sabi star 83
Sage, brown 214
   common forest 215
   large blue 97
   rusty 214
   soft blue 213
Salad thistle, dune 258, 331
   Namaqua 258, 331
Salie, bloublom- 213
   bruin- 214
   grootblou- 97
   strand- 214
Sambreelblom, geel- 278
Sambreeltjie 182
Sambreeltjies 323
   Namakwa- 323
umuSa omncane 94
Sandholly, paperfruit 221
Sandlelie 274
Sandlily, forest 29
Sandpypie 160
Sandroos 179

Sandrose 179
Sandui 29
Satinflower, blue 148
Satynblom 148
Scabious, Cape 241
Scaevola 102
Sea boneseed 115
Sea nightshade 205
Sea pink, creeping 207
   dune 206
   Saldanha 206
Sea pumpkin 260
Sea rose 209
Seeplakkie 102
Seerooglelie 47
Sehalahala 88
Sehlakoana 113
Sehlolo 66, 112
Sekitla 42
Senecio, grey-leaved bush 325
Senko-toana 108
Sentkannetjie 291
Septemberbos 187
Septerpluimbos 236
Setima-mollo 91
Sewejaartjie 244
   pienk- 108, 245
iShasha-kazane 64
uShayabhici 41
umShelezana omhlophe 100
iShongwe 84
uSiboniseleni 86
Sidvwana 55
uSikisiki 95
Silver carpet 106
Silver pea 192
Silver tree 226
Silwerboom 226
Silwerbos 224
Sjambokbos 325
Sjielingbos 302
Sjokaladeklokkies 82
Skaapbos 328
   stink- 328
Skaapkaroo 321
Skilpadbessie 186
Skilpadbos 187
Skilpadteebossie 246, 326
Skynloodkruid 119
Slaaibos 258, 302, 331
   kus- 258, 331
Slakblom 219
Slangbessie 205
Slangbos, katstert- 241
Slangkop 25, 272, 276
   blou- 31

Index of vernacular names

Slime lily, bushveld 26
  common 132
  Drakensberg 26
  greater 133, 272
  Nelson's 27
  sandveld 132
  warty 272
Slugwort, common 219
Slymlelie, bosveld 26
Snake berry 205
Snakebush, cattail 241
Snakeflower, common 152
  Outeniqua 152
  summer 151
Snake-head, large 25
Snakelily, cockatoo 126
  common 276
Snotrosie 176
Snowbush, common 222
  grey 222
Sôe 334
  wit- 334
iSolelemamba 97
Somerpypie 151
Sooibrandbossie 91
Sopubia, silvery 99
Sorrel, common 177
  golden 177
  grand duchess 178
  large 309
  Namaqua 308
  oblique-leaved 65
  red-eyed 309
  rock 308
  sugarstick 178
  yellow-eyed 177, 308
Sosaties 166
Sourfig 61
  dune 173
  Hottentot 173
Spekboom 61
Spekbos 182
Spider iris, sea 142
  yellow 280
Spiderhead, golden 232
  long-stalked 231
  pinleaf 231
  sandveld 231
Spike lily, stinking 127
Spinnekopblom 142
  geel- 280
Spinning top 223
Spiny tortoise berry 186
Sporrie 178, 179, 310
Springbok painted petals 289
Spurge, golden 165

Squill, large blue 31
  tall white 24
  white 25
St John's wort, small 65
Star-flower, medicinal 33
  ribbed 33
  stiff-leaved 33
Starlily, common tumbling 128
  Namaqua 270
  seaside tumbling 128
Starwort, yellow 114
Steekhaarbos 248
Sterblom 33
Sterretjie 275
Stilbe, pink 198
Stinkkruid 248
Stinkskaapbos 255
Stinkweed, cluster 248
Stoepjakaranda 97
Stokroos, wilde- 70
Stompie, maanhaar- 237
  rooi- 237
  vlei- 236
Stonecrop, white 62
Stoneflower, false 300
  silver 300
Stork's bill, clove-scented 185
  hedgehog 304
  lesser 185
  magenta 184
  sandpaper-leaved 183
  scarlet 184
  seaside 183
  silver-leaved 305
Strandboontjie 80
Strandroos 206
Strawflower, brown-tipped 243
  fiddle-leaved 243
  sea 243
Streptanthera 286
Streptocarpus, crimson 101
Sugarbush 240
  African 104
  broad-leaved 237
  brown-bearded 241
  chestnut 239
  common 104
  Drakensberg 104
  sandpaper-leaved 239
  shuttlecock 238
  silver 105
  waterlily 105
  Welwitsch's 105
Suikerbos 240
Suikerkannetjie 288

Suikerkelk 313
Sukkelbossie 220
Summer swallows 212
Summer swifts 212
Sunbush, western 230
Sundew, rose-flowered 176
Sunflax, common 178
  showy 179, 310
Suring 177
  geeloog- 177, 308
  groot- 309
  Namakwa- 308
  skuinsblaar- 65
Sutera, scarlet 103
Suurvy 173
Swartoognooi 93
Swartstorm 73
Swarttee 117
Sweetpea, narrow-leaved 80

T'aibie 192, 312
T'iena 306
T'kaibe 321
T'koeibee 303
T'neitjie 305
T'noutsiama 297
T'samma 82
Tamarak 132
  wit- 133, 272
inTebe 23
Teele-e-kholo 51
inTelezi 45
Tephrosia, creeping 80
Terblansbossie 69
Teringbos 209
iThalelimpofu 65
umThekisana 116
iThethe 81
Thistle, spiny berg 113
umuThi wamadoda 90
umuThi wechanti 108
Tickberry, common 255
Tinderleaf, true 221
Tjienk 133
  bont- 133
  geel- 134
  Transvaalse 27
Toffee-apple 230
Tolletjiesbos 223
Tontelblaar 221
Toontjies 301
Traveller's joy 63
Tree sweet pea 195
Trekkertjie 255
Trewwa, baster- 164
  ewwa 163

Index of vernacular names

pienk 164
rooi 163
Trompetters 94
Tsamma melon 82
inTsema 84
Tulp 143
  geel- 144
  pienk- 281
  rooi- 143
Turbina 87
Turflelie 279
Turkeybush, crested 186
  greater 186
  Namaqua 312
Turkey-chick 160
Twinleaf, coastal 182
  four-winged 302
  penny-leaved 302
  scrambling 182
Twinspur, Drakensberg 103
iTyolo 63

Uintjie, blou- 145, 280
  Hottentot- 145
  pouoog- 281
  soet- 145
  vlei- 146
Uzura 84

Vaal River lily 45
Vaalertjie 192
Vaaltolbos 223
Valsmoeraskruid 94
Varkblom 125
Varkoor 62
  geel- 24
  pienk- 23
  witvlek- 23
Varkslaai 297
uVelabahleke 44
Veltheimia, winter 274
Velvet bean 78
uVemvane 69
uVemvane olukhulu 69
Vernonia, quilt-leaved 109
  silver 109
Vexatorella, Kamiesberg 319
Vierkleurtjie 131
Vingerkanna, rooi- 296
Vingerpol 165

Vingertjie-en-duimpie 299
Vingertjies 219, 316
Viooltjie, fraai- 273
  Karoo- 274, 314
Visbekvygie 171
Visboontjie 80
Vlambos 236
Vlamlelie 41
Vlam-van-die-vlakte 74
Vleiblommetjie 149
Vleilelie 45
Vlieëbos 205
Vlieëpisbossie 65
umVuthuza 63
Vuurhoutjies 196
Vuurlelie 140
  geel- 44
Vuurpyl 130, 268
  Basoetoe 37
Vygie, bont 171
  copper mat 298
  ertjie- 299
  giant mat 298
  Karoosneeu- 310
  krans- 60
  mat 174
  mountain 60
  rooi 171
  tooth-leaved rock 172
  volstruis 298
  white beaded 299

Waboom 238
Water star 135
Waterblommetjie 125
Waterbos 202
Waterlily, blue 63
Waterphlox, greater 126
Waterslaaibos 292
Watersterretjie 135
Watsonia, Drakensberg 53
  firecracker 151
  Knysna 150
  Natal 53
  Overberg 151
  Pillans' 53
  purple 150
  Table Mountain 150
  wax-flowered 149
isiWesa 44

White lady 62
Widow pea, common 191
Wild aster, Baker's 116
  grey-leaved 251
Wild cucumber 82
Wild dagga 214
Wild foxglove 98
Wild garlic 138
Wild lilac 109
Wild pentas 91
Wild senna 74
Wild sesame 98
Wild stock 179
Wild thistle, large 331
Wildedagga 214
Wilde-ertjie 80
Wildegranaat 92
Wildemagriet 116
Wildemalva 184
Wildepatat 86
Wildesonsoekertjie 109
Wildevingerhoedjie 98
Wildewinde 86
Windowseed, dark-eyed 328
  golden 328
  Namaqua 329
  Springbok 329
  sticky 255
  winter 255
Wine cup 149
Wireweed, common 326
  shrubby 246
Wood iris 49, 146
Wurmbossie 248

uXhapozi 64

Yellow snow 326
Yellowfaces, common 216
  common 318
Yellow-head, alpine 88
  common 89
  lesser 89
Yellowweed 254
Yellowwort, alpine 92
  painted 209
iYeza lentshulube 69

umZonde 73

Glossary

A

actinomorphic: radially symmetrical, divisible into equal halves in 2 or more planes

alternate: applied to leaves when they are arranged on the stem such that each one is inserted between the place of insertion of two on the opposite side of the stem

annuals: plants which complete their lifecycle, from seed germination to flowering and seed production, within a year and then die

anther: the fertile part of one of the male organs, comprising the pollen sacs and the connective but excluding the stalk or filament

anthesis: the stage of floral development at which the pollen is shed, usually coinciding with the full opening of the flower

axillary: arising along the stem in the angle formed by a leaf or bract and the stem

B

beak: sterile portion at the tip of an organ, especially the fruit in Geraniaceae and some Brassicaceae

berry: fleshy, indehiscent, many-seeded fruit containing no hard parts except the seeds

bract: leaf-like appendage at the base of the pedicel in most flowers, the flower arising from the angle between the bract and the stem

bulb: underground or surface organ formed by the much swollen leaf-bases of the plant attached to a small disc-like stem from which the roots issue, the organ not renewed totally each year

C

capsule: a dry, non-fleshy fruit comprising more than 1 carpel, usually dehiscent

calyx: collective term for all the sepals, particularly when they are more or less joined together

carpel: a unit of the gynoecium (female part of the flower) when this is compound and the units are fused together

cladode: flattened, leaf-like branch or stem

compressed: flattened from the sides

connective: sterile tissue connecting the pollen sacs of an anther

corm: subterranean organ formed by a much abbreviated and much swollen rhizome which is renewed annually and which is covered by dry leaf bases

corolla: collective term for all the petals, particularly when they are more or less joined together

corymb: racemose inflorescence in which the lower flowers have longer pedicels than the upper

D

deciduous: falling in season

dehiscent: bursting or splitting open at maturity, used of fruits that shed their seeds and of anthers that rupture to shed their pollen

dioecious: of species in which flowers of separate sexes are borne on different individuals

disc: specialized part of the receptacle, usually producing nectar, within the calyx or corolla and stamens; the central part of the flower head or capitulum in Asteraceae as opposed to the rays

discolorous: with the upper and lower surfaces distinctly differently coloured

E

exserted: of stamens which protude beyond the mouth of the corolla

F

filament: the stalk of an anther, usually thread-like

floret: small flower, especially the flower of daisies; disc florets: the central florets of a daisy, having 5 small equal petals each; ray florets: the outer florets of a daisy, having a single very large strap-shaped petal-like lobe each

G

globose: nearly spherical

H

herbaceous: soft and not woody (of plants); green and leaf-like (of sepals)

I

included: of stamens which are completely enclosed within the corolla

inferior: applied to the ovary when the other floral organs are inserted above it

internode: the part of the stem between the sites of leaf insertions

involucre: a ring of bracts, usually surrounding a cluster of flowers

Glossary

M

monoecious: of species in which flowers of separate sexes are borne on the same individual

N

node: the part of the stem at which a leaf is inserted

nut: a hard and indehiscent one-seeded fruit

nutlet: a dry and indehiscent one-seeded fruit or part of a compound fruit

O

opposite: applied to leaves when they are arranged on the stem such that each one is inserted opposite another on the other side of the stem

ovary: part of the female organ consisting of one or more chambers containing the ovules

P

palmate: shaped like a hand, thus lobed or divided from a common point

panicle: a branched inflorescence in which each branch ends in a flower, the youngest flowers in the centre and the oldest having been produced beneath these

pedicel: stalk of an individual flower

peduncle: stalk of a group of flowers or an inflorescence

perianth: the sepals and petals together, particularly when they are similar

persistent: not falling or decaying in time

petiole: the stalk of a leaf

plumose: feather-like

R

raceme: an unbranched inflorescence in which the flowers are stalked or pedicellate, the oldest at the bottom and the youngest at the top

receptacle: the portion of the axis on which the parts of the flower are inserted

rhizome: underground stem producing rootlets and the apex bearing stems or leaves

S

sessile: attached directly to the stem without an intervening stalk

shrub: a woody plant smaller than a tree and without a single trunk but with several main stems from the base.

spathulate: spoon-shaped with a narrow claw and expanded blade

spike: an unbranched inflorescence in which the flowers are sessile, the oldest at the bottom and the youngest at the top

spathe: large bract enclosing a flower cluster

stamen: one of the male parts of the flower, comprising an anther and its filament

staminode: rudimentary stamen producing no pollen but often functioning as a petal or nectary

stigma: tip of the style or style branches which pick up the pollen grains during pollination

style: the thread-like stalk connecting the ovary with the stigma

stipule: a leaf-like or linear appendage, usually in pairs, at or near the base of the petiole in some plants, sometimes transformed into spines

succulents: plants which store water in their swollen stems or leaves and which can survive periods of drought by drawing on these water reserves

superior: applied to the ovary when the other floral organs are inserted below it

T

tepal: sepal or petal when no distinction is made between them

tuber: a much swollen root or part of a root

U

umbel: an unbranched inflorescence in which the flowers are stalked or pedicellate and arise from the same point at the tip of the peduncle, the oldest on the periphery and the youngest at the centre

W

whorled: applied to leaves when they are arranged on the stem such that three or more are inserted in a ring

Z

zygomorphic: bilaterally symmetrical, divisible into equal halves in 1 plane only